# HANDBOOK OF NARRATIVE PSYCHOTHERAPY FOR CHILDREN, ADULTS, AND FAMILIES

# HANDBOOK OF NARRATIVE PSYCHOTHERAPY FOR CHILDREN, ADULTS, AND FAMILIES
## Theory and Practice

*Jan Olthof*

Translated and edited by Beverley Jackson and Gertha Sijbers

**KARNAC**

First published in Dutch in 2012 as *Handboek Narratieve psychotherapie voor kinderen, volwassenen en families: theorie en praktijk* by Uitgeverij de Tijdstroom

First published in English in 2017 by
Karnac Books Ltd
118 Finchley Road
London NW3 5HT

Copyright © 2017 by Jan Olthof

The right of Jan Olthof to be identified as the author of this work has been asserted in accordance with §§ 77 and 78 of the Copyright Design and Patents Act 1988.

All rights reserved. No part of this publication may be reproduced, stored in a retrieval system, or transmitted, in any form or by any means, electronic, mechanical, photocopying, recording, or otherwise, without the prior written permission of the publisher.

British Library Cataloguing in Publication Data

A C.I.P. for this book is available from the British Library

ISBN-13: 978-1-78220-299-8

Typeset by V Publishing Solutions Pvt Ltd., Chennai, India

Printed in Great Britain by TJ International Ltd, Padstow, Cornwall

www.karnacbooks.com

*For Marleen*

Mother and child by Omer Gielliet

*For Thérèse*

The Virgin Mary by Omer Gielliet

*"I think that if you can muster the patience to spend your entire life painting pictures of potatoes, and only then, you might end up learning what a potato is. Every day you will see new shapes and colours. The potato will look different each time, not because the potato changes but because you yourself are constantly changing and constantly comprehending that potato from within a different inner world".*
*Toon Hermans*

*(From an exhibition of paintings by the Dutch cabaret artist Toon Hermans in Het Domein museum, Sittard, in 2010)*

(Reproduced with kind permission of Stichting Toon Hermans)

*Ithaka*

As you set out for Ithaka
hope your road is a long one,
full of adventure, full of discovery.
Laistrygonians, Cyclops,
angry Poseidon—don't be afraid of them:
you'll never find things like that on your way
as long as you keep your thoughts raised high,
as long as a rare excitement
stirs your spirit and your body.
Laistrygonians, Cyclops,
wild Poseidon—you won't encounter them
unless you bring them along inside your soul,
unless your soul sets them up in front of you.

Hope your road is a long one.
May there be many summer mornings when,
with what pleasure, what joy,
you enter harbors you're seeing for the first time;
may you stop at Phoenician trading stations
to buy fine things,
mother of pearl and coral, amber and ebony,
sensual perfume of every kind—
as many sensual perfumes as you can;
and may you visit many Egyptian cities
to learn and go on learning from their scholars.

Keep Ithaka always in your mind.
Arriving there is what you're destined for.
But don't hurry the journey at all.
Better if it lasts for years,
so you're old by the time you reach the island,
wealthy with all you've gained on the way,
not expecting Ithaka to make you rich.

Ithaka gave you the marvelous journey.
Without her you wouldn't have set out.
She has nothing left to give you now.

And if you find her poor, Ithaka won't have fooled you.
Wise as you will have become, so full of experience,
you'll have understood by then what these Ithakas mean.

*Source: C. P. Cavafy,* Collected Poems
*translated by Edmund Keeley and Philip Sherrard*
*(Princeton University Press, 1992)*
Republished with permission of Princeton University Press

# CONTENTS

*ACKNOWLEDGEMENTS* — xi

*PERMISSIONS* — xiii

*ABOUT THE AUTHOR* — xv

*FOREWORD TO THE ENGLISH EDITION*
Psychotherapy as a craft — xvii
*Peter Rober*

*FOREWORD*
Voices of many sources of inspiration — xxi
*Wibe Veenbaas*

*PREFACE* — xxv

*INTRODUCTION* — xxix

*PRELUDE* — xxxv

## PART I: ASPECTS OF NARRATIVE THINKING

*CHAPTER ONE*
Nomadic thought: thought on its travels — 3

*CHAPTER TWO*
The house of language — 33

*CHAPTER THREE*
The language of the body: the role of the body in narrative psychotherapy — 67

*CHAPTER FOUR*
Narrative space: the "third space" — 81

*CHAPTER FIVE*
Abduction and the logic of metaphor — 111

*CHAPTER SIX*
Creating and structuring a therapeutic context — 133

*CHAPTER SEVEN*
Developing a therapeutic framework — 173

## PART II: NARRATIVITY IN ACTION

*CHAPTER EIGHT*
Finding a therapeutic script — 207

*CHAPTER NINE*
Stories from beyond the horizon: on dissociative attacks and on stories-as-yet-untold — 233

*CHAPTER TEN*
Birth stories: listening to children — 249

*CHAPTER ELEVEN*
Blended families — 273

*CHAPTER TWELVE*
Fatherly love — 285

*EPILOGUE* — 297

*CONCLUSION* — 301

*AFTERWORD* — 313

*REFERENCES* — 315

*INDEX* — 323

# ACKNOWLEDGEMENTS

This book is a tribute to the scholars, philosophers, mystics, poets, novelists and other writers, film-makers, actors, athletes and sports coaches who have inspired me. It is a tribute to the landscape of life and the many people who have crossed my path in the course of my journey.

First I want to thank the clients I have met over the past thirty years, for their trust and for everything they enabled me to learn about life. I want to thank my supervisees for allowing me to discuss some of their case histories. Their voices too are heard in the polyphony of this book. And I want to thank the numerous colleagues and team members with whom I have been privileged to work.

The years I spent at Vijverdal psychiatric centre had a decisive influence on my later practice. The psychiatric patients I encountered there taught me many important things. My partnership with the colleagues at Vijverdal has remained a source of inspiration to the present day. I want to thank them all, through Mark Richartz, then professor of clinical psychiatry, and Aart-Jan Vrijlandt, then director of treatment services, who placed their trust in me and allowed me the scope to develop my own approach within the practice of psychotherapy.

I want to thank Alfred Drees, clinical lead of Bertha Krankenhaus in Duisburg, Germany, who was a great source of inspiration while I was working at his clinic. I also want to thank my friend, the psychologist Jürgen Schmidt, with whom I worked in the same period.

I want to thank the family psychiatrist Walter Oppenoorth, and through him all the team members with whom I worked in over twenty-five years at the RMPI, Barendrecht (known as Yulius since its recent merger). Walter Oppenoorth presided over the family department for over twenty-five years, and together with the other team members he developed a consistent philosophy of treatment. I feel extremely privileged to have been able to work alongside him and many other skilled and enthusiastic colleagues in my time there.

I also want to thank Peter Spijkers and Theo Aerdts of Boddaert outpatient centre for children and adolescents, and Jan Doelman, Cees Theuns, and Jos Vanhoutvin of Kempenhaeghe Epilepsy Centre.

I am grateful to Frans Boeckhorst for his valuable comments and advice, Walter Oppenoorth for his careful reading of the text, Joke Hilhorst for her enthusiastic contribution to our editorial team, and Ton Hilhorst for preparing numerous delicious meals.

I should like to thank my editor Gertha Sijbers for our nomadic journey, and her companion for the English edition, the translator Beverley Jackson. Together they ensured that the text was consistent and ready to go on its travels.

I should like to thank Wibe Veenbaas for his Foreword and for his help in difficult times.

I am grateful to Jacqueline Wils and Paulien Kuipers, who were an immense support to me and my family and with whom I shared many long talks around the kitchen table. They were also enduring sources of professional inspiration on our shared nomadic journeys.

The sculptures of my esteemed friend Omer Gielliet, priest and sculptor, and frequently my guide and mentor, occupy a special place in this book.

I want to thank my deceased friend Thérèse, teller of stories, and a muse to me and many others. It was her narrative verve that inspired the "story" theme.

My greatest thanks are to my wife Marleen, mother of our children Laura and Lars. She died in 1998 after a shared life of over twenty-five years. The story of her sickness and death is woven into the fabric of this book, which is therefore also a tribute to her.

This book is dedicated to Marleen and Thérèse. I gave the first copies of the Dutch edition to my children Laura and Lars, to honour our past, to celebrate our present, and to nourish the becoming of our future in love.

*Jan Olthof*

"All my writings were given to me, one piece at a time, by a thousand different people and a thousand different things".

—*attributed to Johann Wolfgang von Goethe*

# PERMISSIONS

Unless specifically listed below, all reprinted material was free of rights or belongs to the author/editor and was (re)produced by the author/editor of the handbook. Where in order, the artist/photographer is mentioned below the illustration in the manuscript. In some cases acknowledgements for the depicted item have been left out to protect the privacy of anonymised clients.

Grateful acknowledgement is made to the following sources for permission to reprint material in this book:

## Epigraphs

The quote from Toon Hermans that introduces this book is used with kind permission of Stichting Toon Hermans.

The quote of Charles Eames as epigraph to Chapter Five is used with permission of Courtesy Eames Office, LLC, © 2016 Eames Office, LLC (eamesoffice.com).

Kind permission was granted by the heirs of Herman De Coninck to use a line of his poem *De Plek* (De Coninck, 2011, p. 180) as epigraph to Chapter Seven and to quote fragments of his poetry in Chapter Two (Hemmerechts, 1998, p. 111 and p. 145).

The quoted words of Gregory Bateson as epigraphs to Chapter Six (Bateson, 1979, p. 15) and Chapter Eight (Nachmanovitch, 1982, pp. 34–44) were used with kind permission of The Bateson Idea Group.

The quoted words of Wendell Berry as epigraph to Chapter Nine are copyright © 1997 by Wendell Berry, from *The Unsettling of America: Culture & Agriculture*. Reprinted by permission of Counterpoint.

Marc Chavannes gave us permission to use his quote as an epigraph to Chapter Ten.

## *Other copyrighted material*

"Ithaka", the poem by C. P. Cavafy (as translated by Edmund Keeley and Philip Sherrard) was republished with permission of Princeton University Press; permission was conveyed through Copyright Clearance Center, Inc.

Toon Tellegen was kind enough to permit us to freely translate and use (fragments of) his work for the benefit of this publication.

The work of Jef Hutchemakers, part of the collection of DSM Art Collection, was reproduced with permission.

Stefan Cools gave us permission to depict his work and Jeroen Olthof gave his kind permission to depict his work and use his photographs.

The University of Television and Film Munich (Hochschule für Fernsehen und Film München, www.hff-muenchen.de/) gave their kind permission for using the poster for the documentary film *The Story of the Weeping Camel* (with thanks to photographer Juliane Gregor for her help).

Permission to reprint the lines about truth from the poem "Preludes" by Tomas Tranströmer was received from The Lion Publishing Group.

Every effort has been made to trace copyright holders and to obtain their permission for the use of copyright material. The author apologises for any errors or omissions in the above list and would be grateful if notified of any corrections that should be incorporated in future reprints or editions of this book.

# ABOUT THE AUTHOR

**Jan Olthof** (b. 1952) has worked as a psychotherapist since 1984. In addition to his own private practice, he also provides diverse other services. He teaches, trains and supervises young colleagues newly active in the field of systems therapy, and is registered in this capacity with the Dutch Society of Relationship and Family Therapy (NVGR). He has also been attached to the family psychiatry department of Yulius institution for mental health care in Rotterdam as a systems consultant since 1985. Jan Olthof founded the School for Systemic Training at Bunde in the Netherlands.

# FOREWORD TO THE ENGLISH EDITION

## Psychotherapy as a craft

This is a book about craftsmanship, rather than science. What a refreshing change.

*Craftsmanship: neither economics nor science*

Science reigns supreme in most discussions of psychotherapy nowadays. Psychotherapy has to be based on a DSM diagnosis and the therapy itself must be evidence-based. Indeed, it sometimes seems that the world of therapy has undergone a transformation into a marketplace at which people offer evidence-based products for sale and all are intent on maximising their profit. Everything revolves around protocol and on the randomised clinical trials that prove that the protocol works. One protocol is compared to another, and policymakers—unimpeded by their rudimentary assumptions about what the practice of psychotherapy entails—decide which will be the best value for money. In other words, in the world of psychotherapy, as in other spheres of life, free-market thinking has gradually moved centre stage. Economic competition is generally believed to lead to better quality. In fact, as we now know, economic competition often drives up costs and erodes quality. In any case, that is what has happened in the world of mental healthcare, resulting in municipal services that are unaffordable, with the added bonus of disappointed and demoralised care workers. It will be some time before the failure of this model for municipal healthcare really gets through to the policymakers, and until then, we—the people who try to help people who are suffering from psychological distress—must put up with this madness.

It is therefore a relief to see that Jan Olthof, in writing this book, radically breaks ranks with the present-day canon and resolutely chooses to focus on psychotherapy as a craft. For what is so frequently overlooked in these times—even though, ironically enough, the scientific evidence has repeatedly demonstrated it—is that psychotherapy is a relationship in language. It is a conversation between people. One is suffering, and the other listens. That is the essence.

## *A relationship in language*

Language is central to psychotherapy. Not commonplace or digital language, but language in all its complexity. Language with its many layers and different shades of meaning. The language of gazes, hesitations, silences; the language of facial expressions, raised voices, and sentences that are often marked by a conspicuous tension between the words. Even if the words in a sentence contradict one another, they nonetheless combine to tell a story, and the tension between words may indicate that it is a complicated story in which no individual word seems adequate. In psychotherapy we are indeed often dealing with language that evokes rather than describes. For in speaking, the listener is always present, and the speaker's words are the oil paint of the impressionist painter that every listener becomes.

## *Craft and skills*

This book focuses above all on expressive language and on the therapist's craft of dealing with that language. The emphasis is on listening and speaking, always mindful of the fact that listening is a precondition for speech, and that speech is an invitation to the other to tell a story.

Jan Olthof urges the importance of expressive language in both speech and listening. For it is in the client's expressive words that the story that cannot be encompassed within a description lies. In the client's metaphors emerges the difference between the words that try to describe but fall short and that person's physical experience of the story that he or she wants to tell.

If the heart of therapy lies in what escapes from descriptive words, and if evocative language is all-important, psychotherapy becomes, for client and therapist alike, an unknowing quest. It involves roaming with a map that does not—can never—coincide with the territory … the nomadic quest for somewhere to rest, where everything falls into place, but somewhere that cannot be more than a place to linger temporarily, ready to move on.

Jan Olthof calls his book a nomadic journey. And it is quite true that the book, like psychotherapy itself, is a process of roaming and lingering. On our travels we pass Bateson and Deleuze, Bakhtin and De Shazer … But we also encounter some queer characters that we seldom encounter in books about psychotherapy, such as the Dutch comedian André van Duin and the Italian writer Luigi Pirandello. We meet the Belgian poet Herman De Coninck, the German philosopher Peter Sloterdijk, the Japanese sculptor Tajiri, the British rock band Supertramp, and Johan Cruyff, who needs no introduction. Unexpected meetings that enrich the journey, giving it greater depth and brighter colours.

## *Narrative knowing*

If this book is about psychotherapy as a craft, and if expressive language is at the heart of it, does that mean that this is an unscientific book? No, but the underlying vision of science is not the vision that is dominant today.

A useful commentator here is Jerome Bruner, the cognitive psychologist who shaped narrative psychology, and who was a great source of inspiration for Michael White. He states that human beings have two modes of cognitive functioning, which lead to different kinds of knowledge (Bruner, 1986): paradigmatic knowledge and narrative knowledge.

Paradigmatic or logical/scientific knowledge is rooted in scientific, mathematical thought. It leads to rational knowledge, often expressed in abstract formulae such as $E=mc^2$. The ideal of this form of knowledge is a formal, mathematical system of laws and propositions that describe reality and explain it in terms of causality. It is objective, context-free knowledge: the knowledge is true and can be used, regardless of the social context, and consequently enables one to make reliable predictions. This is the kind of knowledge with which science is associated.

There is a second kind of knowledge: narrative knowledge. This is knowledge that arises from telling stories. What counts here is not truth but plausibility: while scientific knowledge convinces on the basis of its truth, a story convinces by virtue of its authenticity. Stories are characterised by particularity. They allude to specific events at a particular place and time. Stories are "context sensitive": each time afresh, there is a "negotiation of meaning" between narrator, story, and listener. Narrative knowledge is wider in scope than paradigmatic knowledge: it is not confined to what can be measured, but also says meaningful things about essential aspects of life, such as love, death, and God.

Traditional societies relied heavily on oral literature and attached great importance to stories: stories determined the identity of cultural groups, through sacred texts such as the Bible and the Koran, and through the myths that provided answers to the world's mysteries. Legends and fairy tales warned of the dangers of life and told the existential stories of heroes who attacked dragons and children who lost their way in the dark forest.

With the Enlightenment came liberation from religious dogmatism and superstition, and rationalism and technology moved to the forefront of Western culture. In today's knowledge society, narratives are no longer taken seriously, certainly not by key policymakers or scientists. Paradigmatic scientists are casually dismissive of stories, labelling them "superstitions", "fiction", "subjective", or "unproven". In our modern technological society, stories are not seen as providing legitimate grounds on which to justify particular choices, or on which to base a policy. The demand is for figures, measurements, and calculations. "Serious" people value stories primarily as entertainment, as ideal fodder for novels, TV series, and films. Stories are described as "exciting", "hilarious", or "moving".

For a narrative therapist like Jan Olthof, however, stories are not entertainment. They are the domain in which he practises his craft. That is where his skills lie, and through stories he can find ways, in a tentative quest for meaning, of establishing a connection with each individual client. That is how he serves his clients, by constructively helping them in their search for meaning and significance in their nomadic journey through life.

*Professor Peter Rober*
*Institute for Family and Sexuality Studies*
*KU Leuven, Belgium*

*FOREWORD*

# Voices of many sources of inspiration

Rose window, Chartres Cathedral. Photo © Bridgeman / Hollandse Hoogte

When my friend, colleague and kindred spirit Jan Olthof told me that the manuscript of his latest book was nearing completion, I was delighted. I was also pleasantly surprised when Jan did me the honour of asking me to write a Foreword to the book. Given our shared passion for the narrative perspective of psychotherapy, I had no hesitation in saying "I'd be happy to!" Then, once I had read the entire manuscript, I was reduced to silence—silence and the flavour of admiration at this rich account of the many dimensions of our profession and the dedication and meticulous attention to detail that it requires.

This would be no easy task: how could my Foreword both introduce and illuminate this book, and do justice to the multiple perspectives of its content? How could I open up the book in such a way as to offer a window to the vistas that unfold in its pages?

For a while I sat pondering and basking in the silence. Then, from within that silence, a single vision swam to the surface: the rose window of Chartres Cathedral, near Paris. The image took me back to that sun-drenched square, and the moment when I crossed the threshold on which countless feet had trodden before me. I felt absorbed into the vast, dusky space of the cathedral's gigantic stone body. We were many. Whispering voices, shuffling feet moving forward hesitantly. Attracted like moths, we arrived at a glorious area illuminated by thousands of dancing coloured lights. The cathedral guide explained: "The stained-glass windows represent the cathedral's soul," adding that glassmaking was once a highly venerated craft. Sand, ashes, fire and coal were combined so as to produce translucent glass. It was laborious work, redolent of alchemy. By varying quantities and pace, glass thickness and melting time, craftsmen learned how to produce all the colours of the rainbow. The result was a glorious profusion of colour brought to life by the effect of light. The inclusion of impurities in the glass added vitality to the light's refraction.

The rose window of Chartres Cathedral is a beautiful symbol for what this book has to offer. The circular window represents a magnificent polychrome cluster of perspectives. It is buoyed up by five equally vibrant lancet windows. The great theme of the rose window is the birth of light out of darkness. The colours stream out radiantly from the dim surroundings and reveal their inner light. All human beings harbour this same mysterious power, which dark times cannot extinguish, however many times the light appears to have been cut off in our existence and in that of our ancestors.

*Handbook of Narrative Psychotherapy for Children, Adults, and Families: Theory and Practice* is a title that conveys the many facets that this book will explore. Indeed, the book serves as a rose window that shines its light into narrative psychotherapy. Jan Olthof takes the reader on a nomadic journey around the different sections of the window: each one provides its own light and its own vantage point. Together the windows make up a wonderful spectacle of colour and vibrancy. Along the way our guide honours numerous traditions, which he watches over, preserves, and passes on. Thus, the voices of many sources of inspiration make themselves heard in this work, with their different timbres and vibrations, all helping to achieve wholeness. The beauty of the work lies in its preservation of clarity. Our guide knows that he must not confuse the many perspectives with the traveller or the map with the landscape, for this would drain the healing field of its vitality.

Olthof has given us a gem of a book that describes the multiple layers of professional expertise that are involved in narrative psychotherapy. The book inspires, illuminates and provides much food for thought. It is a book with an invitation: "Build a nest and wait for a bird to settle there".

Building such an enticing nest calls for great craftsmanship as well as knowledge of the architecture of healing contexts and frameworks. It also relies on the use of one's heart as a sensory organ. This book is about the entire range of such knowledge. It is about developing the ability to build nests in which the underlying causes of symptoms that have been drifting in worlds of oblivion can find their way home. A nest for those parts of the story that have not yet discovered the supportive cohesion of the surrounding fabric.

Only a writer who has himself made inner and external journeys with immense commitment could have written such a book. It is an ambitious work that epitomises painstaking dedication to detail: the quest for precisely the right step, sound, tone and rhythm, knowing when to speed up and when to slow down.

It is both a textbook that illuminates essential kinds of expertise and a book of stories, relating highly expressive encounters in the world of therapy. It describes the art and technique of real listening in an effort to understand the other. "Real listening" means paying close attention to the story that the other person is telling through particular expressions and other uses of language. It means listening with the heart—the "inner ear"—not only to the symbolism of a story but also to the stories that symptoms have to tell. Olthof writes about the marvellous phenomena that occur once we learn to "comprehend": how, once the connected story is found, symptoms can immediately settle into place and the story can spontaneously unfold. It is extraordinary how someone's entire body relaxes when he or she hears that what they have tried to express has been understood. Something is released, something is liberated, and at the same time something that appears to float free is retrieved, reattached, sometimes followed by a deep sigh: "Yes, that's how it is." In that sense, this book also describes the mystery of encounters between individual human beings. I hope that this book will be a source of illumination and inspiration to many of our dedicated colleagues.

*Wibe Veenbaas*
*Phoenix Opleidingen*
*Utrecht, The Netherlands*

# PREFACE

The book that lies before you is an account of a nomadic journey. It is a sequel to *De mens als verhaal* (published in 1994, in Dutch only), which I wrote with the psychiatrist Eric Vermetten. It tells of my journey through time, across over thirty years of practice in psychotherapy in diverse contexts and places.

The first of these contexts is my own practice, within which I frequently act in a supervisory capacity for other therapists and institutions. Before I started my own practice in 1984, I worked for a number of years at Vijverdal psychiatric clinic in Maastricht in the south of the Netherlands. Some of the stories relate to that period, such as that of Mrs Johnson, described in the Prelude, who maps out the course of this journey.

Then there is the psychiatric training centre at the Bertha Krankenhaus in Duisburg, Germany, where I taught methodology in the supervision of family and systems therapy for six years. It was there that I gained inspiration for the method of the "team as therapeutic medium", which is discussed at length in this book.

Another important location is Yulius centre for child and adolescent psychiatry in the town of Barendrecht, where I have worked as a consultant in the family psychiatry department for over twenty-five years. When dealing with multi-problem families it is particularly important to devise a sound framework for therapy, precisely because so many complex forces are at work. The book describes the methodology of creating this framework in detail.

The same applies to the Boddaert outpatient centre for children and adolescents, to which I was attached for over ten years and within which we refined the method of the "team as therapeutic medium".

Finally, I want to mention Kempenhaeghe Epilepsy Centre in the south of the Netherlands, where I worked on a project aimed at gaining a better understanding of dissociative fits in the 1990s. Several of the stories related here originated at that centre.

All these locations provided me with inspiration for this book, and each one furnished stories that trace my journey through the landscape of narrative psychotherapy.

## *A handbook*

I hesitated long and hard before deciding that it was right to call this book a "handbook". After all, I might be arousing the impression that the book presents a blueprint for psychotherapy and that it contains concrete instructions for the creation of a reproducible model. You will not, in fact, find any such blueprint or linear instructions here. At best you will be aware, when you have finished the book, that after every session you will need to start again, with a fresh outlook and from an attitude of active *not-knowing*.

Even so, I decided to adopt the epithet "handbook", because many of the examples presented here may inspire you to shape your own therapy in creative ways. In that sense it is indeed a handbook: a book that you can hold in your hands to go on a journey through thirty years of therapy. You will read about successful courses of therapy and others that stagnated, about the tentative beginnings of therapy and the struggle to achieve a good result. It is a handbook to the extent that it can help the reader to pay careful attention to what clients say and to think about the significance of their words; to think in terms of context and framework; to consider when a context is therapeutic and when it is not. If a context is not therapeutic, however good and well-intentioned the therapy may be, the efforts will nonetheless stagnate or lead to a recurrence of the original problem.

This book is a handbook insofar as it seeks to encourage therapists to use the logic of metaphor and the logic of abduction to forge links and connections with the realm of art, fiction, poetry, film, drama and dance—and also, of course, with the realm of science.

It also seeks to draw attention to the phenomenon that the problems presented by clients are frequently duplicated within the team that tries to help them. This repetition should not be seen as a problem originating with the client, but noted with interest as providing a source of knowledge and a way of attuning oneself at a deep level to the clients' inner world.

All the various stages of human life are dealt with, from birth to old age, and children are emphatically invited to speak about their own experience. The child's voice is often lost in psychotherapy. All too often we find people talking *about* children instead of *with* them. When children are referred for therapy, it is common to separate the children from their parents. The child is "examined", tested or given individual therapy in the playroom while parents receive parental guidance. This book emphatically urges involving children in therapy, giving them a voice and regarding them as fully fledged participants in the therapeutic process. Children possess knowledge and in the examples described here the children and parents are often seen together. It becomes clear that therapists frequently overlook the aftermath of extremely dramatic and traumatic births—births that can lead to multiple symptoms, as several examples will show. I describe cases in which it proved to be possible to forge a link between a problematic birth as an untold story and symptoms that appear when the child is a little older.

It was Françoise Dolto who highlighted possible approaches to extremely young children, informed by her conviction that we are knowing, linguistic, autonomous beings from the moment of conception. This insight makes Dolto one of the book's sources of inspiration. Birth, as a story that is stored within the body, indicates the significance of the place of the body in narrative psychotherapy. You will encounter many examples here of what I call "the landscape of the body" or "the narrativity of the body".

While parents and children are generally seen together, that is not to say that the therapist does not work with them separately. In the approach that I wish to propagate, however, this cannot be done until a therapeutic context has been organised and a shared framework has been agreed. The creation of a therapeutic context and a framework for therapy therefore provides the leitmotif that runs through this book.

You will often encounter types of "knowing" in these pages. The ultimate "knowing", however, springs from an attitude of *not-knowing*, as Lynn Hoffman calls it in her book *Family Therapy: An Intimate History* (Hoffman, 2002). It is this attitude that I want to advocate in this book—that of active *not-knowing*, the ideal attitude in helping us to attune ourselves to the client and his or her world view and cultural background; to the client's life story and mode of expression, and to his or her unique choice of words and idioms. In the quest for the appropriate therapy, it is often a struggle to return to this attitude of not-knowing, and from within this attitude to rely on the sources that are present in the client, the collaborative relationship, and the therapeutic team. Not-knowing means keeping an open mind and this will help us to turn our clients' knowledge to the best possible advantage. This attitude also appeals to our own knowledge as care workers: it encourages us to use all our experience, knowledge and skill as contributions to the therapeutic process and the therapeutic relationship. In this context, *knowing* and *not-knowing* are engaged in a constant dialogue.

Furthermore, this basic attitude is inextricably linked to the understanding that each course of therapy must be tailored to the individual until it is a perfect fit, a view derived from the teachings of the renowned psychiatrist Milton Erickson, who conducted groundbreaking work in the realm of hypnosis. He taught us that it is the client's own structure, not the psychological theory of the psychotherapist, that must provide the basic structure. This structure is reflected in the person's particular use of language, which rises to the surface from the unconscious. This specific, original use of language can be heard whenever a subject is broached that is deeply embedded in the person's inner world and in which heart and soul are involved. "Ordinary" language often proves inadequate in such cases.

Milton Erickson also provided the foundations for hypnotherapy as related in several of the case histories presented here. Erickson sees the unconscious as a treasure chamber full of potential and creative solutions. Our collective unconscious contains the knowledge that can enable us to forge new links with each story that is presented by a client and to plumb this treasure chamber as a source of inspiration. This book too seeks to link up with this treasure chamber. It therefore does not contain any specific instructions for psychotherapy. Rather, it urges psychotherapists to use their inventiveness to find individual, creative solutions. It calls for passion and attachment, relationships and loyalty.

The reader will encounter a great many case histories, sometimes in the form of just a few fragments from a session, while at other times an entire course of therapy, extending over many sessions, is related in detail. This helps to clarify the process whereby therapist and client together search for an appropriate path and framework, illustrating the structure of the dialogue and the struggle that sometimes ensues before it is possible to progress. In some cases I have also included the client's reaction to my description of their therapy.

Terminology sometimes varies: for instance, a "family system" may at times be referred to as a "complex dynamic system". I also use the terms "client" and "patient" interchangeably. The term "patient" is appropriate given its original meaning, "suffering". Regardless of terminology, however, the crucial point is that narrative psychotherapy focuses on meaningful relationships. In the first case, of course, these are the relationships with other members of the nuclear family. However, members of the extended family and others belonging to the client's circle may also be significant. The place of the carer and the care system in the larger whole must be addressed explicitly. So we refer to the "therapeutic system", in which the therapist will need to inscribe himself or herself hierarchically, sometimes adopting a high, sometimes a low status, as appropriate in each particular case.

As I noted at the outset, this is a nomadic book. In time, it travels in a zigzag fashion from 1980 to 2012. It also travels through a range of landscapes: psychotherapy, supervision, consultation, team supervision and team consultations, and education. It is an intertextual book, with abundant references to writers and thinkers and many contributions by clients, supervisees and colleagues. The text thus rests on the creative endeavours of numerous others; it is built on many other people's ideas and owes to many a debt of gratitude. At the same time it is an account of my own creative process, the creative links I forged between all these nodes and the pattern I developed in the process.

On this journey, the book dwells on the wealth of numerous encounters and exchanges and the loss of loved ones. It contains the soul of loyalty, love and sacrifice, of experiences of life and death. It is about the love felt by parents for their children, by grandparents for their grandchildren, of siblings for one another, of children's love for their parents and the love among life partners. It travels across the generations and tells the stories of my meetings with people ranging in age from eighteen months to almost ninety.

It is my hope that the stories in this book will inspire you to apply similar approaches in your own creative way, as I myself was inspired by the stories of teachers and colleagues, and by the wisdom of my clients—adults and children alike.

# INTRODUCTION

In the course of this journey through the practice of narrative psychotherapy, the terms "narrative" and "narrativity" will crop up with great frequency. I should therefore like to start by reflecting on the meanings of these terms. Both derive from the Latin *narrare*, meaning to narrate, convey, recount. These words have a wealth of associations.

Among the meanings of "to convey", according to the OED, are:

- to tell, impart;
- to transport, carry, take from one place to another. A ship may be shifted or conveyed, for instance, from one berth to another.

In order to *recount* an event, it may first need to be *recovered, retrieved,* brought back close from somewhere far away. Damage, too, can be *recovered*.

Bearing all these associations in mind, the following chapters will reflect on the practice of narrative thought. Narrative thought is the framework that is needed in the psychotherapy practice described here, in order to *retrieve* and *convey* the life experiences that have been stored in the body and converted into symptoms: the damage must be recovered, converted into language, related. The stories must be retrieved from somewhere far away, sometimes from far beyond the frontiers of consciousness. A person needs to be able to put the damage that has been caused into words, to "narrate" it. Narrating events can help someone to rally, recoup lost energy, and recover (Veenbaas, 1994). This process takes time, just as it takes time to convey a ship from one berth to another. The shift to a different berth creates a new perspective, from which the world looks different. We might say, perhaps, that "relating" is "recovering".

Developing a story about ourselves gives us a sense of coherence and identity. We are as we relate, we become the story that we narrate about ourselves. Each of us is his or her own story.

The many examples that will occur in the following pages are narratives, encompassing and implying all the meanings and associations listed above.

Our reality is a narrated reality. We relate it in order to familiarise ourselves with what is strange, to make existential events and the themes of our life manageable. To do so, we need our fund of narratives: a stock of stories that make up a collective unconsciousness, stories with which people in different cultures have sought along with us, and before us, to find answers to the great questions of life.

When incomprehensible things happen in our lives, we must be able to develop a story about them; we have to be able to relate what has happened. To do so, we need to allow our imagination to speak, thus venturing, as Kundera puts it in *The Art of the Novel* (Kundera, 2002), into "landscapes inaccessible to rational thought": passion, pain, desire, love, faith, the creation of meaning, loyalty.

Narrative psychotherapy makes an explicit appeal to the imagination. To allow the imagination to express itself, the focus shifts constantly between art and science on the one hand, and between knowledge and skills on the other. Art, literature, film and theatre, dance and the world of sport are welcome guests in our consulting rooms, and are often invited to participate. They contribute to the fund of narratives.

Part I, "Aspects of narrative thinking", opens with Chapter One on nomadic thinking. If we want to allow the imagination to express itself, thought must be set free to travel and to become nomadic. Nomadic thinking is essentially an invitation to allow our thought processes to leave the citadel of fixed knowledge and to abandon fixed meanings as far as is possible, creating a free space for meanings by undertaking a journey. Instead of reducing reality to the One, reality is made present in its diversity, multiplicity and difference. So Chapter One involves a shift from the One to the Many. We open ourselves up to the world of difference, or *différance*, as some may prefer, and enter the world of active *not-knowing*, leaving the old certainties at the door.

We shall be constantly tacking back and forth between this nomadic thought and a quest for new order and structures, cohesive patterns in complex dynamic systems. When our journey is fruitful, we find such a cohesive pattern along the way, once the imagination has been allowed to speak. Narrative psychotherapy seeks to engage all levels of human existence. Relationships occupy centre stage: our relationships with our bodies, the relationships that exist *within* our bodies, relationships within the nuclear and the extended family and with all significant people in our lives. The concept of "story" does justice to this world of relationships.

Chapter Two focuses on the world of language, text, textual analysis and imparting significance. As a therapy of relationships, narrative psychotherapy is dialogical in nature. This dialogical quality is not construed as a supplement to monologue, but as a meeting in the world of relationships—a meeting of voices and stories. The world of stories takes us to the interpretive nature of the practice of psychotherapy. Psychotherapy is conducted through the medium of the spoken word. We are storytellers, narrative subjects, and words have a multiplicity of possible meanings.

Chapter Three gives the body and the language of the body a place in narrative psychotherapy. The body is described as the place of language, the bearer of our life stories. Language touches the body. Our history and our life stories are inscribed there: our bodies speak, move, narrate, elucidate. Our life experiences dwell within our bodies. Events choose a particular part of the body as their dwelling place, and so the body may sometimes "shoot its mouth off". The English language has one or more expressions for almost every part of the body.

Chapter Four focuses on the narrative or "third" space. This book construes the dialogical as a cooperative endeavour, as a meeting of people collaborating around a particular theme. In psychotherapy that theme is usually a problem, a symptom, a conflict or a physical complaint that has not yet been understood. The theme is then seen as the third element in the dialogue. This third element—or third space—is essential if we are to do justice to the stories.

Chapter Five describes the logic of metaphor, the logic that we need in narrative psychotherapy in order to allow the imagination to express itself. Classical logic can subsequently help us to create a certain order.

Chapter Six focuses on the creation of a therapeutic context and Chapter Seven is about making a therapeutic framework. You are welcome to browse, travel, and "lose your way", but you will always be called "to order" at some point. Indeed, you can always return to that order—which in this book is the therapeutic context and the framework for therapy.

Part II, "Narrativity in action", focuses more explicitly on the practice of narrative psychotherapy. We find here that narrative psychotherapy focuses on action, on the here and now, and on the reality as experienced by the body.

This part opens, in Chapter Eight, with a discussion of enactment and therapeutic efficacy. I drew inspiration here from the ideas on enactment of Salvador Minuchin, one of the pioneers of family therapy. Enactment involves "acting out" or "staging", a powerful strategy that is associated with therapeutic efficacy. The aim is to make a session trigger a difference—a significant difference for both client and therapist. If the dialogical encounter (to use Bateson's term) constitutes a difference that actually *makes* a difference, this encounter will also prove enriching for the therapist. Therapist and client—whether the client is an individual or a family system—embark on a particular journey by way of their encounter. To achieve this, something has to happen: travel equals experience. Chapter Eight also shows that language is action, that the sentences spoken by the client can be enacted, thus facilitating subsequent action by giving these sentences a reality, as it were, an existence in space.

In the subsequent journey through narrative practice, readers will encounter numerous examples. They are related by a narrator who is frequently the writer, the therapist. But I would encourage you to inscribe yourself in this narrator's voice and journey from this perspective; to join this voice, and through it, to join your clients, your colleagues, and your own mentors. The stories may possibly resonate with those of your own clients and help to forge new links.

Chapter Nine discusses dissociated stories, stories that are told through dissociative processes. These are untold stories that are nonetheless present in the body. They contain the "not yet told". They are related by the body through a loss of consciousness and they seek a narrator and translator to furnish the text. The stories cannot yet be articulated in language. The therapist will try to find the appropriate language and text for the trail and clues left by these attacks. The quest for significance can be read as a travelogue.

In Chapter Ten we hear the voices of children and stories of (largely traumatic) births. Birth stories too are frequently untold; they are preserved by the body without being expressed in language or text. This chapter explores the link between traumatic births or hospital admissions at a very early age and symptoms that develop in subsequent years. This discussion is based on the principle formulated by Françoise Dolto that children are entitled to be given the information that relates to the existential facts of their lives. It was Dolto who placed babies on the agenda of psychotherapy and demonstrated that they possess consciousness—that they *are* consciousness.

In Chapter Eleven you will read the stories of "blended" families. Here too, the focus is on children's voices—children who show how hard it is to find a new sense of belonging when families fall apart. The number of blended families is increasing, and more and more children are growing up amid all kinds of complicated connections. I present a number of stories from my practice to set up a dialogue in which we can search together for answers to the problems that accompany blended families. The need for an "architecture of living" emerges: a vision of the way forward when forming a blended family.

Finally, Chapter Twelve turns to the subject of fatherly love. In blended families in particular, the importance of the father's role stands out in sharp relief. Part I of the book focuses largely on the female, earthly and affective qualities as an important source of knowledge and describes the role of the feminine-maternal, the attachment to the mother. However, since psychotherapists find themselves increasingly confronted by identity problems among boys, and since important spheres of life such as day care and primary school have become largely dominated by women, this chapter focuses on the position of the father, especially in relation to boys. In this chapter, I urge the need to allow the male and female voices to be heard in equality and harmony alongside one another. I also point out that boys and fathers may well benefit from a different use of language, and I appeal passionately to fathers to be present in their children's lives.

Some of the elements that have been discussed during the expedition through the narrative practice come together in the epilogue, in the story of the boy who soils his trousers: the love of a father, the precarious equilibrium in newly "blended" families, the stagnation of development, the usefulness of working with arrangements of Russian nesting dolls, and "parts integration" in exploring untold stories that are stored in the body.

Finally, I want to dwell on the question of the direction in which narrative thought may move in the present era. The journey through postmodern thought, through the world of difference and different voices, the world of local, place-bound and contextual knowledge and the world of different kinds of knowing, has given us the adventure of the journey. However, we still find ourselves sitting on a bench under a tree, as at the end of Chapter One, pondering together on ways in which the practice of narrative psychotherapy may develop.

This final chapter is entitled "The end of the journey: from modern to postmodern to diagonal". If the "great stories" are structured vertically and nomadic thought is structured horizontally, and if the stories are linked as in a rhizome, meeting, branching out and creating a network, the next phase in the development of thought may well be a form of "practice", as suggested by the German philosopher Peter Sloterdijk in *You Must Change Your Life*. Sloterdijk invites his readers to embrace the practice of climbing the mountain and responding to a transcendental call. Climbing the mountain means ascending diagonally, whether or not in a zigzag path. It will be clear that this book is open-ended and contains an invitation to embark on a new journey.

Up the mountain, Sinaï 2007. Photo: private collection

*PRELUDE*

Flowering magnolia outside the consulting room, with thanks to Joke Klomp and Ton Hilhorst

## Mrs Johnson

Mrs Johnson, 65 years old, had been admitted to a hospital psychiatric ward. She had a tired and depressed look about her. She was withdrawn and largely kept to her room, at the end of a dreary corridor. Standing in front of her wardrobe, she said:

"I don't have any clothes!"

A nurse came in, and pointed out the various dresses hanging in the wardrobe.

"Here they are, Mrs Johnson, your clothes are right here!" she said.

Silence …

Mrs Johnson looked at the wardrobe again and said:

"Yes, but I don't have any *clothes*!"

The nurse remained friendly:

"Here they are, Mrs Johnson, look! Here are your clothes!"

Silence again … then:

"Yes, but I don't have any *clothes* …"

The nurse became a little impatient.

"Now just follow with me and look, Mrs Johnson: one, two, three, four dresses. And a skirt. And here's a sweater. Plenty of clothes!"

Mrs Johnson stood there silently, peering at the clothes in her wardrobe and then, timidly, said:

"Yes … but I don't have any *clothes*!"

At this point the nurse started to lose her temper.

"Mrs Johnson, now come and help me count: one, two, three, four dresses, a skirt, a sweater. You have more than enough clothes to wear!"

Dismayed, Mrs Johnson stared at the wardrobe, flinching a little at the nurse's tone. The nurse could not understand that Mrs Johnson didn't see the clothes in her wardrobe. To her it seemed as though she was deliberately being foolish.

Watching this scene play out, with the eyes of a junior psychologist, I blurted out in my youthful enthusiasm:

"Maybe Mrs Johnson means to say that she feels *undressed*!"

With a little jolt Mrs Johnson turned around and looked me in the eye. It was an instant reaction, and the grief in her eyes was palpable. We had made contact. That moment marked the beginning of a story that developed over time. It also marked the starting point of Mrs Johnson's therapy.

That scene took place some thirty years ago, when I first started treating patients in a psychiatric context. I have never forgotten Mrs Johnson and I can still picture her standing there, shoulders bowed, standing helplessly in front of a wardrobe full of clothes. That was the beginning of my quest for the value and meaning of metaphor and story. How is it possible that you can make contact with someone just by uttering a little sentence like "do you mean, perhaps, that you feel undressed"? And how or why did Mrs Johnson become stuck in a pattern of fixed reactions as the nurse kept confronting her, with the best of intentions, with the reality of her clothes hanging in the cupboard?

The phrase "feeling undressed" in reaction to "I don't have any clothes" established a relationship. When Mrs Johnson was confronted with the "reality" of her clothes, she felt resentful. In classical logic I can point out the clothes in a wardrobe and count them. In this way I can prove that there are indeed clothes in the wardrobe. If Mrs Johnson denies this perception of reality, she must be either mad, wilfully uncooperative, or demented.

Yet, when someone says to her: "Wait a minute, maybe you mean something else. Maybe you mean to say that you feel undressed and maybe this is the only way you can express it", there is an immediate reaction. This metaphor turns out to be a starting point for therapy.

The nurse joined in and we all became Mrs Johnson's allies on her road back to health. We learned that Mrs Johnson's five children had all left home within a relatively brief space of time. Mrs Johnson was having difficulty coping with the fact of having an empty house. She felt as if she had failed as a mother, but she could not put this feeling into words. It had confused her and the bewilderment was visible in her features. Yet when she heard the sentence "I feel undressed", it resonated immediately.

What followed was family therapy with Mrs Johnson, her husband, and their five children. The painful process of their leaving home was discussed. All five children had found it very difficult to leave home, and all confirmed that Mrs Johnson had really been a good mother.

Mrs Johnson was now able to find words to express herself, and to explain how difficult the whole process had been for her. She made rapid progress, and started to feel better. Soon she was ready to return home. We had managed to get her "dressed" again!

The two sentences "I don't have any clothes" and "I feel undressed" are part of a landscape that connects them. This landscape is the subject matter of the book that lies before you. Mrs Johnson became my guide in this landscape and she marks the beginning of the journey described in this book.

# PART I

## ASPECTS OF NARRATIVE THINKING

CHAPTER ONE

# Nomadic thought: thought on its travels

*"A good traveler has no fixed plans and is not intent on arriving"*

—Lao Tzu

### Introduction

This book is based on the premise that if the nature of human beings is "storied"—that is, made of stories—and a story is a text, the most helpful diagnostic tool is textual analysis. The foundations for this narrative paradigm for psychotherapy were laid in the earlier work, *De mens als verhaal* ("The storied nature of humankind"; Olthof & Vermetten, 1994). The present book takes up the same thread and continues this journey around the world of language in psychotherapy. Words combine to make sentences; sentences combine into paragraphs, and a succession of paragraphs constitutes a chapter. Taken together, the chapters make up a text—a story, in the present context. A narrative paradigm for psychotherapy is based on the assumption that thought is multifaceted and multivocal, and embraces difference—that is, in the post-structuralist sense of *différance*.

Embracing this narrative perspective, psychotherapy tells the stories of thought's travels, the places visited by the words, the memory of language, local conditions, and contextual and place-bound knowledge. It speaks of embodied, affective, and earthly wisdom. Basing itself on the text, the actual words that are used, this book travels through history, through universal narratives or *grand récits*, through mythology and art. It travels through poetry and literature, and through films and plays.

We label this narrative, storytelling thought, using a term coined by Gilles Deleuze, "nomadic thought". Nomadic thought in philosophy is inspired by the spirit of postmodernism and by the concept of *différance*, as developed by philosophers such as Michel Foucault, Jacques Derrida, Luce Irigaray, Deleuze, and Jean-François Lyotard. The philosophers of *différance* frequently invoke Nietzsche as a primary source of inspiration. With nomadic thought as a travelling companion, psychotherapy can draw on different domains of knowledge without the need for thought to take up permanent residence in the citadel of fixed meanings.

Psychotherapy can pass through familiar domains, such as biology, psychiatry, and neuroscience. It can pass through narratology and the world of stories and other texts; through semiotics and semantics, religions and mythologies, novels, fairy tales, and films. It can travel through time and through history, which relates how others have expressed answers to the same questions, in other places and other times. On its journey, thought can pass through philosophy, literary theory, theology, and narrative-based schools of psychology and sociology. This implies that nomadic thought can have more than one "home base". It returns from its journeys, tells its travel tales, and reflects on the experiences gained along the way.

In consequence, this is an intertextual book. It inscribes itself into many other texts and draws inspiration from many texts to make new stories. It forges new links between numerous texts and makes new tracks, revealing new approaches to the practice of psychotherapy. It allows itself free rein and creates an open space that provides scope for a constant proliferation of different ways of thinking and different creative approaches.

This book embraces *différance*, and the above-mentioned thinkers were key sources of inspiration. Perhaps because narrative psychotherapy has drawn such inspiration from the philosophers of *différance*, its development has been strongest within systems thinking and family therapy. In systems thinking, narrative psychotherapy rests on the shoulders of numerous progenitors, without whom family therapy would not exist.

Gregory Bateson was the first person to apply systems thinking within the world of psychiatry and psychotherapy. He set up a research group on communication in 1952. Besides communication processes in families, the group also studied other subjects, including animals at play. The project continued until 1962. Bateson's main associates in this work were John Weakland, Jay Haley and Richard Fisch. Haley describes the history of this project, which had a strong influence on psychotherapy, with regard to human relationships and communication (Haley, 1981). Don Jackson joined the group later on, when the focus shifted to communication processes in the families of people diagnosed with schizophrenia. It was then that the term "double bind" was coined—a concept that would later become very widely known.

The research team drew inspiration from Milton Erickson, who founded the field of psychotherapeutic hypnosis. Erickson brilliantly highlighted the power of language, context and suggestion in the many creative and inspiring approaches he presented in case histories. Bateson's research team trained with him, studied his work, reflected on it, and disseminated it.

The idea of working with entire families was a paradigm shift: previously, therapists had worked solely with individual clients, and the primary conceptual and therapeutic framework was psychoanalysis. As the 1960s progressed, various therapists started involving family members in sessions with clients. These included Salvador Minuchin in Philadelphia, who treated patients from disadvantaged, poverty-scarred families. Minuchin's associate Dick Auerswald subsequently cast his net even wider, including members of the extended family, neighbours, and healthcare services.

The Child Guidance Clinic, the institution headed by Minuchin and Auerswald, was very active in training family therapists, and some of its staff—such as Haley and Braulio Montalvo— later attracted followers of their own. I myself spent some time there as a guest, observing their work.

The Mental Research Institute headed by Paul Watzlawick and John Weakland was founded in Palo Alto. Together with their colleagues Richard Fisch, Don Jackson, Virginia Satir and Janet Beavin, they wrote a great many articles and books, two of which— *Pragmatics of Human Communication* (1976) and *Change* (1974)—were truly groundbreaking. These books were based on the ideas developed by Bateson's research group. Watzlawick, Weakland and their associates were prolific researchers, and trained numerous therapists in what was initially called communication theory and later became known as social constructionism in psychotherapy.

Two groups were formed in Italy: one in Milan, around the child psychiatrist Mara Selvini Palazzoli, and another in Rome, the central figure of which was Maurizio Andolfi. At the Ackerman Institute in New York, therapists such as Peggy Papp, Peggy Penn, and Olga Silverstein introduced a feminist approach to psychotherapy, along with theories of gender, class, and culture. These early developments of family therapy are described in Lynn Hoffman's book *Foundations of Family Therapy* (Hoffman, 1981).

Up to then, families were seen—under the influence of systems thinking—in terms of a reality to be observed from a distance, whose dynamics could be decoded. The notion of a participating consciousness, or observer-dependent observation, had not yet achieved currency. Bateson's group started to study the dynamics of family interactions and the context surrounding each individual. The period during which families were viewed as units or entities that could be observed and described had been accompanied by an upsurge of enthusiasm for charting patterns and circular processes. Terms like homeostasis, feedback and rule formation were borrowed from systems thinking.

This was the earliest experimental research into communication patterns. On the one hand, the trend led to a depreciation of the therapist: after all, certain mechanisms could be examined, it was believed, separately from any particular person, time, or place. Meanwhile, a contrary movement grew up that saw the therapist's role as crucial, particularly in experience-based approaches to working with families, as exemplified by Nathan Ackerman, Carl Whitaker, and Satir. These therapists developed a style of their own from which many drew inspiration. People were still searching for fruitful concepts. Another influential figure was Iván Böszörményi-Nagy, who developed the concept of loyalty within families and generations (Böszörményi-Nagy, 1986, 1987).

The earliest developments in systems thinking, sometimes referred to as "first-order cybernetics", highlighted equilibrium, steering, regulation, and control. In the 1980s, under the influence of two very different bodies of theory—social constructivism and quantum mechanics—the focus shifted to studying reality. It became clear that the observer influences reality in the process of observation. There is no objective, external reality; reality is constructed by the observer, while actively ordering his or her observations. The influence of biology and constructivist ideas emerged in the work of biologists such as Humberto Maturana and Francisco Varela, and that of the scientist Heinz von Foerster and the philosopher Ernst von Glasersfeld (Dell, 1985; Efran & Lukens, 1985; Maturana & Varela, 1992). Maturana and Varela introduced the concept of the "autopoietic system", a system that organises itself. Absorbing elements of these theories, family therapy too started to focus on the therapist's influence as an observer and on the participating consciousness with which reality is constructed.

At the end of the twentieth century, language and semantics moved centre stage: family therapy came to be seen more as a dialogue or conversation in which people construct meaning. Systems were regarded primarily as *linguistic* in nature, and rather than focusing narrowly on the family, attention widened to include all the participants in this conversation around the problem. Anderson and Goolishian coined the phrase "problem-determined system" (Anderson & Goolishian, 1988). The practice of psychotherapy took on a narrative quality (Bruner, 1999), and nomadic thought made its entrance.

In Milwaukee, Steve de Shazer and Insoo Kim Berg devised their "solution-focused" approach (Berg, 1994; De Shazer, 1985). In Norway, Tom Andersen worked on creating a "reflecting team" (Andersen, 1987, 1991). In Australia and New Zealand, Michael White and David Epston introduced the ideas of postmodernism and the philosophy of Foucault into family therapy through what they call the "dominant discourse". They developed ideas about the externalisation of problems to liberate clients from a "problem identity" (Epston, 1994; White, 2007; White & Epston, 1990).

The above brief journey through the history of family therapy has inevitably left out a great many names. This outline is intended solely to emphasise the fact that this book could not have been written without all the developmental work done by our predecessors. For a detailed history of family therapy, readers are referred to the works of Lynn Hoffman (Hoffman, 1981, 2002). Although some of these earlier methods and views are now seen as outmoded, and certain schools of thought are described rather dismissively as "modernist", family therapy could not have matured to the form it has today without them.

Before looking in detail at the practice of narrative psychotherapy, we also need to take a brief tour of the *philosophical* background. The ideal of progress has occupied the centre ground of Western thought since the Enlightenment. The primacy of reason, it was held, would lead humanity to achieve evermore progress on its way to a truly humane society. This post-Enlightenment or "modern" thought is based on the principle that human beings are fundamentally reasonable creatures, and that reason will naturally lead to the further evolution of humankind. Still, with the shocks sustained by the horrors of the Second World War and its death camps, confidence in the reasonableness of human beings was shattered in the latter half of the twentieth century. We have gradually been forced to admit that the primacy of reason is a myth. Indeed, it is a myth that leads to the exercise of power over, the domination and exclusion of, large groups of human beings, making them into refugees. Postmodernism, as an umbrella term for many ways of thinking in diverse fields— such as art and architecture, philosophy and psychology, history and theology—therefore seeks to define an alternative to the belief in progress through the operation of reason.

Postmodernism can be seen as a kind of marking time, a space for retreat, an interspace from which to explore possible new avenues of thought. It is a juncture or hub at which many paths come together and from which many paths depart, paths that lead to unknown destinations, that need to be trodden, described, and discovered. Growing doubts as to which path to pursue may lead to cynicism, despair, relativism, or solipsism.

Rosi Braidotti, inspired by the work of Deleuze, sees the nomad as an alternative to the reason-driven human being, and nomadic thought as a viable alternative (Braidotti, 1993a). We can take the concepts of "marking time" and/or "space for retreat" as denoting a haven or "free space": a space cleared of fixed meanings in which freedom can be recaptured, allowing new ways of thought to evolve. Indeed, the title of Braidotti's book on the subject (*Beelden van de leegte*) means "Images of the void". A "free space" can restore the liberty of thought, enabling it to break away from the stranglehold of the dominant discourse, shuffle off the primacy of reason, and follow a path away from the great main road of rational thought.

In this void or "free space", feminist thought too feels the freedom to strike out along new paths. *Différance* is a key concept in feminist theory. Braidotti, following the other theorists of *différance*, argues that Western thought has functioned through the binary oppositions of dualist tradition, which thus places "the other"—other human beings and "the other" as an abstraction—in categories separate from the subject. In consequence, "different from" becomes "less than". *Differing from*, or *différance*, are words and phrases occupied by relations of power. Just as *different from* becomes *less than*, so too does *other* become *worth less* and *inferior*. Many groups are excluded on this basis of this dualistic thinking in terms of binary oppositions. Differences are not respected but subsumed into, and reduced to, one standard unit. Thought is reduced to a common denominator, within which truth, rationalism, order and unity are the main principles with which the subject is postulated and positioned in opposition to and above the object, human beings in opposition to and above nature and the body, men in opposition to and above women, white in opposition to and above black, and the Western world in opposition to and above the rest of the world. Differences must be erased and subordinated to a hierarchy in which the One is supreme. Identity is created by unity and concord: one Voice, one Identity, one Centre, one dominant mode of thought that adheres to the primacy of Reason and Nietzsche's "will to truth", and which, by thinking in terms of power, excludes large sections of the population and numerous ideas from that supreme One. Difference is subordinated to unity. The primacy of Reason, *Logos*, has become a powerful instrument of exclusion: the exclusion of other modes of thought that do not correspond to the Logos.

Difference-based thought seeks to avoid a dualistic perspective, and instead to define difference in positive terms. This opens up space for different modes of thought. Luce Irigaray has examined the ways in which the Logos excludes the feminine, and sets out to devise a feminine mode of speech, writing, and imagination: *parler femme* and *écriture féminine* (in Braidotti, 1991; Rhode-Dachser, 1982).

Lyotard posits "micrologies" as alternatives to the *grand récits* or metanarratives of and about the truth, which reveal the dominant male discourse (Lyotard, 1984). A micrology or "little story" is bound to a specific time, place, context, and person. A micrology is not related to "truth" or "unity"; rather, it conveys something of the complexity of life, it reveals something about the absent, the invisible, the silent, and the concealed (Assoun, 1987; Deleuze, 1976, 1993; Foucault & Deleuze, 1981; Scheepers, 1987). Deleuze refers to this mode of thought as *nomadic*, which denotes a critical interrogation of thought and ideas. *Nomadic* in this sense means peripatetic, in motion, becoming and moving in a particular direction. Ideas thus become mobile, vibrant identities, which resist occupation and exclusion. Nomadic thought seeks to release thought from the straitjacket of the Logos and give it back its liberty, vitality, beauty, and difference: all the paths are opened up again, and the beaten—not to say time-worn—paths can be abandoned. New stories can come into being and tales told about alternative routes.

Nomadic thought roams by definition across disciplines. It identifies and gathers valuable ideas from a wide range of sources, and discovers new applications and combinations eclectically along the way. It creates a consciousness of the situation-bound nature of assertions, of local knowledge, and relative truth, and it deconstructs claims to universal assertions and universal truth. The emphasis is squarely on connections, context, and intertextuality—links between texts from different fields, polyphony, and allowing many voices from different contexts and times to be heard, voices that may constantly combine to form new harmonies. Thought may follow different routes and end up in the same destination, from which it may depart, converting fixed "knowledge" into a new temporary "truth".

The organising principle of this thought is the positive value it accords to difference and multiplicity. Difference is accepted as giving and making space, as added value, and as *arriver entre* (Deleuze, 1993). Memory amalgamates the many forms of knowledge and the travel experiences of different travellers at different times. This "counter-memory", as it is sometimes called, is the memory that resists the thrust of oblivion. It encompasses a body of oral traditions, local knowledge, and stories that have been discarded or deleted from the dominant discourse—those that are either untold or have been forgotten.

Given the wide sweep of these travels, nomadic thought is the thought of adventure and liberty. Deleuze uses the phrases "becoming nomadic", or "deterritorialisation", for the abandonment of a fixed place, a fixed meaning, and fixed frontiers. Nomadic thought also leads to a different view of the subject, which, rather than being seen as pivotal, the citadel's control centre, governing the surrounding area, is seen instead as a conglomerate of different coexisting selves, different aspects and levels of experience, which memory, again, holds and amalgamates. Identity, here, is not a fixed concept or congealed position, but a retrospective notion. Identity is not laid down in advance, as a prior condition; at best it may be discovered retrospectively. Braidotti writes: "Identity is a backward journey through places we have been" (Braidotti, 1993b). Memory turns this journey into a story.

A story is the integration of these co-functioning selves. This integration is not a given, but the result of maturity. We are born polymorphous and multifaceted. Cohesion is a result—the subject is de-central. Deleuze uses the image of the rhizome for this subject (Deleuze & Guattari, 1976). A rhizome is an underground system of roots, which has no defined beginning or end; it may begin or end anywhere. It has no "main entrance", but many points of access. A rhizome may be broken at any point; but the ramification process will constantly continue. As another feature of the rhizome, Deleuze refers to the principles of connection and heterogeneity: any point of a rhizome can be joined to any other by connecting lines. A rhizome has no fixed centre, no unit functioning as its centre. The emphasis is not on the separate points, but on the lines. Any place may indeed be designated as the centre, simply by marking boundaries.

In the metaphor of the rhizome, thought relinquishes the notion of a fixed, permanent centre, and is instead engaged in a quest for originary sites or authentic identities. The connecting lines can be broken at any point and time. These ruptures, however, do not carry meaning: the structure of the rhizome simply carries on developing. For a rhizome has what Deleuze calls "lines of flight", lines along which its organisational structure continues, and which constantly refer to one another. The organisation regroups along these lines of flight. A rhizome has lines along which it is structured into parts, layers, and segments, and deterritorialising lines, along which the rhizome is continuously expanding. The World Wide Web is an example of a rhizome.

The organisational structure of a rhizome cannot be identified, bounded, or fixed. There is no fixed structure—or primary genetic axis, to use Deleuze's term. It is impossible to produce a representation of a rhizome: this, indeed, is the quintessence of nomadic thought. After all, Deleuze's criticism of the philosophy of representation is that it is a thought cast in terms of control, which deems itself capable of ordering, arranging, and classifying what *is*, and thereby of representing an identity. For in a representation, the mutual distinctions between entities—that is, *différance*—are subordinated to what they have in common. In other words, difference is subordinated to identity, and thought then focuses on recognising what is identical instead of distinguishing what is different. Representational thought claims to supply a true account of *what is*, whereas in fact, Deleuze argues, it can only give an account of the part of reality that is capable of representation.

Nomadic thought is an "as if" mode of thinking, which makes imagination possible. It maps out new lines along which thought can travel. The "as if" philosophy does not pin down, does not claim to posit reality with the assurance of a mathematical equation. Nomadic thought refers to an intimate mutual bond, and "as if" thinking is a strategy that takes from the past what is necessary and useful on the journey to the new stopping place. Some things from the past are transformed, taking on a new meaning in the new location. Nomadic thought, then, is the affirmation of fluid boundaries. If the subject is seen as multifaceted and as a link between the different juxtaposed selves and parts, which are kept together by memory, there is no controlling unity or absolute centre. Instead, identity is polymorphous. However, there is still cohesiveness, connection, and an organising principle. There is an affective bond, driven by desire.

Nomadic thought does not necessarily imply a roving style of thought without any home base. Rather, it implies a mode of thought that is capable of creating homes in different places. It does not suggest enforced displacement or refugee status, but a transition to a subject that has relinquished all claim to fixed boundaries.

Nomads are in origin peoples who worked pieces of open land outside the city. The clan elders would assign the pasture to the tribe's members. The word "nomad" derives from the Greek word νόμος, which means both pasture and law (rule, convention), while the related word νέμειν means to assign a plot of land as pasture. In a city, the city exercises power within its walls, land is owned as property, and the law applies. Nomadic people, however, live in an open space without fixed frontiers or walls. The boundaries separating different members of the tribe are fluid. Nomads thus inhabit a different, more horizontal, power structure than that of the city.

Again, the rhizome metaphor is illuminating here. A rhizome is not structured vertically or hierarchically, but horizontally. In nomadic thought the emphasis is on connections, driven by affective forces, and on merging and undergoing transformation into new forms. So there is nothing at all romantic about the term "nomadic thought" or the concept of ideas "becoming nomadic". The term should not be taken to imply the impossibility of developing a stable basis for thought, or of finding a fixed site or location. Travelling too can be an "as if" process that takes place in the imagination: "the nomad is not necessarily one who moves: some voyages take place in situ, are trips in intensity … nomads are not necessarily those who move about like migrants. On the contrary, they do not move; [though] nomads, they nevertheless stay in the same place and continually evade the codes of settled people" (Foucault & Deleuze, 1981, p. 62).

To ensure that these travelling thoughts and the imagination are constantly allowed to express themselves, a fluid form of perception is needed—perception like running water, water connected to the permanence of the earth. This perception must focus on the now. Deleuze has a particular view of the now. He sees it as consisting of three aspects that are all present simultaneously: the now of the past, the now of the present, and the now of the future. This simultaneity manifests itself in the body. For the practice of psychotherapy, this means that the now can be actualised, and that both the past and the future can be inscribed in the now. Viewed thus, psychotherapy is not speaking about the past—*there, then,* some time long ago—but speaking about the influence of the past on the present and how the present may *become* in the future. The present is hence a place of becoming, of potential, of orientation to the multiplicity of possibilities. The present is a sluice gate that opens, allowing the attention to be truly, completely focused on the here and now. Within this space, possibilities may unfold, and qualitative shifts may also occur.

The journey takes place along the boundary between knowing and not knowing, and thus becomes an act of the imagination: words escape from the meanings assigned to them and lead a life of their own. They are no longer representative but affective (Deleuze, 1976). Nomadic thought can lead to a form of uninterrupted presence, an integration of conscious and unconscious aspects, a trance-like state, as described by Milton Erickson (Erickson & Rossi, 1979), in which the mind floats freely and travels, with a wide focus and nonetheless full of vitality; a state in which thought is sharpest and the inner landscape brightest, without being clearly defined. This thought extends to a maximum depth and breadth, without any controlling orchestration performed from the camera angle of the ego. The focus is not sharp. It is a sideways, lateral kind of thinking, travelling along diverse landscapes and inner locations, imagining paths that lead ahead and that lead back, where presence may be here and there at the same time. In this mode of thought, the body is an active source of knowledge. The American poet and thinker Adrienne Rich states:

> I am convinced that "there are ways of thinking that we don't yet know about" [Susan Sontag]. I take those words to mean that many women are *even now* thinking in ways which traditional intellect denies, decries, or is unable to grasp. … In arguing that we have by no means yet explored or understood our biological grounding, the miracle and paradox of the female body and its spiritual and political meanings, I am really asking whether women cannot begin, at last, to *think through the body*, to connect what has been so cruelly disorganised—our great mental capacities, hardly used; our highly developed tactile sense; our genius for close observation; our complicated, pain-enduring, multi-pleasured physicality. (Adrienne Rich in *Of Woman Born*, pp. 283–284)

We encounter the focus on the physical aspect of thought earlier, in Nietzsche, who proposes conceiving the subject as a physical entity. Nietzsche reproaches philosophy for its neglect of the bodily roots of human subjectivity (Braidotti, 1991). Through the body as a source of knowledge, feminist thought and nomadic thought converge.

## Embodied, affective wisdom

Braidotti, like Adrienne Rich, urges a return to the physical roots of the thought process, to its libidinal, unconscious foundations. She sets out to explore ways in which women can develop a truth that is embodied, rather than being separated from the body. Passion and desire are inscribed in knowledge, as well as sensory sources and affectivity, as forces that can liberate us from dominant patterns of thinking. Nomadic thought actually goes in search of affective wisdom and has faith in its roots. Irigaray (Irigaray, 1993) writes that when women are obliged to remain silent about their experiences, they convert this self-imposed silence into physical symptoms such as muteness and masochism. She also refers here to embodied wisdom and physical experience as sources of knowledge, which have been silenced and transmuted into physical symptoms. Signs for which there are no words degenerate into symptoms, says Kristeva (Kristeva, 1987).

Just as nomadic peoples watch over their pastures, live with the earth, and help the soil to be fertile, thought becomes fertile by acknowledging its earthly, physical roots. Irigaray too implicitly advocates nomadic thought, when she writes of women destroying encoded forms, and thereby rediscovering their nature. She refers to these female forms as "never to be completed in a single form … ceaselessly becoming" … the becoming that comes from travelling (Irigaray, 1993, p. 103).

## Earthly wisdom

In nomadic thought, earth or soil is far more than the ground we stand on: it is fertile soil or humus: loose, warm, and moist. Here, earth is connected to water. Water flows and is fluid; it has no centre and its essence cannot be pinned down. It resembles the unconscious. Humans develop in amniotic fluid; their earliest nourishment is fluid, from blood and oxygen to milk and voice. The first home is not a tight-fitting repository; the embryo's security derives from a space that expands with time.

In nomadic thought, within the meadows of "as if", the earth is fertile, moist soil. There is also air, and difference that is valued. Difference itself makes up an interspace, in which relationships of difference add space: a space *of* and *for* words. Relationships of difference are metaphorical: the metaphor describes how the *relata* are connected. This connection cannot be defined by some central significance. The interspace of and for words, the space for relationship, is dialogical, allowing for a *you* as subject who can share the space with the subject *I* without becoming one. We feel connected in the interspace and share this space. There is no objectification of the other: we are both subjects.

## The interspace

The interspace is a space of tranquility; a silence providing space to breathe and to gain inspiration, to find words to express what we need to express and to develop a dialogue. The client may be stifled if a therapist encodes his or her words with predetermined meanings. Irigaray urges the importance of allowing space for breathing in speech, asserting that breathing is central to truth (Irigaray, 1996, p. 121). Speech often consists of non-listening and non-breathing, with words filling up the silence. An interspace allows breath to be converted into experienced, breathed words; we recall that the very word "inspiration" means filling with breath. This breathed language is tactile and affects the body. It does not seek to define a truth, a reality or an object outside the body or to link words to existing codes or "truths" (ibid., p. 124). In the interspace, the tone, modulation and choice of words matter just as much as content. The emphasis is on relationships, with questions taking precedence over imperatives. This implies a preference for verbs that invite dialogue and are predicated on connectedness—intransitive verbs used with prepositions such as "to", "between", and "with", instead of transitive verbs that risk reducing the other to an object. The interspace is a space that makes coexistence possible.

The psychotherapist tries to insert herself into all the modalities of the client's expression. In hypnotherapy, this is known as "pacing" (Bandler & Grinder, 1976, 1979). This includes paying attention to the rhythm of the person's breathing, his choice of words, the favoured imagery, silences, pace, pitch, and trying to create space to enable the client to recover his breath. The client, here, is the "code". In a dialogical contact, the two participants will often fall into the same respiratory rhythm: the words provide breath, and the breath provides words. The tactile quality of language adds value, constitutes subjectivity.

Irigaray advocates a different kind of language. She proposes transforming verbs that are generally used transitively, like "to love", into intransitive forms—"I love to you", the title of one of her books. The effect of this verbal transformation is to create an *interspace* in the relationship between subject and object, or as we shall later call it, a *subject–object–free space*. In the sentence, "I love you", both the *I* and the *you* are assimilated into the space by the *I* as subject, and by the *I*'s actions or desire. The sentence "I love to you" does away with this hierarchy. In adding the preposition "to", Irigaray suggests a movement towards the other, acknowledging the other, the *you*, as a subject.

This mode of speech creates a context of cohesion and imagination. An interspace is a space of *becoming*, a space without any predetermined code or truth, a space for the not-yet-coded. In this space there may be silence—but not the oppressive kind of silence, which makes the other responsible for filling it. It is not an enforced or imposed silence, but a silence that allows for openness. The interspace allows for what Foucault calls "parrhesia"—roughly, "frank speech". We may note that the word "interest" derives from the Latin *interesse*, "to be between". In other words, interest has to do with a relationship, with one's attention being present in the space between the speaking participants.

In the daily newspaper *De Volkskrant* of 15 January 2011, neuroscientist Susan Greenfield discussed the illuminating research findings of a recent project with a group of underachieving children who believed that they had been born with low intelligence. Their poor performance, they thought, came from their "stupid genes". Once they had been taught that brainpower is highly sensitive to the surroundings, since brains are malleable and adaptable, they understood that they could alter their brains by undertaking certain activities. They did so, and their performance greatly improved.

Greenfield's example shows that messages can both harm and heal. Messages serve as organising principles that drive the entire body and can instil a belief, for instance, that someone has "stupid genes". This message is like a sealed code, a closed narrative. The other message, that brainpower can be influenced by the surroundings, creates a different context: if you send the brain a different message, different impulses, you can change yourself from an underachiever to a high achiever, from "stupid" to "clever". The messages are active in the landscape between inside and outside. What is outside does not enter the inner world directly, but by means of a message, which acquires significance through an interspace.

Bateson (in Charlton, 2008, p. 38) uses the term "interface", for instance, for the points at which our body interacts with the outside world. Drawing distinctions is an active process, and ultimately a linguistic act with which we decide whether a thing lies within or outside the boundary of the distinction. These boundaries are permeable, however, as far as the body is concerned, just as the skin is our connection with the outside world. The skin is like a landscape, an interface—or interspace—between inside and outside. The skin reacts to differences, and receives news about differences.

Bateson says that if we want to find a rich variety of wild plants or animals in the natural world, we have to search along the interfaces. On the edge of the forest, on the banks of a swamp, that is where we will find numerous species interacting with each other. That is where we need to look; that is where we can observe change. Mental life consists of, relies on, and originates from this meeting at interfaces where differences meet and something happens. The interface between opposites is an area of transformation. The energy of transformation is generated by balancing on the edges of the interface. Interfaces are markers of identity.

Poets have a more lyrical way of expressing it:

> Nothing exists that does not touch something else.
>
> (Jeroen Brouwers in *Bezonken Rood*, 1981; trans. BJ)

And:

> Two truths approach each other.
> One comes from inside, the other from outside,
> and where they meet we have a chance to catch sight of ourselves.
>
> (Tomas Tranströmer in "Preludes", 2011)

That is why it is important for psychotherapy to organise a context of love at this interface, thus enabling a form of cooperation that can influence every level of bodily function. This implies the use of loving language, a language of kindness and affection, which respects and protects all important relationships.

Infants too are linguistic beings. A fascinating book by Caroline Eliacheff describes the practice of psychoanalytical therapy with infants in a children's home in Paris (Eliacheff, 1993). Many of these children have been removed from their parents in dramatic circumstances. They are treated for extremely severe *physical* growth and development disorders by using *language*!

Eliacheff studied under Françoise Dolto, who states that children are autonomous, knowing, linguistically endowed beings from conception. The child possesses language and assimilates meaning as soon as it is born. From birth, it starts to make its voice heard. It receives love and hears speech. Eliacheff writes that since a child is linguistically endowed, its body can express more than the merely biological. The symbolic activity of a child who cannot yet speak manifests itself through all the bodily functions that do not need to be learned. Attempting to attach symbolic significance to a child's functional disorders does not imply that the child does not undergo medical examination and treatment. But language-based therapy sometimes produces astonishing results: functional disorders may simply vanish, even in cases in which it is not entirely clear what aspect of the child's psyche is involved.

Language is the body's mediator. It is as if life experience searches for a place in the body, and marks it as a signifier. Thus, the language of the body can be translated into meanings. This translation can only take place in the interspace.

In the interspace, the therapist can become immersed in the client's life story, and feel how her own body resonates with it. The client's related and embodied story in turn touches the interface of the therapist's body and inscribes itself there. If interpretation is then deferred, as far as possible, the imagination can express itself, and if the imagination is allowed free rein, states Eliacheff, it becomes possible to "translate" something that was initially experienced as unintelligible (Eliacheff, 1993).

Eliacheff asserts that in a session with a child, the therapist's own body is where the effect is felt that the words and events have had on the child's body. The therapist translates this effect in words, and these words in turn impact on the child's body. In that sense, the body does not speak, but it is the place of language (Eliacheff, 1993). If the words are exactly right, they have a healing effect on the child. The body indicates the reaction to the words with great precision.

That is also the difference between loving language and confrontational language that organises conflict and resistance. That is why clients are often so glad to hear the words, sentences, and meanings that fit exactly and feel exactly right—as if they had been invented for them and do justice to their own unique experience. How much can a single glance not tell us? And a handshake? But where does the handshake "live"? In my hand? In your hand? In the two hands together? The handshake lives in the interspace. It inhabits the system "I and the other" and the landscape in between. The landscape, the interspace, is the dimension of the unconscious.

Bateson speaks of a participating consciousness in the system of "I and the other" and the "ecology" into which we are inscribed (Bateson, 1972). The interface is as a domain of interaction that two people create with each other in the interspace and inscribes itself as language and sign into the bodies of two people who are bound together in interaction. Both undergo a physical reaction through and by means of the handshake, by processing the consciousness of the handshake, the bodily landscape, the interspace, and the related language. No two handshakes are the same, and in this space, the attribution of meaning, meaning that is deeply experienced and bodily felt, plays the central, interpretive role. To me, the firm handshake that almost hurts may convey that the person is happy to see me, in which case the painful sensation in my hand may become a sign of happiness. On the other hand, precisely the same handshake may be construed by me as the other's determination to gain the upper hand, and arouse in me a reaction of alarm, disappointment, or belligerence. The meaning I attribute organises the biological processes. Happiness organises a happy body; pain may cause withdrawal and disrupt the relationship.

We also find the concept of an interspace in the *team as a therapeutic medium*, as described in my earlier book (Olthof & Vermetten, 1994), in which team members have an opportunity to react immediately, allowing the language of their body to speak, expressing images, associations, and fantasies without recourse to pre-existing codes. This approach does justice to "local knowledge", each person's own life experience, and to the differences between team members—without any hierarchy. There is no question of the strongest—or the majority—setting the rules. Experience with this approach has shown that if all differences can be expressed, a pattern or mosaic emerges organically, a pattern in which all team members feel acknowledged. We shall discuss this process at length below.

In the interspace that this approach allows to form, the body too can fully inscribe itself and speak its own language. The body is inscribed in language, and the language of the body is the language of relationship—a poetic and narrative language that differs from the language of text, discourse, and argument. In the shift from objects to relationships, language also forges mutual connections, and does so through imagery, especially metaphor. According to Bateson (in Bateson & Bateson, 1987, p. 30) metaphor is "the logic upon which the biological world has been built". The language of text, discourse, and argument tries to order the different views into a majority and a unified whole. It takes away the space for the other, and for other truths. It deprives reality of relationships and its narrative quality, treating reality as if it were the sum of its parts, as in a mathematical equation. In contrast, the interspace, as described above, is the world of "as if", of multiple realities, in which the body can speak.

In the language of discourse there cannot be a "stone on my stomach". Even so, the stone may be part of an experienced and breathed reality. The body speaks in narrative language, the language of "as if". A headache may feel like a tight band around the head, but no trace of any such band will be found within the objectifiable world. Even so, the tight band that is experienced by the body may tell a story: what thoughts have to be kept in? What thoughts are not allowed to escape? What must not be said? What fear is being protected? Within the world of "as if", it becomes possible to travel into the story of the band, explore its colour and change it in the imagination. In this world, we do not need to discuss whether the band is really present. We need only to enrich it and to change its conditions—varying, strengthening, uniting them (Deleuze, 1993, p. 139). The experienced reality of the band around the head has many languages and many voices.

The film *Il Postino* depicts the relationship between the exiled Chilean poet Pablo Neruda and the postman who brings the poet the piles of letters he receives every day on his island of exile. Proud of having been entrusted with this prestigious task, the postman starts reading Neruda's poems. He is moved by the lyrical language, and wants to learn about metaphor. Neruda teaches him, and as they sit on the beach together, at the edge of the sea, Neruda recites a poem about the rhythm of the sea. The postman says: "The lines go up and down my body; they carry me along, they make me a little seasick". The back-and-forth movement of the words is comprehended by the body and experienced as a bodily back-and-forth movement, causing a sense of nausea.

Thus far, we have discussed the elements earth and water, which belong to earthly wisdom, and the element of air, which might be regarded as part of the interspace. The next element is fire. Agnès Vincenot is cautious when dealing with this element. She notes that in Greek mythology, fire is the domain of male immortality. Fire is subjected to a goal; it is harnessed to rule. In the smith's forge, metal is melted down and cast in moulds; fire is used to fashion and solder items of jewellery. Fire is on the side of processing and of art (Vincenot, 1990). While earth, water, and air connect the world of human beings to those of animals and plants, fire, in contrast, is an element that separates these worlds. Fire is used to heat, to make vehicles, and to prepare food, but it also has a dangerous side, in that it can easily degenerate into an instrument of domination or war, and a means of punishment. In Western history, women have perhaps suffered most from the domination of fire as a means of punishment.

Fire can be a greater force than—and pose a threat to—a human being. One client related a dream, in which he came home to find islands of fire scattered around the living room. Not a blazing fire, but more like the flames of a paraffin stove. The fire was not yet consuming or destroying, it was on the surface, but it was nonetheless dangerous. In the dream, the man did not panic at the sight, though he did immediately turn the stove off. The stove heated stones that continued to radiate heat for a long time afterwards. The man deduced that there was something wrong with the pipes, which were delivering the fire outside instead of inside. Something had to be done about them, since the fire would wreak havoc if it carried on like this. While focusing on this dream in the therapeutic process, the man acquired the insight that it was only through the fire of others that he could get moving—not, as yet, through any fire of his own. He saw that the pipes needed to be rerouted, so that the fire could come from within.

Fire can also be linked to light, to passion, to the sun, to fertility, and to warmth. It can be a life-giving force, and becomes dangerous only when it is separated from the other elements. Vincenot proposes exploring the possibilities of fire in order to further expand our images of life, to connect the fluidity of the flames to currents, moods, intuitions, and vitality, without clearly defined shapes or boundaries. From this perspective, the flame becomes a sign of life, of desire and passion—the unconscious source of physicality and of affective, passionate thought.

## Mimesis as a strategy for change

At the beginning of this chapter we touched on the way in which the prevailing masculine discourse or *Logos* subordinates feminine thought. It treats the feminine as a derivative of masculine *signification*, or as Rosi Braidotti and Suzette Haakma put it (Braidotti & Haakma, 1994), "I think, therefore she is". We might even say that this dominant discourse makes the assumption "I think, therefore she may exist". The feminine owes her existence to "me", the male subject. For "the feminine", we might substitute "the psychiatric patient", "the foreigner", "the other". In each case, the distinction is ordered by the Logos according to a dichotomy: more-less, sooner-later, higher-lower.

The other must be controlled or excluded. The exclusion of *unreason* leads to the exclusion of everything that is traditionally derived from it, such as the sensory world, dreams, passion, and the body. According to Deleuze, this mode of exclusion of *Being* is determined by the law of the negative, in which difference serves only to reinforce the One as a model or to establish the One as a foundation.

Irigaray describes the social and cultural order as patriarchal and phallocentric. Its fundamental principle is the suppression of the maternal and the feminine. Irigaray posits that this maternal-feminine order was the origin of the culture's thought, but that it was suppressed by the Logos when patriarchal culture developed. This principle of feminine origins is reflected in babushka nesting dolls. Babushka is an affectionate Russian word for grandmother. The nesting dolls tell a story about the feminine principle of life, the successive generations who are born from the bodies of women. The use of nesting dolls as a valuable therapeutic aid will be discussed at length in this book.

The way in which we deal with the earth and the soil that nourishes us reflects the problematic relationship that exists between women and their mothers as well as men's quest for a mother (paraphrased from Halsema, 1998). The maternal-feminine constitutes the unconscious layer of culture, and is never forgotten altogether. Irigaray's passionate thought focuses on the way in which women are represented, and explores ways of expressing the feminine, which the patriarchy excludes. She seeks to explore new ways of thinking in which women can create the necessary conditions to become a subject, for a mode of speech and writing that does not remain captive in the categories of the Logos. She concerns herself with the difference between man

Figure 1.  Collection of babushka dolls in the practice.

and woman, and the articulation of sexual difference, in and through which the woman—as *the other*—can express herself in her own way, shaping an identity that corresponds to her physicality, at every level. Irigaray asserts that the body is mediated by language (Irigaray, 1985).

Irigaray does not refer to nomadic thought, but like Deleuze she tries to channel thinking in different ways in order to articulate the feminine. Her strategy for change relies on mimesis, meaning imitation: she starts from the patriarchal order, and then seeks escape routes from it. The strategy of mimesis involves repetition, but not unmodified repetition. Irigaray's version of mimesis involves playing with the discourse, seeking to reveal what was supposed to remain hidden. This mimesis echoes and duplicates voices and impressions without appropriating them; it reflects from a free space. Once this playful repetition has revealed what had remained hidden for so long, it becomes possible to move towards a new mode of thinking, writing, and speech.

Irigaray sets out to achieve change by transforming language, by creating a different "house of language", in which one can speak subject-to-subject with a language that remains in contact with the mother-origin and with the body, *parler femme* and *écriture féminine*. Speech and writing together develop the conditions for a feminine subject position. From the free space, the mimetic strategy holds up a mirror to the patriarchal order. Until then, the woman's reflection in the mirror has been distorted to correspond to the man's image. The patriarchal discourse freezes the woman to an object, and deprives her of the opportunity to reflect herself. In the free space, the mirror is turned around, so that the man can see the patriarchal thinking, his own thinking, in the mirror.

In addition, the mirror gives the woman an opportunity to rediscover ancient pieces of wisdom and to develop other images of her existence that have yet to be realised (Irigaray, 1993). If the woman, in mimesis, adopts the role that has been assigned to her, but does so in full awareness of what she is doing, this is in itself an affirmative reversal of the subordination, and the start of undermining it (Irigaray & Burke, 1980).

Now that the Old Stories and ideologies have largely been dispelled by postmodernism, they have left a void. Braidotti sees this void as fertile, free of old interpretations and ready to be reinscribed with new meanings, a void in which feminine thought can take root. There is a beautiful passage about the fertile void, written by Dag Hammarskjöld, the former secretary-general of the United Nations. Inaugurating the new meditation room at the UN's headquarters in New York, in 1957, he formulated his thoughts as follows:

We all have within us a centre of stillness surrounded by silence.

This house, dedicated to work and debate in the service of peace, should have one room dedicated to silence in the outward sense and stillness in the inner sense.

It has been the aim to create in this small room a place where the doors may be open to the infinite lands of thought and prayer.

People of many faiths will meet here, and for that reason none of the symbols to which we are accustomed in our meditation could be used … .

…

But the stone in the middle of the room has more to tell us. We may see it as an altar, empty not because there is no God, not because it is an altar to an unknown god, but because it is dedicated to the God whom man worships under many names and in many forms … .

…

There is an ancient saying that the sense of a vessel is not in its shell but in the void. So it is with this room. It is for those who come here to fill the void with what they find in their centre of stillness. (source: website www.aquaac.org/un/medroom.html)

### *Fertile soil*

Expressing the above argument in the imagery of nomadic thought, we could say that a nomadic tribe will create a settlement in a fertile spot. Nomads need fertile soil to provide sustenance. They respect the earth, and if a particular place is no longer fertile enough to nourish a new harvest, the tribe will move elsewhere. They may scorch the earth—that is, treat it with fire—to revive its fertility, so that it can be worked again later. Nomads treat the soil with care, because they know that one day, many seasonal cycles later, the circle of their travels will be complete and they will return. A nomadic tribe does not mark off or appropriate territory, but designates fluid, temporary boundaries. It does not see itself as the owner of the land, but settles there and works the soil. Nomads see themselves as guests, guardians, and servants of the earth, receiving food in a reciprocal process of give and take.

Nomadic thought cannot be imposed on someone—liberty is an intrinsic part of it. An imposed mode of thought is automatically linked to power and exploitation: it involves one person using "the other" for his own thought, his own benefit and future. Once the other has given enough, he can be cut loose. Such an approach cancels out the responsibility and reciprocity of relationships and ties. Nomadic thought, in contrast, develops from within. It springs from a decision to undertake a shared journey, form connections, and accept responsibility for the earth, the body, the other, and mutual relationships. Like the tribes described above, nomadic thought does need terra firma of some sort, a place to be, a seedbed for growth, a home base. But when the thinking starts to congeal, it moves on.

### *Liberated language*

Nomadic thought operates through the language of metaphor: through relationships and connections, the language of the imagination. It is a physical, earthly, sensory language. The *team as therapeutic medium* endeavours to create a free space in which its members can speak nomadically in a liberated language, travelling through history and time, through the body and the ambience of a space, by using free association, the images that spontaneously come into the minds of team members when a patient is introduced and discussed. The basic principle is that the kind of language that is liberated—that is allowed to be affective, earthly and physical, passionate and full of fire, and in which words can say where they have been—can forge a deep relationship with the patient.

In the 1980s I worked for a time at the Bertha Krankenhaus in Duisburg, Germany, where the clinical lead was Alfred Drees. There, after a patient had been discussed in an initial round using the established language of psychiatric discourse, it was standard practice to focus on the same patient again in a second, "fantasy" round. In this round, everyone could speak freely in the language of unfettered imagination. Drees referred to these free-ranging fantasies as magicians who materialise in our heads—artists who recreate realities and turn them into different ones, or shape-shifters who can assume different colours, attire, roles, chameleon-like, as the situation and mood require. They pop up in conversations, in rooms, and pass through the walls between rooms. They surface in covert thoughts, and if we give them free rein, they transform not only ourselves, but also the other participants in the conversation. These persons will then see themselves in a different light. The essential task of these magical beings, it seems, is to reveal shifting horizons and to make movement possible. They play the role of brightening spirits. Whenever things have become obvious, when they are taken for granted and therefore immovable, these spirits emerge and push themselves to the fore. Since they may cause unease, they are often banished from thought edifices and power structures. Humour and light-hearted language are the favourite playmates of these elfish creatures of the unfettered imagination (Drees, 1995).

In psychotherapy as well, unfettered fantasies may surface—as shadows, archetypes, or symbolic figures that try to forge links between experiences that have become calcified or blocked and new possibilities and landscapes. The shape-shifters try particularly hard to help those who are hemmed in, stuck in a blind alley from which escape seems impossible. Drees gives the following example (Drees, 1995, p. 14), which I summarise here.

Marie, a 54-year-old patient with terminal cancer, knew that she did not have long to live, but was unable to speak to anyone about her fears. Marie's family were also afraid to bring up the subject of her approaching end with her. The patient's chief physician consulted the psychiatrist, Drees, and confessed that he felt inhibited when he attended Marie, with her big, searching eyes, on his rounds.

Drees accompanied him to see Marie, and after introducing himself to the attending nurse, he expressed his consternation about the gloomy surroundings: there were no flowers, colours, drawings or paintings in the room. Looking out of the window, he noted that the weather too was sombre. Marie asked the chief physician about the latest test results. The psychiatrist met her eyes and asked how she was feeling. She looked at him vacantly without answering. There was an oppressive moment of silence. Then Drees told the patient that he knew about her poor prognosis and her inability to speak about it, and that that was why he had come. He said that he was shocked by the greyness and rigidity of her facial features.

After another brief silence, he asked whether he could describe a few fantasy images to her. Marie agreed. So he told her that he saw a long line of people dressed in grey monks' habits, possibly attending a funeral, in a long procession stretching across a wide plain. Looking more closely, he saw that they were walking past a fence with barbed wire, behind which he saw wooden crosses without any names. It was a dismal picture. A forest of wooden crosses, clustered higgledy-piggledy. At that point, the nurse joined in. In a cheerful, almost jaunty tone, she said, "That's funny! At first I saw images just like the ones you just described, all dark, dim, and dreary. But then I suddenly thought of my last holiday. I was in the mountains with my husband and our two children, and we got caught in a thunderstorm. We found an overhanging rock and sheltered under it. The storm passed, we'd only got a bit wet, and we had a fantastic view of the valley. We …" Marie suddenly interrupted her and started talking. The tears streamed down her cheeks, but she was laughing as she talked. She told them that she and her husband used to go hiking in the mountains every year, in the autumn. Then, four years ago, her husband had had a heart attack and died. She hadn't been back to the mountains since then. Now she launched into lively recollections, full of detail, of the time they spent in a mountain village and the good relationship they built up with the innkeeper at the Gasthof to which they used to return every year.

"I really ought to write to him," she said.

The tears were still streaming down her cheeks, but at the same time, the happy memories lit up her face. The clinical lead, surprised by the patient's revelations, dropped his keys on the floor. This made Marie laugh, and she told them that during one of these mountain walks, her husband had dropped the car keys—into a ravine. As a result, their holiday lasted a day longer than planned. After her story, Marie looked exhausted but very grateful. She asked the clinical lead to get a priest to come and see her. "That one with the short hair, you know? The one with the mischievous smile."

It was remarkable that these fantasies, spoken in a free space, had such a profound effect on the patient. In spite of the seriousness of the situation, the psychiatrist and the nurse together created an interspace by offering images to nourish her memory and her imagination. They first asked her consent, and then simply presented these fantasy images to her. The images moved of their own accord, and the patient could choose whether or not to make contact with them, in her own way. The interspace thus created became an additional space in which the patient could breathe and allow her tears to flow. Notwithstanding all the pain and grief, the space also unlocked happy memories, even laughter and gratitude.

In this way, free-ranging fantasies enter the world of "as if". They can have a liberating, healing, and spiritual influence. This world of "as if" is converted into a "reality" that can have a salutary impact on bodily processes. They move in a different sphere of knowledge, and are archetypically linked to the collective unconscious, as described by Jung. Everyone has access to this collective unconscious. Every care worker is attached to it in some way. As this example shows, most people have been in the mountains at some time in their lives. In their contact with the patient in the world of psychotherapy, each care worker has different experiences, and finds different ways of relating or "tuning in" to the patient. In this process, care workers draw on their own images and memories, their own backgrounds, life experience, and understanding.

The images create an interspace. The care workers respond to the patient's own story as openly as possible: what thoughts, feelings and fantasies are conjured up? What mood do they experience, and what atmosphere do they feel in the physical surroundings? What happens to them, in a bodily sense? How do their bodies react to the patient's story? Their free-ranging fantasies are then offered to the patient as a kind of bridge, a connection offered in a bid to reach the patient, whose self is often locked into a blind alley, like Drees's patient, described above. Drees argues that these free fantasies act as a catalyst to achieve a change of mood, of consciousness, behaviour, and mentality.

In the *team as therapeutic medium*, team members use their free-ranging fantasies, as well as all the bodily and sensory impressions they receive, as they "tune in" to the patient. The mood and atmosphere in the space may be conducive to this process. The care workers relate their fantasies freely, without any predetermined goal. The images are neither interpreted and reduced to the subject who is articulating them, nor interpreted to the patient. They float freely in space, making it possible to enter new landscapes.

## Narrative psychotherapy

To move by way of nomadic thought to the practice of narrative psychotherapy, let us follow Deleuze a little further.

Scientific concepts frequently relate to abstractions, reducing the singular, the individual, to the manageable identity of a conceptual image. They generally fall into one of the following categories:

- Identity: the concept is always applicable in the same way.
- Opposition: there are two opposing concepts, each being the negation of the other. There is a clear dichotomy: either this or that. The concepts cannot coincide, overlap, or refer to one another.
- Analogy: the concept is a reflection of the thing itself.
- Resemblance: the things have something in common, on the basis of which they are united in an identity. (Romein, Schuilenberg & Van Tuinen, 2009, p. 117)

Deleuze's position is very different. In his view, concepts are *not* fixed: each is a manufactured coupling or assembly of a number of heterogeneous elements in a unique consistency, whose nature is transformed as soon as new elements are added or old ones removed. A concept is never universal, but always provides an answer to the actualising question: "why here-and-now?" It shifts with the construction of specific circumstances through what Deleuze calls "vital anecdotes".

It seems to me that the term "concept" can be replaced here by the word "story".

To summarise this in schematic form:

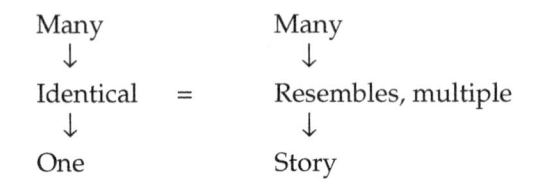

```
Many              Many
 ↓                 ↓
Identical    =    Resembles, multiple
 ↓                 ↓
One               Story
```

In the practice of narrative psychotherapy, we use the term "dialogical encounter" in this context. Such an encounter can be seen as a shared "becoming" surrounding a particular event. Vital circumstances are created through vital anecdotes. Deleuze refers to the intensity of the encounter. Ideas and concepts, cultures, fiction, poetry, art, and film—collective forms of knowing are offered in the encounter, and resonate together. An "open" encounter is one in which concepts are related to circumstances rather than to essences. It is not about arguments or debate. According to Deleuze, all one need do is to explore the problem indirectly, pass the terms back and forth, add something, relate them to something else—but without ever addressing the problem explicitly. As Romein remarks, concepts reflect concrete events rather than abstract essences (Romein, Schuilenberg & Van Tuinen, 2009, p. 25).

In the encounter, what the participants know is always inscribed in the dialogue and immanent. In the same way, the scientific, philosophical knowledge is immanent and is constantly being re-created and expanded. The science of representation asks: What *is*? Vital encounters ask questions like: How? Where? When? In what case? From what perspective?

This is not about reasoning or debating, but setting scenes. Vital ideas, vital anecdotes, are the chance elements of the encounter; they are formed at intersects and nodes; they develop in the intervals and interspaces that Deleuze calls *entre-temps*. It is in these as yet amorphous interim moments that the creative, vital force originates.

Deleuze refers to a person's life history as an oeuvre. Each oeuvre is a journey, a particular course, and consists of a conglomerate of texts. For psychotherapy it is important to prod these texts into motion—certainly if they have congealed into a "problem story". Movement is generated by drawing convergence lines. Psychotherapy could be described as a process of making and organising movement, the nomadic journey to the *zone of difference*, which Deleuze calls a *landscape*. A disorder or problem can also be regarded as a landscape (Kuipers & Olthof, 2005). The convergence lines consist of exploring what is not said, but is nonetheless inscribed in the text. The zone is present in the unsaid or in certain details.

Movement is generated by enlarging the details, exploring the meanings of words, and drawing convergence lines from the dominant to the more peripheral meanings of words. This makes it possible for the story to escape from its dominant meaning. Then we have to dig down into the soil we are standing on, in the manner of archaeologists. The practice of narrative psychotherapy is like archaeological research in the ground on which the here and now has been built. This ground contains tradition, small stories, historicity. It is not all-embracing or universal. Whatever is found in this soil is situational and context-bound, and knowledge that is found in this soil is relative with respect to the wider reality. Here and now, in this place and in this context, an answer must be found.

The psychotherapist is aware of the place-bound nature of the knowledge that has been unearthed, and the interpretive nature of his or her approach to it. Interpretation is unavoidable, but it is impossible to arrive at an interpretation with universal validity; one cannot revert to unitary history or an interpretive framework of universal validity. The stories that are extracted from the soil possess pragmatic significance, which is necessary to give meaning to the existence in the here and now. If we see the knowledge as relative, this might lead to a form of nihilism or a non-committal, passive response. But in Deleuze's view, while the knowledge must be placed in perspective, this approach must be supplemented by an affirmation that kindles enthusiasm, an invigorating passion, a cheerful disposition. This should include space for confusion and insecurity, for impasses and contradictions, for stagnation, speechlessness, and chance occurrences. With these, we can map out the contours of our existence. Psychotherapy, too, can instil enthusiasm, affirmation, and appreciation. Placing things in perspective includes a quest for the liberating moment, the new wisdom.

Drawing on Nietzsche's "Three Metamorphoses", the basic attitude of therapy distinguishes three guises: the camel, the lion, and the child. The camel is weighed down by the burden of established values; the lion shakes off these values, and the child creates new values (see Romein, Schuilenberg & Van Tuinen, 2009). In the *second naïveté* (Ricoeur, 1969), psychotherapy can give rise to a new alternative moment, engender enthusiasm, create, and become art. The practice of narrative psychotherapy seeks constantly to re-create, to find a fitting truth that can apply here, at this moment in time. The psychotherapist and client explore the soil together, and then—still together—they create a new raison d'être, affirming the new enthusiastically by drawing convergence lines from the existing order. Psychotherapy benefits from the creation process that takes place in and through the meeting between the therapist and the client with his or her experiential world. The constant movement is characteristic of nomadic thought, and indeed gives it its raison d'être.

### The nomadic therapeutic team: the team as therapeutic medium

Many of the families who come to the family psychiatry department of Yulius Centre for Child and Adolescent Psychiatry (the former RMPI in Barendrecht) have been referred there for clinical treatment by a children's judge. Such cases often involve extremely complex problems and a large nexus of forces extending in all directions, abounding in missteps and conflicts, all of which makes it difficult to identify an organising principle and to devise a useful way of orchestrating the therapy. If children have been placed under a supervision order, or in different foster families or institutions; if the situation involves several biological fathers or complicated divorces; if there are serious conflicts with the parents' families, compounded with multiple psychiatric symptoms, a strong, flexible and creative team will be key to devising a sound plan.

If there is the added complication of a complex care system, with diverse therapists concerning themselves with the children's suffering and perhaps identifying shortcomings in parental care; if the mother needs trauma therapy while the parents also need joint supervision of their parenting skills; if there is a request for a psychiatric diagnosis as well as a prescribed medication regime; if the foster parents or care workers from other institutions, grandparents and other relatives influence the treatment and adopt different positions in relation to the children, all such complications place a great strain on the team.

Within the care system, a therapist may act on the basis of his or her own set of assumptions, with great effort and dedication, and subsequently run up against another therapist who acts with equal energy and commitment from a different set of assumptions, in a different part of the complex system. In such cases, conflicts within a family may be reflected and repeated within the team—they are naturally driven into it, as it were. This may cause tension within the team, and team members may get caught up in the same movements as the family conflicts, often without being aware of it, and end up organising a repetitive form of these conflicts.

When dealing with a large field of forces, there is a need for a multivocal, "nomadic" team—that is, a team that can function nomadically. A nomadic team operates on the basis of a number of principles, rules, and axioms: it has a specific methodology and a specific vision. The method employed by a nomadic team can be divided into several phases.

In phase I, the team becomes acquainted with the patient and his or her family system. The care history is discussed, along with biographical data, the family situation, the research data, and the medical and psychological diagnosis. The world of the facts that are related is arranged into a certain order, as is customary in the consultations of a multidisciplinary team. The data arising from the case history—as well as hetero-anamnesis, where appropriate—are discussed, and a diagnostic picture emerges. This phase is often very time-consuming. The nomadic team will have the necessary discipline to stop at some point, if necessary, and to proceed to the next phase.

Phase II will be called here the "nomadic phase", as described in an article co-authored by Peter Rober (Olthof & Rober, 2001). The team members are asked to adopt an open attitude to the patient's story, and to allow free rein to their own associations and images. Each is asked to say how his or her body reacts to the patient's story, and these bodily reactions are discussed. The team members take note of the atmosphere that has arisen in the room. Resonance is an important concept here. To do this in a disciplined way, the team observes three basic rules, which will be discussed in the remainder of this chapter.

## *"Alles ist der Patient" (Drees, 1995)*

Everything that occurs within the team in response to the contact with the patient and his or her family system is channelled back to the patient. This rule serves as an axiom, a point of departure. It does not mean that everything that happens is actually *caused* by the patient. The basic principle here is that all team members are acting to promote the patient's treatment, and conduct themselves so as to become—together—a therapeutic medium, a medium that is capable of absorbing influences and exploring their significance. The team members resonate with the patient's story and place everything they themselves experience in the service of the treatment.

Each team member will be sensitive to certain aspects of the patient's story, depending on his or her own life history (Elkaim, 1997). Every team member will construe and interpret what emerges in a particular way, thus articulating a specific part of the story. In this way, multiple voices are expressed in the team, a polyphonic quality that does justice to the complexity of the patient's story and prevents a one-dimensional approach. Dealing with this multivocal response within the team is not easy.

Most teams of psychotherapists go in search of the best approach, the truest explanation, the "real" diagnosis—the best story. Then they try to reach a conclusion that bridges the differences that have been expressed, or to reach agreement, either by adopting a majority view or by ordering the different views hierarchically, thus silencing the minority. Experience shows that voices that are silenced often end up leading lives of their own, and even correspond to, and resonate with, voices in the larger system of the patient, which are also stifled. A voice that is not heard in the team frequently reflects a voice that is not heard in the patient's own system. A team that is under strain and/or has to absorb many external forces often tries to adopt a universal method, thus excluding "the other" and difference. In other words, the problems that are played out within the family are repeated in processes in the team. I have previously described this metaphorically (Olthof & Vermetten, 1994) as a type of "viral infection".

The nomadic team sees the positions adopted by team members as reflections of the positions adopted within the patient's family or surroundings. Coalitions in the team are seen as derivatives of coalitions in the context of the patient. An atmosphere in the room is regarded as an atmosphere that may be present in the patient's home. Two quarrelling parents will often be mirrored in quarrelling team members. Symptomatic experiences in the team are used as indicators of the patient's symptoms. The silence of certain team members or the pressure exerted on them to speak and to adopt a particular position is seen as a reflection of processes within the patient's family. Criticism of team members is seen as belonging to the dominant story that underlies the patient's suffering. What may not be said in the team may possibly also refer to what may not be said in the patient's family. The symptoms are repeated in a mimetic form (IJsseling, 1990). If the silence of certain team members can be studied as a repeat of what takes place in the patient's family, it adds value and "space" to the dominant story. Together we can exaggerate the "row" I have with one of my team members, since we know that this "row" actually benefits the patient's treatment and is a kind of repetition that has much to tell us. Everything we experience in our conversations is seen within the nomadic team as resonance, thus creating a *subject–object–free space* or "transitional space", to use Winnicott's term (see Drees, 1984, 1991, 1995).

Of course, the patient's behaviour could also be construed as a reaction to the team's response. It is certainly true that the team members also transfer their own material to the patient. They are obviously expected to reflect on their own behaviour and on their own primary processes. Practice has shown that the axiom "Alles ist der Patient" is a salutary rule, which helps to defuse many team conflicts. The transfer of material from team members to the patient—counter-transference—dissolves in the free space if team members are given the opportunity to indulge in free association and to allow the primary process to be articulated as much as possible.

## *Protecting the subject–object–free space*

Phase II is protected by the subject–object–free space that ensures that the primary process of the team members is not attached to specific relations between subject (the narrator) and object (the substance/theme). All the associations that arise within the team are detached from both subject and object. Team members can speak freely, and their utterances are not seen as conveying "truth", either about themselves or about the patient. They are construed within the framework of phenomenology: that is, the "phenomena", or experiences, are not seen as the characteristics of the team members or the patient, but as impressions of a receptive, attuned and resonating organism that has opened itself up to care, as a therapeutic medium, and that relates its responses as freely and openly as possible.

The free space is a space in which utterances are completely unconstrained. As time passes, as the team members feel a growing sense of real security and freedom to articulate their fantasies, a deeply felt, structural link is forged in this free space between the team and the patient. Heated exchanges may occur, and positions may be adopted: all such events are construed as repetition, as a mimetic process. Past experience has shown that it becomes possible, after a time, to accurately feel the patient's symptoms. A team member who feels listless and apathetic, and who is not involved in the process of team consultancy in any way, may interpret this feeling as a story and a resonance, and pose the question: who, in the patient's close environment, would feel like that? A team member who feels a constant urge to mock or laugh at aspects of the serious story may be rebuked and corrected because it is an inappropriate response, as would usually happen in a non-nomadic team. Alternatively, the person might be asked to explain the urge. Humour—even completely inappropriate humour—may have a liberating effect for a team that is experiencing strain or pressure. It can also provide important information about what is going on in the patient's world. Any team member who starts daydreaming during this phase, perhaps recalling the film he or she saw last week, a film that has nothing to do with the subject under discussion, may be asked to say something about that film. It often turns out that certain aspects of this film do in fact provide new interfaces with aspects of the patient's story.

Protecting this free space requires enormous discipline within the team. The further the team can go down the path of unfettered speech (or parrhesia) in this phase, the stronger it becomes, and the more inspiring and creative the care it can develop. The team members derive a sense of elation and exuberance from feeling that all forms of knowing can be articulated, regardless of the person's age, gender, experience, or field of expertise—regardless of status. In addition, the method makes it easier to avert and resolve conflicts within the team, and even reduces the absenteeism that is frequently caused by corrosive conflicts. The team members are assured that the free space will be truly respected as such and that spontaneous ideas will not be held against them or seen as a description of the relationship between team members. The more space the team members have to differ, the better they will be able to lay bare the aspects of the patient's story that have not been related.

Team members together form a nomadic team if they can place their own judgement processes, their need for interpretation, and the forcefulness of the *desire to know* in perspective; if they do not keep the patient's story at a distance, as a reality that says nothing about themselves, but on the contrary, place their own subconscious in the service of the patient, in the safe knowledge that what their subconscious relates will not be held against them.

Working together in this way is like a team race in a cycling event. For years I have had a photo of the Raleigh team of many decades ago that celebrated so many successes in the Tour de France hanging on the wall of my consulting room, a photo flecked with coffee stains, which to me symbolises this process of collaboration. The captain, Jan Raas, represents the person within the team who ensures that all voices are heard, that no one falls by the wayside, and who protects the subject–object–free space.

## Resonance and its incubation period

It takes time to allow the images to develop, and to give the body the opportunity to inscribe itself in the patient's story; to enable an atmosphere to grow from the information obtained in the initial phase. The team meeting generally has time constraints, which may lead to this "incubation" phase being rushed. This is unfortunate, since a wealth of information from other sources of insight may be lost. Time saved in the short term is likely to lead to slower progress further down the line. In addition, this rushed approach may prevent the team from developing to its full potential, making it ill-equipped to handle the complexity of the patients' problems. It is therefore important, precisely in this initial informative phase, to go straight to the nomadic phase, before any discussion or exchanges of views. This nomadic phase may be of varying duration, depending on time constraints. In any case, it must be followed by a third, concluding phase.

We could label Phase III the "narrative" phase. In it, team members reflect on the events of the nomadic phase. They detach themselves from the positions they had taken up, from all that emerged in the "free space", and from their own, emotionally coloured, view. In this secondary, reflective process, professional experience and conscious analysis are helpful in creating order in, and attributing significance to, the primary processes. Diagnostic categories now take on living, inspiration-filled meaning. Generally a gestalt takes shape: a mosaic, a connecting pattern. By this point, the patient's story and experiential world have been furnished with more context and depth. The multivocal responses of the nomadic team do more justice to the complexity of the patient's story and the system in which it is embedded than the univocal responses of a team that tries to identify a single truth.

In this phase, a concrete, manageable treatment plan is devised, in the form of a therapeutic framework. This framework is presented to the patient and all those who are closely involved with him or her, and elaborated in joint consultation. Because of the team's working method and the careful attunement to the patient's story, the patient and family members generally experience this framework as an enriching proposal. If everyone concurs, therapy can start from this common base. Once everyone is in agreement, the narrative cycle is complete. If family members reject the framework, it often means that certain voices were overlooked, ignored or suppressed during the team process. It is our experience that family members will be very willing to help with modifying the framework in such cases, to complete the narrative cycle. It has also been our experience that if this cycle is not completed, and therapy is started anyway, it generally breaks down and/or gets stuck.

The members of a nomadic team thus travel through time and space and through diverse voices and positions in themselves, large and small, hard and soft, trying to *embody* the insight they acquire. They travel through conscious and unconscious layers to past and future, looking back and looking ahead. There are no constraints of chronological or logical accountability. Diachronic travel is permissible, and lines of thought are not continuous or linear, but discontinuous. Multiple paths may be followed from the diverse intersections that arise. There is no symmetry, and the patterns are dissonant, multivocal, and interlinked.

After the patient's biographical details and story have been articulated in the first phase, and the second phase has been enriched by the free space, the third phase involves choosing a fertile seedbed as a provisional base. Here, a framework with fluid contours is drawn up, with which the prospect of altering the symptoms can be organised. Devising a framework in a fertile base can be seen as offering a textual interpretation, in which the patient can decide whether it rings true. Umberto Eco reminds us that a text remains a text: infinite interpretations may be possible, but not all will be admissible (Eco, 1990). We may not be able to say which textual interpretation is best, but we can say which ones are wrong; we can also experience which ones ring true and are appropriate to these people and these problems at this moment in time.

The therapist can be seen as an ethnographer, a traveller who describes, rather than someone who lays bare a pathological structure. Alternatively, he or she might be described as an anthropologist, who describes a certain group, culture, rituals, form of society, and use of language. The nomadic team speaks the language of the imagination, of relationships and metaphors. The team speaks in terms of narratives. A storyteller is not concerned with "facts as information" but with "facts as experience". It has even been suggested (by Baudrillard in "The implosion of meaning in the media") that information destroys meaning and signification.

The term "story", as used here, may, in the wider meaning of the term, refer to a performative text, a linguistic or non-linguistic system of signs: a statue or a piece of music, a play or a drawing, a comic strip or a work of art. In short, it may be something that is represented and encapsulated in text within a particular culture (Meijer, 1996). The story takes us to the interpretation of text and brings us back to the imagination. After all, as Eco says: when you are unable to construct a theory, you tell a story. And telling stories is narrativity in action.

The nomadic team does not adhere to a fixed order of diagnostic procedure. A good and careful diagnostic procedure, in accordance with professional insight, is always an important part of the nomadic team process: here, however, this procedure is widened to include phenomenological, embodied diagnostics. The nomadic journey can begin from any point and at any time. There is no fixed goal, and the journey has neither a fixed purpose nor a fixed destination. It starts with and from all the local knowledge possessed by those involved. The boundaries between disciplines become blurred, and the nomadic journey goes beyond mere assignation to diagnostic categories, which strips reality of its narrative quality and deprives symptomatology of context. Assignation to diagnostic categories gives the signifiers the power of interpretation. This reduces the story to an average standard, an analogy that can be fitted into a protocol.

Diagnostics can be used nomadically. A nomadic team seeks to adapt its thought processes to patients' own theories of their reality, preserving values that are vital to the patient and family members. However, the team also seeks to ensure that the story from which the patient is suffering is not constantly retold and repeated in the same way. It sets out to view symptoms as a text that can be interpreted in many different ways. Within the text, threads are woven, connecting it to other texts and contexts. Threads are woven to parents, brothers, sisters and other important people, and other textual interpretations are sought besides the obvious ones that may initially be put forward by the team members.

Foucault has written of the "order of discourse": those who are given, or who claim, the right to speak, have the power to define reality (Foucault, 1971). With this in mind, the nomadic team tries to spread the right to speak, believing that there is no ultimate truth and no ultimate expertise. This diffusion, it is hoped, will lead to a similar diffusion within the patient's world. In a sense, then, the nomadic team appeals to unconscious knowledge that is inscribed in the body and connected affectively, a knowledge that tells stories about each person's individual existence. Mobility, flexibility, passion, desire and cheerfulness are all encouraged.

By these means, the patient's story and experiential world become inscribed in the world of the team. The story journeys into the world of the individual team members, of the relationships among its members and between them and other institutions. It sets off echoes of voices. A nomadic team acts on the basis that letting go of one's own perspective may act as an enabling condition for the other. However, it is not possible to let go of one's perspective until a position has been taken; in other words, after the team member's voice—followed by the echoes of other voices—has been heard.

To advocate nomadic thought is not to champion a facile pluralism. Rather, it is a passionate plea for the recognition of the need to respect complexities and to find forms of action that reflect these complexities without drowning in them. Nomadic thought involves setting out different travel routes alongside one another, but without setting them up in conflict or competition until the strongest one remains. Where conflict arises, it is admitted, as a mimetic repetition. Roland Barthes (Barthes, 1973) expresses the hope that difference will imperceptibly take the place of conflict. According to Braidotti, difference does not cover up or conceal conflict: it is reclaimed from conflict; it is beyond and beside it (Braidotti, 1991).

Within the nomadic team, too, difference is reclaimed from conflict. This working method, however, also implies a mimetic repetition. Conflicts that arise within the team are only nominally conflicts: they are protected by the rule that all interactions and all subjective positions are placed in the service of the patient and channelled back to the patient. Conflicts within the patient's own experiential world, as articulated and expressed in language, recur with a similar use of language within the team. The language used by the patient recurs as problematic language in the team. How often do teams not find themselves using bellicose language, full of war metaphors, the language of battle? Braidotti writes that "language is a virus" (Braidotti, 1994). How often do we not find discordant language among the members of a team?

I am reminded of the title of a famous play by Luigi Pirandello: *Six Characters in Search of an Author*. In the nomadic phase, the team members too are characters searching together for an author, a signifier of the text. In the narrative phase, the patient and the team, together, become that author.

The physicist and philosopher of science André Klukhuhn has said in an interview (Klukhuhn, 1995) that scientific progress does not bring us closer to reality. Reality "retreats as we approach, like the horizon before a traveller". So at the end of progress we find ourselves sitting on a bench under a tree again, in the manner of Plato and his pupils, says Klukhuhn: at least, if there are any trees left by then. We too look for this bench as the point of departure for our journey, in the knowledge that we shall return here at the end of our journey, enriched by our travel experiences, with answers, and also with new questions. And we know that after a while we shall have to set off with our questions once again. We are thrown back, as always, on our own resources.

Klukhuhn says that when traditions become fragmented and truths crumble, the result is often a form of nihilism and meaninglessness (Klukhuhn, 2003). For if there is nothing left that is "true", what is the point of adopting any position at all? When there are no longer traditional truths to use as benchmarks for assessing thoughts and actions, Klukhuhn goes on, it takes immense effort, meticulous care and responsibility to form the best possible opinion from the multiplicity of available options and to adopt a position. The greatest challenge of today's world is combining an acceptance of the relative nature of our own convictions with a determination to stand up for them nonetheless.

I adopt a similar approach in this book: putting one's own truth and positions in perspective, while at the same time arguing from those positions in dialogue with the other. One's own perspective engages in a dialogue with the other to enable the other to take shape, to give a reply. Inspired by Emmanuel Levinas, I would say, "I respond, therefore I am". Human beings are responsible for their responses and for their relationships with others. The awareness of the end of progress is therefore not an idealistic or absurdist position, but an enabling condition. In the space that has been freed and emptied, from which old meanings have fallen away, new responses can be inscribed and new images may present themselves.

In their illustrated history of Western and Oriental philosophy, Bor, Kingma and Petersma (1995) assert that diversity has now become acceptable in philosophy. The effort to arrive at a comprehensive truth, one that is timeless and valid in all contexts, apparently belongs to the past. Truths can coexist in non-hierarchical perspectives. There is no longer a single instance that can determine or gauge truth. Knowledge is a consensual domain. Thus, the narrated truth and narrativity make their return to philosophy, giving imagination a chance to flourish.

This book is a plea for ardent thought, for therapeutic care provided with passion, responsibility, and consideration. Narrative psychotherapy seeks to formulate carefully considered answers to the patient or client, and to all those with whom he or she feels connected. The thought involved in arriving at these answers takes place in dialogues, rather than from any centre. Deleuze describes this as thought that emanates from peripheral flows. Like a rhizome, it moves in all directions, may branch out and form new connections. It can start and end at any point—which can then become a new point of departure. The thought is inscribed in the body, the insight is connected to the body; it is formed from and by the body. Knowledge thus arrived at is tested in relation to the body. Ideas are events, active states of consciousness that rest on affective foundations. Braidotti advocates that those setting out on the nomad's path do so with a cheerful spirit, full of passion, desire, and a sense of comedy. When this cheerful spirit speaks, the language is lived-through, embodied, and vibrant.

In their emphasis on dialogue, nomadic thought and narrative psychotherapy highlight the importance of choosing words with care, and listening carefully to the words that are spoken. For this reason, the next stage of our journey is to the "house" in which this language lives.

CHAPTER TWO

# The house of language

*"Words were originally magic"*

—Sigmund Freud

Figure 2. Sculpture of John the Apostle by Omer Gielliet. With thanks to Joke Klomp and Ton Hilhorst.

## Introduction

There is no need of Christian belief or theology to appreciate the implications of the opening words of the Gospel of John, in the New Testament, on the central importance of words in human life. "In the beginning was the Word". It goes on: "and the Word was with God, and the Word was God" and later "and the Word was made flesh, and dwelt among us".

The Greek version of this Gospel opens with "en archei", which is usually translated "in the beginning". Jan Nieuwenhuis notes, in his book on John the Apostle, *Johannes de Ziener* (Nieuwenhuis, 2004), that the original Greek does not have a definite article: the text reads, "in beginning". That is more of a qualitative description than an indication of time, more of a fundamental than a moral determinant. It refers to origins, genesis, principle (Nieuwenhuis, 2004, p. 428). This opening qualifies and signifies a becoming, an organising principle: from the beginning, continuously, overstepping time. It is a word that looks ahead rather than back; it does not relate a past, a "then", but a now. It is a continuous beginning, a new commencement, an "again and again". The opening words are also: "In [the] beginning was the Word". This means that the Word was already there. It was not created, it did not come into being; rather, it *was* and it *is*. It stands above past, present, and future. "Time does not apply to the Word. It simply *is*, on principle. There is never anything without the Word. There was never a time in which the Word was not there. All things, including people, are dependent on the Word; indeed, they originate from that Word" (Nieuwenhuis, 2004, p. 429).

"In beginning was the Word", and this refers to speech itself: the powerful, creative speech of God. For the first few verses of Genesis, in the Old Testament, state that God *spoke* to begin making life on earth. From his mouth came a word and this word created. "The Word is therefore a creative power that evokes existence and life" (ibid., p. 430).

Nieuwenhuis states that everything that is, was created through the Word, and that creation is the articulation of that Word. In Psalm 148:5 we read: "for he commanded, and they were created". Without the Word there is no creation, says Nieuwenhuis, since the Word is the message. The Word is a living Word, is speech itself, and speech itself is a creative act. The Word is in motion and does not stay where it is; it goes, happens, and takes place. It enters into time.

The Word was made flesh, and "flesh" signifies that our human condition is fragile, vulnerable, and finite. The Word came among us. In a hard and chaotic world, the Word entered to create order in the chaos.

## The word never forgets where it has been

Language is expressed in speech or writing. So the Word creates, makes something begin, enters time, and engenders something. The word re-creates reality. Something exists as it is expressed in so many words. The words, precisely *these* words, create and bring to life. The way in which something is named is how it exists among us. It becomes a reality in the way in which it is named. The words that are spoken lead a life of their own, as it were, outside those who have articulated and heard them. They originate from the speaking human being and detach themselves from that person. That is how words circulate among people.

Psychotherapy, of course, is oriented towards biology and the neurosciences, towards medical thinking and medical pathology, psychiatry and its diagnostic system of classification—but psychotherapy also belongs to the domains of semantics, semiotics, textual analysis, and textual interpretation. Just as in my earlier book *De mens als verhaal* (Olthof & Vermetten, 1994), stories are at the heart of this book, and I inscribe myself in a narrative science that has been developed in philosophy, narratology, theology, and history. Should psychotherapists not consult poets and writers, playwrights and choreographers, film directors and visual artists? Should they not enlist the aid of literary theory, linguistics, and hermeneutics? And of film narratology and mythology? Philosophy and Bible studies?

Psychotherapy proceeds via the spoken word. It relies on linguistic acts and verbal communication: in short, psychotherapy is a linguistic activity. So why has psychotherapy concerned itself so little with language? If language is the tool of change, should not psychotherapists be first and foremost textual and linguistic experts? And perhaps linguistic artists as well? Language and words map out the road to change. Even if a mode of psychotherapy is given that relies on non-verbal treatment, even then, the meaning of the session needs to be articulated in words at some point, even if only in the very last minute, with a single sentence that forms the context for the silence. Language, significance, and interpretation make up the core of narrative psychotherapy. What is said in so many words? Who speaks, and who says what? What do the words mean? What is the history of these words in this particular speaker?

On our nomadic journey, we shall now make a brief excursion to the work of the Russian linguist Bakhtin, using the insights of Maaike Meijer (Meijer, 1996), Hubert Hermans (Hermans & Kempen, 1993), Jaakko Seikkula (Seikkula & Amkil, 2006), Peter Rober (Rober, 2005) and Arne Saeys (Saeys, 2004). Bakhtin famously affirms: "The word never forgets where it has been". Words travel, have a certain history, they are spoken in a linguistic community and pick up well-known and more obscure, divergent meanings along the way. They go through consultation rooms, school playgrounds, gymnasiums and theatres; they visit classrooms, symposiums, and the marketplace. They can be found in pubs, outdoor cafés, and restaurants.

For Bakhtin, the subject is dialogical and life is by its very nature dialogical (Bakhtin, 1981). Life means engaging in a dialogical relationship with "the other and the surroundings". This relationship is embodied and inspired. Hands, legs, gestures, mind, and the entire body take part in the dialogue. Language consists of dialogical interactions with others, in which every verbal expression focuses on that other and acquires its significance in the ever-developing context that is created in the course of the dialogue.

The dialogical self consists of multiple voices and multiple positions in the dialogue with the other. Even in the dialogical self's dialogue with itself, several different voices will be present. Each word is always also an answer, and as such anticipates the word uttered by the other. Being engaged in a dialogue means that linguistic genres and linguistic registers are being created through communal meanings in an intermediate space. The word does not reside in the system of language, but in dialogical interaction. Bakhtin uses the word "heteroglossia" to indicate the existence of different linguistic genres and linguistic registers. The language of science is different from the language of journalism. The language of the law is different from the language of economics. A wealth of languages can be distinguished: of politics, of commerce and the marketplace, farming, information science, and psychotherapy, to name but a few. Every group has its own language and its own linguistic domain.

Bakhtin also refers to recollections as a dimension of language—the memory and the historicity of language. Words have already been everywhere, and have had different meanings in different places, in different contexts, and at different times. Every group has its own dominant colloquial language, but no single word in that language has a fixed meaning. Through the multiple layers of language, the word acquires its dialogical orientation. Amid the dialogue between different languages within society, dialogues between different individual voices continue to flow. Words enter the intermediate space, the intersubjective space, and are incorporated into a dance of significance. A linguistic expression acquires context only in relation to the other person. It has a theme, that is to say, a unique, non-repeatable meaning in the specific context. It also has a certain semantic content, which remains the same in different situations. This semantic content can be looked up in dictionaries. The word or phrase used may also have a particular bias, that is to say that a selection is made from the multiple possible meanings to determine what the word or phrase will mean in this context, here and now. The different layers of meaning come to the fore in differences of context, place and person.

Each text is always in dialogue with other texts. As Kristeva observes (in Kristeva, 1987), "any text is constructed of a mosaic of quotations; any text is the absorption and transformation of another". She goes on to explain that every word is rooted in a tradition, and that this tradition remains audible, like an echo, with each new use. Words have memory, and the person who hears the words or reads the text allows the textual memory to surface and gives his or her own meaning and interpretation. Texts are connected across time, they are intertextual, related diachronically. Meaning comes into being in the context with the other and in a text's relationship with earlier texts. Every word, every sentence, and every text inscribes itself, and the existing meaning takes on an additional meaning in the meeting with the other. These additions transform a text into a new text. In this way, a woven fabric of texts is created. Intertextuality is regarded as the dialogical aspect of language.

Maaike Meijer distinguishes the following (Meijer, 1996):

1. The dialogue between the word and all other words that already surround the object to be described. What you want to say has already been said and named many times before, and on the way to the object, the word encounters many other words. Indeed, you can only see what you want to talk about in the light of all the words that have already touched it. The word finds its own meaning by passing through all existing meanings.
2. The orientation of the word, phrase, sentence or other expression towards the listener or reader. Every linguistic expression is oriented towards an answer and directed towards an active listener. The horizon of expectations makes itself felt in the text before the answer is given.
3. Every word has been used thousands of times before, it has a history, and "does not forget where it has been".

Bakhtin refers to all these forms of dialogical interaction as intersubjectivity, while Kristeva uses the term "intertextuality". There is a large field of possibilities within dialogues that take place between therapist and client, a field that needs to be bounded: a common space for meaning needs to be created. The dialogue will then take place in a particular genre of the language, which is in turn part of a discourse. Roland Barthes sees significance as being created not so much by the author as by the reader. From this perspective, the client is the reader of his or her own text, and never stands outside or above it. The "I" as reader is already a multiple of other texts, and the "I" as speaker is already a chorus of voices, already polyphonic.

In the dialogue, the text is transformed and commented on, and it acquires a new role and position in the new context. Old meanings continue to resonate as well. Dialogue is often construed as the counterpart of monologue: stories told as monologues are added up and enter into conversation. This suggests implicitly that a good therapy is dialogical and consists of creating a dialogue between monologue stories. But here dialogue embraces the meeting of multiple voices in an intermediate space. Rober (Rober, 2005) gives the example of eight-year-old Eric, who says to the therapist, in a family session which includes his parents: "I don't want to talk, I want to make a drawing". Rober says that these words can be understood as an expression of his deeply felt desire to make a drawing. Making a drawing, inspired by Bakhtin's dialogical vision, can mean a great deal if we focus on the social context in which these words are spoken. This sentence is related to other sentences, other words that have been spoken inside and outside the session. For instance, there are the words of Eric's mother, who is worried about the fact that Eric cries every time she leaves him at school. He also cries when his parents go out and he has to stay at home with a babysitter. His mother is concerned about Eric and has said several times that it may be necessary to go and see a "talking doctor" and to explain to this doctor why he cries so much. Her words are linked to the words of his father, who agrees with the mother and adds that Eric should also talk to this doctor about his fears and insecurities. There is also a connection with one of Eric's friends, who goes to see a therapist every week and has told Eric that he doesn't like talking to the therapist. There is a connection with the words of Eric's teacher, who has complimented him on his beautiful drawings. And there is also a connection with a documentary that Eric has recently seen on television, about a boy who goes to see a therapist with his parents and then hears that his parents are going to get divorced. When Eric saw that documentary, it reminded him of the rows between his father and mother and he was afraid that his parents too were going to get a divorce.

From the perspective that is offered us by Bakhtin, we can say that all these words and sentences are connected and create different meanings. In this way, a simple sentence like "I don't want to talk, I want to make a drawing" may mean a great deal. From a position of actively "not-knowing" the meaning of the words, the therapist can explore them and tease out the intended meaning.

In the process of actively not-knowing what a word, phrase or expression may mean, a text is interrogated and introduced into a semantic space. As Derrida puts it, a text is an open system that interacts with its context. Every text must be read deconstructively. In narrative psychotherapy, symptoms and complaints are linguistic expressions that have no fixed meaning, no meaning attached to an "equals sign". Things are similar rather than identical; the focus is more on differences than on correspondences. In a representation of reality, a master signifier is presupposed. In the world of "similar", the world of "as if", the focus is on making interactive meaning possible, far more than on discovering a central, universally valid meaning attached with the logic of a mathematical equation. In the dialogue with parents and child, the meanings resonate, and a relevant significance can be identified together. We might also say a sign is attributed.

Signifying also means attributing significance. "To signify" is a verb—it is about supplying signs, imparting meaning. The word, the sentence, the text and the story can be seen as a process instead of independent words used by the writer or speaker. The universe of meanings must be confined to practical, embodied knowledge, a knowledge that is implicit and that implies a "knowledge of how to go on". Embodied knowledge is knowledge with felt meaning, here and now, in the dialogue between these people, in this context.

Dialogical understanding creates something new. This is not a conception of dialogue in which it is the therapist's task to interpret the client's story. A dialogue in the Bakhtinian sense refers rather to a kind of dialogue in which one person's meaning comes into contact with someone else's. Thus, even small children can be knowing, active signifiers and full participants in the therapeutic process. In dialogue, meaning has to be added from outside. After all, the existing meanings are not sufficient to eliminate the complaint or symptom. The dialogue needs to be enriching and to add meanings.

As Bakhtin puts it, the subject is polyphonic, and its diverse voices have a dialogical relationship with each other. In dialogue, diverging points of view are together embodied by characters. The client's text can be seen as a polyphonic novel, or as polyphonic music. In polyphonic music too, voices adopt different spatial positions, follow independent melodies, such as to produce a collective musical expression.

The Dutch psychologist Hubert Hermans too refers to the polyphonic, dialogical self, in his books *De echo van het ego* ("The echo of the ego"; Hermans, 1995) and *The Dialogical Self* (Hermans & Kempen, 1993). This self adopts relatively autonomous "I-positions" in an imaginary landscape. The "I" can shift position and move through space. Each position has its own voice. This polyphonic self is a narrative self, structured in time and space. In Hermans's polyphonic self, the omnipotent subject has likewise been superseded by diverse "I-positions" that are situated alongside one another in time and space. Hermans refers to a juxtaposition in which divergent viewpoints are associated in dialogical relationships. He refers to the polyphonic novel as described by Bakhtin, with the disappearance of the omniscient narrator. The diverse characters are no longer subordinate to the narrator; each tells his or her own story. The juxtaposition he refers to focuses on the relationships between the different storylines and the quality of those relationships. Juxtaposition creates added value that transcends the individual voices and viewpoints (ibid., p. 28). Thus, Hermans's polyphonic self too emphasises difference and multiple positions, a simultaneous presence in space of positions that may even be contradictory. This is like polyphonic music, which derives its beauty from the simultaneity of contrasting melodies (ibid., p. 31). We also see this in Greek laments such as *miroloi*.

Hermans refers to four aspects of the polyphonic self:

1. The "I" can adopt multiple positions;
2. From each position, the "I" can tell its own story, taking account of the temporal dimension;
3. Positions and voices are juxtaposed: they are brought so close together that the "I" can move back and forth between the different positions and voices;
4. The movements are dialogical in nature.

We might add a fifth aspect to these:

5. Each voice is linked to, and "inhabits", a particular part of the body. Tom Andersen (in Hoffman, 2002, p. 165) says "Voices must have homes".

In a more absurdist sense, we encounter the polyphonic and multiple self in Pirandello's *One, No One, and One Hundred Thousand* (Pirandello, 1992), in which the protagonist is astonished to discover that he is not a single individual but in fact harbours 100,000 different personas. This discovery is precipitated by a casual remark made by his wife, who asks him, as he stands in front of the mirror, if his nose is not crooked.

## *Text-focused reading*

Steve de Shazer distinguishes between text-focused and reader-focused reading (De Shazer 1994). If we were to see psychotherapy as a conversation, and a conversation as an exchange of spoken words, we could classify the words spoken by therapist and client as a "text"—a text that is heard or "read". These exchanges may embrace non-verbal expressions, which will then need to be invested with linguistic significance, such as the little boy who keeps tearing his hair out, discussed later in the book. The therapist is a reader of the client's text, and should read the text as literally as possible—that is to say, without any personal assumptions based on his or her own interpretive schemes. Text-focused reading means reading the text that is said or written in so many words. It is the text of the quotation, of what is literally said.

This literal text is then subjected to textual analysis. This means reading the text from within, and bringing it to the surface, to its outer frontiers or margins. Textual analysis searches for what is omitted, magnified, or diminished, but retains its focus on the text, continues to take the literal text itself as its point of departure. Reader-focused reading, in contrast, is an interpretive process. The therapist interprets the meanings and significance of what the client says. The therapist is here the signifier who ascribes meaning, meaning that acquires greater value than the meaning that the client himself or herself can apply. All too often, as therapists, we do not hear what clients say, but *think* we hear what they say and interpret their words on that basis.

In text-focused reading, it is the client who is both author and master signifier of the text. In therapy, the client's text is often part of a dominant story of suffering and pain: a problematic story. Together with the therapist, this text is taken to its marginal limits. In many cases, the text at issue is one that is always spoken in the same way, one that no longer admits any nuances or new meanings. The therapist leads the text, via that which is spoken-in-so-many-words, through dialogue, to new meanings. For in general, words have certain dominant meanings, meanings that tend to occupy the foreground. These are the meanings that can be looked up in the dictionary. In addition, one can consult an etymological dictionary, as a kind of archaeological lexicon. For in addition to a word's dominant meanings, it often possesses peripheral meanings, which are further to the background—frequently meanings that the words have possessed in other times or specific contexts.

Just as similar stems in different words point to a shared origin, many words have layers of meaning, constituting a semantic archaeology.

Besides their dominant and peripheral meanings, words also possess associative meanings. Through the client's text, what we may call the "semantic margins" can be explored. Within these semantic margins, associative meanings play a role, meanings that are attached by virtue of sound, tone, or analogy. In addition, words may be split up, subsequently following different paths of meaning, as we shall see below. In these semantic margins, the text is stretched: one reads the text from the inside out, and around the text, and the text is brought from inside to the surface. This is the realm of intertextuality and deconstruction. The therapist, as the reader of the text, forges his or her own associative connection. The therapist's own context and history inevitably creates a sensitivity to certain aspects of the client's text. Furthermore, the client's text leads the therapist to other texts. Numerous connections between meanings are possible; words always refer to one another, make each other into a text, and texts also refer to one another. Bakhtin's aphorism, "The word never forgets where it has been", and the different meanings that words have had, come to life in these semantic margins. There is an open, active dialogue in an intermediate space.

It is often a joyful experience when client and therapist find the "right word", the word that fits exactly. The body reacts to the right words with a feeling of relaxation, warmth, tingling. Or with a sigh of relief. The body knows what the right words are. They often need to be tracked down, discovered and excavated in an archaeological expedition. According to Lacan, the subconscious is structured in language, and we are therefore connected to one another in a collective subconscious.

Text-focused reading requires us to keep to the words, sentences and imagery used by the client, and to forge connections with this imagery—to remain within the client's linguistic domain. If the problems are articulated in terms of music, music is the linguistic domain. If language and images from nature are used, nature is the linguistic domain, with all the words that go along with it: growth, organic, weather, the rhythm of day and night, the tides and seasons, sunlight, hot and cold, hard and soft, water, nourishment, manure, compost. A linguistic domain excludes certain other words. The word "instrumental" does not belong in an organic linguistic domain, "installation" does not belong with development, "force" does not belong with growth. Freezing is naturally linked to thawing, loosening to fixed. In the semantic margins, associations can be made on the basis of the client's text, which can thus be widened, deepened, expanded, or reduced in size. The following pages give examples of text-focused reading and the subsequent textual analysis. In these examples, the client's words and phrases form the point of departure and the therapist attempts to go from the client's words to a different text, one that evaluates or relates to the original utterances.

Psychotherapy is often predicated on the assumption that meanings are known and shared, and the therapist "reads" the text with the meanings that he or she knows and assumes to be known to the client. A simple sentence like "Now I'm getting all the blame as usual", spoken by a client, evokes a well-known meaning of the word "blame". The therapist "reads" this meaning and adopts it. But "blame" may contain a multitude of meanings, depending on context and history. If the meaning is assumed to be known, the question that is omitted is "If you say that you get all the blame as usual, can you tell me what 'blame' means to you, and what it means in your family? What happens when you get all the blame?"

The word "blame" can then be illustrated using an object or attribute. In the session in which a client spoke this sentence, it was a handbag. "Suppose this handbag is the blame. What happens with the blame if you get all the blame? Who do you get the blame *from*? Where do you put that blame?" The handbag may then be placed on the client's lap, under her coat, behind her back, or under the chair. It may be visible or concealed, it may form an obstacle or hindrance, it may be light or heavy.

When a man says to his wife, in a conversation with the therapist, "You're always watching me", this sentence will sound like an accusation, especially if said in a particular tone of voice, and the meaning will almost certainly be taken for granted. In narrative psychotherapy, however, the question will be asked: "What does watching mean? What does 'You're always watching me' mean?" The therapist adopts an attitude of actively not-knowing the meaning of "watching". Together with the husband and wife, the therapist writes the word "watching" down. Who watches who? What are you watching? What does the word "always" refer to? Does it refer to all time, to all the time there is? "All the time there is, you watch me, just like others watch me", perhaps? What does it mean for the husband if his wife watches him? It may perhaps refer obliquely to a care context: you watch out for me, as one may watch a child, perhaps. It may refer to a lack of space: you're too close, I can never get away from your field of vision.

Suppose that the client says, in this case: "If they watch me, it means that I have no space, that they're too close", the reproach "you're always watching me" implies a strong desire for space. In the text, the problem shows the way to the solution. There is a desire to be out of sight. A more associative meaning evokes the relationship between "to watch" and "to be seen": "You watch me, but you don't see me".

In the case of the husband who says this to his wife, this is what the words turn out to mean: "You're always watching me, but you don't see me. And if you don't see me, I'm weighed and found wanting. I long to be seen and at the same time to be thought good enough".

By way of the semantic margins in which the therapist, in his or her capacity as a reader, assumes the meaning of even the simplest words to be not-known, a context is created for new meanings. This calls for a completely open attitude, one of actively not-knowing what words mean. Or the knowledge that words never forget where they have been, and that they may hold a world of meanings within them. Within these semantic margins, new words can come into existence, and words may acquire new meanings.

*Nightmare*

Sonia, eight years old, came to see me, together with her mother, because she was troubled by recurrent nightmares. Sonia, her mother, and I obviously all knew perfectly well what a "nightmare" was. But did we really know? Sonia often woke in the middle of the night in a terrible panic; fear racked her body, which shook with emotion.

"Shall we have a look and see what 'nightmare' really means?" I asked Sonia. We looked the word up in the dictionary, which told us:

"A nightmare is a dream that frightens a sleeping person"

That was the meaning we already knew—the first and dominant meaning of the word. Then we looked up the word's etymology:

In Middle English, a nightmare or *nightes-mare* is described as "a female spirit or monster supposed to beset people and animals by night, settling upon them when they are asleep and producing a feeling of suffocation by its weight". The element "mare" originally meant "a kind of goblin supposed to produce nightmare by sitting on the chest of the sleeper". Other languages supply additional dimensions. In Old Church Slavonic, we find *mara* with the meaning of "emotion", and in some Russian dialects, *mara* means "phantom, vision, hallucination". In Dutch, *mare* can mean a story or news. This is what Bakhtin calls "heteroglossia".

So we found meanings as different as "night monster" and "night news". At night, we might conjecture, news is circulated by a nocturnal sprite or goblin. Associatively, the word *mare* can be linked to French *mer* (sea), and *mère* (mother). Perhaps the child was frightened at night time without her mother, perhaps she was afraid of drowning in the sea or of being washed away, and felt a keen need for someone to watch over her and protect her from danger; did she miss her mother at night time? Perhaps she was dreaming of her grandmother, who had recently died? In this way, we paused and reflected on the intermediate and intersubjective space in which the world "nightmare" is inscribed. Sonia was an active participant in this quest for meaning.

Reflecting on a word in this way, looking it up in the dictionary, considering its many different meanings, created a space in which three experts were able to speak and were knowledgeable. The eight-year-old child had her own form of knowledge, or wisdom, beyond her own embodied and inspired experiences with nightmares. She too was connected to the language's collective memory. Children frequently come up with surprising ideas in such situations. The space is free for interpretation and significance, thus exemplifying the principle of co-creation, dialogue, and cooperation.

Sonia ultimately took on the role of "master signifier" and we continued the dialogue with the meaning with which she identified most closely. It became clear that Sonia was terrified that her own mother would die if she failed to pay sufficient attention. Granny had died very suddenly and without being able to prepare for her death. In her great grief, Granny had entered the house and was haunting Sonia's bedroom at night and in the domain of her sleep like a goblin. In an open dialogue, it became possible to discuss Granny's decease, the funeral, sickness and death. And the nightmares stopped.

In some cases, new words may be coined in the course of the dialogue, as in the following example.

### Dislusting

A 55-year-old woman used the word "dislusting" when describing her lack of sexual arousal. (Translator's note: The original Dutch text is about the coinage *afzinwekkend*, a portmanteau word created accidentally from *afschuwelijk* (horrible) and *weerzinwekkend* (disgusting). The word *zin* in the latter is a very rich word, which can mean liking, but also sense.) This word is clearly a contamination of the words "disgusting" and "lust". And since we immediately understand what the word is intended to mean, we might easily let it pass. Even so, this slip of the tongue turned out to fit precisely with what she is trying to express about the context of sexual tension in which she had been forced to live as a young child. We analysed the word together, with the context she had described. She was referring to something to which she felt an aversion. We split the word "dislusting" up into its three syllables, and wrote them down on a big sheet of paper. Together we reflected on the meaning of this slip of the tongue.

First the part "lust", with its connotations of sexual desire. Instead of "lusting", lust was gone, producing "dis-lusting". The lust that might have been there had vanished, or had been repelled. The lust that had been discarded referred to the relationship she had had as a young woman with an older man, who was also her mother's lover. The man had made sexual advances to her. On the one hand she felt aroused, a sense of "lust", while on the other hand it disgusted her that this man, who was having a relationship with her mother, was making advances to her. While the incident gave her a certain sense of superiority to her mother, she was nonetheless appalled to find herself in this position. The "lust" that had been aroused, the young woman's burgeoning sexuality, was smothered. The lust became disgust, dis-lust, her sexuality withered and froze into a stifling impediment. The young woman's urge to reach out in love had been blocked, in relation to the older man and to her mother.

The text therefore served as a diagnostic tool. The young woman did not have any sexual dysfunction; rather, an external intruder had abruptly aroused and then stifled her sexual responses. What initially appeared to be a mere slip of the tongue proved to lay bare the connection between lust, shame, and disgust. Sexual arousal, when it occurred, was now inevitably accompanied by revulsion.

This story helped the woman to understand her own lack of sexual excitement in her marriage: her senses had been smothered.

For textual analysis we must read in a text-focused way, always taking what is said in so many words as the point of departure. For narrative psychotherapy, in the client's text, it is important to be attuned to keywords, core expressions, details, and symbols, which possess energy and represent embodied and affective knowledge. These keywords and core expressions are metaphorical utterances that appear in the form of surface details.

Van der Hart et al. (in Van der Hart & Schurink, 1987) refer to "metaphorical core expressions". The word "core" refers to the intensity of these expressions and to an important "value area", to use a term coined by Hermans (Hermans & Hermans-Jansen, 1995). They are utterances that contain a nucleus or grain of truth. *Core* does not mean that it contains the core of the client's text. Core expressions are usually said casually, in a subsidiary clause, in the sideroads of language. They are often overlooked or forgotten along the main highways of speech. Metaphorical core expressions serve as stopping places, little bus shelters where the speaker can wait, reflect and gather strength before the next leg of the journey. They may become indicative and fertile metaphors if the therapist adopts them and repeats them back to the client.

Metaphors are also important ingredients that help to create a framework for psychotherapy and to ensure that the client's language is preserved. If the therapist picks up such expressions and uses them, he or she remains connected to the client in the same intermediate space. All too often, therapists translate their client's literal words into the words that they (the therapists) are accustomed to speaking. In that case, the psychotherapy compels the client to adapt to the therapist's language—often without an interpreter. It is not inconceivable that the client's original words may get lost in translation.

Metaphors are also ideal instruments for describing relationships. In a metaphor, the relationship remains the same, while the *relata*—whatever or whoever are being compared—can be replaced. Metaphors make it possible to explore multiple meanings. No two people discuss the same symptom or complaint in the same way, and our language, dominated as it is by digi-speak, is inadequate for the subtle discussion of emotions. For this, we need metaphors, poems, or stories, and our ears should prick up whenever a client says: "It's as if…" Here language becomes fluid and flows, and this language is a point of departure, or "line of flight", as Deleuze calls it, providing direction for the therapeutic framework.

## *Meaning of metaphor*

According to the Oxford English Dictionary, metaphor is:
- the figure of speech in which a name or descriptive term is transferred to some object different from, but analogous to, that to which it is properly applicable;
- an instance of this, a metaphorical expression.

The word *metaphor* derives from the French word *métaphore* and ultimately from the Greek μετα- (corresponding to Latin *trans*) + φέρειν (to bear, carry): etymologically, then, it means carrying over from one linguistic domain to another. It is related to the words *transfer* and *transport*. The Dutch writer Jan Wolkers has said that imagery must be used extremely sparingly. Images should be used only when they possess some dramatic power and really add something to what is being described. "I later understood that such images bring you into contact with the black box, the symbolic world of the subconscious, or whatever name you want to give to it" (Brokken, 2006, p. 131).

Lacan, we recall, asserts that the subconscious is structured in language, and that the language of the subconscious is the image or the metaphor. A metaphor always describes the relationship between individuals or between a particular person and the world. That is why metaphor is pre-eminently the language of systems. Metaphor brings to life an image that can act as an organising principle, describing numerous interactions.

As the Belgian poet and essayist Herman de Coninck says:

> As a grandfather loves his grandson,
> imagery puts an arm around something.
> An image has to be a few sizes too big,
> like a winter coat. An image brings reality
> back home with it as grandfather takes his grandson home
> when his first girl has said it's over.

or:

> I carry my sleeping daughter
> up the stairs just as a poem
> carries words. Language is a father.

Herman de Coninck in
Kristien Hemmerechts, *Taal zonder mij*
*(translated for this publication by BJ)*
*Reprinted with kind permission*

Let us look at a few examples of textual analysis, in which core sentences are analysed. We shall also look at examples of core metaphorical expressions, some of which were articulated with great intensity during psychotherapy, while others were related en passant as trivial details in the story. The phrases or expressions were analysed for their dominant and peripheral meanings. They were split up, and lines were drawn linking each sentence and each word to other words and meanings. By way of associative meanings, the semantic margins were explored, and within this space, new meanings, twists in the story, possibilities and solutions could suggest themselves.

## Textual analysis

In the following paragraphs, the instrument of textual analysis is applied to a number of key utterances made by several clients in the course of their therapy.

### *I feel as if I'm in the process of decomposition*

This sentence was spoken, during one of her first therapy sessions with me, by a woman who had been admitted to a psychiatric institution some time earlier. "I'm in the process of de-composition". The woman spoke of herself here as the protagonist, and at the time of speaking, in the "present", she was in the process of decomposition.

*Being in the process* describes something that is ongoing. It may be active or passive. It may imply that there is a force that is stronger than her, which is responsible for this process. Alternatively, it may imply active participation.

*De-composition* refers to the many meanings of "compose": what is initially "composed" may separate or dissolve; a composition, made up of connected parts, may fall apart. Decomposition also carries within it an allusion to putrefaction, rotting away.

Thus, being *in the process of decomposition* presents an image of the future on the one hand, of being at the mercy of a situation, while on the other hand it may convey an active picture: an active process of decomposition is going on, a process in which composite wholes are lost and communal connections dissolve. The patient said that she was a bad mother, since her children had left home. In her eyes, the fact that they had left home meant that she had failed.

I decided to start by placing the decomposition process in a temporal perspective that could be indicated on a horizontal axis. I asked her to show where she stood on this axis, representing a scale between an imaginary beginning and end of decomposition (taking up a position is an act, an active operation: a determination of place). She placed herself three-quarters of the way towards the end of the scale. I then focused on the final quarter, and said,

"Is this the last phase of decomposition, which leads to the end, to death?"

"Yes," she said, when she had fixed a place for herself. Then, once she had concentrated on the final quarter of the axis that she had drawn on paper at my request, she chose different words to express her situation, saying:

"I'm ready for the scrapheap." The meaning here refers to a feeling of lacking all value or significance, of almost being thrown away.

I then chose two directions along which to structure the dialogue:

- Where did the process of decomposition begin?
- Can I translate your sentence "I'm ready for the scrapheap" into "I feel 'dumped' or 'rejected'"? (Translator's note: The Dutch word used here for "dump" is *afdanken*, a verb for "to discard", "get rid of" that (oddly!) contains the word for "thank").

The conversation then proceeded along these two lines. The woman explained that she had been given away to a foster family when she was born, and that that was where the process of decomposition had begun. In this foster family she was subjected to a very unpleasant regime, a kind of totalitarian state, as if she were a citizen with obligations and no rights. "I felt I'd already been dumped when I was born".

I then asked the patient to accompany me on a journey to explore new meanings. Using a hypnotic form of language, I asked her questions that I then strung together to make a new story. She started on an internal process of exploration. I allowed space in between the questions, moments of silence, when I saw that the questions were triggering an internal exploration in her.

> Is it possible that ever since you were born you've been trying to form a whole composition, to make connections, and that you have become more and more entangled and tied up in this process?
> …
>
> Is it possible that once you had a family of your own, you undertook, together with your husband, to ensure that these connections would never be dissolved, that they would exist forever, in the same state as that in which they were first composed?
> …
>
> Is it possible that you were terrified that these connections might be broken, afraid of dissolution, of decomposition?
> …
>
> And if you are afraid of decomposition, now that you have finally felt what it means to compose a family, to have ties, is it not possible that what you like most would be to tie your husband and children to you, to ensure that these ties, this connectedness, will never be lost?
> …
>
> And perhaps you cannot imagine otherwise than that once your children start developing their own ties, their own connections, with the outside world, this can only lead to decomposition, to the loosening and disintegration of the ties with you?
> …

> Is it possible that your children are happy to compose your family, but that they don't want to be tied down, and that you find it impossible not to tie them down, because you lost your own connections so early in life?
> …
>
> Is it possible that the composition, the connection, that you have experienced with your children must therefore never be changed, and must remain the same forever?
> …

After this, a contemplative silence ensued, and I decided to place the emphasis on the therapeutic relationship. This was because at the psychiatric ward the woman had developed the habit of constantly clinging to anyone who tried to help her, and this clinging had led to a recurrent pattern of rejection or "dumping".

> Suppose we decide, together, to compose a therapeutic relationship, to forge a connection, in which I try, as your therapist, to help you find ways of reconnecting with your children. Perhaps your children don't want to be tied down, but they do want to have a tie, a connection with you, and perhaps they don't want to dump you, but to thank you for everything you've done for them. But if I forge a connection with you, are you going to tie me down, so that I would have to take you everywhere with me, so to speak? If you do that, I would have no choice but to detach myself again. Then the therapeutic relationship would be de-composed, and you would feel rejected or "dumped" again. Could we compose a connection that helps you explore the ties with the people who are dear to you? At the end of this conversation, can I translate your words "I feel that I'm in a process of decomposition" into the words "I long for connections, I long for a life in which I feel connected to the people who are dear to me"?

In this way, the therapist can use the client's literal words, her own language, what is said in so many words, to explore the multiple meanings of the words that have been articulated, and to lead the problematic meaning that has inscribed suffering and pain by way of the same words to different meanings. Here, the words "I feel that I'm in a process of decomposition" were resolved, through the words' multiple meanings, into "I long for a life in which I feel connected". The focus on the process of rotting or putrefaction, with its associations of death, was transformed into a longing for life and for the experience of connectedness. The initial emphasis on passivity, on being at the mercy of forces inexorably carrying on a process, was changed into an active process of exploration, in which the therapist could be of help—always providing that the patient agreed with these new meanings.

This example of textual analysis shows how it is possible to draw on the multiple meanings of a word, by way of sentences or key metaphors, to define an intermediate space. Then, through peripheral and associative meanings, this intermediate space can become a semantic space that draws lines enabling the client to leave the problem story behind her, and to travel to a new horizon with new prospects for the future.

Let's look at some more examples.

## Conductor of trains

"I don't want to be the conductor, only of the trains," said a four-year-old boy to the district nurse who had come for a house visit because the boy was displaying symptoms of intense anxiety. What a wise sentence, if you knew the family context! The boy's mother had numerous physical maladies and had been admitted to hospital for surgery on several occasions. His father was often abroad on business, and was absent in his role as a father, although he dearly loved his son. With all the insight of his four years, the little boy said that he was the conductor of the train called family, and that he didn't want this role! He was happy to be a conductor of trains but not of the family.

## Something is changing in that body

"Lately I've had the feeling that something is changing in that body" spoken by a man aged seventy. After a pause, he added "and that I'm going to have to take more care of myself."

The man had been widowed a few months earlier. For years he had devoted himself intensively to caring for his sick wife, and he had carried on helping to take care of her until her death. The man did not refer to "my" body but to "that" body. Might that mean that in caring for his wife, he had been compelled to completely disregard himself? That he had been dimly aware of numerous signals of pain and stress but felt obliged to ignore them? That he had been unable to attend to them because there was something bigger and more important—his terminally sick wife, whom he had to support? In the hierarchy of meanings, his wife's suffering was of a higher order than the pain in his own body. Was he compelled to disown his own body in order to help relieve or respond to his wife's suffering? Had he been forced to transform *my* body into *that* body?

There he sat before me, shattered and despairing. There was pain and stiffness everywhere in his body: his neck, his shoulders, his back. He had been having trouble sleeping, and when I went to get him from my waiting room, where he had been waiting for a while, I found him asleep there. He had decided to ask for help, and in the course of our conversation he felt understood, he surrendered a little. Something broke through to the surface.

I suggested: "Can *that* body become *my* body? Could you now start taking care of *that* body and take up ownership of your body again, so that it becomes *my* body? Is it time, now, to start taking care of *my* body? Could the mourning process include, or show the way, from *that* body to *my* body? If you have been taking care of your wife so intensively, and for so long, you have almost become part of her."

At the man's home, everything had been left in the same state as in the final phase of his wife's life. The wheelchair, the slippers, the cupboard with towels and underwear, the bottle of pills beside the bed, the clothes on the chair … everything was still standing or lying in exactly the same place. The room had become a kind of museum, in which time had stood still. When the parish priest came to visit, he said, with the best of intentions, "I think it's about time to clear up!" The man felt that this displayed a lack of understanding for his situation. Frozen in time … Just as when something is taken out of the freezer to thaw, it would be a very gradual process in his case. Where would change begin? It seemed as though nothing in the outside world could have any influence; only some movement within him could start something. This movement appeared to be slowly, cautiously, stirring … Exactly where the movement began could not be determined, but one thing was sure: thawing starts in warm surroundings.

In the following session, the man said that he had put on his "bold shoes" (*stoute schoenen*: "de stoute schoenen aantrekken", literally "to put on your bold shoes", is a Dutch expression meaning to take the plunge). He had driven around the hilly landscape of the province of Limburg and entered a café where he and his wife would often go to have a drink. The café was very crowded, however, and he could not bear the noise of voices, the clatter, and the cheerful atmosphere … As he told this story, I was suddenly reminded of the title (not so much the content) of a book by the Dutch writer Anton Koolhaas: *Sensitive Skin* (1986). When you're in mourning, your skin is very sensitive. The sounds of the café hurt; they confronted him too much with the loss of his wife. So he got back in the car and drove on. Unable to find what he was looking for, he ended up returning after all to the same café. By then it was quieter. He ordered coffee and ham and eggs. It felt like a big step to do such a thing: "Ordering ham and eggs, just for myself." To do this, he had needed to put on his "bold shoes".

I took his images literally, and turned "bold shoes" into externalised objects. What does it mean to put on your "bold shoes"? Bold, in this context, means brave, fearless. Many Dutch expressions featuring shoes have equivalents in English. Shoes symbolise a person's circumstances: "How would you act if you were in *his* shoes?" "I wouldn't like to be in *his* shoes". "Only the wearer knows where the shoe pinches" … and if you put on "bold shoes", you prepare to do something for which you don't really have the courage.

Following this reasoning, the man's "bold shoes" helped him to do something that he would not otherwise have dared to do. The shoes were bold—meaning that they took him down paths other than the beaten track, followed different routes. They might be just a little bold or extremely bold: they might gradually branch off from the regular route, or go in the opposite direction. Whatever the case may be, every change is "bold".

I asked him to put his "bold shoes" by the front door, to remind him that it was fine to get moving, bravely and slowly. "To mourn" is a verb: it requires action. Perhaps his "bold shoes" might help him take the necessary action, and be part of the process that would help him go from *that* body to *my* body.

*A piece of my heart is still lying there on that hill in the woods*

During a supervisory session, my supervisee, the psychologist Yvonne van den Brekel, presented the case history of an eighteen-year-old woman—let us call her Eline—who had said these words. We analysed the sentence together.

The sentence refers to a conversation that Eline had had with her mother at the age of twelve, during a walk in the woods. Eline felt trapped in the consequences of her parents' divorce. Both her mother and her father now had new relationships, and Eline felt as if she inhabited a no man's land between them. She lived with her mother and fiercely protested at the formation of a new family, with the two children of her mother's partner. Eline had lost her place. She says that she had been a very difficult child at the time, and had behaved unpleasantly to both of her parents' new partners. The crucial conversation in the woods was about the fact that she wanted to live with her father. Eline and her mother quarrelled, but her mother could understand her daughter's decision and even found it something of a relief, since the father's partner could take over the task of caring for Eline. "I can still see my mother walking down that hill in the woods, away from me." And it was when recalling that moment that she said, "A piece of my heart is still lying there on that hill in the woods."

If we split up the literal text, what is said in so many words, into its constituent parts, we get: A piece of my heart—is still lying there—on that hill in the woods.

A piece of my heart. "A piece" implies a relationship between part and whole. The whole is a heart and the part is a piece of the heart. It is logical to ask how that part relates to the whole. Which part of the whole? What proportion of it? You might say: if half was left in the woods, we are talking of a broken heart.

Lying there. Lying is a state, a position. On the one hand, "lying" is a participle from a verb, which may imply action. But if someone or something is lying, the picture this evokes is of a state, a fixed position. It is *still* lying there. "Still" implies duration, an extension of time. It has been lying there for six years, which implies that it is unlikely to move and change of its own accord.

And where is this piece lying? It is lying on that hill in the woods. The place has been defined: it is lying *on that hill*. Not any old hill, but very specifically *that* hill. That experience in those particular woods, in that particular place, on that particular moment of that day, is still present in exactly the same way in her memory. If a piece of the heart is missing, lying somewhere, it implies that the heart is incomplete. The therapeutic movement could therefore go from incomplete to complete. What needs to be done in order to make the heart whole again? What—or who—has to move in order to accomplish this? And the movement is *from* lying *to* … what? A related question might be whether there is also a piece of her mother's heart still lying in that place in the woods.

Eline also talked about the position she had found herself in, as a twelve-year-old girl: "I had to lead my mother's life." Eline constantly adapted to the lives of others; that was the theme of her therapy. It exhausted her, made her head feel very heavy and tired, and she sometimes felt she could scarcely remain standing. Her head was full of concerns as to whether she was dividing her love fairly between her father and her mother. Was her heavy head trying to tell her, perhaps, what a heavy burden it was to lead her mother's life and her father's life, and the lives of others on top of those? Was that why it sometimes felt as though her knees were giving way? Might that piece of her heart on the hill in the woods not be a piece of a different heart? The heart of expectations, the heart of loyalty and parentification, the heart of the intermediate space in between mother and daughter? Perhaps that piece did not actually belong to her *own* heart. After all, if a piece of her mother's heart was also still lying there, did that piece not also belong with her mother? Could the pieces, perhaps, be buried together there? The little pieces of disappointed expectations, the pieces of excessive demands and having to do too much? This exploration made it possible to create new meaning.

*A wheelbarrow won't move unless it's pushed*

This sentence was spoken by a sixty-year-old man in a particular phase of his psychotherapy. He remembered his mother saying this sentence, and told the following story.

> My father was laid off after serving his company faithfully for twenty-five years. He felt very hurt and upset. That was in an era when there was scarcely any social security. My father seemed lost in self-pity. At some point my mother lost her patience, and decided to give him a bit of a push in the right direction. She gave him an ashtray with the inscription: "A wheelbarrow won't move unless it's pushed". It helped to give my father the impetus he needed, and soon afterwards he found a new job.

The man himself had recently been "laid off" after twenty-three years of marriage. During those twenty-three years, they had kept each other in a stranglehold. They were heavily dependent on each other, and neither had a life of their own to speak of. In the course of the therapy, it became clear to the man how heavily he had relied on his wife, and the extent to which his wife had been expected to care for him like a mother. He felt very sad and hurt, and was inclined to drown his sorrows in drink. That would be theatrical and would be a kind of revenge on his wife: "Just look at what you're doing to me!" It would make him a tragic hero. But his mother had always taught him: "Be a big boy!" That is an expression that you don't hear much anymore. It is not useful anymore, we no longer want to hear it. Perhaps it was used so much in the past in order to suppress all sorts of emotions.

"Be a big boy!" used to arouse strong feelings of opposition in him. His reaction would be to get ill, using illness as a form of resistance. Then he could no longer be expected to be a "big boy"; he was excused, and knew he could count on his mother—and later his wife—to take care of him. As we talked, however, it turned out that the expression "Be a big boy!" also had another significance for him. He explained how proud he was of his parents:

> My parents are both well into their eighties, and in all their stubbornness they are vigorous characters. I think that my mother's mental strength helped prevent me sinking into depression—still helps me now. I think that my mother's spirit has been activated in me, and that I have to get myself moving ... I'm not a wheelbarrow anymore!

### *Psychotherapy and the process of interpretation*

*A hand*

A hand appeared, high up in the sky.
Everyone looked up.

It's quite possible that this was just any old hand
that someone had discarded
and that had got caught up in a rising current of air.
If not, there's surely another explanation.

A finger pointed straight at us.
But that might mean anything, absolutely anything.

*(From Toon Tellegen, 2000, translated for this publication by BJ)*

When asked who we are, we answer with a story. In dialogue with our fellow human beings, our story takes on shape. We explain what we have done and where we come from. We talk about our families, our work, our plans and ideals, our disappointments. We explain how we look at the world. In dialogue we shape our story, refer to events, and arrange them into a meaningful whole. In dialogue we develop a cohesive story about ourselves, and select from the world around us whatever fits in this story. This gives us a sense of coherence and continuity. We are as we say we are, we become how we talk about ourselves—we are our own story. In this way, the world of which we are part becomes a familiar world with an intelligible story.

When we are struck by incomprehensible, sorrowful, fateful or absurd incidents in our lives, we feel compelled to weave them into a story. We need to be able to place the events in a significant context and to relate them. If we are unable to create a cohesive story, we are overwhelmed by feelings of fragmentation, disintegration, senselessness, and passivity: instead of being participants, we become passive spectators. We lose contact with the world and ourselves, stop telling our story—or at best we keep telling the same story in an evermore compacted form, a single-track, one-dimensional tale. We tell an evermore constricted version of the reality that is causing us increasing suffering, or we continue to tell the same story, again and again, without changing or adding anything.

Many of those who present themselves as clients to psychiatrists, psychotherapists, and youth care services are incapable of telling anything other than a fragmented story about themselves—from broken families to broken people; from broken people to broken stories. They are no longer authors of their own stories, but merely the listeners to, or readers of, a story that others have created for, with, and about them.

Narrative psychotherapy sets out to help clients develop or retrieve their own stories. A narrative text may take on diverse forms: a story, a poem, a novel, the lyrics of a song, a fairy tale. It may also be a non-linguistic text: a film, a piece of music, a play, a drawing, or a symbolic image that tells a story. In this sense, symptoms and complaints can be viewed as untold stories, stories that have been excluded or marginalised, or stories that have been told again and again in the same congealed way.

In his book *The Ant's Departure* (published in Dutch; Tellegen, 2010), Toon Tellegen gives a brilliant example of the myriad meanings that may be attached to a single event. The ant's departure baffles all the other animals; no one has any idea why the ant has gone. Each one tries to find an answer to the mystery, to instil some significance into the ant's departure. In the absence of any written explanation, every creature interprets the enigma in his or her own way. The following paragraphs on these diverse reactions could well be used as the basis for an entire manual of psychotherapy!

> The *squirrel* squeezes his eyes shut, concentrates very hard on thinking of the ant, and at length he sees the ant in front of him. And since he can see the ant, the ant cannot have gone anywhere! However, as soon as he opens his eyes, the ant has vanished again.

> The *penguin* thinks to himself: *I am always gone, but no one even notices.* No, they don't go looking for me, they say: let him freeze to death; let us never have heard of him.

The *cricket's* solution is to walk back and forth in his room, to poke his head out of the window and to call out: "He hasn't gone! Of course he's still here. Why would he have gone anywhere, he can't have gone anywhere, and he wouldn't want to go anywhere. Go away ... what a lot of nonsense!" He goes to see all the other animals, and to each one he says: "He hasn't gone anywhere!" And he calls it out so loudly and so often that he starts thinking to himself: "Phew! That's a good thing! He hasn't gone away at all!"

The *sparrow* responds to the event by giving some lessons in going away. Lesson 1 is about *Going away.* Lesson 2 is about *Coming back,* and Lesson 3 is about *Staying away.*

The *aphid* feels ashamed and doesn't dare to show himself in public. He hears two creatures talking about the ant's departure and wondering why it might have happened. The aphid cringes. "It's all because of me. The ant obviously thought: that terrible aphid—must stay away from him! Must get away from him!"

The *frog's* thoughts are completely different: "He left because he wasn't able to croak. That must be it! And he feels ashamed because of it. That's why he has gone." Then he jumps up, thinking: "But surely, he didn't need to do that! Not everyone has to be able to croak, after all!" He sits down again and thinks to himself: "I could have taught him to croak, couldn't I? Not croak really beautifully, I mean: I couldn't have taught him an outstanding croak, but a reasonable croak all the same." He looks around him. There's no one there. "An acceptable sort of croak, anyway," he thinks to himself, "I could have taught him *that*, at least. I should have insisted more, and told him more about croaking; then we might have croaked together."

The *crow* says that the ant hasn't gone anywhere. He keeps pointing to a particular place, and when the other animals look behind the tree, they don't see the ant there. "Of course not," says the crow, "haven't you ever heard it said of someone that he is 'a sight too clever for those around him' or that he knows how to fool people? Because that's exactly what the ant is doing with me right now—fooling me."

The *butterfly* chooses a different epistemological solution, and says: "Perhaps he's calling out to us right now: 'Where are you?' And we can't hear him. So let's all start calling out: 'We are here! We are everywhere!'" He calls out, but no one answers.

The *wasp* cries out: "You just stay away!" And "I'm really glad you've gone. Don't ever come back, and if you do come back, I'll chase you off again straight away!" He calls out these things for hours, and the other creatures get angry with him, because they miss the ant and they *do* want the ant to come home. The wasp answers: "I want him to come back too, I'm being perverse! That's what it's called!"

The *crab* thinks: "This is the end of the ant! If he comes back after all, it will be too late. I shouldn't really think like this, but it keeps going through my head. It's all over with the ant, it's over for good, over, if he comes back it will be too late; this is the end of the ant!" These are horrible thoughts and he begs his thoughts to go away.

The *secretary bird* advises following the ant to the letter:
"If you don't, you'll never find him. If you do, you may meet him some time in the future in the written word or in phrases or some other written thing. Life is lived to the letter!"

The *carp* has a better idea, and gives the pike a guilty conscience:
"I can quite imagine that the ant has gone."
When the pike asks him what he means by that, the carp says that he doesn't want to hurt anyone and that one can easily think of reasons why someone like the ant would not want to be around here any more. For instance, if he has had more than enough of someone.
"There are some things that we simply know, dear old pike, indisputable things. That's what they're called. They're also called home truths."
And he goes away, leaving the pike feeling utterly wretched.

The *mouse* thinks that the ant is hiding, and that there's nowhere better to hide than in a word. So he goes in search of him, in all the words he knows. But he can't find the ant.

The *swan* understands perfectly why the ant left, since there's nothing elegant here, it's all uncouth, mucky, and higgledy-piggledy. Everything's dry and stained and sloppy! The swan makes a list of all the reasons why the ant may have left.

The *owl* writes a letter to the ant:
"If I had gone away, I would have left a note that said: don't come looking for me, don't call out for me, don't be sad, don't miss me, but do write. I'm writing to tell you that I've discovered something. It's that if I write to you, you're not gone! You're gone in real life, but not in my thoughts."

The *hippopotamus* thinks that the animals ought to surprise the ant: "We should decorate his house, bake some cakes, and think of presents to give him. Then he's bound to come back!" Because he can't imagine that he, hippopotamus, wouldn't come home if his house was decorated and everyone was eagerly waiting for him to return and certainly not if it was all prepared to be a surprise!

The *beaver* blames himself, and says:
"I should have built a wall too high for him to climb over."
He imagines the ant standing in front of his wall and saying: "Oh! I hadn't expected that."
And if the ant hadn't been able to climb over the wall, the beaver would have invited him home with him to have some cake.

The *toad* thinks that the ant must have exploded with anger, just as he so often explodes with anger himself. He does wonder what it was that made the ant so angry that he exploded. "It must have been something terrible," thinks the toad, "perhaps someone insulted him."

The *caterpillar* thinks that the ant has not gone away but has changed into something else. Not *someone* else, but *something* else. Something else, something you can't see, possibly something that hasn't arrived yet. These were enigmatic words and difficult thoughts.

The *woodworm* does not mind that the ant has gone: as if going away were more important than boring holes in wood. Suddenly, however, a thought strikes him: "If all the wood were gone, and there was nothing left to bore holes in, what would happen then?" And he gets on with boring more holes, with relentless energy. "Just bore holes," he thinks, "Don't think!"

The *lobster* has a book that contains everything that does not exist. He often leafs through it, and one day he encounters the ant in that big book. And he goes around saying to everyone that the ant has not gone, since he never existed.

The *snail* and the *tortoise* philosophise about the idea of going away, especially about going away *well*. The snail says that going away well means going away slowly. So if you go away better, you go away more slowly, and if you go away even better, you stand still, and if you go away *even better* than that, you disappear. That is all they have to say.

The *earthworm* and the *mole* talk to each other about what could have caused the ant's departure. The earthworm says that it was much too dark for the ant here, and mole says that it was much too light for him.

Each creature interprets the ant's departure in a different way. Could one possibly conceive of a more wonderful palette of human emotions and thoughts? Could one possibly imagine a better way of explaining how many solutions there are for cognitive dissonance? Tellegen succeeds in creating a "multiverse" of meanings. Each creature reasons from within his own world view, from within his own epistemology, his own autopoiesis, thus producing a different interpretation of reality. Taken together, these interpretations constitute a world of stories, in which no one story is truer than the next, because none of the stories can be confirmed by the ant.

So many different truths cannot easily coexist within a community. Generally efforts are made to achieve a consensual domain, in which the truth with the greatest support is elevated to "the Truth". This "Truth" becomes a discourse, the discourse to which Foucault refers. In a discourse, certain groups or individuals claim the right to judge and the power to give or deny others the right to judge, or to determine what is meaningful and reasonable and what is not. In other words, significance and interpretation have to do with power.

Take the following fragment from Lewis Carroll's *Alice in Wonderland*, for instance. Alice, puzzled at Humpty Dumpty's use of the word "glory", asks him to explain:

> "I don't know what you mean by glory."
> Humpty Dumpty smiled contemptuously.
> "Of course you don't—till I tell you. I meant there's a nice knock-down argument for you!"
> "But glory doesn't mean a nice knock-down argument," Alice objected.

> "When I use a word," Humpty Dumpty said in a rather scornful tone, "it means just what I choose it to mean—neither more nor less."
> "The question is," said Alice, "whether you can make words mean so many different things."
> "The question is," said Humpty Dumpty, "which is to be master—that's all."
> Alice was too puzzled to say anything, so after a minute Humpty Dumpty began again. "They've a temper, some of them—particularly verbs, they're the proudest—adjectives you can do anything with, but not verbs—however, I can manage the whole lot of them!"
>
> (Carroll, 1992, p. 254)

## *The world of interpretation*

It is no easy matter to decide when an interpretation is correct. What we can do, however, is to say which interpretations don't fit, and we can establish where there is a subjective feeling of well-being. In that sense, psychotherapy does not have evidential value; rather, it has the power of expression: stories can persuade, appeal to someone's feelings, impart a feeling of beauty and enchantment. They may be elegant and aesthetic, focused on connections, cooperation and love.

Details in the main lines of a story may be important points of transformation. Even so, they can easily be missed. In that case, perhaps there is a different way of entering the story. Hearing the details is a matter of chance, it may depend on serendipity. In the words of Ben Okri:

> The beautiful thing about even the most superficial attempt to collide with the secret lives of others is what can only be termed the aesthetic of serendipity: the accidental discoveries, the widened horizons, roads opened by lightning flash into the forests of reality. (Okri, 1997)

Symptoms and complaints can also be seen as untold stories, excluded or marginalised stories; stories that have become dissociated and detached from the shared context. Stories in themselves to which no significance can be attached in isolation, stories searching for an author and a listener. Stories require interpretation if connections are to be made and a cohesive whole discovered. Complaints may also be congealed stories, held captive and locked up within language.

For instance, I still remember my very first work placement, in a large wing for people with a mental impairment. From what its inmates had initially seen as a temporary settlement, the wing had become a permanent place of residence, a destination without any prospect of a new journey. A destination of congealed stories, frozen in time and language, audible only in the form of sudden snatches of sentences, divorced from context and significance, isolated and almost shorn of significance, but still … One of the patients who lived there was Tony, who cried out all day: "Did you tear those trousers, Tony? You mustn't do that, Tony! Did you tear those trousers, Tony? Did you do that, Tony? You mustn't do that, Tony!" And then he would hit himself hard on the forehead. If these sentences are spoken a hundred times a day, and the man hits himself on the forehead a hundred times a day, does anyone still listen to him? And would Tony himself still be able to explain where these sentences come from? For Tony, it was impossible to add a single word to this sentence. His story had become stuck in his brain, but what had happened in his life, and what was the significance of those torn trousers? And the blows to his head? There must have been many lines in his life story! Tony, in any case, no longer had any words at his disposal.

Therapist and client together search for the semantic space in which to tell the story and to interpret complaints if they are not accompanied by a clear explanation. The world of interpretation is not the world of mathematical equations; rather, it refers to the world of analogies, similarities. The therapist's role as all-powerful signifier is deconstructed, and the reality is interpreted as a narrated reality with an "as if" quality. Significance and interpretation are given in dialogue.

The following example shows what happens if significance and interpretation are attached to a patient's words in a one-sided manner.

*I love my parents*

A supervisee who has only just started working in psychiatry told the following story, which she had found very upsetting:

One morning she saw a man and a woman, evidently a married couple, come into the hall of the clinic. They sat down and waited for the woman's admission to be arranged. The supervisee went up to them because the woman was crying and was very agitated. She briefly sat down beside the couple and asked them who they were waiting to see. Then a care worker came to get them. The woman's agitated state worsened. She had evidently been receiving treatment for some time and was afraid of medication. The patient was shown to a room, together with her husband and the care worker. The supervisee followed the couple, since she could see that the patient was deliberately going limp, falling to the floor. Close to the room in which the admission interview was to take place, the patient did in fact collapse on the floor. She appeared to have lost control: she was foaming at the mouth, her eyes were rolling, and she started cursing and using obscene language. The supervisee heard her say:

> I love my parents, I love my brothers ... those damned drugs ... everything's being destroyed ... the whole world is rotten through and through ... Go to Hell! ... I don't want any pills ... I love my parents ... I love my parents.

The woman was restrained and spoken to, and pressured to accept the medication, with the argument that it would help to make her feel calmer. Her husband was very upset, he appeared confused, and tried to provide what comfort he could to his wife. People attracted by the noise stood around watching from a distance. The supervisee stroked the woman's back, trying to provide silent support as the patient continued screaming her sentences. It was the first time she had experienced a crisis situation in her fledgling career in psychiatry. Later on she told her colleagues that she found the experience extremely harrowing, and was given the advice to keep a greater distance in such situations in future.

What could the connection be between being forced, or not forced, to take medication and the sentence: "I love my parents ... I love my brothers"? Taking medication appears to have the significance for the woman that she doesn't love her parents and brothers—even, in fact, that taking pills is "destroying everything".

What would happen if this crisis were not seen as a "crisis", and care workers were to make contact on the level of the language the patient used? If they were to say: "Talk about how much you love your parents. Is there someone who says that you don't love your parents?" What would happen if she was asked what these pills say about her love for her parents? Apparently the sentences she utters are heard as meaningless language, as congealed language that is merely repetitive. The sentences have been stripped of all meaning and are therefore no longer heard. The context of the hall in a psychiatric hospital, of a crisis in the public space, of the room in which there will be talk of medication and admission, organises a dominant discourse within which the patient's words are heard only as an illustration of a clinical picture. This context makes people deaf: indeed, how often are we care workers not "deaf"?

## The magical significance of words

In his book *Words Were Originally Magic* (De Shazer, 1994), Steve de Shazer describes the magical origins of words. This magic can still be conjured up if words are given the space to have multiple meanings. De Shazer discusses the linguistic philosophy of Ferdinand de Saussure. De Saussure distinguishes surface and deep structures of language, and these structures stand in a hierarchical relationship to one another. De Shazer compares surface structure to conscious thought and deep structure to unconscious thought. In structuralist linguistic philosophy, it seems as though the code of deep structure can be deciphered—as if the unconscious has its own language that can be mastered, a code that can be interpreted and determined.

This code might be deciphered with the aid of omissions that can be tracked down in the surface structure of language. However, De Shazer argues, following De Saussure, deep structure too may have its gaps and omissions. We can never be sure that we can find them. In the centre of the structure is a hole; the structure is open to interpretation. In this void, the hierarchy vanishes: surface and deep structure reform into the same level, converge into a single line. This means that there is no longer any fixed anchor to which meanings can be attached, no Archimedean point from which significance can be inferred.

Lacan fills in this gap in significance with the aid of the phallus as master signifier, with the "Law of the Father" as the primary authority in the symbolic order. Derrida, in contrast, says that the existence of this gap is an essential possibility, a precondition for finding other meanings (Derrida, 1982). There is an endless chain of meanings, a play of meanings, a positive condition of possibilities, of becoming. It is precisely in the gap that a fertile vacuum of interpretation may be formed, enabling new meanings to be found that escape from the dominant structure of "the Law of the Father". Nomadic thought, thinking in terms of difference, fills in this void with a new mode of speech and writing. This void is teeming with imperceptible energy, which could take on new forms at any moment.

The realm of the void, so quantum physics teaches us, contains mysterious riches (Chopra, 1989). The void should not be filled up with interpretation that creates presence from what is absent; rather, the absence should be seen as transcendental. Derrida uses his concept of deconstruction (he actually prefers the word *soustraction* = extraction) to detach words from entrenched meanings. He tries to follow the text beyond its intended significance and to push it to its limits, to the margins, the secrets and silences that determine the significance of the text.

Philosophy should relinquish for good its illusion of omnipotence in relation to significance, and return to the endless play of signs, the connections with other texts and other significances, which can be connected to one another again and again in a constant succession of new ways.

A link might be posited here between psychotherapy and art, because it is in that fertile void that the creative process can germinate. Let us listen to what the poet and essayist Bert Schierbeek has to say. In his essay "Een broek voor een octopus" ("Pants for an octopus") he discusses the creative process (Schierbeek, 1965). He hears a Spanish construction worker sighing: "This work is harder than making a pair of pants for an octopus." The man uses this common Spanish expression to express how exhausting he finds his job as a construction worker: he is puffing and panting, groaning and sweating. After he has voiced this metaphor he gets on with his work with all the appearance of having forgotten the words. But the words haunt Schierbeek. He recites them to himself, and the words keep buzzing through his head; they have long since lost their denotative, communicative and descriptive significance and take on a life of their own.

This new, independent significance is what Charles Peirce calls "firstness" (Peirce, 1960). The words detach themselves, take on a meaning of their own, fill the space and travel to different contexts, different signifiers. They go in search of new content and forge connections to new words. They escape from one context and are found elsewhere. Schierbeek says that words start off living within their limitations, in their meanings: "They are not yet 'drained of meaning'. It is only once they are drained of meaning, once they are empty, that they can become signs. Words are weighed for so long that their weight eventually vanishes. Then they become manageable and it is then that the miraculous creative process can begin" (Schierbeek, 1965, p. 12).

The words themselves become signifiers, they become an organising principle and free up the semantic space for other meanings, giving rise to a poetic universe. These words are "heard" in the breath of the person who speaks them, they become discoveries, inspirations. Schierbeek refers in this context to an area of tension, a force field onto which the word falls, setting off vibrations throughout the entire extraordinary network of feelings, thoughts, things, people, phenomena, and apparitions. The entire creative process thus consists of a succession of moments in which "discoveries" impinge on the field of tension and set it vibrating in its entirety. As a result, the discovery is elevated to a new height; it becomes part of a force field to which it had never belonged before, and alters its consequences.

According to Schierbeek, the "discovery" automatically acquires a place in the pattern, and the maker already suspected beforehand that this discovery was in the offing—a place has already been prepared for it. While in the throes of creative tension, the maker appears to encounter only those things he can use—they arrange themselves with a kind of inevitability in the as yet unknown pattern. The maker has to discover a different order in the things and words, and so he actually finds, to his own surprise, what he was not looking for. According to Schierbeek, while we often refer to an "open ending", we speak far too little about the concept of an "open beginning". The path is made by the imagination.

Words do not belong to anyone; their power is inherent to them and anyone can activate them. They can be reconnected to other words and become a fresh organising principle: poets must liberate the words from their fixed place and significance, fill them with new energy and rhythm. Schierbeek refers to the necessary quest for the "zero point of significance … the zero point in which things and people slumber. Sleeping, they are ready to be roused, awoken in colours, shapes, scents or words" (ibid., p. 47).

In this way, associative links come into being: lines that detach themselves from the words' fixed meaning and reattach themselves elsewhere with a fresh meaning. From within an "open beginning", the logic of abduction—discussed at length in Chapter Five—can do its work. It is therefore essential that we take the client's own spoken text, literal quotations, as our point of departure. If we think we have heard what the client said, we may well interpret it without the words having truly "sung". What matters is that the words repeated are the actual words that were used, that what was said was what was actually said. That is the key point when it comes to "text-focused reading". Text-focused reading takes the text as the point of departure and analyses it in its own right.

So if the text is taken as the point of departure and words are taken literally, they can start echoing, spreading, while the person who spoke them has forgotten ever saying them. As soon as the words have been spoken and truly heard, they no longer belong to the client and take on a power of their own. They enter the "poetic universe" and the "semantic space". Then they can draw lines to each member of the team, who will hear these words in accordance with his or her own nature and in his or her own way. Once all the information has been presented, the team sets to work, in its capacity as a therapeutic medium: it proceeds from an open beginning towards an open space and allows the words to detach themselves from their original context. The team starts searching, starts working, and is willing to wait for something to be found. It is willing to inhabit a state of not-knowing, to go to the "zero point of meaning", where it may enlarge or diminish, rotate and detach. Information that comes from daydreams, images and associations that are raised, the atmosphere that develops in the room, distractions and intermezzos, it is all part of the process. A mosaic is gradually formed, a creation, a material shape that forms the foundations for the treatment framework that will be constructed in the following phase of the process, and that will be developed by analysing and reflecting on information from the open space that was referred to in Chapter One as a subject–object–free space.

## Crisis? What crisis?

In this subject–object–free space, we experience time as real, lived time (durée), a concept coined by Henri Bergson. Sometimes the experience of lived time breaks through; this is what happens in daydreams, meditation or contemplation, in looking at art, or in other experiences calling for heightened concentration, such as sport—experiences in which we lose our sense of linear time. In the impartial gaze, *real, lived time* has an opportunity to come to the fore, as Bergson puts it, because during the creative process, the artist distances himself from the ego with its functional actions and descends into the deeper layers of his being, which, like *real, lived time*, is dynamic and in a permanent state of flux. If we want to experience *real, lived time*, says Bergson, we must "let life take its course" (Hermsen, 2009, p. 62). So in this open space, we can focus our attention on art, novels, poetry, film, drama, and sport, and in this space we can constantly move.

According to Bergson, *real, lived time* is what creates difference: not so much differences in relation to other people, but internal differences, so that the changing or emerging nature of everything that exists comes into sight. This requires a more intuitive mode of thought. *Real, lived time* differs from economic and linear time, and it is also linked to different experiences of time: there is an ego that acts in accordance with the principles of practical intellect, and a second ego that Bergson calls *le moi profond*, which is linked to a dynamic *real, lived time*. It is also important to note that these two aspects of self are engaged in constant dialogue.

In psychotherapy, too, which is inscribed in economic time, it is crucial to allow time and space for *real, lived time*. If the team functions as a therapeutic medium, it goes through both these processes of time. In *real, lived time*, nothing is lost, as Bergson puts it: the memory records, in the form of memory-images, all the events of our daily lives as they occur in time; every moment is new and unrepeatable. Only memory makes it possible to experience *real, lived time*. Everything we have experienced is present in our memories as an *élan vital*, which provides the driving force underlying every life process. This *élan vital* is movement, and it is important to pause, to stand still, if there is a great deal of movement.

When a crisis arises, for instance, people often respond by moving quickly. Clock time imposes itself and actions are dictated by Chronos. Precisely at moments of crisis, it is important to connect ourselves to *real, lived time*. We should endeavour to look in the opposite direction, away from what is tugging at our attention. As Johan Cruyff liked to say: "You should always look to see where the ball is *not*." This calls for stillness in the midst of movement, and movement in the midst of stillness. It requires you to look behind you when your attention is being directed in front of you, and vice versa. "I'm not interested in the player with the ball, but in what is happening at the other end of the field," said Cruyff (Baartse, 2007; Winsemius, 2004).

A team is often confronted with the pressure of circumstances. This pushes them to look in only one direction, focusing all their attention on a single point. With a couple that is embroiled in a bitter conflict, all attention focuses on this strife. Even so, the *real, lived time* can be experienced if we go and sit next to their little daughter and ask her how it feels for her to hear and see her parents fighting with each other like that. The process is interrupted, as it were: there is a moment of stillness. Create a difference; do something else! The patient who throws herself on the floor in the hall of the hospital, and who cries out as she lies there, foaming at the mouth and eyes rolling in her head: "I love my parents! … I love my brothers!" attracts all the attention, and her behaviour is defined as a crisis. A crisis organises the actions and responses in a peremptory way. And yet even this movement might be brought to a standstill if someone were to sit down restfully beside the patient and respond to her words: "I love my parents".

In 1975 the rock band Supertramp released an album called *Crisis? What Crisis?* This phrase has stuck in my mind, and has often helped me in crisis situations in a family or an institution. A situation is actually *turned into* a crisis as soon as it is labelled as such. The Chinese character for crisis can mean two things: danger and possibility/opportunity. In the case of a crisis as danger, immediate action must be taken, and any postponement is dangerous. In the case of a crisis as possibility, acting too fast is often part of the problem, and exacerbates it. I remember a patient from my first period of practical training who lay in front of the lift, shaking uncontrollably and thrashing with his arms and legs. Everyone walked around him and people were calling for emergency assistance. Then someone passed by and reacted in a completely different way. He said: "Move out of the way please, I'm from the technical department." This remark was so completely inappropriate in the context that the patient looked up at the man in astonishment and stood up. This made it possible to enter into dialogue with him.

So if we inhabit a world of interpretation, it is of the utmost importance how we go about naming. Words create a reality; they structure a particular linguistic domain. What we call something becomes part of the reality. Malou van Hintum wrote an article that appeared in *de Volkskrant* of 5 January 2011 under the heading "There's no such thing as difficult patients, only complex treatment situations". The article was about "Ambivalent connections" by the social-psychiatric nurse Bauke Koekkoek, a PhD thesis submitted at Radboud University of Nijmegen. Koekkoek argues that carers exercise a great deal of influence when they call a patient "difficult". In his experience, it is more appropriate to refer to complex treatment situations, to which the care workers have not yet found a satisfactory response.

This seems to me exactly right. A treatment situation becomes complex if there is no clear framework, no clear therapeutic context. Sometimes the circumstances of a "difficult" patient's life are so complex that care workers are simply incapable of finding an adequate response … or rather, not one of the available options is adequate. In such cases, the description "complex treatment situation" is more helpful than the stigmatising label "difficult patient", which singles out the individual in a negative way. Patients are seen as difficult when there is no good framework and no good plan: in consequence, the therapeutic relationship becomes an ambivalent connection, whereas the best prognosis for successful treatment depends on a good therapeutic relationship. When a community is created—that is, a community of people with some connection to the problem who can help to deal with it; when those most directly involved with the patient, such as family members and friends who belong to the "conversation community", are given an active role in the treatment, this often creates a larger support base in the search for a helpful response to a complex treatment situation.

The periodical *Filosofie magazine*, dedicated to philosophy, has a regular "Dilemmas" column with readers' contributions. In one issue (2011), the mother of a schizophrenic son writes as follows:

> About seven years ago, our adult son suddenly broke off contact with his family. This was followed by compulsory admissions to psychiatric institutions—three times. Sometimes I would spend an entire day sitting next to the telephone; these were days on which the attending physician had promised to call back and by the evening I was still waiting. Finally I managed to get some information from a student doctor, who mentioned in passing that our son had been diagnosed as schizophrenic. The institution did not wish to say any more, since our son had asked them not to.
>
> How are you supposed to respond to this, as a parent? It seems to me that the concept of "autonomy" has gone too far in the healthcare services. Don't get me wrong: I too believe that patients should be able to take control of their own lives, as far as possible. But it is common for people with schizophrenia to become paranoid for a time and to even refuse all contact with their families. These things tend to go in waves. In the meantime, I have fetched my son back from the United States three times. Then he tells me: "Mum, Mum, I love you so much." He himself has said that he doesn't want to leave us at all, but that sometimes there is something in him that takes over.
>
> In spite of all this, most of the care workers act as if our son is a normal person who is capable of making decisions autonomously. When we raise the alarm, they sometimes simply

keep us at a distance. Of course the care workers have to assure themselves of the family's sincerity; some family members can be toxic. But at the institution where our son was staying most recently, they were able to see that in the initial months he derived a great deal of support from us. In such a situation you surely don't stop all contact if he suddenly says that's what he wants? I should emphasise that we often have no idea how our son is, or where he is. Unfortunately we are now dependent on the willingness of individual doctors to cooperate with us. If they don't want to, there's nothing we can do. I believe that the family should be systematically involved in the treatment. After all, care workers are always to some extent—as one of them recently said so eloquently—passers-by. They only see our son for a short while. But the family is there for ever.

### *Horizontal and vertical polyphony: open dialogue*

The Finnish psychologist Jaakko Seikkula developed the "open dialogue" approach to psychiatric crises in the sparsely populated region in the north of Finland, near the border with Lapland (Seikkula & Amkil, 2006). A team made up of members from different disciplines visits the family at home if there is a crisis, or sets up a meeting and discussion somewhere else. Seikkula and his colleagues take it as an absolute principle that the person's family and social network should always be involved. If a psychosis develops and there is a sudden crisis situation, they immediately ask who should be there and who is important in the patient's life. Besides the patient's immediate and other family members, these may include friends, neighbours, or co-workers. All these people are invited to the meeting. Creating a context for an open dialogue means adhering to the following principles:

- the patient is never discussed in his or her absence;
- no decision is taken without the family's involvement;
- no discussions take place with the patient alone;
- families are part of the treatment;
- there are open meetings, without any advance planning, without any protocols or textbook guidelines;
- the process is not steered or controlled;
- it is therefore essential for those concerned to be able to cope with uncertainty.

The psychotic stories are discussed when everyone is present. Those who are not present are nonetheless brought into the discussions by asking: what would he or she say if … Seikkula calls this "speaking with the voices" (Masterclass held in Amsterdam, 19 May 2011). The referring physician or other professional is invited to the meeting, since the patient is never discussed on the telephone. There are no hidden agendas. This creates a safe context in which to maximise the resources of the client and his or her surroundings. Seikkula draws inspiration from Bakhtin's dictum: "Life is living in the polyphony of voices. Dialogue between voices is the basic human experience" (Bakhtin, 1981).

In a meeting with an open dialogue, there are therefore a great many voices. These include not only those who actually come and sit in a circle and join in the conversation—what Seikkula calls "horizontal polyphony"—but also the voices that live inside us and with which we live when a particular subject or person is being discussed: "vertical polyphony". If a patient starts talking about the one he loves, the voice of the one *I* love will sound inside *me*. If I'm talking to a patient about his brother, the voice of *my* brother will also make itself heard in *me* in the way we speak to one another. In this way, external and internal voices interact.

All those who take part in the conversation start at the same time, thus creating a shared history. This ensures transparency. The conversation focuses on resources and cooperation, on respect, and there is an effort to refrain, as far as possible, from critical comments. Decisions are taken communally, and therefore enjoy the necessary support. The aim is to generate a new language for those experiences that lack words, or for which the words do not yet exist. Since there are no hidden agendas, the conversations are not followed by internal consultations. Anything that has to be said and asked is said and asked during this meeting. The inner world is outside and the outer world is inside. Shotter calls this kind of participation on the part of psychotherapists "witness thinking"—thinking *with* instead of thinking *about* (Shotter, 2010).

In this way, Seikkula and his team are often able to devise responses to complex treatment situations. Seikkula reports a dramatic fall both in the use of medication and in the number of admissions to psychiatric clinics. Instead of diagnosing the patient, thinking and speaking about him or her and thus effectively isolating the patient, a conversation community is created within which the patient is absorbed and within which those involved cooperate. It is a form of being together with and around a patient in crisis. Take the following example:

> In a ward of a psychiatric hospital, a number of patients became anxious and confused because one of the male patients was pestering them and sexually harassing them. This was not discussed openly, but the subject gradually came to the attention of the staff through chance remarks that were overheard. The customary procedure would be to discuss what should be done at a confidential staff meeting. In this case, however, it was decided to set up a conversation community, and to hold a meeting in the main hall for all team members and all the patients. This included the man who was accused of sexual harassment, who attended solely in the capacity of a listener. Everyone else's voice was heard; everyone told his or her story. There was an open discussion on whether or not to allow the man to remain on the ward. Remarkably, everyone expressed his or her opinion, without exception. This created the necessary support and forged a sense of solidarity, at which it was decided to keep the man in their midst. A "together" had been created, and no one felt alone anymore; everyone felt the community's support. From then on, the harassment could no longer be swept under the carpet; it would be transparent and brought to the surface. This is an example of "witness thinking"—thinking "with" each other, instead of decisions being made over the patients' heads. The meeting released remarkable forces: the women on the ward felt reassured by the solidarity expressed by those around them, and were no longer afraid of the man. The stories made a great impression on the man, who was grateful when they decided that he could stay. This sense of gratitude facilitated the process of his own care and assistance.

The polyphony of an open meeting also has a different logic, one that may be called (borrowing a term from Deleuze) a forgotten or suppressed logic. Deleuze illustrates this logic with a passage from Lewis Carroll's *Alice in Wonderland* (see Romein, Schuilenberg & Van Tuinen, 2009). Alice loses grip of herself; she loses the sense of her own well-defined identity. She becomes smaller and then larger in rapid succession, and experiences a series of baffling transformations. Size no longer provides a fixed frame of reference, belonging to her identity. Instead, small and large are attributes that lead lives of their own, as though separate from her. Shrinking and growing are things that happen to her, they become active processes instead of features of her "being", in the classical sense of the word. The process is played out between opposing poles and is in constant motion, in a kind of uninterrupted simultaneity. Alice does not grow larger without being smaller; big and small imply and refer to each other. This constant, uninterrupted motion exercises a tractive force in both directions.

In the same way, attributes can lead lives of their own within an open, dialogical meeting. Toon Tellegen gives a marvellous description of this in a poem in his collection *Daar zijn woorden voor* ("There are words for that"):

> I had to say something.
> I looked around me. Who was there?
> I saw desire to get away, with his restless eyes,
> and doubt in his long grey coat.
> I saw ambition, bumptious but lame,
> and aversion to this and now.
> It all depends was there, hunched over
> —on a stool in a corner—when would he ever not be there—
> and sense of duty with his gigantic eyebrows,
> that's almost all he is.
> I saw the despair sisters, teetering on white high heels,
> they kept on looking in their bags
> and sometimes met each other's questioning eyes.
> I also saw ennui and lethargy, their backs
> towards me, and vanity, suspicion, hubris,
> oh-so-obvious . . .
> But where was shame, my shame?
> I looked around, looked up, and down,
> and suddenly I saw her, out of breath, and stammering:
> "Am I late?"
> "I ... ," I said.
>
> *(From Toon Tellegen, 2005, translated for this publication by BJ)*

In this poem, shame is still an attribute of the speaker; it is "my shame". The other attributes are spectators and events; they overcome the speaker and his vibrant ideas and anecdotes. They each have a certain relationship with the speaker and refer to one another. They are all there. A logic of this kind is helpful at a nomadic meeting. With the attributes that initially belonged to the subject's identity a journey can be set in motion, a personal story can be told in relation to the subject. This logic creates the possibility of a ceaseless becoming. Chapter Four on the third space and Chapter Five on abduction discuss this logic as an active event with which, and through which, a relational whole, an open system, can be created. Attributes can be linked, giving rise to new links; new lines can be drawn that can make the constant process of "becoming" a reality.

In this way, all the different types of knowing and wisdom can resonate with and off each other. Deleuze says that it is nonsense to want to "think past Plato". Not because we have replaced Plato, but because we *cannot* replace Plato. Criticism is completely pointless (Romein, Schuilenberg & Van Tuinen, 2009, p. 31). In nomadic thinking, forgotten and rejected knowledge remains important. We stand on our ancestors' shoulders—in philosophy, in psychotherapy, and in our personal lives. Ideas from the past, which no longer "mean anything" to us, are nonetheless part of our knowledge. They still belong. The "no" is not a distinctive category, as in the logic of representation, but an intrinsic part of our knowledge.

So in a psychotherapy meeting, the answers are not fixed: on the contrary, we need to find an answer to a complex problem, each time afresh, in the here and now, at this particular meeting, with what is happening in this place right now, with the knowledge of all participants being freely expressed. The context is the enabling condition for this response. The knowledge is present below the surface, and the archaeology of knowledge lays bare the different layers that have preceded our current knowledge, which are immanent in our present knowledge and emanate from it. This approach, in philosophy and in psychotherapy, replaces negative, oppositional reasoning with a joyful, positive mode of thought. Affirmation and appreciation as living ideas—that is, a joyful form of knowledge and a joyful practice. On this basis, the practice of psychotherapy becomes an open, affective sojourn in intermediate spaces (Braidotti, 2004), a process of becoming, a process situated in the local practice of transformations enacted in response/responsibility.

To mould the archaeology of knowledge, this practice relies on a quotation-based approach; in other words, many voices are heard in the meeting, not just those of the participants. "Speaking with my mother's voice is a gesture of solidarity" (Braidotti, 2004, p. 41). In the intermediate space of an open meeting, ideas become nomadic, space can be created for other voices, with the aid of quotations. Nomadic thinking helps those involved to remain true to themselves and to others: after all, the subject constitutes himself or herself in relation to others, and the meeting with the other carries within it the realisation of mutual dependency. That is why the thinking is geared towards the longer term. The meeting takes place through the embodied self.

Chapter One referred to the power of the embodied self to be moved and to move others, with the aid of a metaphor: "the body as a landscape". A landscape has a history and provides soil for archaeology; it has fluid transitions and frontiers. A person's biography is inscribed in the landscape of the body. The body is thus layered, like a layered text, composed of the surfacing of memories. Social codes too are inscribed in the body. In the landscape of the body, diverse codes cross one another: different lines, different areas of the landscape intersect and overlap. "Embodiment is an intimate form of signification" (Braidotti, 2004, p. 32). This intimate form of signification is the subject of the following chapter.

CHAPTER THREE

# The language of the body: the role of the body in narrative psychotherapy

*"There is more wisdom in your body than in your deepest philosophy"*

—Friedrich Nietzsche

## Introduction

In Chapter One we reflected on "embodied" and "affective" wisdom. Following the philosophers of *différance*, we sought to show the body's place in thought, thus connecting knowledge and wisdom to their physical roots, in line with Luce Irigaray's "spirituality of the body" (Irigaray, 2002). We noted that language acts as the body's mediator and resides in the body; life experience searches for a place in the body and marks it as a signifier. Language touches the body: words can caress, comfort, soothe the body; they may be harsh, make us blush, or make our hearts race. Words can instil feelings of shame, make us clench our fists in frustration, or open our hearts. Language elicits physical responses: words can cause physiological changes. We now know that abusive language can cause physical pain and that it affects the same parts of the brain as physical pain.

Traumatic experiences and early memories that predate linguistic consciousness also leave marks on the body. These marks are signs, visible clues that reveal something. As Julia Kristeva says, signs for which there are no words degenerate into symptoms (Kristeva, 1987). Signs reside at the semiotic level, the level of signs (Greek σημειωτική), which precedes language. This is the level for which no words have yet been found and to which no significance has been assigned: it is embodied consciousness without language.

In the Dutch documentary *Meeting John Berger*, the British writer John Berger describes his life among the farming communities of the French alpine villages. He is fascinated by the human face and draws portraits of the people around him. He tries to capture the markings on their faces as closely as possible: their features, with all their wrinkles, lines, and inscribed furrows, tell a life story: people's biographies are written on their faces. These markings belong to the level of semiotics: they are not related in logical language and are not part of the semantic domain. Rather, they are the untold stories that are etched into the body. Although this is the prelinguistic level, it can nonetheless be converted into language. Clients can be helped to translate, to put into words, what has been inscribed in and on their bodies.

Dennis Potter's television series *The Singing Detective* presents a striking example of a biography that is inscribed in the body. The protagonist, crime writer Philip Marlow, is in hospital, afflicted by psoriatic arthritis. Barely able to move, his suffering is inscribed on and in his body, like a big untold story. At one point, during the doctors' rounds, feeling reduced to an object as he lies there helpless and exposed to the gaze and interpretations of doctors and nurses, he yells despairingly: "If I don't tell someone, if I don't admit it, I'll never never beat it." Even so, Marlow is obstinate and hardly capable of talking about his life. He keeps the doctor at a distance. His torrent of abuse combined with periodic fits of weeping prompts a referral to a psychiatrist, whom Marlow warns that if he were to actually start talking, he would spew gallons of filth. Any therapist willing to engage with him would have to be able to deal with all this filth. Philip Marlow is not aware that in the plot of *The Singing Detective* he has told his own life story through the various characters, including that of the detective himself.

The psychiatrist has read Marlow's detective story on a semiotic level—that is, as a book filled with signs and marks that tell the story of his patient's life. As the therapeutic relationship develops, more and more memories and stories emerge from Marlow's hardened and horny skin, his inflamed joints. Marlow gradually starts to connect the different narrative layers in his book with his own life story and the "inscriptions" on his body. As the stories are released from his body, his body becomes more mobile. The semiosis is given significance and an embodied meaning. Thus, the body is animate matter, touched by the word, and speaking through the word. The body articulates itself: it becomes narrative.

The body is a landscape of stories, and symptoms are the untold stories that leave behind traces and clues. According to Deepak Chopra (Chopra, 1993), the body is the platform that allows experiences to manifest themselves. "Old cells make up the map of our life experience", he says. The body has a memory and carries all our memories and life experiences. That is why we speak of the "narrativity" and "landscape" of the body. Let us use an example to explore the landscape of the body in more detail.

*"It feels as if I live inside a bell jar"*

This is how Dorothy, forty years old, described how she felt. She had been referred to me for multiple physical ailments without any identifiable somatic cause. Her primary symptoms were in the abdominal and intestinal region: severe pain, constipation, and bleeding, along with symptoms that she ascribed to the menopause, such as hot flushes, panic attacks that "went to her head," and headaches.

We studied the description "it feels as if I live inside a bell jar" as an important text, and I asked her where in her body she felt this bell jar. As if it was obvious, Dorothy explained, "The bell jar goes over my head and arms and reaches down to my waist." It is surprising how often clients find it simple to link a key metaphorical image to a place in the body. So the bell jar just covered her abdomen and intestines. Then she said: "When I look at my childhood photos [she was the eldest of seven siblings, and her father made numerous snapshots of her], I see a happy and lively child until the age of five. After that, the photos show a withdrawn, shy, and introverted little girl. As if the zest for life had gone and been replaced by fear."

Dorothy went on to say that when she was five she and her siblings were placed in a children's home for the first time. It happened very suddenly, because her parents "needed a break." Their marriage was very unstable. They could no longer cope with raising the children, and her mother had many physical ailments. This abrupt removal to a children's home or foster family was repeated several times. As we pondered the bell jar theme, the client said that this feeling had originated around then. "I've never really lived. I've always felt like a marionette, who did whatever had to be done." Together we examined the different meanings of the word "bell jar". Why is something placed under a bell jar? What is the function and significance of a bell jar? "It keeps something fresh," she replied. "Cheese, for example, is sometimes put under a bell jar. But after a while, the oxygen runs out. There's no life in a bell jar."

Together we set up the following framework: part of her ended up under the bell jar when she was about five years old, but wanted to get out: it needed space and air, it needed to breathe. Another, livelier part lived outside the bell jar, but its space was limited by the bell jar. The part in the bell jar was surviving rather than really living. The other part continued to develop after the age of five and had mainly known anxiety, since she was made responsible for her siblings and for dealing with her parents' marital troubles.

The part that developed into adulthood quickly acquired a maturity far beyond her years: this part had been weighted down and has never really been able to enjoy life. External stimuli—a song on the radio, a word or phrase—could sometimes hurl her consciousness back to life inside the bell jar, bringing headaches, shortness of breath, and a feeling that everything was going to her head. Now that she was an adult, she was able to re-emerge from the bell jar after half an hour, but she lived in constant apprehension of the next attack. We agreed to find out, together, how we could free that five-year-old child from the bell jar.

Dorothy had tossed out the phrase "as if I live inside a bell jar" almost nonchalantly. However, she carried with her the embodied experience of life in a bell jar. It was only when we focused on her symptoms and on her life history that she produced this image, and she was astonished at its aptness and accuracy—it was a perfect description! She could describe every detail of the bell jar: how it fitted over the crown of her head, down over her shoulders and arms, all the way down and past her waist.

Though invisible, the bell jar was acutely present in Dorothy's embodied experience, as a present non-presence. A key image of this kind can be seen as an organising principle. Chopra (Chopra, 1989) describes this area of bodily consciousness as "quantum space", an area of silent, invisible but present energy that directs physical reality and causes it to materialise (see also Rosenblum & Kuttner, 2006; Van Lommel, 2010). You might say that "life inside a bell jar" clarified how the client's body was organised and how it ascribed meaning to the multiple physical symptoms. The energy of Dorothy's symptoms manifested itself in the form of a bell jar. She required only the briefest moment of concentration to physically experience the sensation of the bell jar: all her bodily functions, from the level of individual cells to organs, were "in a bell jar". At every level, then, in her entire physical body, her life was mere survival, starved of oxygen and deprived of sufficient living space.

We turned to consider the predicament of cells and organs—and foetuses—stuck inside a bell jar. The client related that both her pregnancies had miscarried. It was as if the foetuses too had been unable to grow, starved of oxygen and deprived of space by the bell jar. Thus, the bell jar could be seen as an organising principle or connecting pattern (Bateson, 1979), permeating all levels of consciousness and matter.

At my request, she drew the bell jar. Regarding the drawing, she said "It reminds me of my intestines and my heart." Having suffered from a chronic intestinal disorder for years, she had recently developed cardiac arrhythmia and a sense of agitation. When we took a closer look at her drawing, she said that the story of her childhood had been stored deep in her intestines and that she had only recently managed to manoeuvre the story out and up to the surface. Now it had reached her heart, so to speak. In a sense, then, she needed "to pour out her heart", but she feared the inevitable flood of feelings and possible emotional collapse. It therefore seemed sensible to build in a kind of safety valve, a device that would help her to break up her story into manageable portions, easing the transition from the internal to the external world. Having started off deep in her intestines, the story had moved to her heart, and now it was almost ready to acquire its own raison d'être in the outside world. Dorothy drew a valve on the top of the bell jar, which calmed her heartbeat, giving a sense of control and relief.

The childhood trauma had inscribed itself in Dorothy's body. She herself had attached the significance: "I am to blame for my parents' rows and for my mother's sickness and sorrow. My very existence is too much for her." While outside the bell jar the part of Dorothy that was not permitted to live struggled on, the part devoted to mere survival; her life that had to be protected languished inside the bell jar.

### The silent space

In the above case history, the key metaphor led the client's consciousness, through a meditative process, to the silent interspace. This is a deep level at which we do not "think" but simply "are" thoughts, where we become a stream of thoughts and the body is a body of consciousness. At this deep level, our organs can think, and cells can "speak": just as in Dorothy's drawing, body and soul coalesce in a free space that contains the wisdom of the connecting pattern, and from which the physical body can be spurred on to change and thus heal.

The concentration needed to reach this silent space requires a different approach to time. This is a creative process, which necessitates the courage to start with an open mind, without preconceptions, clearing a space for the memory of language in the Bakhtinian sense: "the word never forgets where it has been". Every word we use is steeped in tradition: the echoes of all the times and places in which it has had a meaning linger in every new usage. Language has its own memory. Once we accept this, our listening is guided by a different logic and a different perspective on time.

We recall Henri Bergson's distinction between clock time and what he calls durée (see Chapter Two), in which, surrendering to intuition, we are able to sense the organic relationship and continuity between past and present. In this durée, the deeper self and its associated

Figure 3. Odilon Redon, *Les yeux clos*, 1890 Oil on canvas, 44 × 36 cm; Musée d'Orsay, Paris.

consciousness converge. Non-spatial, indivisible and non-quantifiable, durée is a stream of continuous becoming and, as such, a *subject–object–free space* full of creative potential. Each moment is new, unique, and unrepeatable, and carries the whole past in it.

We can only enter the silent space by slowing down, that is by asking—together with the client—what Kunneman calls "slow questions" (Kunneman, 2009). It is in this space that chance discoveries can be made; from here the perfect word or metaphor may emerge. It is here that the language for interventions and spontaneous, non-logical ideas can form, words that can connect with the still unsaid. In this space, the world of patterns, an image can emerge that reveals the essence of organic relationships.

Deepak Chopra writes of the mysterious realm that inhabits empty space (Chopra, 1989). It is in this space that the ideas, creations and language that connect us all at a deeper level originate, and that form materialises. This form may be a thought, an idea, a metaphor, the image of a work of art, a revelation, which suddenly takes up time and space and manifests itself as a change affecting the entire body.

This is the start of a transformation of thoughts into biological processes, and this transformation takes place in an interspace, a space that is vibrant with energy and consciousness. When an idea, wish or intention is formed, it acts as an attractor, organising the surrounding energy into a pattern: the result is a physical reaction throughout the body's biochemical processes.

Memories of painful events initiate the same current in the body as the events themselves, because there is no biochemical structure outside consciousness: every part of our body is fully aware of how we think about ourselves. The body can thus be conceived as a process, a stream composed of experiences that are expressed physically. Our consciousness creates biological information: even the slightest change in our consciousness creates a new pattern of energy and information. Thus, a sense of happiness may manifest itself at the molecular level, while anxiety can permeate our body to the extent of producing anxious cells. The body reacts strongly to connections with loved ones—the hand that is held during difficult moments, a pat on the shoulder, a tender touch, appreciation or a sense of togetherness. Related to this is the elevated pain threshold that can be noted during coordinated movements, such as those of a sports team. Joy, sadness, anxiety, tension, and love affect every part of the body in distinct ways: tears of sorrow have a different biochemical structure from tears of joy.

In psychotherapy, unique words can emerge from this silent space when given the opportunity. "As if I live in a bell jar" can thus be seen as a verbal constraint on life and body that affects every organ: every part of the body is aware of the bell jar. Restrictive thoughts and emotions limit and cramp the body as messages that reach the cells regulating our immune system and weaken them, communicating these emotions to the cells themselves.

As therapists, we seek to join with our clients in sending healing messages to and from the silent space. The therapist can create a power-based context or a context of love: in a power-based context, the whole atmosphere will become rigid, defensive and tense; in a context of love, the atmosphere flows in a positive embrace.

Daniel J. Siegel (Siegel, 2010) describes an experiment in which subjects were asked to sit still, close their eyes, and concentrate. Then the researcher would say "No!"—first quietly and gradually getting louder: "No, no, no, NO!" Subjects were then asked to describe the physical reactions elicited by the word "no". The exact same procedure was then repeated for the word "yes". The physical reactions to "yes" were significantly more positive. In a number of subjects, "No" prompted a tightening sensation, a constriction, a shutting-down; in some cases even anger. "Yes" elicited in some subjects an uplifting, energising feeling, with a sense of relief and release. There was no right or wrong response; the feelings described were the reality of these individuals' subjective experience. Siegel hypothesises that "No" tends to precipitate the person into a reactive state, possibly with elements of fight, flight, or freeze, whereas "yes" fosters a receptive state. These two basic aspects of internal experience, reactive or receptive, are crucial elements with which we can become familiar. Reactivity shuts off presence, whereas receptivity creates it (Siegel, 2010). That is why appreciative language is so important: it is not only loving and appealing, but also healing and calming.

We need to find words that enable love and connectedness, harmony and cooperation to develop. Narrative psychotherapy aims to restore connections. When connections have been broken or damaged, when consciousness has become split within a relationship or family, the body is in fight mode: the consciousness of the client who felt as if she lived in a bell jar was split into two parts—one inside, one outside the bell jar. If the bell jar is transformed, the client's consciousness too will change, generating different organising processes in the body. There will be a different attractor, eliciting a different form.

If the therapy focuses on the significant words used by a client, and on a "close reading" of them, these words will gain in intensity. If new meanings are found in the semantic playing field, these new meanings will create a different organising principle, which will in turn organise the body differently. After all, psychotherapy is concerned with deeply felt and physically experienced meanings—with felt meaning. This is why the client is the ultimate signifier, who must respond affirmatively and agree heart and soul: deeply felt significance permeates the whole body.

## The landscape of the body

Words can heal and bring peace to every level of the body. That is why we are so happy when we find the word or expression—metaphor—that most aptly describes the relational field. In the following examples of the landscape of the body, different parts of the body tell their story.

### In one ear and out the other

A 65-year-old woman, Carol, had facial pain near her left ear. Fifteen years earlier, a similar pain had affected her entire face, and hypnosis had proved an effective treatment. She explained that she had not had any recurrence for years, and was delighted. Now that the pain had returned, she had decided to act fast. Since I was busy writing this book, I could only fit in a single appointment. I asked Carol whether she thought that her unconscious mind could tune in to the previous treatment, and eradicate the pain in one go, using hypnosis. Could she ask her unconscious mind to open up to the story linked to the pain, and thus to help to banish the pain? Carol agreed to this strategy, and when she arrived the next day, she told the following story.

> I was widowed more than four years ago. My husband—I'm sure you remember him—was so ill, he gradually became weaker and sicker until he died. All that time I took care of him, lovingly, right to the end. Then I was alone for three years—a lonely period, since all the rest of my family live far away. Still, I'm not one to give up, and I struggled through it all. I looked after a woman through a long illness, and after her death I married her partner, John. He had been widowed before, and both relationships had been unhappy. Still, we got together and now we're married.
>
> I gradually learned that John had numerous unresolved issues with his family, his children, his deceased wife, and his previous partner. Since he did not deal with them, I ended up in the firing line: terrible accusations and curses, not directed at me, but I still hear them. I hear so many terrible things …

At this point Carol started crying. I linked the pain near her ear to all the terrible words and phrases that had entered that ear, words not intended for her. I said: "That ear has heard so many awful things," deliberately saying "that ear" so that we could listen to the story of her ear, as it were. This externalised and relocated the pain around her ear to a third space. Moreover, by concentrating on the story of her ear she was able to enter a trance and dissociate herself—the woman who was listening and engaged in dialogue with me—from "that ear". I went on: "So much has intruded that has caused pain, pain that the ear has been unable to deal with. It was simply too harsh. Yet because what you heard wasn't intended for you, we could ask the other ear to help. After all, you know the expression 'In one ear, out the other'." She understood what I meant, and I could see that my explanation affected her. The context became therapeutic, laying the foundations for a link with the successful treatment fifteen years earlier and the memory of the hypnosis we had used then.

Inducing hypnosis, I presented my proposal for treatment:

All the things that have been unjustifiably said to you, and that have nothing at all to do with you, were too harsh for your left ear. They can all leave again, either via the "return to sender" route or through the other ear.

While the client was in a hypnotic state, I repeated the story, stressing the pain and unhappiness the words had caused her to feel. She replied: "And now it's all in my stomach!" Agreeing, I continued:

Yes, it's all in your stomach. And now it's allowed out, through your right ear and through your tears. I know you well enough to be sure that you can reflect honestly on your own contribution to these situations. You are already carrying enough baggage. You are very strong, and you can carry that baggage, but no more. Your husband's past, his unresolved problems, are too heavy for you, and weigh you down. You can return the unpleasant things you have heard. They can leave your body through your right ear.

After a long silence, Carol said "I can feel it moving across my forehead, from left to right." The movement had been initiated.

I said: "Your unconscious mind has found an exit for the pain and a way to release you from it. Just take your time for this process."

Again Carol remained quiet for a long time, in a deep trance. I occasionally asked where the pain was located, and she said that it was moving closer and closer to her right ear. Then she said: "Now the pain has gone completely!" She looked at me with shining eyes.

### "Blood is thicker than water"

A patient, Margo, remarked in one of her psychotherapy sessions that a large red mark had suddenly appeared on her neck. It was inflamed and very itchy. Then she talked about the party she was planning to organise for her seventy-fifth birthday for the whole family, especially those related to her "by blood." She had made an appointment to see a specialist about the unsightly mark on her neck, not wanting it to spoil her appearance at the party.

Margo had lost her mother in childhood and had been sent to boarding school. She had already done much to process her childhood traumas during the therapy, and in this particular session she was feeling well and in good spirits. She had printed photographs from key periods of her life on the invitations, including one taken when she was about thirteen, when her "blood relatives" had taken her in after her expulsion from boarding school. The photographs told the story of her life, and had prompted questions from many recipients. The "burn wound" developed while she was answering these questions.

"Blood is thicker than water," her stepmother had declared on Margo's wedding day, as she "delivered" her stepdaughter to the groom. As Margo repeated these words to me, the mark became extremely painful and inflamed. We focused on this, and I asked her to consider the possibility that this was the place in her body where that sentence had branded itself into her, where her body had stored the memory of those words. If so, this was a narrative spot with its own story. The mark became more painful as we discussed the wedding day and her stepmother.

I suggested that this sentence could now be released from her body, given that she had been happily married and, though now widowed, was doing well. Margo concentrated intensely on the mark, and using EMDR (eye movement desensitisation and reprocessing), we were able to neutralise the pain, and to erase the brand and the sentence from her body's memory. By the end of the session, the pain and burning sensation had vanished. The following day she called to say that she had cancelled her specialist's appointment, since the mark was no longer bothering her!

*The story of the trembling hands*

I published a story about a woman who was troubled by trembling hands in an earlier book (Olthof & Vermetten, 1994), and the publication led to the following new story.

A young research manager called Peter phoned me after reading "the story of the trembling hands" in my book. The story had affected him deeply, he said, since he suffered from the same malady, though fortunately he could keep his hands under control fairly well if he had to give a lecture or chair a large meeting. He joked: "It's fine as long as I make sure my cup is only half full of coffee."

The story had prompted him to reflect on his life story. He had always assumed that his trembling hands were an isolated symptom, and now began to consider the symptom's origins, a possible narrative context:

> I'm number six in a family of twelve. We often had to stand in rows and stick our hands out to receive punishment. We were struck hard for the slightest misdemeanour. Anyone who pulled their hand away would be struck harder still. For years I made light of this childhood punishment, actually trivialised it. Now I suddenly realised what my hands were telling me: they were afraid of censure, since censure could mean punishment. My hands were used to punishment, so they were frightened

to show themselves. So I would always avoid standing around empty-handed or holding my hands out; any disapproval, and they might be struck.

Peter now realised that whenever other people were watching him closely, this fear resurfaced, although he had learned to control the symptom well. But the reason for his call was that after a long period of pondering this narrative connection, staring into space, he had reclaimed his own story, and now no longer suffered from trembling hands. The story had cured him "by remote control"!

*Abandoned lungs*

In a therapy session, Stan, aged forty-eight, described his sense of abandonment when he lay alone upstairs as a young child, frequently ill, wishing his parents were there. While describing this feeling and concentrating on his body, one particular childhood scene suddenly returned in all its terror: when he was five, other children had pushed him into the water. Unable to swim, he sank and fought his way back to the surface again and again with sheer muscle power. Although he eventually reached safety, the experience had impressed itself on his consciousness as a narrow escape from death.

As he relived this scene, his lungs reacted violently: they told the story of his near-drowning. He coughed up mucus, as if he could still feel the water deep down in his lungs. Reliving this terrifying event proved to be cathartic, symbolically purging his lungs of the water that had lingered there for all those years, essentially stifling him. The sense of abandonment, the lack of help when he had almost drowned, the feeling that he had to do everything for himself: it had congealed into a story that had taken up residence deep down in his lungs. Together, we witnessed the cleansing of Stan's lungs that resulted from reliving the childhood experiences, and the return of the breath of life.

Stan's story confirms the proposition that the body stores the memory of a traumatic history: the water had lingered in Stan's lungs as a non-present presence. Chopra has written at length about such perceptions arising from the storage of untold experience in the body (Chopra, 1989). The stored experience acquires a fixed form that demands constant time, energy, and attention. Consciousness can absorb an imprint in much the same way as wax. Once this imprint has solidified, our consciousness organises itself around it, and symptoms develop as inscribed and fixed signs. But if our consciousness examines this imprint in the silent space, and identifies its context, the symptoms can dissolve, becoming a stream that can materialise in many new ways and assume new, creative forms.

In all these stories, a key metaphor mediates between body and biography. The story that is locked up in the body can unfold through physical symptoms; the process of cognitive structuring takes place later.

*The Book of Job*

Finally, to illustrate the relationship between the body, illness and health, let us consider the Old Testament story of Job. After all, however long we reflect on the role of the body in psychotherapy, and however many examples we examine, the relationship between body and spirit, illness and health remains at heart mysterious. Ultimately, this is a sacred space, within which we can speak only with reverence, restraint, and humility. We have seen that this silent space is also the space of potentiality, of possibilities; the space from which healing can take place. The Book of Job is about this space. The following paragraphs are indebted to Ellen van Wolde's discussion of the Book of Job (Van Wolde, 1991).

Job is a godly man who leads an upright life, a man whom God calls his servant. Job is also a man of considerable substance, an eminent man of great wealth, with many sons and daughters. Then God and Satan meet. God challenges Satan by proudly telling him about his pious servant. In return, Satan challenges God, saying that it is only because Job is blessed that he remains pious; if he were to lose everything he has, he would surely abandon his faith. God maintains that Job will remain steadfast. They make a wager: God agrees that Satan may deprive Job of all his wealth, on condition that he spares Job's health.

Job is accordingly struck by disaster: he loses his children, his servants are killed, his oxen and camels are stolen, his vast estates are plundered, and he is left destitute. However, Job does not give in to despair, but courageously accepts the situation as it is. He does not assign motives to God or apply the logic of causality, the logic of "why" and "because". Nor does he complain, reasoning: "the Lord gave, and the Lord hath taken away".

Job sits on a dung heap with his friends nearby. They visit him and comfort him, but after seven days they are unable to cope with the lack of significance, the absence of any explanation for the calamities that have befallen one who has lived such an exemplary life. There must be some explanation—something wrong with Job or with God, or with the relationship between the two.

One friend tries to persuade Job to abandon his faith; another assumes that Job must somehow be to blame for his woes. Job resists this pressure, remaining firm in his belief that he has not transgressed, and firm in his faith: he asserts that God too has done nothing wrong. His friends find it unbearable to stay close to Job without any explanation. Still Job does not waver in his faith.

Then God and Satan meet again. "You see," says God, "such a faithful servant, such unshakeable faith." Satan concedes the point and praises Job, but challenges God anew: if Job were to lose his health, he would surely abandon his faith. Again God meets the challenge, giving Satan the liberty to strike Job again, provided he spares his life.

Job falls ill: covered with sores, he lives on the dung heap. His wife and friends again urge him to abandon his faith in God. Job despairs. He calls on God to account for himself. His truth no longer seems to apply. In the story, this is followed by a hymn to wisdom. All the impressive achievements of mankind have not yielded wisdom.

Job and his friends reason as follows: if I had done something wrong, then I would probably deserve all this, then God would have had a reason to punish me with this fate. But I haven't done anything wrong, so I don't deserve this fate. This is the principle of payback or retribution. It is a logic based on causality:

> if you obey these rules and regulations …
> if you live healthily …

>    if you work hard enough …
>    … then …

Later in the Book of Job, this mode of reasoning is demolished. Job's notion of truth proves untenable. He is confused: the truth he thought he knew, along with all the rules he had learned for obtaining happiness and wisdom, prove invalid. What follows is a process of disintegration in which Job understands that he himself is no longer the measure of things.

According to Ellen van Wolde, the Book of Job is layered like an onion. Each truth can be stripped away to find a deeper or newer truth, and so on. By the end we realise that truth is layered, and that this layered quality is itself the essence of the text. Each layer has its own wisdom.

In his reply to Job, God says that in the beginning, when he made everything, he found wisdom, and that wisdom is an unending process. Wisdom cannot be reduced to a place or a moment, but is in constant motion. Fixed standpoints turn out to be temporary, providing answers that suffice only for a limited time.

The same applies when we are afflicted by illness and suffering. When clients come to us who are weighed down by grief, pain or incomprehensible calamity, it is all too easy to revert to the principle of retribution, to causal explanations: which rules or procedures did the client flout, to prompt this situation?

>    You're ill because …
>    You're depressed because …

Psychology abounds in answers: suppression, denial, neglect, failure to act, too much or too little of something. Yet however scientifically sound these answers may be, they are time-bound and relative. The answers may come from the domain of science, or that of religion and spirituality, they may have their origins in so-called common sense or in New Age ideas, or they may derive from the lessons of history, for instance.

Years ago, while driving I used to listen to a phone-in programme in which people could speak to a church minister. Like Job's friends, these ministers started off by being comforting, empathic, and encouraging. They suggested beautiful texts for contemplation, and urged callers to pray. Many callers found this enough. Occasionally, though, a caller would say, obstinately, "Yes, but I've prayed for hours already." The minister would respond that this was excellent but perhaps even more prayer was called for. Most callers would stop at this point and accept the minister's words of wisdom. But occasionally a desperate caller would be left persisting: "I've already done that, I've prayed endlessly."

And just as Job's friends were eventually unable to stay with him in the absence of any logical explanation, the ministers were eventually reduced to saying: "God has his reasons, God never does anything without a purpose." This indirectly referred to the retribution principle: you must be to blame somewhere along the line! This does not only apply to church ministers: psychotherapists, priests, coaches, advisers, doctors, teachers—all eventually take the same approach.

But Ellen van Wolde writes of the consolation derived from not knowing, from not being able to know, which can lead us to surrender to a situation as it is, without a single answer to the question of why. At the end of the story, Job is a happy, wealthy man once again. He joyfully embraces the renewal of his good fortune. The Bible does not clearly explain why Job was struck by misfortune, or why his situation was eventually reversed again. Perhaps the story illustrates "God's Grace".

The Book of Job makes it painfully clear that our usual mode of reasoning and our reliance on causal connections do not suffice. Such reasoning is individual, and bound by time and space. Whatever answers they may provide are only provisional. Suddenly, all our certainties and assumptions appear inadequate. However complacent we may feel, the positions and standpoints we adopt give way beneath us.

In narrative psychotherapy we therefore prefer to speak of "moving points" rather than positions or "standpoints", precisely because of this relativity of the truth. Moving points shift in relation to the standpoints of others. Nomadic knowledge tells us about time-bound and context-bound aspects of truth and wisdom: truth is always relative, a home base that temporarily feels comfortable, and can provide the right answer for a time. Moving points lay no claim to absolute truth. As such, they serve as hosts for narrative knowledge, home bases for stories—and for their beginnings and endings. After all, we cannot live without answers, without purpose and meaning. Job, too, had his story.

The above examples illustrated the principle of textual analysis; we examined the archaeology of language, and analysed the layers of meaning in words and phrases. Now that we have packed our suitcases with language, and given the body a role in narrative psychotherapy, we will continue our journey, to the space where this language can come alive.

CHAPTER FOUR

# Narrative space: the "third space"

*"Music is the silence between the notes"*
—Claude Debussy

## Introduction

The discussion of nomadic thinking and the nomadic team touched on the "House of Language" and looked at the nomadic and poetic use of language, which has its own logic: the logic of metaphor. Metaphors revolve around images, and an image that arises in an open dialogue can be regarded as the third element, the "third space". In the third space, narrative psychotherapy can create a system, a complex of relationships; it can generate new meanings, pursue new avenues, and help to make new stories. How this space works in the practice of narrative psychotherapy will be described in this chapter.

It has often been said, for instance by the jazz pianist Oscar Peterson, that in jazz there is no such thing as a wrong note. No note is pure or false in isolation. It is the second note that brings harmony or dissonance. Two notes together await a third, and the three notes together then make up a chord. The minimum unit of interaction contains three components: "To know two … necessarily requires the presence of three … A triple somersault is necessary to see relationship" (B. Keeney in Flemons, 1991).

Narrative psychotherapy revolves around creating a third element or third space to allow a story to take shape. If one person says to another: "You treat me like a bull in a china shop," it is an accusation of insensitivity and carelessness. The speaker feels vulnerable and not "seen". Each of the two inhabits an individual world, the *first space*. Their relationship is the *second space*. The metaphor is the *third space*, an image that comments on the relationship. The third element can be created from within the relationship, brought to the surface from inside, or introduced from the outside, as we shall see below. If only the first and second spaces are used, the interaction stays within a dominant discourse, a problem story of accusations and resentment. Discussing the relationship from one of these spaces is too limiting. The exchanges stay in the same linguistic domain: "You're too dominant, too insensitive; you don't see me." Then comes the reply: "You're over-sensitive, I have to watch my words, you always overreact." A therapist who inscribes himself in this linguistic domain becomes part of the problem.

The third space creates new openings for speech. Then lines can be traced from the dominant discourse of the first and second spaces, "lines of flight" (Deleuze) that make new connections possible. It is here that a relational field can be described, and a new story can be shaped. The triad is the unit of analysis in family therapy. It's like tactics in soccer: Johan Cruyff always urged the need for triangles: they create the freedom to pass the ball to one of two other players.

## The narrative space

Let us look at the practice at Boddaert outpatient centre for children aged six to twelve. Each child had distinct problems, life stories, and reasons for referral. To create a good therapeutic context, it was necessary to inscribe each complex of symptoms in the family story, and to define an accepted framework for therapy in the triad consisting of parents, child, and care system. The children had to understand why they were there and what the treatment plan would be, to create a basis for cooperation, with each child taking an active part in his or her therapy. The next step was to enable the children to *tell each other* why they were there. Many of the problems were similar: divorce, the absence of a father, question marks about their parentage, a parent suffering from depression, unemployment and poverty in the family, abuse, drug problems, and incest.

Children can understand and help each other, but creating the appropriate space for it is essential. This intermediate or "third" space functions as a framework in which children can express their problems and where they can take stories that are difficult to tell. This framework makes it possible to reflect on the behaviour of the group and of individual children. It constantly establishes links with the home situation, creating a "narrative space".

For the Boddaert children, a narrative space was created by developing a story, based on the philosophy set out in the previous chapters. The story was about two spiders, Pip and Pippa, and was presented in the form of a letter.

To the children of the Boddaert Centre,

Hallo, we are Pip and Pippa, the Boddaert spiders.
Some of you have heard of us or even seen us. But we didn't always live at the Boddaert Centre. We arrived a few months ago. We hid for ages, because we didn't know who might be out there. We looked at you from our dark corner, up behind the big green plant. We saw what a mess you sometimes make! But mostly you seem to be having a nice time. You're probably wondering what we're doing here. So here's our story.

We spiders have existed for thousands of years. We were born in Web, that's spider land, where spiders grow up, play, and go to school. At school we learn important things like how to make a web and how to catch flies. We also learn that people—boys and men as well as girls and women—are frightened of us and think we're yucky, and do terrible things to us. We saw scary horror films: there's a poor spider sitting nicely just over a reading lamp, and suddenly—wham! It's too horrible for words, a big flappy shoe coming from nowhere.

So when we learnt all that and saw those films, we wanted to stay nice and safe in Web. But our king, Tarantula the Second, had other ideas. He chose a hundred spiders to go to the Land of Humans to improve our image *over there*. That means, what Humans think of us. He wanted us to prove that spiders are not scary at all, and there's certainly no reason to squash us! Well! Did we want to go to the Land of Humans? No we didn't! Still, we did feel a bit proud to be chosen. We decided to go. We had a few lessons on how to start a fan club, and some classes in self-defence, and off we went: to the Netherlands. We hugged all our spider friends and family, and set off, with our legs—all eight of them!—shaking and wobbling!

We arrived somewhere called Utrecht, at a big station. Suddenly we saw our cousin, Ali. He had left Web years ago and we hadn't heard from him all that time. So we were really happy to see that Ali was alive and well! We talked all night about his adventures in the Land of Humans. It was very upsetting. Ali's house had been wrecked again and again. Humans are constantly dashing about with dusters, and some tried to kill him, with fly-swatters, shoes, and cushions, but up to now he'd survived. He limped a bit, but apart from that he was fine.

Ali gave us your address. He said it's nice and quiet here, except between three and seven on weekdays. And that it's messy here, not so much dusting, so our houses wouldn't be wrecked so much. So this was a great house for spiders, an ideal place to begin our mission. Well, I can tell you we like it here, and we plan to stay! You're very nice to us. So this seems the right moment to start on our mission. Remember? We've got to help Humans and spiders to get on better, and improve our *image*. We're going to start by learning about Humans: what do Human children like to do, what do they find important, funny, scary, sad, and why? We'll send the results to our king. But you won't see us much. You're a bit noisy and rambunctious so it's a bit dangerous: we're very small, you know!

We'll write to you often, and hope you write back. So if you want to tell or ask us something, don't hesitate, just do it! Put the letters up in the corner behind the plant. We hope that we'll all have a nice time and learn a lot about each other, and most of all that we can help make a real friendship between Humans and spiders.

Best wishes from<br>
Pip and Pippa<br>
(This story was written by Rinie Moonen and her colleagues)

The children listened to the story and they loved it. They enthusiastically embraced its fantasy world and its narrative framework. The spiders instantly became an important part of life at the Centre. The children immediately informed newcomers about the presence of Pip and Pippa and encouraged them to write to them. None of the children tried to "unmask" the spiders. They left the imaginative world, the secret of communication, intact. The presence of Pip and Pippa thus formed a "sacred space" (Bateson & Bateson, 1987) for everyone.

The children immediately started writing to the spiders, leaving their letters in the "postbox" in the corner. They wrote about their sadness, their pain and secrets, including their home lives. The content of the letters remained secret. The letters were answered by Pip and Pippa. Of course the children knew that the group leaders were writing the letters, but no one ever broke the spell. It was a shared magical illusion that created extra space and possibilities.

Each letter received a personal reply. Although this was a lot of work, it also created space, since there was a spectacular improvement in the group atmosphere. The children experienced each letter as a special gift. They never asked each other about the content. The world of the letters was a protected, free space that everyone respected. Once a week "Pip and Pippa" wrote to the whole group, reflecting on the children's behaviour and their trials and tribulations rather like a Greek chorus.

The letters to the children, including the group ones, provided a context for questions. After all, "Pip and Pippa" were studying the behaviour of human children; they were not-knowing, non-powerful. The letters were framed in a reflexive (never moralistic) tone, to preserve the free space. This carefully constructed space provided an ideal context in which to encourage solidarity, to explain the problematic behaviour of individual children to the other children, and to ask them to help each other. The group leaders always adopted a position of not-knowing to ask their questions. Some of the letters were long, while others consisted of a single line. Here is one from Fred:

my dad is in prison, love Fred.

Fred had apparently been unable to discuss this secret with anyone. Pip and Pippa reacted from the position of not-knowing: what is a prison? Why do people go there? Fred went on to describe his relationship with his father, how it felt to miss his father, how he interpreted his father's behaviour. Through this dialogue, Fred was encouraged to share his secret with the other children in his own good time.

Other children in turn told their stories, and discovered that they were only able to tell such personal stories through the "third space". This narrative space was thus drained of all preconceived codes and meanings. It was set up explicitly to enable children to attach their own significance to their life stories. In their letters, "Pip and Pippa" asked only what things meant. The spiders were naive, non-threatening, foreign, and a different species, yet related to the children nonetheless. They could ask anything, deconstruct any significance, and make suggestions from a free position. This promoted what Foucault calls parrhesia, candid speech or "truth speaking" that helps to constitute the self. In the free space, the children were the writers and readers of their own life stories, constituting themselves in relation to the other children and the group leaders.

Once a week, the children were asked to send a group letter to Pip and Pippa to tell them how things were going in the group. The supervisors sometimes helped them compose the letter. Pip and Pippa occasionally "accompanied" children to help them with a difficult task, hospital tests or admissions, or in a difficult period in the family. When Annelies had to have an operation, she asked tearfully if Pip and Pippa would write to her while she was in hospital.

The children's letters started out light-hearted, with questions like "Do you have cars?", "How do you make a web?", and "Do you like fish?"

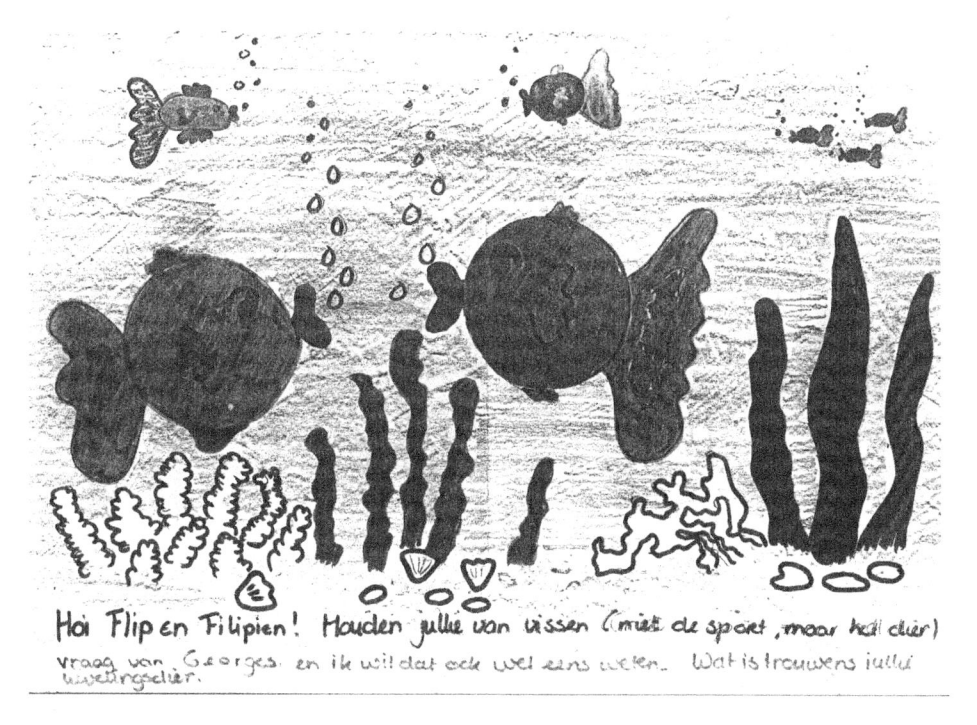

Hoi Flip en Filipien! Houden jullie van vissen (niet de sport, maar het dier) vraag van Georges en ik wil dat ook wel eens weten. Wat is trouwens jullie lievelingsdier.

Figure 4. Do you like fish?

But after a while they became more serious:

Hallo,

Joe has left the Boddaert Centre and I miss him. Daddy and Mummy had a row with a man in the street. Daddy is in a tiny room because he got angry with someone. Mummy took Daddy some clothes. Someone hurt Daddy with a knife. Polices came to the house, Auntie Netty was there with Augie.

love, Jantine

Some wrote about experiences in the group, others about personal experiences, such as Sam, who wrote:

Hello I am Sam. At home and almost everywhere I feel BAD. If I feel bad I get very hyper and I don't want that.
  SO I WANT TO ASK YOU PIP AND PIPPA COULD YOU PLEASE HELP? I HOPE SO
  please Pip and Pippa
  love Sam
  Kis xxxxxx ses Sam

Sam had a very hard life, growing up in a violent family. He had numerous behavioural problems at school and in the neighbourhood, and also made things difficult for everyone

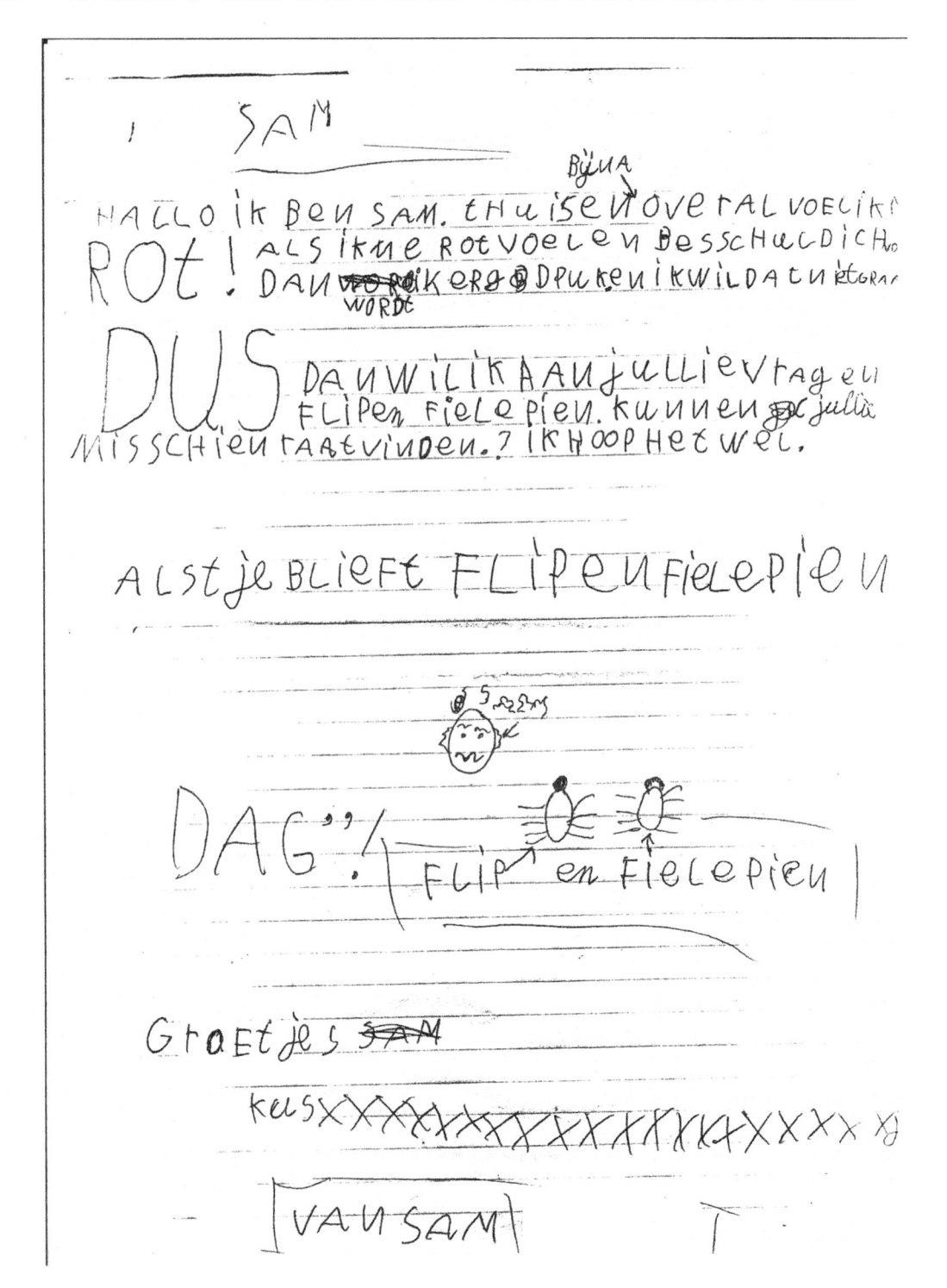

Figure 5. Sam's letter.

in the group. Normally you would say an outpatient group could not deal with him. But through Pip and Pippa, the other children were urged to help Sam. His home situation was explained, placing his problematic behaviour in a context and attaching a compassionate explanation. The children were asked for their help and support. Still, since nothing could be done to remedy the painful home situation, it was clear that Sam would have to be referred to a clinical setting. To avoid any suggestion of blame, or the notion of Sam being "excluded" because of impossible behaviour, the group leaders sent two letters, through Pip and Pippa, one to Sam and one to the group as a whole, including Sam. Here is the group letter:

Hello everyone!

We got a very sad letter from someone in your group, someone who has a very difficult time at home and gets very angry about it. Yes, it's Sam! Sam asked us to help, but things are so difficult at Sam's house that we can't really solve it. So we've decided to go the Land of Web to ask King Tarantula.
 While we're away, we'd like to ask you to do something:
 We see how nice you are to Sam and do your best to help him. That's not always easy, 'cos we see that he makes things difficult for himself and for you. But you care a lot about him, and he cares a lot about you. Remember the presents he gave to Mark and Sander, writing on them "presents for two friends"? … Sam needs lots of help … How about you, his Boddaert friends, making a present for him? One he can take home, that will remind him of how much you care about him, when life is really hard.
 You could make a cuddly toy or something for his room, to help him when he's all alone and sad. We're sure you can think of something, and that the group leaders will help. Thank you! We'll write again when we get back from our trip to see the king.

Love,
Pip and Pippa

And here is the letter to Sam:

Hallo Sam,

Pip and I got your letter. It made us really sad, and we talked about it for ages. We've already seen how difficult things are for you, and how hard you are trying, and no one seems to know what to do. Now, you and Rinie and Marga and the rest have decided to ask someone else to help. So it looks like you have to go and live somewhere else for a while. You're not just very tired but also very angry. Angry with everyone. We understand why. You just want to play, but it's so difficult at home that you keep thinking about how horrible things are.
 We don't know what's the best thing to do either. So we're going on a journey to ask our king Tarantula. So it will be quite a while before you get a real answer to your letter. That's why we're writing now, to tell you we see how difficult things are for you, and that's why you sometimes do things you don't want to do. We think you're a great kid! We love you, and so do lots of other people. See how hard the other children try to make things better for you? That's because they love you. Think of that, when things are difficult.

Now we're off, back to our land to see our king. We hope he will give us some good advice. See you soon, Sam! Good luck, we're rooting for you!

Three big fat spider hugs,<br>Pippa

It would be some time before Sam could be admitted to a clinical unit. Until then, he would need the group's support to get through this difficult time.

Although this intervention did not provide any structural help, it did prevent Sam's exclusion from the group, in spite of his disruptive behaviour. After the group letter was read out, it was touching to see the other children reaching out and including Sam. They made him lots of presents to take home, which amazed and thrilled Sam, who was used to rejection and punishment.

The narrative space was thus useful both at individual and group level. It enabled discussions of the children's home situations with them and with their peers. It created a climate of compassion, and helped to minimise rows and conflict. In short, it created a truly therapeutic climate.

### Lars and the Real Girl

The film *Lars and the Real Girl* provides a fascinating example of a narrative space. The young man Lars comes to stay with his brother Gus and the latter's wife in a remote, sparsely populated community. Lars has immense trouble with human relationships, bordering on autism. He gets a job, and is well liked, but is unable to respond to offers of friendship or the romantic interest of co-worker Margo.

One day Lars announces that he has a lady visitor. He introduces his new friend, who turns out to be a life-sized doll, "Bianca", ordered from an adult website that one of his colleagues had mentioned. She comes with her own life story: she is a wheelchair-bound orphan of part-Brazilian descent, eager to help people. Alarmed at Lars's delusional state, his sister-in-law sends Lars and "Bianca" to Dagmar, the family doctor, who doubles as the local psychologist. Surprisingly, Dagmar decides that the best way to help Lars is to go along with the fantasy that Bianca is a real person.

As time goes by, everyone is persuaded to join in the fantasy: the family, co-workers, even the local church minister. From the start, Bianca's presence has a salutary effect on Lars. He treats her as a real person, and becomes more sociable. Crucially, Bianca becomes "the third element", helping to heal the brothers' relationship. We learn that the brothers lost their mother many years ago, after which Gus left home, leaving Lars to cope with their father's deep depression. Gus realises that he had effectively abandoned Lars, "sacrificing" him to their father's grief, and that Lars's development had stalled as a result. He is now able to see Lars as an equal, to appreciate the consequences of his actions, and to apologise. Through Bianca, Lars also gains a sense of his own sexuality and develops a sense of responsibility for others.

Dagmar goes through the motions of regularly checking Bianca's blood pressure and vital signs, thus gaining Lars's confidence. Bianca's regular "health checks" provide a framework for Dagmar to talk to Lars about his life with Bianca. Lars takes Bianca everywhere with him, dressing her up fashionably and doing her make-up. Her presence acts as a conduit: he becomes gregarious and even accepts party invitations.

Once Bianca has played her role, Lars is ready to respond to Margo's interest in him, but he cannot be "unfaithful" to Bianca. The unspoken solution is that Bianca becomes "ill" and "dies". Lars has re-established contact with his family and his own past, and is now able to respond to those around him. He no longer needs Bianca. Margo comes to stand beside him at Bianca's "funeral" and they clasp hands.

Bianca's arrival helps to create a third space: for Dagmar and Lars, who become partners in helping her, and for Lars's brother and sister-in-law, whose relationship with Bianca helps them to establish an authentic relationship with Lars. In the third space created by Bianca's arrival, Lars can resume his stalled development. The intervention of Bianca creates a space in which healing can take place. The magic is left intact, Lars's vulnerability is protected, and his soul respected.

## The bull and the china shop

Poetry too provides examples of a "third space". Take these poems by Toon Tellegen, for instance:

> Once I wrote a poem
> and the poem stood up, took a step backwards
> and looked at me—
> suspiciously and haughtily as only a poem can

And:

> "Hello bull," says the china shop,
> "better stay away for a while."

*(From Toon Tellegen, 2005, translated for this publication by BJ)*

In the writing process, the poet constitutes the first and second spaces in relation to his or her poem. If the poem acquires a voice, "stands up" and occupies a position of its own, this opens up the third space. The metaphor of "a bull in a china shop" posits a hierarchical relationship in which a large, unsubtle person deals insensitively with the other's vulnerabilities. Tellegen changes the usual formulation, adopting two narrative subject positions: the bull's story and that of the china shop. But there is a third space, the relationship between the two subject positions: "better stay away for a while." The china shop is troubled by the bull. The two narrators and two subject positions—two perspectives—open up the world of relationships, of possibilities. The rest of the poem shifts to a third perspective, that of the observer, who looks at the bull and the china shop and says that the china shop is his soul, but then goes on to wonder what that roaring bull says about him.

> The bull stands at the door,
> but doesn't need a doorknob.
> He sniffs up the autumn smells—
> smells rain and stormy winds—

pricks his ears, rushes straight ahead—
that china shop's my soul, I always knew,
but that bull
that comes thundering along once more,
crushing everything in its path
and bellowing all the time:
"I'm right!"
what does that bull say about me?

*(From Toon Tellegen, 2005, translated for this publication by BJ)*

### Externalising the problem

Michael White introduced into psychotherapy the idea of "externalising the problem" (White & Epston, 1990; White, 2007). White objectifies the problem—not the person. Clients often tend to identify with their problem—the problem *becomes* their whole identity. This creates a dominant story about the "problem person" that makes someone feel powerless. White gives the problem its own separate identity with a particular intention: he sees it as having arisen as a solution for something else, with its own tactics and strategy. Detaching the problem from the person's identity makes it possible to look for alternative stories, alternative truths about the person's identity, creating options for different courses of action to move his or her life in a different direction. It does not absolve the person from responsibility for tackling the problem; rather, it creates space in which this responsibility can be shouldered. The conversation can then be organised around an externalised problem, and the person's influence on the problem, and vice versa, can be explored. The problem is defined as a story, rather than as a representation of the truth about the person. It becomes possible to examine the consequences of the order imposed by the dominant problem story, to look for exceptions, to see what resources are available that might provide different information about the person. White tries to mobilise the person's inner resources in the direction of a different future, a different identity, towards a solution (White & Epston, 1990).

One of White's best-known examples is about a girl who is referred to him for faecal soiling. White and the girl together invent a name for the soiling—Sneaky Poo. The soiling influences the child's identity, not only outside and at school, but also, and to a large extent, at home. The more frequent the episodes, the more she is identified with the problem, so that faecal soiling becomes the organisational principle of her personality. The problem is *sneaky*. It works slyly and secretly, evading the girl's waking consciousness: without realising, she has suddenly soiled herself. Together with the family, White explores ways of joining forces to outwit Sneaky Poo. They search for exceptions, occasions on which the girl has succeeded in being stronger than Sneaky Poo.

White's creation of a context of cooperation generated energy, spontaneity, and vitality. The therapeutic process could include playful elements, creative ideas, and plans. The girl and her parents all acquired a new self-respect. Moreover, instead of a struggle between the first and second space within the family, everyone now focused on the third space: Sneaky Poo. The redefinitions united the first and second spaces in a new approach in which they tackled a third space together.

Lynn Hoffman (in Kenny, 1988) refers to a problem that organises a system, thus shifting the focus from behaviour to the level of ideas and significance. In other words, a system is created of people who are involved in conversation about the problem and in deciding what it signifies. And if the people in the system who name the problem are high up in the hierarchy of significance for the client, the client's identity becomes problematic. Goolishian and Winderman write: "systems do not make problems; languishing about problems makes systems" (in Kenny, 1988, p. 135). A context in therapy is all too often one of talking about the problem, which has the effect of strengthening the problem's identity. The therapist thus joins the ranks of the dominant interpreters of the problem.

Externalising the problem means setting up a conversation that aims to detach the person—linguistically speaking—from the problem identity. The method is not so much a technique as an all-embracing attitude and a philosophy about the subject, which links up with Foucault's ideas on the dominant discourse and its exclusion procedures, and with thinking in terms of *différance*, in which identity is seen as plural and multivocal. The following paragraphs are based on an article by Bill O'Hanlon (O'Hanlon, 1994), describing the different steps involved in this narrative strategy:

### 1. The first step is finding a name for the problem, one that everyone can accept

This initiates the linguistic separation between the person and the problem. Once the problem has a name, it has a separate identity.

A six-year-old girl called Jenny at the outpatient clinic was in the habit of making an incredible mess at home. Not just an ordinary mess, but a mega mess. It was quite a project for her: she scattered washing powder round the house, spread toothpaste on her mother's underwear, buried sticky wrappers under the new sofa cushions, urinated in various corners, smeared faeces around the toilet, and delighted in walking across a clean floor in muddy boots. Her distraught parents started to hate their daughter, who they saw as deliberately setting out to drive them mad.

Whenever Jenny was told off, she gazed in wide-eyed innocence, as if she had no idea what she might have done. She always promised to mend her ways. She told her therapist at the outpatient clinic that she couldn't withstand the urge to make a mess. "I have to do it," she said.

Trying to think of a name for this problem, we decided to call it Piggy. It's a good name, since it could be a cuddly toy, but also has associations with mud and a pigsty. Then we set about reconstructing Piggy's story.

### 2. Personify the problem

The problem acquires human shape, has an intention and a purpose, tactics and strategy. It has an origin: it was once a solution for something. It was born from good intentions and doesn't know that times have changed, that the client now finds it a nuisance rather than a support. Efforts can be made to cooperate with the problem to achieve a change of direction.

Jenny explained that Piggy had appeared when she was very sad, around the age of three. She doesn't remember what happened, but one day Piggy appeared and whispered in her ear that she should make a mess. In the team, this reminded us of the film *Drop Dead Fred*, which is about the "imaginary friend syndrome". In this film, Lizzie is an unhappy girl with a friend, Fred, who is invisible to everyone except herself. Fred is mischievous, thinks up plans, and comforts the girl. He also represents her anger towards her parents and the outside world. Lizzie and Fred have great fun creating chaos, and their conversations comfort Lizzie enormously.

Similarly, Piggy represents Jenny's anger towards her parents, especially her mother. Instead of equating Jenny's identity with making a mess and with anger at her mother, it became possible to explore her little friend's motives, to pinpoint the times at which he appeared, and to figure out what responsibility Jenny might take for restricting Piggy's role. Jenny started making drawings about Piggy and the way he had entered her life. This opened up a space in which the lost story of what had happened when she was small could surface, with Piggy as the third element.

Devising an accepted name for the problem makes it possible to move all the characteristics that have been attributed to a person, assigning them instead to the problem.

*3. Investigate how the problem that started out as helpful has now become discouraging, making the person believe it is indispensable and part of the person's identity*

The language is not used deterministically to say that the problem is the cause. Instead, narrative language is used: Piggy tells stories, whispers, tempts, persuades, convinces. A space for reflexiveness is created.

Once the problem has become detached from the person's identity, the person's relationship to the problem can change, opening up room to manoeuvre.

*4. Search for alternative truths and scenarios, and situations in which the client has successfully resisted the problem's influence*

Some writers refer to exceptional situations, situations in which the problem is resisted (see O'Hanlon & Weiner-Davis, 1989; White & Epston, 1990). Client and therapist can together marvel at these, try to figure out how the client successfully resisted, and what the exceptions reveal about him or her. Next, they try to expand this successful strategy. This creates a context that implies that change is possible, that the client may acquire more influence over the problem, diminishing it. Sometimes they muse about a moment in the future when the problem and its influence will be gone. They ponder how the client's life and relationships will look in that new future. The entire approach is solution-oriented (Cauffman, 2010, De Shazer, 1982, 1985, 1988).

*5. The therapist and client go in search of "historical evidence", alternative sources and stories that will make it possible to see the person in a different light*

Within the views of contextual therapy and thinking in terms of loyalties (Böszörményi-Nagy & B. Krasner, 1986; Van den Eerenbeemt & Van Heusden, 1983; Van den Eerenbeemt, 2009), the next step is to identify the client's strengths, what the client has sacrificed through the problem, and how the problem may have helped to protect others: for instance, helping mother to bear her grief, distracting attention from the parents' marital difficulties, uniting the parents in their care for another, shouldering the burden for one of the parents.

One can also search in earlier generations for alternative stories about the family, stories that contrast with the problem identity. Through what White calls "remembering conversations", old stories can be revived, helping the client to connect with important figures in his or her life, ancestors, neighbours, key figures from the past who matter in the present. They provide a feeling of belonging, of community, contributing to a multivocal ego and a feeling of coherence, a bond with significant people.

In this way, clients reclaim ownership of their own stories, and a joint quest begins for alternative stories. The inquisitive, affirming therapist will encourage a fascination with life and show an interest in the neglected aspects of self, and the untold stories. White also mentions the search for affirmative "witnesses", people who appreciate the client, and bestow respect and recognition (White, 2007).

For instance, Jenny was helped to make a book that told the story of Piggy, with drawings and a comic strip. The other children in the group were also asked to help—Jenny made a terrible mess of her food and other things in the communal area. Her personal hygiene was poor and she acted provocatively. The children were informed about Piggy's presence, who Piggy was, and what its aims were. They were asked to act differently to Jenny and to help her by ignoring Piggy.

This created an empathic context in which problematic behaviour could be ignored and the negative attention that had previously been dominant could be redirected. Jenny found it increasingly rewarding to adopt a more cooperative mode of behaviour, and this could be named as the influence she was acquiring over Piggy. She had started out as a figure of fun, but now she gradually secured a more important place among the children. As time went on, she was able to play in a carefree manner with the others.

The group leaders made a compilation from the film *Drop Dead Fred* in which the imaginary friend Fred shows why he was needed—it was because the girl was unhappy. They also showed it to Jenny's parents, to help them to reinterpret their daughter's behaviour. In addition, Jenny wrote a letter describing Piggy's arrival.

> I am Jenny. Now I'm happy, but sometimes I'm very angry. Mummy sometimes swears at me. She tells me to go upstairs but I don't.
>
> Daddy used to go to the pub a lot. He used to drink lots of beer. Then, when he came home, ... Mummy and Daddy shouted a lot. They sweared very loud. So I was scared and ran next door ... Mummy and I were afraid that scary things would happen.
>
> Daddy and Mummy had lots of rows cos Jenny made a big mess. They got cross and shouted at each other. I always made a big mess cos I was angry at Mummy and Daddy cos they were always fighting. I hated that. I was sad and it made me cry, cos Daddy was away a lot. I threw everything around and made a terrible mess. Daddy hated it too and so he went out a lot. So Mummy was left at home all by herself and she had to clear everything up and that was lots of work. Then she had to start all over again cos I made a mess again. I liked that, I enjoyed winding her up. I was cross with her, because once I woke up and Mummy wasn't there when I was scared and I called her. I was all alone and I went next door. Mummy was there too—that was lucky.
>
> When I was little I couldn't get to sleep. I had horrible dreams. ... About that Daddy had to go to the police station or that the police was coming to get us and we all had to go to prison.
>
> I don't fight with Mummy so much now and I can stay up later. We watch TV together and sometimes people come from Mummy's work and they play cards. We don't fight so much at home. I do

miss Mummy now that she has to work a lot in the evening but I'm happy for her too. It gives her something to do and she earns money and it's all sorted now, cos Daddy comes to sit with me.

This letter does not yet outline a new identity, but Jenny had managed to express the context of her problem and to link her behaviour to the home situation. She described her parents as part of the problem, which meant that the responsibility to change no longer rested solely on her shoulders. The family had many other problems, and from then on they could gradually be discussed.

### Orientation towards the third space

A client's key phrase or metaphor, written on a flip chart and used for textual analysis, can function as the third element. Therapist and client focus on this text together as the third space. The third space creates a collaborative relationship between therapist and client, a joint effort (much like a client's arrangement of nesting dolls) around the sentence written there, the chosen symbol. The third space is in the middle. Anyone can join in around it, drawing on their own position and their knowledge, which is of equal value. This facilitates conversation, dialogue, an exchange of ideas.

Alternatively, the third element can be introduced from outside the therapy, without there being any immediate relationship with the therapy, to create sufficient distance. Lenaerts (Lenaerts, 2009) writes that such an element must not refer directly to the problem at issue. Its relationship is indirect; it makes the space larger. In this case the third element comes from another world, one that knows nothing about the problem being discussed in the therapy, but that shares associative connections with it. It helps to forge a relationship of equality between therapist and client. Its approach is oblique, embracing whatever is needed in terms of protection.

The third space may be provided by a mental image. In the following example, therapist and client together focused on the image of a steel band that was clamped around the client's head and told a particular story.

### A steel band around my head

A woman of thirty-five had anxiety and panic attacks, nausea and fits of vomiting, and constant splitting headaches. When I asked her what she observed in her body during these attacks or what she felt in her body while she was telling me about them, she said that it felt like a tight steel band round her head, pressing against her temples. There were screws at her temples that she could turn to make it tighter or looser. She noticed that if she concentrated on these screws and loosened them, she was able to influence her physical reality through her consciousness. We set out to figure out the possible significance of that band around her head. Then she quickly recited a list of emotional traumas she had suffered over the years. One child died shortly after birth, and the following pregnancy had been harrowing. She barely allowed herself any time to mourn the loss of her baby. Everything raced along without a break:

> It just went on and on … Eventually I couldn't keep up, my thoughts were in danger of exploding. I think that's where the band came in. It came to help me keep my head, to stop me losing myself.

After a few months of therapy, the client was able to pick up the thread of her life again, and she could gradually loosen the band. She needed it less and less. She was able to thank the band for the significant role it had played.

The metaphor "like a steel band round my head" functioned like an image in the third space. The language of the imagination belongs to the intermediate space, the world of "as if", of multiple consciousness and multiple reality. Within the world of "as if", much more can be true than in the world ruled by equations. The metaphor helps the body to find the space it needs to inscribe itself in the client's relationship with her body, which then acquires space to breathe.

The paternalistic discourse governed by a single "master signifier" banishes the narrative element from reality. It imposes a rigid logic and dismisses the reality of "as if". In this world, people do not have steel bands round their heads. But as a metaphor, the steel band can tell a story: which thoughts had to be kept together? Which thoughts must not escape? What needed to be protected? How was the band attached, and what colour was it? Within the reality of "as if", a change in the colour or material of the band can alter reality. A change made in the person's imagination impacts on her physical reality. Consequently, when the client loosened the screws, her headache was less severe.

## The power of metaphor

Only the language of analogies is strong enough to discuss emotions. Grief, fear, pain, mourning, joy, pride, and enthusiasm all require vivid imagery if we are to do justice to the quality of these emotions. A metaphor is not so much a figure of speech as a way of thinking. Our subconscious thinks in images and speaks in metaphors. To discuss the world of relationships, we need metaphors. A metaphor is a linguistic register that opens up a linguistic domain. How can we discuss love? We need metaphors: the sun, fire, a warm bath, butterflies, fuel … there are an infinite number of possibilities. Metaphors organise our consciousness, creating order and structure.

Metaphors channel our thoughts, structure stories, and organise the way in which we discuss our lives. We live by metaphors (Lakoff & Johnson, 1980; Lakoff, 2004). Where this book compares supervision to soccer, the linguistic domain of sport organises our mode of thought and speech: we use words such as team, cooperation, plan, line-up, and organisation, and phrases such as putting the ball in play, and the midfield game.

The keywords in a metaphor often embody problem and solution at the same time. Textual analysis can sometimes lead us from problem to solution, within a single linguistic domain. For instance, when the client says "A piece of my heart is still lying there on that hill in the woods" (see Chapter Two), her metaphor opens up a linguistic domain: wood, bench, walk, greenery, silence, serenity, peace, birds. The therapist can then organise the discussion within this linguistic domain—the domain is large enough to accommodate it. The fact that a piece of her heart is still there implies the possibility of looking for and finding this piece, and perhaps bringing it back.

The world of the image does justice to the narrative structure of our lives. It helps us to explain and listen to the stories of others. The image is therefore articulated in one or more metaphors, which may incorporate oppositions.

In narrative psychotherapy it is generally important to remain within the given linguistic domain, to make the therapist–patient connection as scrupulous as possible. However, if a particular metaphor only organises a struggle, it is desirable to go from the linguistic domain in which the problem is inscribed to a different one, in which a solution may be found.

### Narrative elements: story tracks as a third space

In 1992 the Cologne-based sculptor Gunter Demnig started an art project to commemorate the countless victims of National Socialism who had been dragged from their homes, transported to concentration camps, and murdered. In front of the houses whose occupants had been taken away, cobblestone-sized slabs or Stolpersteine (lit. "stumbling stones") were placed, with the people's names inscribed in brass plaques. One stone, one name, one person. They tell the casual walker who stumbles upon them that in the house he or she is standing outside once lived people who were taken away to be murdered because of their religion, politics, ethnicity, or sexual persuasion. The stones serve as "counter-monuments", memory tracks that tell the story of the indescribable suffering of the Holocaust victims. They tell the story of those who are absent, that they may not be forgotten. Or, in the words of Gunter Demnig, citing the Talmud: "A person is only forgotten when his or her name is forgotten".

Stumbling stones have been placed in about 600 cities, towns, and villages throughout Germany and Europe, and the project is still ongoing.

Here are some other examples of story tracks.

Figure 6. Stolperstein in the city of Maastricht, The Netherlands. Photo: private collection.

*Onna*

In early April 2009, a major earthquake struck the Italian region of Abruzzo. Images of the devastation wrought in the city of L'Aquila went around the world. A Dutch official noticed that one of the villages in the ravaged area bore the same name—Onna—as a neighbouring village in Holland. The echo stirred his compassion and moved him to launch a relief campaign. The shared name activated a series of connections: fellow human beings, fellow Europeans, fellow villagers. The councillor encouraged the local population to help the people living in the Italian village of Onna. "The power of four letters," mused the journalist who interviewed him.

*King Arthur's stone*

A client visited the ruins of Tintagel Castle, which is associated with Arthurian legend. From the rocks at the summit, he looked out over the sea, pondering his life and the process he had gone through in psychotherapy. The stones lying on the ground told him stories, and he took one away with him to give me. Today, it lies on the table in my consulting room. This warm stone, which fits precisely into my palm, evokes the story of the Knights of the Round Table. It symbolises quest, such as the quest for the Holy Grail. It tells of self-sacrifice and perseverance, of endurance, of having a purpose in life. It tells of loyalty and solidarity, of a higher purpose in the hierarchy of significance that justifies supreme effort. Sometimes, if a client sees the way ahead as posing an insuperable challenge, I hand over the stone and talk about the Knights of the Round Table and the client who brought me this stone from the environs of Tintagel Castle.

*The washing line*

In the documentary *It's Been a Lovely Day*, the film-maker Jos de Putter records the last four seasons on his father's farm. The film is a tribute to his father, who is forced to give up his farm, since none of the children wants to take over. De Putter follows his father, asking him about his life as a farmer and the history of the farm. His father struggles to tell his story. The pain it causes him to relinquish his life's work and his farm, which has been handed down from one generation to the next for so long, is palpable. He has no words for his grief, and the film-maker respectfully allows this silence to hang in the air.

One scene shows his wife hanging overalls up on the washing line. We see and hear the overalls blowing in the breeze of Zeeland. The camera focuses for a long time on this image of the washing hanging on the line—the clothes in which so much hard work has been done. The blue overalls in the sun and wind are silent witnesses to a whole life. They tell stories that each viewer will understand in a different, personal way. The image of the overalls introduces an imaginary narrator with fresh perspectives, helping viewers to gain a new sense of the miraculous nature of everyday life.

*Chalk and box*

A client arrived at a therapy session with a small tin box. Pasted to the lid was a tiny blackboard. The box contained a small pack of tissues and a piece of chalk. The client explained that the box symbolised gradual progress, a process that was accompanied by floods of tears and constantly triggered new words. She wanted the box to help other people too. After each session, she wrote a new word on the little blackboard: *love, metaphor, I, enough, ehh* … The box created an intertextual interface for other clients, who constantly looked at the latest word, and sometimes added one of their own. In this way, the box ended up narrating processes we all go through.

*The story of a handkerchief*

Twenty years after his mother's death, the Dutch musician Gé Reinders found a half-decomposed handkerchief, with a still-legible inscription in embroidery stitch: "Vught, barracks 4 and 7: Ravensbrück, Munich".

Reinders wrote a book about his quest for the story of his mother's internment. He reconstructed his mother's life by talking to concentration camp survivors, interviews that culminated in an exhibition at Amsterdam's Verzetsmuseum (Resistance Museum) showing the embroidery made by women in the camps.

The name "Onna", a stone from the hill by Tintagel Castle, washing blowing in the wind, the box with a piece of chalk, and the handkerchief that had belonged to Gé Reinders's mother can all be seen as narrative elements that can help to reveal new aspects of reality and to change the course of a story. They might be called "markings" in the tradition of Dag Hammarskjöld (Hammarskjöld, 1964).

Importantly, a narrative element can evoke a feeling of beauty without fulfilling any external aesthetic criteria, a response that Allman has called the "aesthetic preference" (Allman, 1982a, 1982b). The narrative element necessarily accords with the client's experience and the theme that is being addressed. While close to the client, it also introduces a certain distance, creating an open space in which new significance can be formed. Imagination remains the key guiding principle. A narrative element can be seen as a pars pro toto with added value, in that it encompasses an entire social environment and tells about the client's relationships with that environment. What is depicted remains within the framework of a story and is not interpreted, giving rise to the space and freedom in which personal significance can be created.

*Tajiri's knots*

The sculptor Shinkichi Tajiri (1923–2009) is famous for his knots, which he has made in diverse materials and shapes in many parts of the world. One of them stands at Schiphol airport. This sculpture represents a junction of routes and pathways, of arrivals and departures, of meetings. Each knot is a metaphor or pars pro toto for the world of travel and the travellers themselves. To each individual, an airport or station represents a different reality. It may signify a wait, full of desire, for a lover returning home after a long journey. It may signify the sorrow of those left behind when a loved one goes away. Or it may simply stand for the everyday reality of the commuter.

Many clients see therapists as people with the power to have words signify what they want them to mean, people with expertise that supposedly makes it possible to read clients' "actual" texts and to fathom their true intentions. When Mrs Johnson says "I have no clothes" (see Prelude), her words have congealed into a text that is no longer understood. The client who cries "I love my parents" has probably repeated this text umpteen times, as a result of which it is no longer heard as a significant assertion. Yet it is possible to give words back their magic, to breathe new life into them.

Narrative psychotherapy emphatically encourages the client to become the author of his or her own text and the ultimate, decisive signifier. Indeed, it seeks to give a text even to those who no longer have any words, who have been crippled and discouraged by life, and who have lost the desire to speak. In this case, a story can be offered that reflects the client's social environment in a more or less mimetic form. The client's verbal and non-verbal responses will indicate whether the story resonates and possesses emotional significance. Only an affirmative response can close the narrative circle. However elegant and attractive a story may be, if it does not resonate with the client, it is at best a literary endeavour rather than a therapeutic story.

## *The story as the third space*

As we saw with Pip and Pippa, a story can be used as the third element or space. Coming from the outside, it offers a safe context and a framework within which the client can be identified and recognised. Gardner (Gardner, 1971) has developed a wonderful technique that he calls "mutual storytelling". He helps children to talk about their lives, to connect with their own reality, by telling stories that are not analysed or interpreted (see also Bemelmans, 1978; Oaklander, 1978; Oudshoorn, 1979, 1980; Olthof & Vermetten, 1994). Such stories provide a safe space. The therapist then replies with a story that follows the structure chosen by the child, with the same characters and events, and gradually adds new elements to the story, suggesting changes and possible solutions, to see if the child picks them up. The child retains the role of "master signifier".

### *Yusuf and the troubadour*

Yusuf was a partially sighted boy, twelve years old at the beginning of the therapy. Along with his mother and elder half-sister he had fled from a traumatised, war-torn country, with the financial aid of fellow countrymen in Europe, and joined the father, who was already living at an asylum centre. At some point the father shut himself up with Yusuf, threatening to kill them both. The boy escaped death, after which came a long series of travels, temporary stays in different countries, years of horror. The two children somehow survived as their mother got drunk, frequently vanished for days on end, and worked as a prostitute at home. In the mother's absence, Yusuf's sister took care of them both.

After all these chaotic wanderings, the two children finally ended up in a Dutch foster family where they could feel safe. Caring for these severely traumatised children naturally placed a huge strain on the foster parents. Besides the complications that inevitably accompany a new attachment, behavioural problems at school, in the neighbourhood and at home caused constant disruption. The foster parents' capacity for love, tactfulness and perseverance was taxed to the utmost.

Yusuf was bullied and got into fights because of his poor sight, and his continued presence at school hung in the balance. The foster parents sought help for Yusuf, and also for themselves, as the children's carers. A network of volunteers was created, from families willing to have the children to stay occasionally to farmers who invited Yusuf to tend and ride their horses. He also received individual help, to promote his social and emotional development and to catch up at school. All in all, it was an ambitious programme. Within all this, however, there was no room for structuring his life story. Yusuf himself had no "text", no words to tell his story; he could scarcely say a thing about it. Nothing came out beyond occasional scraps of narrative. It became clear that he was terrified of his mother, and of being abducted by people from his own ethnic community. But the barrier preventing him from speaking out was too high.

Yusuf quarrelled with everyone, especially women, whose authority he refused to accept. It seemed sensible to strengthen the "male line" and to give him a clearer role in the world of his foster father, Leo. To help create a safe space to tell his story, a space remote from his everyday life, Leo and I devised a frame story, which was passed on to Yusuf, with an invitation to reply.

This was the first letter, with the framework:

Dear Yusuf,

You know that we sometimes go and see Jan, who knows all about our family and gives us good advice. The other day, Jan mentioned a French song about a troubadour in the Middle Ages, which had made him think of our Yusuf.

The song is about a king who is sad because he has no court troubadour to sing to him about the goings-on in his kingdom. The king decides to send a messenger around the kingdom to find a suitable minstrel. One day the messenger hears a troubadour making beautiful music. Overjoyed, he sets off back to the palace to tell the king, who goes to hear for himself.

The king is delighted with the troubadour, and asks him to come and live at court and to sing for him.

But the king is wise. He realises that he can't keep the troubadour for himself; everyone must be allowed to share his songs, music, and stories. So he gives the troubadour a special royal badge, commending him to people all over the kingdom. The singer occasionally returns for a few days, sings and plays new and old songs to his king, before setting off around the kingdom again. The troubadour sings about goings-on at court and in the country, and everyone loves him. The king is far-sighted. He doesn't think only of his own pleasure, but also of what is best for the men, women and children in his kingdom. He always encourages the troubadour to do his very best, and as you can imagine, that's pretty impressive!

Your Mum and Dad

Mediaeval chivalry seemed the ideal framework because we knew that Yusuf was argumentative, easily offended and competitive, and liable to become defensive and bossy. His poor sight and his traumatic history heightened his vulnerability. So we tried to create a hero with whom Yusuf could identify, and hit upon a troubadour because of his striking talent for music.

The king represents the good father who bolsters his son's self-confidence. The two are related by choice rather than biologically, similar to Yusuf's bond with his foster parents.

The troubadour is given a special position at court, enhancing his self-esteem, and a special mission, one that does justice to his talents. He goes around the kingdom, bringing good cheer. His stories and songs comfort the people.

This framework gave Yusuf an opening: it enabled him to tell his life story through the experiences of the people in the kingdom. Instead of talking about himself directly, he could do so through others. Crucially, neither the relationship between Yusuf and the troubadour nor that between Yusuf's experiences and those of the people in the kingdom was ever spelled out. The framework provided a free space, an invitation, and enabling conditions to tell a story.

Yusuf seized this opportunity. The stories were precious to him, and he often asked Leo if Jan had another one. He never asked anything else about Jan—who he was or where he lived, for instance. The spell was never broken. As time went on, the framework generated a whole book of stories.

This is how it worked. Leo gave Yusuf the framework of a story, and Yusuf responded with a story of his own, which Leo brought to the consulting room. Then we wrote a new story for Yusuf together. Leo's wife, Anna, would then read it to Yusuf at bedtime. They often discussed the stories, but always within the story framework—its relationship to his own life was never mentioned. So here too, the spell was never broken.

The stories accompanied Yusuf in his turbulent life for over eighteen months. They enabled him to attach significance, symbolically and unconsciously, to real-life experiences that were too painful to discuss directly, creating a reflexive space for him. The framework created an opportunity to make ego-enhancing suggestions (Hartland, 1971; Edelstein, 1981) and to consolidate his relationship with Leo through the relationship between the king and the troubadour. This indirect form of psychotherapy was adopted because of Yusuf's tendency to be combative in a one-to-one relationship. It enabled me to bolster Yusuf's self-confidence through a fictional Other, thus providing a context for a positive transference relationship that did not become overly personal.

Yusuf's linguistic and storytelling abilities progressed in leaps and bounds, and his stories developed from incoherent phrases and scraps to real narratives. He often adopted suggestions made in our own story—for instance, that music was now his weapon, his "sword", instead of his fists. Because of his special position in the story, his identification with the troubadour, he had fewer and less vehement conflicts. He also resumed his piano-playing without being prompted.

To illustrate Yusuf's development, here is a small selection of the stories. The grammar has not been corrected. In his first story response, Yusuf wrote a poem and a few lines introducing himself.

I'm Yusuf and I'm 12 years old and I can't see very much but I can do a lot of stuff and sing but sometimes I get sad and then I think if only I could see better. But I'm still different to the others and I find that hard to accept if that other one is lucky because he or she can play football. But I can do stuff that those others can't do, like smell and feel better, but that makes me different to the others and then I think why did God make me like that. But God doesn't want everyone to be the same, I do get that. I don't like it though. I'm going into the future with all these people around me who have lots of luck.

This text shows Yusuf's struggles with his disability, with being different. He mentions God, as the supreme signifier. It is God's will that people are not all the same. He is going into the future with the happiness of people around him—there is nothing about his own happiness!

These elements recur in the second story, in which we are also introduced to the world of the refugees. I also tried to help him to identify with the troubadour. The salutation "Greetings" comes from Yusuf himself.

Greetings Yusuf,

I read your story very carefully and I can only say that the picture of the troubadour and the picture I have of you are very similar. I'll go into the story in more detail, so that you understand the king's intentions.

The king noticed that the troubadour made everyone happy at court. He heard that his songs were about happiness, about suffering, about the comfort provided by God, about not having a home or a purpose in life, and about knowing what it's like to have a heavy burden. Some people had lost their families, some were hungry and thirsty, some had been driven out and had to wander around the kingdom, homeless. Yes, the minstrel knew so much about the goings-on in the kingdom that the king decided that he mustn't keep him at the palace all the time but must send him round the country, even though he would really miss him. Because he brought happiness into people's lives. The king summoned the troubadour and solemnly presented him with special royal insignia enabling him to travel freely around the kingdom and to sing everywhere. The king said he should tell the people stories and above all comfort them.

"You're no longer the little singer who happens to meet people here and there. You have a new task now, you're the king's troubadour."

With these words, the king hung the insignia around his neck. The singer felt greatly honoured, but he also had a vague feeling of sadness. He didn't want to be different. What he wanted most was to be just like everyone else. ... But the king explained: "Sometimes God chooses people for something special, a mission. He doesn't want everyone to be the same and do the same ... You're going to bring people happiness, and you'll always come back, because you belong with us and we belong with you. It's God's will that you're so wonderfully different."

The troubadour realised that the king was making a great sacrifice. He understood what his mission was. It was not easy, but with God's help, he was sure he'd succeed. Soon afterwards he started telling his first stories ...

Jan

Yusuf replied:

> Greetings Jan
>
> I read your story. It really made me think. I liked it that you're interested in me and want to help. I'm glad the troubadour succeeded he helps people and that's a good thing! I felt that the troubadour was making people happy. So perhaps people are curious how I deal with my disability. Cos most people don't go to a special school. In the Middle Ages there weren't any. They didn't have any optical or hospitals neither. People are different now. Now I'm going to tell you how I deal with it.
>
> I dont need a stick but I do have a disability and I have to have someone with me if Im in town or if I go for tests for my disability. Im not allowed to cycle in town, so you see people are all different. But Im good at telling stories! Perhaps Ill become a story-teller but I'm good at telling jokes and having fun. And Im good at the piano. That's a gift I got from God.
> The End!!
>
> Cheers, Yusuf age 12.

Here Yusuf starts describing his life, adopting pieces of the initial story: he's good at telling stories. That is an initial identification. Then he introduces his disability. We decided to jump ahead in the story.

> Greetings Yusuf,
>
> Thanks again for your wonderful letter. I certainly want to help you, because I'm really impressed by your words and I'm curious how you deal with your disability. You have a disability, but you don't need a stick. You do need someone to go with you. It's certainly true that you can tell great stories. Maybe you can also tell stories with the piano and make other people happy? Music is a gift from God. You have certainly received this gift. That makes me happy, because you have quite a difficult time. It's true, disabled people didn't have proper help in the Middle Ages. Well, that's what this next troubadour story is about.
>
> The troubadour's second journey was to a new part of the good king's vast kingdom. In one village he met disabled people of all ages: babies, boys and girls, and old people too. They were all treated harshly—gaped at and treated roughly, as if they were inferior. The healthy people never realised that their own health was a gift from God. But the troubadour noticed the disabled people helping each other: a blind woman caring for a toddler with no legs, a deaf boy helping a lame man on his way. The ordinary people didn't even notice.
>
> The troubadour was full of rage and he wanted to hack into the mean people with his sword, or to get the king to punish them with his army and cannons. But just in time, he luckily remembered his mission, so he wrote a song instead. Everyone was shouting, drinking beer and wine and gobbling food. But when he started to sing, they all fell silent. He sang about the heroic deeds of disabled people. His song opened the people's eyes, and the healthy people saw the fantastic ways in which the disabled people helped each other. His second song, about the special gift of disabled people, made many people blush with shame. The young troubadour saw that his music moved the people's hearts. He fell asleep very late, quite exhausted.

Next day he moved on. But later, on his way home, he passed through the village again. He stayed the night there, and was treated with great respect. He saw the changes; he had sung happiness into the village. He shone with pride. "My music is my sword." He decided that music could achieve more than brute force. He was glad with all he had learned and with the mission that the wise king had given him.

Jan

Yusuf replied, and started to describe his own life in specific terms. He wrote that he was sad that his mother was "always thinking about herself" and described a frightening incident with a man wielding a pistol. His narrative goes back and forth between the story of the troubadour and his own life. In another letter he describes being beaten with a belt by a friend of his mother's, and his mother doing nothing to help him. He appears to be referring to experiences in his home country when he writes of the cruel treatment meted out to beggars:

> If someone didn't listen he was punished and his head was chopped off or the people who had done even worse things were hanged.

As a therapist, I might now have picked up on the things Yusuf had written about his background. But there was a risk that he might then stop telling the stories. The "story" quality had to be preserved. It was clear that Yusuf was following my storyline, and still occasionally referred to it. I decided to follow the line.

Greetings Yusuf,

The last stories you sent me also gave me a lot to think about. Here is the next bit of the story.
   The troubadour went off around the country, full of good cheer. He was often showered with gifts and delicious food. He went on his way, full of pride.
   But some places were very different. The troubadour saw children being beaten with sticks and whips while their own mother was watching. He also saw beggars being thrashed, just for asking for something to eat. He wanted to lay into them with his sword. Then he remembered the king's words. He had an important mission, collecting stories, bearing witness and offering comfort.
   So in the evening he sang to the crowds in the square: first, a comforting song for the boy who'd been beaten in front of his mother. Then he sang to the beggars who had been treated so badly. Some people were stuffed with food and drink and sat around belching; others listened attentively to his beautiful voice. As he sang he saw tears welling in the little boy's eyes. Beggars hovering around the edges of the square listened carefully to his second song. Then he felt sure that he had done the right thing, but as he rode home he felt sad.
   Instead of going to the king, he went straight to bed and slept for 20 hours. But the wise king suspected what was wrong, and comforted him with the following words:

Jan

This open end is the essence of the technique of shared storytelling. Yusuf was invited to fill in the king's words and give them meaning himself. As the months went on, Yusuf wrote more and more about his life; as the therapist, I kept to the context of the framework story, however.

At one point Yusuf told a story about "the troubadour's father", who had been cursed by a witch, since which time he had changed, unable to "settle". I pondered that this might mean that the son also felt cursed; his father was no longer in his life. This would have to be addressed in the stories, for otherwise it might be difficult for the son to "settle". I broached the subject indirectly:

Greetings Yusuf,

Well, that was another wonderful story, you're a real story-teller. And it's true, as often happens in stories, not everything ends well. Just when the father has received tremendous applause for his song, the terrible witch suddenly appeared on the stage. With a bolt of lightning, she cursed the father, a disaster. As you wrote, the man could no longer "settle" after that. Now we know that his son is the king's happiness troubadour, wearing the highest royal insignia. But what about that curse? Does it get passed on from father to son? The troubadour worried about this terribly in the darkest places of his heart. It was his own sad secret.

I continued by telling a long story of the son's fear, and a dream in which God heals him, vanquishing the curse. This led Yusuf to respond with a story in which the father is proud of his son, who works through stories rather than brute force.

Then Yusuf started explaining about his nightmares, and his stories, which became more and more detailed, turned into a real battlefield. There were black knights, there was a journey through a haunted forest, there were ghosts and dark holes and the blackness of night.

In another story he introduces an image that may represent his mother: he has "a sick feeling in his stomach" and a whispering voice leads him to "a little deer drinking its mother's milk". Then the peaceful deer are frightened away by a huntsman.

Does thinking of his mother make him feel sick with fear? Do people look at him strangely because of having such a mother? A whispering voice leads him to a primeval image of mother and child.

As the correspondence continued, Yusuf's writing skills improved. His stories had plots, and described a succession of incidents. Just as he himself was now being cared for by loving foster parents, he provides a caring home for the huntsman in his story. In later stories he introduces a squirrel that has "strayed and lost its mother", after which he meets a wild horse that he tames without the use of force. Could the taming of the wild horse stand for his ability to control his own emotions of anger and sadness?

As time went on, the stories became more cheerful. The troubadour feels at home at court, surrounded by the animals. He goes on trips with his horse and the sun is often shining. He has already become a true knight. He is often sent on missions, and each one ends successfully.

The troubadour is surrounded by harmony and he is happy, as one of his final stories makes clear. Yusuf's language has clearly evolved. His vocabulary is larger, and he gradually uses more punctuation.

Greetings Jan

One morning the troubadour woke up and decided to go out to say good morning to the animals. After that he went to his room and thought long and deep what will my next mission be? Since he had nothing to do in the evening he decided to go for a long walk in the woods of course he met the animals that lived in the woods. He kept thinking of the conversation with the king. Suddenly the sun came out it was fine weather all the animals came out to enjoy the fine weather cos the sun didnt shine very often in the kingdom where he lived. Suddenly a pilgrim passed by he wore a brown robe and a chain with a cross on it. The pilgrim looked tired I think he must be very thirsty the troubadour gave him some water. Thank you brother Im so grateful. The troubadour and the pilgrim sat in the lovely field of sunflowers, enjoying the sunshine. Brother perhaps it sounds strange but could you show me somewhere to rest? The troubadour thought would the king allow this shouldn't he ask if it was allowed? But the pilgrim looked very tired and was so hungry the troubadour replied straight away and said yes of course. Come with me. After they walked for half an hour they arrived at the king's palace. Well I hadnt expected something so beautiful and orderly. Are you the kings son? Certainly my boy. The pilgrim went in with the troubadour.

Suddenly the king came in and said troubadour who is that? That is a pilgrim he asked me for somewhere to sleep and perhaps something to eat and drink if its possible Sire. But of course the king showed the pilgrim all over the palace. It was nearly time to eat the tables were already laid and it was almost twelve o'clock. The king came in and announced that dinner could begin. Everyone was happy and ate and drank after a delicious meal the king announced the mission: dear people as you know the troubadour is a good fellow who has helped many people and has cheered up many people but that time has ended and so I want to tell you that the troubadour has a new mission and that is that he is going to learn to be a knight because he has studied all year and so I want him to start the training. Everyone was happy and cheered with satisfaction. The troubadour sang a song to finish after the fine concert everyone applauded.

cheers Yusuf

The troubadour is totally accepted as part of the court. Life is peaceful and sunny and the story acquires more depth. The troubadour is training to be a knight.

These stories gave Yusuf words and a framework for his own text. Just as the troubadour grows in the course of the stories, Yusuf too matured. He managed to keep his head above water, and there were clearly fewer escalating incidents in his life. And although he would occasionally shout, in anger and despair: "Do you think I don't know that I'm the troubadour myself?" the magic was never broken. Alongside the care and support that was organised around him, this story cycle played a useful role in his social and emotional development.

### The landscape of the third space

The journalist Frénk van der Linde made a documentary about his parents' divorce, *Lost Connection*. He interviewed his parents separately, to obtain their individual stories. Later, in an interview in the daily newspaper *de Volkskrant* (14 February 2011) he was asked how his parents had fared since the documentary's release. He replied, "They have agreed on periodic access to the pain." This answer captures perfectly the action of moving the pain to the third space. It is no longer the pain of each parent individually, the first pain, or the pain between them—the second space. They are now connected in a shared pain and have evidently been able to meet again, after years of estrangement.

## A kiss as third element

In a poem by the Dutch writer Remco Campert (Campert, 2000), the kiss becomes the third element or space. Detached from the person who kisses, it moves independently. It searches, with its own reason for moving, seeks a mouth to go to, to press itself against. This line represents a manner of speech, reflects Deleuze's view of attributes—a subject's characteristics. Attributes confer a fixed identity or Self. Deleuze defines the attribute as active and autonomous, detached from the subject. An attribute "happens" and expresses a pure, unadulterated *becoming*. Viewed thus, identity is not a *carrier* of attributes, but is carried in a ceaseless process of becoming.

If a client is asked to arrange a set of Russian nesting dolls, attention will focus on the arrangement of dolls on the table. This creates a cooperative relationship that links the client, the therapist, and the third element or space—the arrangement. The arrangement speaks, acquires its own voice, can move—thus bridging or widening distance. The dolls can shift and look in different directions. Furthermore, the client and the client's problem are thus linked to the externalised image, made visible through the dolls on the table. In this way, the secret, the trauma, the lie, the fear, the suspicion, the silence, can all become *the third element*. Instead of any discussion of a secret that must (or must not) be disclosed, the secret acquires separate narrative agency.

The third element can also be described as a landscape. As the Dutch writer Bernlef once remarked in a radio interview: "I always have to start with a landscape. If I don't have a landscape, the story won't get going." The landscape is the space of becoming, the interspace, the area between subject and object that creates a connection.

## Thirdness

The American philosopher C. S. Peirce refers to the concept of *thirdness* (Peirce, 1960). In his view, the dyad is an inadequate description of the mental world. He distinguishes three categories: *firstness*, meaning the concept of the things as they are in themselves, unseen and prior to any encounter, without context. In therapy, you might say: the separate worlds of therapist and client, without their meeting. *Secondness* is a mode of being in relation to another. In psychotherapy, this is the meeting. *Thirdness* relates to a mental process whereby the first and second elements are inscribed in a relationship and acquire significance. The influence of one subject on another is mediated by a third element: here, the element that constitutes the relationship between therapist and client. This third element may be a theme or idea, a sentence, a text, or an image; it may be an object in space. Linguistically, Peirce's *thirdness* is the triadic relationship between a sign, the object to which the sign refers, and the interpretive thought, which is itself another sign.

A therapist who sets out to heal the client, or to guide the client towards health, is adopting the dyadic position, that of expert and "master signifier". But the third space can help the therapist to adopt a position *alongside* the client, to engage in a cooperative relationship around this third space. Anyone can join, bringing their own life experience and expertise to bear. The resistance that may surface in a dyadic relationship will therefore not arise in the third space of narrative psychotherapy.

We see a graphic image of the third space in Giotto's painting *Joachim and Anne meeting at the golden gate*, to which the German philosopher Peter Sloterdijk refers in his trilogy *Spheres* (Sloterdijk, 2011 (I), 2014 (II), 2016 (III)). In the interspace between the faces of St Joachim and St Anne, we see a third face forming. The third space is generated in the meeting between the two.

Figure 7. *The Meeting of Joachim and Anne outside the Golden Gate*, fresco, c.1305, Padua, Scrovegni Chapel, by Giotto di Bondone.

Figure 8. Detail.

The notion of the third space is useful in the creation of a therapeutic context. Within this context, we develop a framework, one that will serve as the third space for all those taking part in the therapy.

Before discussing the development of this framework, we need to look at the logic on which it will be based: the logic of abduction.

CHAPTER FIVE

# Abduction and the logic of metaphor

*"The details are not the details. They make the design"*

—Charles Eames

## Introduction

A man says: "It's as if my whole chest is full of ants, as if there are ants crawling under my skin everywhere. It gives me a very nervous, hunted feeling. I feel tiny electric shocks everywhere, it's extremely unpleasant."

He presents this description to his neurologist, who is essentially quite baffled. The image "as if ants are running through my chest" can only be understood with the logic of metaphor. It is common sense, of course, that ants cannot crawl around someone's body. Ants move in and across the earth, not through a person's body. The bodily sensation of tiny electric shocks, a crawling, swarming, and itchy feeling, is compared here to ants crawling across the earth. The movements of a column of ants are compared to a prickling movement in the chest, on the basis of shared characteristics. In order to gain a better understanding of the underlying mechanism at work here, and the way in which such metaphors may be interpreted, we shall take an excursion into Bateson's theory of the logic of abduction.

Bateson describes the theory of logical types as expounded by Russell and Whitehead (Bateson, 1972, 1979; Bateson & Bateson, 1987; see also Pakman, 2004). Within this view, the universe is a hierarchy of systems: each system is part of a larger system, which is in turn embedded in a still larger one, creating a hierarchy of levels and meta-levels. Logical classes, logical order, and hierarchy can help to clarify relationships within patterns, and patterns within patterns, all neatly organised into levels, differentiated by logical type. This means separating the different units of systems: from cell to organ, from organ to organism, and from organism to ecosystem.

In the theory of logical types, a distinction is drawn between things, a class of things, and the class of classes of things. The objects referred to have names, and this name itself has a name. The name and the objects to which the name refers belong to different logical types. Birds can sing, but the name "bird" cannot. We can eat the dishes listed on a menu, but not the menu itself. Classical grammar teaches us that a noun is the name of a person or thing. But it says nothing about the *process* of naming. According to Bateson, a noun may relate to other parts of a sentence in different ways. Information is a complex of relationships, not a complex of things. Words may be incorporated into logical arguments, and share the same attributes, as members of the same class. After all, the theory of logical types is based on classification.

The logic of metaphor, however, works in a completely different way. Bateson observes that language stands in the same relationship to the objects it refers to as a map to the territory it depicts. He directs focus away from the map itself to the process of map-making. The names never coincide completely, and never encompass the totality of the objects they name. The process of signifying and interpreting is never complete. There is an open space, an interspace, in the process of representation, and it is in that interspace that the world of possibilities, the world of "as if", comes into being. Signifiers are not necessarily linked to what they signify. To bridge the gap between map and territory there is a need for "news" about the difference between them.

> The bridge between map and territory is *difference*. It is only *news of difference* that can get from the territory to the map, and this fact is the basic epistemological statement about the relationship between all reality out there and all perception in here: that the bridge must always be in the form of difference.
>
> (Bateson, 1979, p. 240)

Let us go on to discuss Bateson's specific use of the word "mind". This concept can help us to think in terms of relationships. The biological world is based on relationships, whereas in our patterns of thinking we focus on content and substance. However, a relationship cannot be understood by adding up the contents.

## Mind

Bateson uses the word "mind" for all processes in which ideas are at work. Ideas are formed by information, and information can be seen as news about difference. So Bateson defines information as "difference which makes a difference". And differences cannot be localised—they are found *within* a relationship. Mental processes, ideas, communication, and patterns are all related to issues of form, from map-making to epistemology, rather than substance. They belong to a world in which consequences are produced by difference, a world in which something that is not there—a nothing, something that is absent—can nonetheless be a cause. Derrida (Derrida, 1978) has criticised the metaphysics of presence—a metaphysics in which there is no place for absence or silence—on which Western thinking is based. In the following poem by Toon Tellegen, someone's absence, their failure to come, has a decisive influence on the evening.

> It's getting very late
> and no one comes
> it's getting later and later
> rain lashes the windows
> and the later it gets
> The lovelier the one who will not come.
>
> *(From Toon Tellegen, 2003; translated for this publication by BJ)*

In classical logic of identity, a primary cause must be:

- simple, that is, without contradiction;
- homogeneous, that is, of the same substance;
- present, that is, identical to itself. (Pakman, 2004, p. 420)

Things are precisely as they are, no more and no less; names are treated as if they were the same as the objects to which they refer. In Bateson's world of mind, however, things are encompassed by differences and by themselves. That is why metaphor is the ideal language for that world. The logic that belongs with metaphor is the logic of *abduction*, a non-hierarchical logic based on coexistence rather than subordination. Bateson derives the concept of abduction from the American philosopher of linguistics, C. S. Peirce.

Classical logic is based on reasoning by induction and deduction, which moves from one "logical level" to another. In the former, general principles are inferred from particular characteristics or events; in the latter, specific characteristics or events are inferred from general premises.

Reasoning by induction, by which a *probable* conclusion is reached, can be explained using an example of the following kind: "Plato, Aristotle and Socrates died; Plato, Aristotle and Socrates are human beings; therefore, all human beings are mortal". The conclusion "are mortal" is attached by identifying Plato, Aristotle and Socrates as members of the class of human beings.

Reasoning by deduction, in which the conclusion is *guaranteed* if the premises are correct, is generally explained using some variation of the following syllogism: "All human beings are mortal; Socrates is a human being; therefore, Socrates is mortal". In this classical logical discourse, the objects are Cartesian: clear and unequivocal, clearly distinguished from one another, and present as reality outside us. The logical types of observation, the distinctions between element and class, are respected, and an attempt is made to get as close as possible to the truth of the territory that has to be mapped. The focus is on causes, in which actors are effective factors that have observable consequences. The discourse is determined by purposeful action. Self-reflexivity must be excluded.

Bateson says that if observation is accompanied solely by purposeful action, what he calls the "ecology of ideas" is disrupted (Bateson, 1972). Whereas classical logical discourse is hierarchical (arguments are based on subordination and superordination), abductive reasoning is non-hierarchical. Stories are woven into each other, and a pattern develops that connects them. Abductive reasoning involves shifts between concepts at the same logical level of abstraction. The logic of abduction corresponds to the logic underlying the construction of a metaphor. It involves following a pattern that moves through different domains, and the differences that are introduced cannot be demonstrably a consequence of, or based on, our interventions.

To avoid getting entangled in the laws of identity and presence, a process of decentralisation is needed. If a comparison is made between a name and what that name refers to on the one hand, and a map and the territory it depicts on the other, this comparison is based on abductive reasoning. A specific pattern is followed through different domains. One pattern does not provide the foundations for another. Rather, they coexist and refer to each other; they are self-reflexive and imaginary. This mode of reasoning corresponds to the "ecology of ideas". The language of this ecology is metaphor. Nature itself consists of metaphors, says Bateson. Psychotherapy avails itself of classical logical reasoning, but it also uses abductive reasoning—as do poetry, art, drama, humour, and dreams. As an example of abductive reasoning, Bateson cites a false syllogism that he calls the "syllogism in grass" (Bateson, 1991):

Grass dies.
Men die.
Men are grass.

Abduction is a process of reasoning that creates a new insight from a recognisable similarity between two or more different situations. Human beings and grass share the characteristic of mortality and are therefore similar, and may be compared to one another. According to classification-based logical reasoning this is nonsense, since grass and human beings do not belong to the same class of mortal beings. The reasoning behind the "syllogism in grass" operates through a correspondence of attributes (Bateson, 1991). Whereas inductive and deductive reasoning identify subjects and assign them to a class, abductive reasoning functions by equating attributes and forming a class based on these shared attributes. Aspects from one part of a system help to make it possible to understand similar aspects in a different system. This practice of comparison and association, of searching for important similarities between different individuals and areas, is crucial to narrative psychotherapy.

This kind of reasoning is linked to what Freud calls the "primary process", the universal basis of all thinking. Metaphors convey the information with which nature creates itself; the transfer operates through "meaningful likeness" (Charlton, 2008, p. 62). Metaphor is not only elegant and aesthetically pleasing, but it is also the kind of logic that underlies the biological world, and an important feature of mental process. Metaphor is a particularly useful form of representation when one is trying to clarify complex systems. What the "syllogism in grass" implies is that grass can serve as a metaphor for human beings and vice versa, on the basis of their shared property of mortality. The Dutch writer Bernlef states, in the Epilogue to his Dutch translation of the work *Memories Look at Me* by Tomas Tranströmer (Tranströmer, 2011): "the power ... comes from finding images that are far apart in logic, but when placed opposite each other nonetheless forge a connection with each other, on the basis of a certain inner consistency".

Freud's "primary process", as Charlton explains, "has no access to negatives, has no tense (no way of operating on past or future), and has no linguistic mood. Primary process usually does not identify things or persons. Its focus is the process of relationship between them. It is primarily metaphorical … and the subject matter is always the relationship between the self and other people or the environment" (Charlton, 2008, pp. 104–105). Metaphor makes it possible to understand relationships and to transfer the relationships that have been understood to other situations. The relationship is preserved, while the *relata*—the things compared—may change. The central issues here are always form, pattern, and connection. Bateson quotes Samuel Butler's proposition that the better an organism "knows" something, the less conscious it becomes of its knowledge, adding "i.e. there is a process whereby knowledge … sinks to deeper and deeper levels of the mind". The primary process has the wisdom of "patterns that connect". The secondary process, conscious thought, has access to only a small part of the mental process. Bateson therefore construes "mind" as the reflection of the larger parts of the natural world around us, and in order to understand the relationships between them, what matters is not quantity but form and connection. Bateson (Bateson, 1979; see also Charlton, 2008) lists six criteria for *mind*, which he uses as a synonym for the *ecology of ideas*, at the beginning of a chapter on "Criteria of Mental Processes":

### *1. Mind is an aggregate of interacting parts or components*

… "the explanation of mental phenomena must always reside in the organisation and interaction of multiple parts" (Bateson, 1979, p. 86). Parts always belong to the whole, and mental function is immanent in the interaction of differentiated "parts" (Bateson, 1979, pp. 121–122). A violinist is a mental system that is part of a larger system: a violinist and her violin, together with her teacher and the orchestra, together with the audience and the concert hall, and all these elements are interconnected. A hockey stick is an extension of the hockey player's arm, and as such it is part of a mental system.

### *2. The interaction between parts of mind is triggered by difference*

The bubble that emerges from a child's bubble pipe may become part of a mental system that includes the child (Sloterdijk, 2011). In the material world, an event has a cause—I throw a stone into a pool, and ripples radiate out from it—and through causes, one system impacts on another. The cause can be measured. In the world of ideas, however, a relationship is always needed between two parts, or between a part at one particular moment in time and the same part at a different moment in time, in order to activate a third component, the receiver. The receiver may be a sensory organ. What the receiver reacts to is a difference or change. Anything that does not change is imperceptible—unless we ourselves are willing to move, adopting a different position or perspective. That is why it is so important that psychotherapy always generates difference and change: a different significance, a different place in space, a different chair, a third component as receiver—such as an important sentence, a symbol, an object or an image.

Difference, however, is not quantitative but qualitative. If it were quantitative, absence would have no effect. As we saw in Chapter Three, the departure and absence of the ant in Toon Tellegen's story *The Ant's Departure* means something different to each animal. The absence cannot be represented in a single unambiguous way; in the open space for interpretation, every animal creates the difference that defines the difference for himself or herself.

Core metaphorical statements such as: "I feel as if I'm attached to a chain"; "I can feel a stone pressing on my stomach"; and "it's like a steel band around my head" are "as if" meanings. The people who say these things know that they are meant figuratively, but the experience is nonetheless presented literally. The stone on the stomach cannot be identified: it won't show up in a photograph. In a material sense, the stone is not present, it has no volume and does not take up any space. Using the logic of abduction, a physical pain is explained using an analogy. In therapy, the "as if" can be made literal, either by deliberately focusing attention on this image—techniques such as focusing, guided imagery, and hypnotherapy work in this way—or by introducing an object to represent the stone, band, or chain. For instance, a cushion may be placed on the client's belly, symbolising the stone, thus introducing the mental world of difference. The logic of abduction takes a lateral route to search for analogies. The heavy weight of the stone that was once felt in the hand is compared to the heavy feeling in the belly. In this way, the metaphor brings the experience closer.

## 3. Mental process requires collateral energy

When I'm riding a bike, I exert force on the pedals to set the bike moving. More force on the pedals increases the number of revolutions of the wheels and thus increases my speed. When I enter a friend's house and I try to stroke the dog that comes to meet me at the door, the dog has his own energy, his own metabolism. He may come closer and allow me to stroke him; he may start growling, because he encodes my approach as posing a threat; he may recognise my smell and happily jump up against me, or he may slink away with his tail between his legs. That energy is already present in the dog, but there is no such energy in the bike, which only starts moving if I provide the necessary energy. The dog's reaction is dependent on the significance he attaches to my behaviour. My behaviour triggers something in the dog, and the dog triggers something in me.

## 4. Mental process requires circular (or more complex) chains of determination

This process drives learning, memory, and knowledge acquisition. My racing bike is incorporated into a mental system of which I am also part. I ride uphill at a particular speed and in a particular gear. If I ride uphill along the same route a few days later, my legs know how to do it, what speed I need to go, in what gear, and how much force I need to exert. That information is stored in the memory of my legs—my legs have learned from experience and they now have a plan of action. Next time I visit my friends, their dog will recognise me, welcome me happily, growl, or slink away again. The dog has learned and developed a memory of our relationship, and so have I. This memory and learning responds to hierarchies of meaning and the codifications that organise themselves in these hierarchies. These codifications ensure that the appropriate responses are given.

## 5. In mental process, the effects of difference are to be regarded as transforms (i.e., coded versions) of events which preceded them

Cause and effect are not the same thing. There is a difference between cause and effect, if both are part of a flexible mental system. A relationship exists between cause and effect, but it is dependent on their codification. Forgiveness is not a logical consequence of damage that is incurred. A wound "knows" how to repair itself. The form of the recovering tissue is determined by the form and differentiation of the wound. A difference has arisen between the part of the body with a wound and the condition of that part of the body before then. The relationship between the body and wound includes learning, memory, and knowledge: the wound carries within it a mirror image of the body part's previous condition and knows how to mend itself; the rest of the body knows how to recover and to absorb the wound into the former state.

*6. The description and classification of these processes of transformation disclose a hierarchy of logical types immanent in the phenomena*

Looked at in this way, mental process or *mind* is omnipresent in the living world. Ideas have no location and cannot be identified; they are non-things. They are immanent, embodied in their examples. However, *mind* cannot exist separately from the body: mental process is present within the physical reality.

## Abduction in practice

The meaning of a particular type of action changes with the context, and especially with any changes in the relationship between those concerned. The context of a job interview can be identified by the line of chairs for the members of the appointments committee, facing a single chair for the candidate. The candidate knows what his or her position is. A different context may be designated by a circular table around which everyone takes a seat. The context of a hot meal served as a buffet is different from that of a meal served at a laid table. A mouse may identify to the cat the context of their encounter by scuttling away. Pupils identify the context for their teacher, who can teach them, and the teacher identifies the context for the pupils. The teacher is the meta-level for the pupil, being in a position to create a given context. The supervisor is the meta-level for someone undergoing supervision, and the psychotherapist is the meta-level for his or her clients.

Messages become intelligible by being placed in a context. This implies that certain behaviour defines or clarifies a context. This "contextualisation of context" is the classification of the messages that occur in that context. In the context of the classroom, numerous events and types of behaviour are familiar and expected. The same applies to the context of a GP's surgery, and to that of a psychotherapy session. These contexts provide an organisational structure, not only for behaviour, but for an entire class of behaviours.

Hierarchy in mental phenomena is approached from the vantage point of codification and interpretation. Every relationship has two sides and needs two descriptions. It always involves the joint actions of two or more people—or two or more parts, creating a third element: a sum that is always more than its parts. Pride, for instance, is a relationship you may have with yourself. In that case, pride is the "joint action", the third element, of the relationship you have with yourself.

Context is part of what something is. Bateson sees context as a collective term for all those events that define for an organism the set of alternatives from which it must make its next choice. Context markers play a key role (O'Hanlon & Wilk, 1987). Many different signals have the function of marking context—that is, of structuring a context within which a certain range of behavioural patterns are expected. If a hero or heroine of a play is in trouble, members of the audience know that this is happening within the context of a play, and there is no need to call the emergency services. They have already received plenty of information about the context: they have purchased tickets and a programme, perhaps dressed up for the occasion, and have taken their seats to watch the actors perform.

Context is also sustained by a constant flow of context markers, or by markers that have a permanent function, such as uniforms. Bateson says that information comes from context as *difference which makes a difference*, towards a new context. The context where the information enters is called the *framework*. A framework, then, is the internal state of an organism within which information must be received. It is the meaning that the organism ascribes to the facts. Therapy consists of transforming the context into a new context, for which new context markers are needed. The transformation of context can also be achieved with the aid of interventions that introduce new meanings, new behaviour, and new context markers to take the place of the old ones.

> A girl who was referred for therapy because she kept telling lies turned out to be struggling to accept the last name she would be acquiring from her mother's new partner. A loyal daughter, she felt unable to refuse, since she had been told she could "choose". Arranging the babushkas, she chose a tiny little doll for her biological father and put a plastic cup over it to make the small doll invisible (there is frequent tension between her mother and father). When the new name is mentioned, she picks up a large doll that she has chosen to be the "fibber" and puts it, almost inadvertently and unconsciously, on top of the plastic cup—as if trying to say: I'm being robbed of my name and I can't say "no". When this observation is related, along with the meaning attributed to it above, the lying acquires a completely different significance, and starts functioning as a completely different context marker. (With thanks to Luuk Hoendervangers)

In the logic of abduction and the world of metaphor, we go back and forth between the world of "as if" and reality. In line with this, our interventions in psychotherapy are based on defining differences that can trigger a new insight, based on the imagination. In the world of mental processes, differences are equivalent to causality. Psychotherapy is a profession that uses both classical logical discourse and the world of "as if", generated by metaphor; it lies in between art and science, between metaphor and classical logic.

## The logic of abduction

The Dutch comedian André van Duin has a sketch in which he presents a good example of the logic of abduction. He and his stooge are boy scouts. The stooge asks André if he wants to learn something about logic. He then puts the following questions to André:

> "Have you got an aquarium?"
> "Yes," says André.
> "If you've got an aquarium, you've got fish."

André nods, thoughtfully, "Yes."
"If you've got fish, you love animals?"
André can only answer "yes."
"If you love animals, you love children."
Hesitating, "Ye-es."
"If you love children, you love people?"
"If you love people, you love women?"
"If you love women, you're not gay!"

André ponders this at length in apparent confusion. You see him switching from one thought to another, following an internal mental process. Then his eyes light up happily—he gets it! Then the stooge asks him to try this kind of logic out for himself. There is an orchestra in the pit, and its conductor is standing on stage. André goes up to him and asks:

"Have you got an aquarium?"
The conductor replies, "No!"

It remains still for a few moments. You see André's brain creaking to absorb this; you see him follow the entire thought process of the questions that were put to him a moment ago. He gazes at the audience, stands there in silence, closes his eyes, and then looks up again with big, joyful eyes to share the happiness of his discovery. Then he looks at the conductor and says triumphantly: "Then you're gay!"

The following anecdote from the world of psychotherapy was told by Betty Alice Erickson about her father, Milton Erickson:

> My brother, Lance, grew up with a heart defect. He gave a talk once where he said that when he was a small boy, he and Dad used to go out and look at trees. They would look at how high the trees were and find the biggest and the tallest trees around. Then they would talk about how long a time that particular tree had lived and how it had taken its energy from the ground and the sun, and then how it had nurtured the squirrels and birds that had made their homes on and within that tree.
>
> (Erickson, 2006, p. 27)

If you look at this story as a psychotherapist, says Betty Alice Erickson, you might say that he communicated to Lance the idea and the suggestion to live a long, good, healthy life. By drawing his son's attention to the tree and its long growth over the years, his son's unconscious receives the suggestion to do the same, and this structures his development along a similar path. The abductive logic, here, is the analogy between the long life of a tree and the suggestion to live a long, healthy life himself.

Symptoms are often exactly appropriate, and literally comment on the "ecology of ideas". For instance, a mother phoned one day to make an appointment for her fourteen-year-old son. She said: "He's so terrified that I might die that he presses his eyes shut all day, as if there is something he can't bear to see" (Kuipers & Olthof, 2005).

*Missing the toilet bowl*

A colleague of mine, the child psychologist Paulien Kuipers, told me the following story:

> A nine-year-old boy systematically missed the toilet bowl when he urinated. Correction, rewards, and punishment were tried, to no avail. The behaviour stopped when it became possible to refer openly to the father's extra-marital affair. The link between the little boy urinating on the floor beside the toilet bowl and the father who was "pissing outside the pot" [a common Dutch expression for adultery] helped, in a completely illogical way, to stop this behaviour. The link between the literal and the figurative is an abductive process. The symptomatic behaviour came to an end; it had performed its task, and the family's problems could be discussed. The focus changed, and the boy was able to move out of the limelight.

*Consultation*

In the "workplace" where I practise along with my colleagues Didier Tritsmans, Nans Klaasen, Gina Devos, Gerdy Konings and Christianne Albertz, the following case history was presented, which illustrates the logic of abduction:

> Didier Tritsmans was working with a client on the theme of expectations. The client was a student who had asked to see us because he had the feeling that he was unable to refuse anyone anything, in particular his mother. The young man had the idea that his mother was so excessively demanding that there was no room for him to lead his own life. There was friction at home if he wanted to make time for his girlfriend; there was friction at home if he wanted to make time to study, and if he wanted to go out, things were worse still. Didier told the group that the young man described himself as someone who was completely incapable of standing up for himself. He always felt obliged to say "yes". The theme widened to include his reactions to other people's expectations. He described himself as someone who felt he had to fit into what other people expected of him. I said: "Hey, this may seem a strange thing to say, a weird association, but I suddenly found myself wondering what it was like when your mother was pregnant with you. Have you ever heard any stories about that?" The young man was silent, looked away, and he clearly had tears in his eyes.
>   When I encouraged him to put what had happened into words, he said: "That's exactly what my mother always says when we have a row: 'You know what I went through with your father'."
>   The story was told again and again: his father had kicked his mother in the belly when she was expecting him. If I understood the story correctly, his mother blamed her son: "If I went through all that *because* of you, and *for* you, you can't turn around and say 'no' now. It's your duty to do what I say and ask of you, without the slightest bit of space for yourself."

The theme of "expectations" is linked here associatively with "expecting a baby". There is no logical connection between the two themes; they are connected to each other as images. The "yes" of the patient's answer, "That's exactly what my mother always says when we have a row," reveals that the student sees this as a "logical" connection. There is no general statement about the connection; the link is only meaningful, only makes sense, to this student with his story. The "logic" is non-repeatable; it is the logic of serendipity and chance connections, a bond created by making a lateral movement. The logic of abduction is applied on the basis of the analogy in the relationship between having to fulfil other people's expectations and what happened when his mother was expecting him.

At the same time, classical logical discourse is also part of this therapeutic process. Didier puts all the communication with his mother of the type "Since I went through all this for you, it's unacceptable for you to ever say 'no' to me" in the class labelled "You must never say no".

All aspects of his behaviour are subordinate to this category. "Saying no" cannot be assimilated as an element of this class. The therapist who wants to help the student make space for himself by "disobeying" the rule and gradually expanding his space to say "no" will push the student into a conflict of loyalties. Conflicts with his mother will escalate, while he is trying to fulfil the expectations of the therapist. A likely outcome is that he decides quite soon that he has "made progress", thanks the therapist, and stops the therapy. For he cannot afford to say no to his mother. There is a strict order between element and class, between types of behaviour that must fulfil the law of always saying "yes". He has to earn his existence by always meeting expectations.

By not talking about behaviour, about the elements of the class, but about the rule—the class—itself, a wider perspective is created, leaving the student space to ponder the question of whether he wants this rule to continue to apply to his life. If another class of behaviour emerges as a new order, liberty will open up again for new types of behaviour.

In this way, the logic of abduction helps us to arrive at the ordering of classical logic: in a zigzag movement between imagination and structure. Narrative psychotherapy seeks to create new connections and lines of flight from the dominant problem story. A succession of new connections and lateral movements may be made. The connection made in this conversation is only an illustration—it might happen in any number of other ways. New connections give rise to what Deleuze calls *assemblage* (Romein, Schuilenberg & Van Tuinen, 2009). An assemblage is the form that this therapy acquires through these connections in this context at this point in time. Further on we shall look at the concept of an assemblage in greater depth.

## Draw a distinction

If we follow Spencer-Brown's imperative, "draw a distinction" (Spencer-Brown, 1969), we can say that drawing a distinction is at the root of every action, decision, observation, thought, and description. A boundary is drawn, with which a whole is distinguished and divided such that one part is inside the boundary and the rest outside it. The observer makes a distinction and draws lines creating an "inside" and an "outside". That is how a universe is created from the first, fundamental and creative act of drawing a distinction. By drawing distinctions, an infinite number of universes can be created. What falls within and outside the boundary is given a name, and this naming is a linguistic act performed by the observer. The name given to a thing is not part of that thing. It follows that the meaning of a name, a naming in language, can never be understood in isolation; its meaning depends on what falls inside and outside the boundary. This is an important point, since it implies that the meaning that is *not* attributed features just as prominently in the thing's definition as the meaning that *is* attributed.

Things that are separated by distinction remain connected; all boundaries simultaneously create a connection; the "yes" defines a "no", and vice versa. Whatever falls outside the boundary and is deemed to be absent is simultaneously present in whatever is deemed to be present. Whatever is defined as desirable also defines what is undesirable. When the request arises in the context of psychotherapy to help relieve certain symptoms, and a struggle is set in motion to distinguish what is present from what is not present, the symptom will manifest itself to a growing extent within this struggle. The struggle against, and opposition to, the symptom connect the two parts that are separated even more closely than before. If part and whole are separated from each other, they nonetheless remain connected. Both are present, and share the same boundary.

If the distinction introduces the word "not", it defines a negation and creates its presence. If the presence thus created is made possible by an absence, by a *not*, the converse is also true: if the presence of something necessarily implies the recognition of something else, its absence is similarly made possible by its presence. In other words, what matters is the relationship between the two.

"The relationship comes first", insists Bateson. If we lose sight of the relationship, an opposition is created, unleashing a struggle: something has to go, to be excluded. Parts are opposed to one another, leading to the maximisation of a variable, which, according to Bateson, creates pathology, since one part tries to control the other part, with which it is connected on a deeper level. It is this struggle that pollutes the surroundings. What is excluded remains linked on a higher level of abstraction: the *not*, the *opposite*, contributes to the whole. The distinction can be completed by linking the two sides of the distinction recursively and by seeing both the distinction and the connection on a meta-level as the relationship between a part and the whole, as a reflection of the relationship between the parts, contributing to the whole (Flemons, 1991, p. 31).

In other words, the dichotomy between *present* and *absent* is a relationship between parts belonging to a particular context that includes both. At the interface of the distinction between inside and outside, in front and behind, first and second, moiré-type patterns arise, which invite us to produce multiple descriptions of our observations. Within these moiré-type patterns, stories and metaphors are generated. "Such contrapuntal weaving can be understood as an exercise in what Bateson terms abduction" (ibid., p. 46). Stories and metaphors follow the logic of abduction.

Multiple descriptions of our observations help to prevent us from getting stuck in the distinctions we are compelled to draw. It is important to speak the language of connection and relationship. Metaphors and stories are fundamentally relational, and the biological world too is based on relationships. A story can be described (following Bateson) as "an aggregate of formal relationships scattered in time to make a sequence having a certain sort of minuet formal dance to it" (ibid., p. 64).

The writer Octavio Paz notes that metaphor upholds the integrity of "not one, not two". He says:

> Analogy is the science of correspondences. It is, however, a science that exists only by virtue of differences. Precisely because this *is not* that, it is possible to build a bridge between this and that. The bridge is the word *like*, or the word *is*: this is like that, this is that. The bridge does not do away with distance: it is an intermediary; neither does it eliminate differences: it establishes a relation between different terms. ... Analogy says that everything is a metaphor of something else. (Paz, 1974, pp. 72–73)

According to Bateson, story and thought are the same thing. We can only think in terms of stories, since there is no other way of observing relationships in a concise form. In a story, all the relationships that you want to consider can be made present at the same time, in images. Negation is something we know only in language, not in experience. This simultaneity of presence and absence recurs in the logic of abduction.

## Present absence

In the world of differences, something that is *not* there can nonetheless be seen (following the logic of abduction, the perception of correspondences) as a cause. The American philosopher Roy Sorensen focuses on this simultaneity of presence and absence as his main theme. His deliberations are about gaps, silences, and shadows. As a guest on the Dutch TV programme *Wintergasten* in 2010, he discussed his fascination with the absent; as an example, he showed John Cage conducting silence. Sorensen calls himself an "apostle of negative metaphysics".

Daniel Libeskind's design for the Jewish Museum in Berlin works with empty spaces, "voids". The architect intended these spaces to represent those who are absent, the many Jewish victims of the Holocaust. One of the spaces, though completely empty, has 10,000 open-mouthed faces coarsely cut from iron, with expressions of fear, despair, terror, and pain, representing the faces of the dead.

Figure 9. Jewish Museum, Berlin. Photo © Jeroen Olthof.

The museum also has a large vacant space with a narrow slit through which a little daylight can enter; sounds from the outside world filter through a number of holes in the wall. This empty space was designed to represent isolation and banishment.

This room encourages visitors to identify with what happened to those who were forced into exile. They can try to imagine what it was like to live in isolation, without the voices and sounds of friends or relatives, with only sounds from the outside world coming through a wall, the same wall that separated the exile from the surroundings. This process of identification may stir a certain resonance; visitors may find themselves resonating with what the space represents. This resonance may in turn arouse certain bodily sensations, thus embodying the world of "as if". The degree of intensity of this response may vary, the "as if" may be experienced as close by or quite remote, and a visitor may be thrown back on a story of isolation and banishment in his or her own history. Feelings and processes may be repeated, and episodes relived. This space thus becomes a universal symbol, a universal story that creates openings for everyone to represent isolation and exile. The empty space is like an interspace between representation and what is represented. Those who are absent are made present in their absence.

Toon Tellegen's book *The Ant's Departure* (Tellegen, 2010) also contains a wonderful account of present absence. Each of the animals gives a different interpretation to the ant's absence; each one assigns a different meaning to this reality. Tellegen thus shows in a literary way that meanings are contextual, bound by place and time. The book is like a polyphonic chorus, none of whose voices is subordinate to another. Each creature has to find an answer to the ant's absence. A "meaningful Rorschach" (Keeney, 1983) must be made. Where is the ant that is no longer present? The emptiness he leaves behind him, the question mark of his departure, is conspicuously present. The empty space is filled with ideas, meaning, and images. The ant's absence is a highly significant presence.

> Where is the letter that was not written?
> Where is the letter that a recipient hopes to receive?
> Where does absence live?
> Where does the memory live of one who has died?
> Where is the slap in the face that was given twenty years ago and that is still present in the memory, and therefore still hurts?
> Where is that callous sentence that the doctor pronounced so unfeelingly at the bedside? That entered like the thrust of a dagger?

Words possess an "energetic charge". Words have their own energy; they have a memory and they land, find a home base, somewhere in the body. They live there, are present there. But no one can register this presence; the presence is absent.

In a passage in the novel *Quiet Chaos* by the Italian writer Sandro Veronesi, the narrator asks himself the following question (Veronesi, 2011, p. 140):

> "Where did this swearword use to be? It came from deep inside of me, but where was I keeping it? ... It was buried deep inside of me, because until this morning, I lived with the

certainty, I repeat, *with the certainty* that it didn't even exist. Where does it come from?" … [His companion replies:] "I don't know, maybe someone else inserted it yesterday."

The swear word has a place in the body, it tells a story. It was absent and exerted influence; it is present and exerts influence. That is why we speak of the narrativity of the body, in which the body is seen as an open space of and for stories, as a text, a language, and sign system. The life story or biography, the history of a person's life, is written on the body, inscribes itself in the body. "Biography becomes biology", in the words of Caroline Myss (Myss, 1997). The words that have been spoken but are no longer there, that have passed into oblivion, have nestled in the body and inscribed themselves as sign and text. Thus, the body can be seen as a field of forces that collide, tumble over one another, forge connections, and keep each other in equilibrium.

The skin, of course, is the boundary of the body as an independent entity. At the same time, the skin is connected to the surrounding area—to the wind, the sounds, the elements, the scents, and of course also to the relevant *others* within the context. Biography becomes part of biology, and biography is a story—with a dominant structure, an organising principle, a plot, a story with proverbial expressions, key words, and maxims: an embodied text, a landscape.

"Where does the stone live that feels so painful, but that does not show up on any X-ray?"

The sadness caused by the ant's unexplained departure is present and tangible in the biology of the animals. Their spirits are heavy, they have lost their way. The sense of loss keeps getting in their way. Every meaning they assign to it lives in a different part of the body—it is always inscribed in the body. For instance, Whale doesn't understand what "gone" means. Octopus tries to explain, and writes the word "GONE" in big black letters on the ocean floor:

GONE

"That's it," he says.
"I can read it, but I can't understand it," says Whale.
"Dearie me, how should I explain it . . ?" says Octopus.
He draws a big fat line through GONE and says that gone is gone now.

~~GONE~~

But Whale stares at him, wide-eyed, and asks: "But where is gone now?"
"Gone isn't anywhere," says Octopus, and scratches the back of his head with a few of his tentacles.
"So where *is* it then?"
Octopus takes a piece of coral and hides it behind his back.
"Gone," he says. Then he eats a huge piece of algae, swallows, and says "Gone!"
Whale shakes his head and says he doesn't understand.
"What does gone look like, actually?"
"Gone doesn't look like anything. Terrible doesn't look like anything either."
"No, but I know what terrible means," says Whale.
They both think for a bit.

Then Octopus grabs Whale with all his tentacles and pushes him under the sand on the ocean floor.
"Now you're gone," he cries.
"I'm here!" shouts Whale in a muffled voice.
"Not for me," cries Octopus.
"I'm here for me!" cries Whale.
A little later they're sitting together again.
"I really understand an awful lot of things … ," says Whale, and he turns his big, mournful eyes on Octopus.
He recites a list of things he understands: irrefutable, indisputable, broke, the village …

"It's only gone I don't understand."
Octopus shows him a book he always has near at hand, which is entitled *Gone*.
It's full of examples: words deleted with big bold lines, missing pages, pages that vanish when you turn them, and even little mirrors in which you see everything except yourself.
"Try reading this," Octopus suggests.
Whale reads the book, but when he's finished, he still doesn't know what "gone" is.

*(From Toon Tellegen, 2010, translated for this publication by BJ)*

If you suffer from periodic loss of consciousness and your mind is often "gone", where has it gone *from*? And where does it go *to*? Where is that *to*, that *somewhere else*?

Where is the apology that was not made, which the client has spent her entire life waiting for? How is it possible that a letter that is written to apologise and accept responsibility for the hurt inflicted by the letter writer creates a sense of relief? Where does the letter live when it has been burned? How is it possible that writing a letter offering an apology, and then burning it, can create a sense of relief? Where does the letter live in the body? How is it possible that burning a letter can cause a physical reaction of relief?

The apology that was not given is nonetheless present all the time. The daughter who hopes that her mother will finally say, on her deathbed, that she loves her, and if the mother does not say these words … where do they live, those unspoken words? How is it possible that, in their absence, they are so overwhelmingly present? The loss of consciousness, the absence of consciousness, takes consciousness to a presence elsewhere, which exerts a great influence on everyday life.

In *Quiet Chaos*, the protagonist, Pedro Paradini, is sitting on a bench outside his daughter's school. He's sitting there because his wife—his daughter's mother—has suddenly died. When he takes the child to school, he promises that he will stay outside the school and wait for her. Over the next few days, he carries on sitting on a bench as long as his daughter is at school. He stops the world, so to speak. He becomes part of a microcosm by sitting there every day and seeing the same people pass by every day. As he sits there, his thoughts return to the past, and he practises remembering. He tries to recall all the airlines he has ever flown with, as the director of a big commercial company. Then he tries to recall the fifty-two girls who allowed him to kiss them, from the time he was a young boy. Then Veronesi writes (p. 54):

Those kisses are no longer kisses. They're nothing. Most of them don't even evince the memory of a kiss. They happened, and maybe even if I don't feel like remembering it now, while I was kissing each one of those girls I was brimming with emotion, and my heart was beating hard, and I felt good: yet nothing has remained, nothing except the authority of this number grouping them all together …

Is it really true that those kisses are no longer kisses? Have they dissolved into nothingness? Are they no longer present? Even though they are no longer present in the protagonist's memory, what he recalls is a kiss from the past, which is present and absent at the same time. Is such a kiss no longer a kiss, does it not exist any more?

The kiss is absent presence and present absence. A kiss that arouses a desire to repeat it is a present absence. Every kiss continues to exist in the memory of the lips. And with the next kiss, the previous kisses make their presence felt, shaping the lips, making the lips multilingual, making them lips that speak. As a result of their past, they become lips with a history, and with each new kiss they can tell a whole story … As Luce Irigaray says: "When our lips speak together" (Irigaray & Burke, 1980).

Figure 10. © Roger Raveel. *Portret van de afwezige (Portrait of the absent one)* 1984, oil on canvas, 40 × 50 cm. Collection of the artist. c/o Pictoright Amsterdam 2016.

We can also find superb images of absent presence in the visual arts. Take the painting *Portrait of the absent one* by the Flemish artist Roger Raveel (1921–2013), which tells of the absent person who has sat on the chair or who is about to sit there.

The scissors on the empty tabletop suggest what is not there—or not yet. What have the scissors been used for, or what are they going to be used for? What other attributes lay on the table? What are the scissors waiting for?

Absence is thus present in our consciousness. The abundant *there* and *not there* is present in the painting, because we fill the space with images, interpretations, associations, questions, and fantasies.

Our deceased loved ones are sharply present for us in their absence. They leave an emptiness that we fill with our memories, with photographs, attributes, a candle, flowers, or a little altar. Coping with bereavement, perhaps, is making present again.

Raveel paints the emptiness in a square. The blank space as absence is bounded by the square that anchors and that makes the emptiness poignantly tangible. You can see the emptiness, as it were: it has been framed. In the same way, you might say that narrative psychotherapy creates a frame—a frame around what-is-not-said, what-has-not-yet-been-said … around absence.

Figure 11. © Sjef Hutschemakers. *Het gebed (The prayer)* 1987, acrylic on canvas, 100 × 90 cm. DSM Art Collection. Used with kind permission.

In the painting *The prayer* by Jef Hutschemakers, we see the absent one in the second cup, the second egg, the empty chair. Who is awaited here? Who is so present on that empty chair? For whom, or what, is the prayer said? Who is not coming, for whom has the table nonetheless been laid? Who is not here? Is the waiting, the prayer, for a *coming*?

Our subconscious cannot fathom the word "not". We therefore have to start by making an image of the "not", with which the absent is made present even though it is not there.

### *The link between classical logical discourse and the logic of abduction*

I should like to end this chapter with a case history that may serve to illustrate the link between classical logical discourse and the logic of abduction.

### *Always catching up*

Rudolf, a man aged forty, decided to start psychotherapy to address his chronic fatigue. He had a congenital disorder, anus atresia, which had given rise to a dual problem with defecation: incontinence and constipation. Combined with this was a problem with his bladder. He had frequent bladder infections, sometimes combined with pyelitis. He was obliged to organise his life around defecation and to set aside a great deal of time for it. His churning bowels often gave rise to stress. More and more frequently, Rudolf was unable to stave off incontinence, as a result of which he had to wash and change into clean clothes. The rinsing of his intestines, several times a week, was no longer as effective as it had been in the past. He had frequent abdominal pain and severe cramps. Rudolf was married and had two children. His growing sons demanded a great deal of attention, besides which he held down a job. He was frequently unable to function because of exhaustion, both at home and at work, and this led to marital tension.

Rudolf explained that he had undergone over thirty operations since childhood. Each time, after the operation and time spent in hospital, he faced the task of reconnecting with his peers in everyday life. He had always succeeded in doing so, but it took a lot out of him. We concluded that he had been saddled with a disadvantage from birth and that he had spent his entire life trying to catch up. Up until now he had always managed to cope, but now he was no longer able to do so. He suffered from chronic fatigue and could not keep up with everything that was expected of him. Those around him blamed him for this.

The story triggered associations in my mind with a skiing class. I had just returned from a skiing holiday, where I'd had lessons in a beginners' group. After a while, some of the group were skiing quite well, while others lagged behind. We often had to wait for the slower ones. All this took place in a companionable atmosphere, however, and as soon as the others had caught up, we carried on. We had been able to rest, while the stragglers had to go straight on.

That, it seemed, was how Rudolf had always carried on. As soon as he caught up, everyone carried on, as if nothing had happened. No one, it seemed, pondered how much effort it took him each time. We decided that a paradigm shift was needed. The initial paradigm was: "How can I catch up? What can I do to restore the situation so that I am in tune with my peers?" The new paradigm would be "Who is in tune with me? Who waits for me? Who adapts his or her pace to mine? Who wants to walk beside me?"

The new paradigm meant that he could go his own way and that those around him could take account of him. Over thirty operations, over thirty times under general anaesthesia, over thirty times recuperating from surgical interventions ... and who stopped to imagine what he had been through?

*Catching up* was the name and heading of a class containing a wide range of behavioural features—elements belonging to that class. *You shall catch up* is a heading for intermediate sprints, perseverance, pushing beyond your limits, joining in, not demanding a place for yourself, never asking for help, ensuring that the outside world never actually notices what it is costing you.

This was the description with which Rudolf presented himself for therapy. What he was asking, essentially, was this: I'm exhausted, please help me, with therapy, to catch up again. But helping him to catch up would remain within the same paradigm and would only serve to exacerbate his exhaustion. The new paradigm, *Going your own way*, removes the word "disadvantage". The word disadvantage implies a norm, that you are behind others, who are further along. In truth, however, he was not behind at all. In view of what he had achieved with his physical constraints and after thirty operations, he was perhaps way out ahead!

The new paradigm helped Rudolf to claim space for himself and to tell those around him that things could not continue as before. He started by telling his wife, and this time really asking her to help him and to provide support for the next operation that he would unfortunately have to undergo. He actually asked her to help him, to join him in the journey of his life. His wife was moved, she had never realised all this so consciously up to now. But she also explained that she had always felt closed out, precisely because he did not ask for help. She always had the idea that he would work things out after all. This fighting in isolation also made her feel lonely in the relationship and excluded. In the new paradigm, they felt united. A different logical order had been created, a different class, to which different kinds of behaviour could belong, as elements of that class.

Rudolf described his reaction to the therapy, which was still going while this book was being written, as follows:

> In the first place, the story of the new paradigm has given me a good feeling! A recognition, and articulation, of my feelings and my struggle. The old idea that I was not good enough, and that this could never change, gave way to more positive thoughts. Thinking back to the struggle I've had to go through so many times, I think it's true that I'm actually very far ahead. I didn't move mountains, I moved entire mountain ranges! I'm still tired (partly as a result of the last operation) but the idea and the knowledge that things can be different give me tremendous strength and give me courage to face the future. At the same time ... a new paradigm ... try and make that shift and ... where do you begin?

The paradigm shift from a sense of being behind to being ahead takes place in the sphere of classical logical discourse. The introduction of a different class makes it possible to identify different kinds of behaviour as elements that logically belong to that class. The paradigm shift came about through abduction, through the chance discovery of an association with pupils lagging behind in a skiing class.

In the next stage of the journey, we shall be looking in detail at the skills and techniques involved in creating a therapeutic context and drawing up a framework for treatment. As described above, nomadic thinking requires fertile soil, a home base for a shorter or longer period of time. Thought goes off on a journey, visits the House of Language, gives words to the body, and takes along the poetic use of language as its baggage. It explores the narrative space and occupies itself with the logic of metaphor and abduction. This is the logic that we need to employ when devising our frameworks for treatment.

CHAPTER SIX

# Creating and structuring a therapeutic context

*"Without context, words and actions have no meaning at all"*

—Gregory Bateson

## Introduction

This chapter deals with the context of therapy. We shall examine the question of when a context is therapeutic and when it is not. We shall look successively at the context and the structuring of a therapeutic context. Creating a therapeutic framework and the quest for an attractor will be discussed in the following chapter.

## Therapeutic context

The word "context" derives from the Latin *contextus*, meaning cohesion, connection. The Latin verb *contexere* (*con* = "with" + *texere* = "to weave") means to weave together, to compose. *Textus* signifies a woven pattern, a continuous series, content, text. A text is an entire complex of articulations in which each element has a particular place. Something occurs in the context of, appears as part of, a weave or pattern, and this larger pattern imparts significance to the part.

Context is the larger, meaning-imparting framework within which something takes place. It tells us about the relationship between the part and the whole. *Context* might also be read as con/text, here signifying a comment on the text. The context of an individual letter is the word in which it appears; the word's context is a sentence; the sentence's context is a paragraph; the paragraph's context is a chapter; and the chapter's context is a book. Each book belongs to a particular genre and has a particular place in relation to a community of writers. The book's publisher, readers, and reviewers make up the context of the book. Every element is part of a larger whole or *class*. It is important not to confuse an element with the class. An element cannot represent the entire class. A child's context includes his or her parents, whose context includes their own parents. The context of parents and child alike includes the wider family. The context of a house is the street in which it stands, and the street's context is its neighbourhood. The neighbourhood's context is its district, the city, the province or county, the country, Europe, and so on. Each element helps to make up the context for another, and context is hence a meta-level of text, and of a higher order. Context gives a text meaning, is a comment on the text, furnishes the text with connections, relationships. Together, text and context produce a meaningful whole, which imparts meaning and cohesion, structuring purpose and direction. The whole structures and creates a story.

An exhibition on the conflict between Israel and the Palestinians in Utrecht Cathedral included a cartoon with the following caption:

> This is the bullet that broke the child that broke the parents
> that broke the family that broke the community that broke the town,
> that broke the state that was seeking revenge from
> the country ... which broke the heart of the world.

A context is therapeutic if all the relationships within that context are structured, if the part and the whole are connected in a meaningful way. A care worker may sometimes want to remove his or her client from their context; for instance, choosing to treat a child alone, without the parents, or a man without his wife or a wife without her husband. The therapeutic relationship that the therapist develops with the female client in such a case may possibly be assigned a negative significance by the woman's husband. As a result, any progress made in the therapy might be reversed in the home situation. The therapist–client relationship may have a negative impact on the client's relationship with his or her partner. Similarly, the relationship that a therapist builds up with a child may engender a conflict of loyalties in the child, in relation to his or her parents. If a school refers a child to a care worker without the willing participation of the parents, the context is not therapeutic. However well-intentioned the care provided, it will be undermined on a different level.

If a team leader requests supervision for a team, and the team interprets this as a vote of no confidence, the context will not be therapeutic for the supervisor. If a heavy drinker is admitted to a detox programme without his wife's involvement, tension will arise when the man comes home for weekends. His wife will feel excluded. After all, she has probably been dealing with all the tensions and conflicts surrounding her husband's heavy drinking for a very long time. If the wife's experiences are not acknowledged, if the clinic does not request her consent before temporarily taking on the man's care during the week, the wife's role is trivialised. Conversely, if the wife and the GP together arrange for the man's admission to a clinic "because things can't go on like this", the context will not be therapeutic for the clinic. In such a case, the man is not a full partner in the care process, and the relationship between part and whole is not structured effectively.

If all the relationships within the context are not structured in a cooperative way, the context is not therapeutic. If the wife and children of the alcoholic man find the home situation intolerable and decide together to have the man admitted for treatment, the man's own role will be diminished. The man can only become a full partner in the care process if the clinic admits him in a cooperative framework: "Do you see how worried your wife and children are about you, and how much they love you? Are you willing to give them a bit of a rest? Will you allow us to help you? How do you feel about the fact that they would like us to take over caring for you for a while?"

If a supervisor proposes family therapy to a therapist under his or her supervision, a *supervisee*, in order to involve the parents and grandparents in a child's treatment, and this does not fit within the institution's treatment culture, the context is not therapeutic. The supervisee will not feel safe or free to talk about the treatment. Should complications arise, he will not feel supported. This will mean functioning within the treatment with the "brakes on". If the supervisor then fails to inscribe himself in the larger whole and advises the supervisee to work systematically in this way, the supervisee will be confused.

The context is therapeutic if the supervisor explores, together with his supervisee, how to obtain consent for family therapy. In such cases, we advise the supervisee, for instance, to ask the team leader's permission to conduct an experiment. First, this acknowledges the team leader's place in the hierarchy and avoids any suggestion that the supervisor is above the team leader. Second, it enables the supervisor to see whether a parallel process may apply: perhaps the supervisee's own position bears some similarity to that of the child at home. If not all relationships that are relevant to the context are structured in a cooperative way, if one part of the whole is in conflict with other parts, the context is not therapeutic. In many cases, this may well be unavoidable. The supervisor serves as the meta-level for the supervisee and his or her team leader, and is therefore responsible for devising the overall therapeutic structure.

The person operating on a meta-level may structure a context of power or one of love. In a context of love, the existing structure is not undermined; there is a cooperative relationship with everyone who belongs to the context. If a mother's children have been placed in care, and a children's judge orders that the mother and her children be admitted for observation to a family clinic, to find out whether her parenting skills are now sufficient for them all to be reunited, this is not necessarily a therapeutic context. If the court has explicitly stated that this is the purpose, the mother will see the clinic primarily as an opponent. If the person appointed as "family guardian" has no confidence in the mother's parenting skills, and the period of "observation" starts off without any other preparation, the care situation is a conflicting context. The mother is virtually powerless. If the context is not structured explicitly, the good intentions will have little positive effect. The answer is to have a meeting in which everyone is involved. The children's judge wants to give the mother a chance. The family guardian could be asked to define the key criteria that must be fulfilled. At what point would he or she judge the mother capable of caring for her children? When would treatment be deemed to have been successful? What is it like for the mother to have so many people watching her movements? What would she like to achieve? How would she assess her parenting skills at this point? What does she think of the court order? Does she see it as a positive chance, as an opportunity?

A meeting like this can create a cooperative arrangement involving all concerned and taking account of everyone's position. Not all positions are equal in terms of significance or responsibility. In this example, the family clinic serves as the meta-level for the care workers, while the children's judge is the meta-level for the clinic. It is the clinic's task to ensure that everyone is admitted within a cooperative framework. Care cannot begin until the context is completely clear. All voices must be heard.

The referral of a child to youth care services or a child psychiatrist often takes place amid a network fraught with conflict. The various participants in that network will often be divided, with some parties opposing treatment or admission. A child's problem may be a derivative of a parental conflict. In such circumstances, a child who is admitted to a facility or started on a course of therapy, without any new clarification, will often interpret it as a form of punishment: "It's my fault, I'm to blame, I did something wrong and I make life difficult for my parents". However well-meaning the help may be, however great the involvement and effort, the child may well experience it as unjust.

Another possibility is that a child's problem is a derivative of a conflict between parents and grandparents, with the child being stuck in the middle of a generational triad. In that case too, some of the care that is offered will meet with resistance. For instance, the grandparents may convey an implicit message to the child that the parents are to blame and that everything will be sorted out: "Grandpa and Grandma are on your side". Once admitted to the clinic, the child is trapped between conflicting loyalties.

In some cases, the initiative to recommend therapy or admission to an institution may originate primarily with external carers or care services: the school, the local (mental) health services, a hospital paediatric ward, or the family guardianship agency. If the child's behaviour has even the slightest protective significance for the family, the child will resist care and, for instance, have frequent run-ins with the group leaders. Children often explain their admission or care with some form of magical thinking:

> It was "because I make my parents sad"; "because I can't get on with my brother"; "because my mother is really upset about my bad grades at school"; "because my bad behaviour caused my parents to get divorced"; "because I have bad thoughts" …

Such explanations often remain concealed, but they play a role in the care situation and impede the therapeutic relationships. The context cannot be therapeutic until the symptomatic behaviour has been placed in a cooperative framework and the child's loyalties have been protected. A child that has frequently been very close to the mother's sadness after a divorce has sacrificed part of his or her development. Once this symptomatic behaviour has been reclassified in this context, admission to a facility can create space to catch up. The facility can help the mother to thank the child for his or her loyalty. The mother can then explicitly give the child permission to accept treatment, to rest, to catch up with something, or to renew contact with the father.

Some children adopt a position in between the parents, thus fulfilling a role in a parental conflict. If referred for care, they will feel split loyalties, construing any improvement in their behaviour, a resolution of symptoms and complaints, as a sign of disloyalty to one of the parents: the improvement would mean that one parent is proved right and the other wrong. Where forces are pulling in different directions like this, therapy has little chance of success. The child will not open up to a therapeutic relationship. If such a relationship is established in spite of all this, it will always discredit one of the parents in the child's eyes. The child may feel he or she is letting one of the parents down. A therapeutic relationship may become a coalition with the child against the child's parents. In this situation, any progress made on the basis of a therapeutic relationship is taken to signify the failure of one or both parents. As a result, the therapeutic relationship is often broken off quite suddenly, with the child regressing to problem behaviour or with the occurrence of a sudden crisis. This may cause therapists to feel rejected or guilty, or to worry that they have done something wrong, thus ending up in the same position as the parents—or as the child.

A child may have the task, within the family, of sustaining the mental or physical equilibrium of one or both parents. This may be too heavy a burden to bear. Such a child may adopt an active or passive "parentified" position by actively supporting the parent; alternatively, it may constantly act in such a way as to require its parents to provide care that is no longer appropriate to its age (Oppenoorth, 1990, 1992). When the child is then referred to a care programme without any acknowledgement of the support it gives to one or both parents, and therapy is started without the child being thanked for his or her loyalty, any form of assistance and any change that is instituted will pose a threat to the parents in the child's eyes. There is then a great risk of the change being reversed. It is only when the child has been thanked and the parents start receiving help along different channels that the child can relinquish the task it has taken upon itself.

## Creating a therapeutic context

The creation of a therapeutic context and the devising of a therapeutic framework both take place at the meta-level of psychotherapy, and do not exclude any school or approach whatsoever. The main emphasis is on structuring the psychotherapy and organising the participants in the psychotherapeutic process, as a team pursuing a specific goal together. This goal is the "attractor" of the complaint within the therapeutic framework, the point that helps to structure all actions within the psychotherapy. Ideally, each participant in the therapeutic process will be conscious of the direction and goal of the care programme and of their own position. You might compare it to the positions adopted by members of a soccer or cycling team. It is all too common for participants in a therapeutic process to pursue an individual course based on their own interpretation. However well-intentioned that person's therapeutic actions may be, they do not dovetail with those of the other participants. The larger and more complex a system is, the more difficult it is to structure the context so as to make it therapeutic.

Take the following example.

### Timo

Timo had a crisis in the final stages of his master's programme. Exhaustion from months of sleep deprivation combined with a fear of failure surrounding the completion of his master's thesis. When he smoked marijuana on top of all this, he developed psychotic symptoms. His brother and sister, both of whom lived nearby, were very supportive, and he received help from a team specialised in early intervention in psychotic disorders. Antipsychotic drugs were prescribed, and he was supervised with care and great commitment. Once the initial symptoms had subsided, Timo found himself in an existential crisis. Not so long before, his status was that of a student who was close to obtaining his master's degree; now it was that of a patient.

Anyone who has ever been admitted to an institution in the medical world can tell you what it feels like to be furnished with a new identity, particularly when the treatment is for a serious disorder. Excellent accounts have been given of this experience: for instance by Erving Goffman in his books *Stigma* and *Asylums* (Goffman, 1961, 1963), D. L. Rosenhan in "On being sane in insane places" (Rosenhan, 1973), and Thomas Scheff in *Labelling Madness* (Scheff, 1975). Timo started living in accordance with this new status; he took on the identity of a patient and ceased to take part in student life. Although the team's intervention was exemplary, it also had the effect of creating and affirming a change of identity. Timo was now a patient; he lived as a patient, and became more and more of a patient every day. All this exacerbated his fear of failure. He withdrew, and from then on things went from bad to worse.

Timo became extremely depressed, partly because he had an adverse reaction to the medication, and foresaw a disastrous future for himself. He had lost face vis-à-vis his fellow students, he could not imagine being able to complete his master's thesis, and developed the idea that his future was ruined. He became suicidal, particularly after a second breakdown at his hall of residence. He started having paranoid delusions and believed that his computer was bugged. These delusions confirmed the picture of a psychotic development.

He went back to allowing his mother to take care of him and generally stayed at her house, far from his university town. I had been treating the mother for some time, and therefore knew a good deal about the family history. Timo spent much of his time with her, and his mother frequently shared her concerns about him with me. She was filled with anxiety about Timo's depression and his suicidal inclinations. A possible serious complication in the context is that Timo was in therapy in his university city, while in practice he was now mostly living with his mother. For the time being, this construction was working.

Timo's mother asked me to help. She and I started by making a plan to help Timo finish his master's degree. Timo had a fixed deadline for submitting his thesis, and this deadline was fast approaching. The thesis was virtually finished; only a few details and bibliographical references needed to be added. We were worried that if Timo failed to complete his thesis and to graduate, it would haunt him for the rest of his life. We also knew that he could not do it alone. Fears would impede him from taking this next step in his development. Since he now had the status of a patient, graduating no longer fitted into the picture he had of himself. I therefore suggested to his mother that we organise a team effort to ensure that Timo handed in his thesis.

The mother agreed to mobilise her daughter, along with one of her other sons and his wife, and together they would help Timo put the finishing touches to his thesis. With one week to go before the deadline, they would not leave him alone with the thesis for a moment. The mother went to see her other children, and they joined in a concerted effort, helping to complete the thesis and submit the official request for the master's degree. Timo defended his thesis, besieged with fears, but managed to stay standing with the support of his family and an assistant attached to the supervisory team. I had no direct therapeutic relationship with Timo at that time, only with his mother. It remained possible for these two contexts to coexist.

Immediately after graduation Timo "fled" to his mother's house, where he lapsed into an existential void and suffered a severe breakdown. In spite of having graduated he was terrified of the future, convinced that he would never be able to stand on his own two feet. He no longer dared to leave the house. His friends and fellow students frequently called him, but Timo did not dare to answer the phone. He had no story for what was going on, and did not know what to say. He had sneaked away from his student room like a thief in the night.

Other telephone calls, from carers who tried conscientiously to keep in contact with him, also went unanswered. When Timo was invited for a consultation to check his medication, he did not dare to travel alone. The medication was causing numerous troubling side effects, but he did not dare mention them. The team knew little about his life and family background, since it had first been called in for crisis intervention. Furthermore, since Timo has graduated, he had abandoned his student room and no longer dared to enter the building, since he did not know what to say to his housemates. He felt ashamed, and increasingly retreated into his shell. He tried to end his relationship with his girlfriend, but she kept calling. He did not dare to answer her calls, but actually opposing her was harder still. He became more and more inaccessible to the team that had been treating him in his university town; he felt lost in a no-man's land and contemplated suicide.

As his mother's therapist, I shared her concerns about Timo. I had no therapeutic relationship with him, but I could see that the context was no longer therapeutic. This was because for Timo, continuing the relationship with the crisis intervention team actually affirmed his status as a psychotic patient. It was precisely this status that had become his existential problem, preventing him from embracing his development on the way to maturity and independence as a graduate. Branded with the status of "psychotic patient", he saw zero prospects for the future. I could see that it was vitally important to intervene in this status of patient. But how?

Timo had no idea where he ought to live. He did not dare to go and pack his things in the student room; he did not dare to travel alone, or to be left alone. His mother decided that he should move back in with her on a more permanent basis, and asked me if I could take him into therapy. The next question was how to create a new therapeutic context. Together we devised a plan: the mother would accompany Timo to a meeting with the care team in his university city and explain the new situation to them. Since Timo was moving back in with his mother, they would ask the team to refer him to me as a psychotherapist. The team was willing to do so, provided there was also a referral to a psychiatrist, to monitor his medication. The mother explained that Timo was having adverse reactions to the medication, but it was difficult for the team to change the prescriptions, with Timo living so far away. In consultation with the team, I asked the psychiatrist Erik de Lange, a colleague of mine, if he would see Timo and collaborate on the treatment. Erik agreed, and held further consultations with the team regarding the referral and medication. We then called a meeting, together with the mother and Timo, and set about creating a new therapeutic context in this new situation. The meeting started with the mother and myself giving Erik the following account of Timo's background.

When Timo was about two years old, he lost his father. The family was abroad, holidaying in a coastal resort. His father was a strong swimmer and often went swimming. One extremely windy day he swam quite far out, and drowned trying to get back to shore. His wife was left to care for their four young children alone. Timo, the youngest of the four, developed severe anxieties, which came to the fore in every transitional phase of his life. A highly sensitive boy, he became wholly attuned to his mother, helping her to bear her grief. The roles of the family became defined and divided: two of the children claimed their places and fought back against life's difficulties. They rebelled against their mother and against the outside world, and at length carved out places for themselves in life. The other two children stayed close to their mother: withdrawn, sensitive, and anxious. As Timo grew older, he chiefly focused on others, trying to fulfil their needs rather than attending to his own development. This is known as "passive parentification".

His sensitivity made Timo popular, but inside he was always anxious and highly dependent on the appreciation of others. He did not manage to forge a place for himself; he lived for others. From early childhood, he wrestled with fears and feelings of depression. Growing up without a father, he stayed close to his mother. Each stage of his development was a heavy burden. It seems that when he at last arrived on the threshold of adult life, he stumbled before taking the last step on the way to independence. Could his psychotic symptoms be traced back to his exorbitant fears? Had he gone through an existential crisis, just before graduation? How could a therapeutic context be created if Timo was hearing two conflicting definitions of himself—two conflicting "voices", as it were? The psychiatric team's "voice" seemed to be saying: "You're a patient, you'll always be a patient; you're never going to amount to anything!" Meanwhile, a second explanation, the "voice" of his mother combined with mine as his therapist, placed his psychotic symptoms in a developmental perspective and linked them to the family's sudden loss of the father. According to this explanation, the loss had placed a heavy burden on all members of the family, and the mother had almost collapsed under the weight; Timo's sensitivity led him to stay close to his mother as a small boy, which also meant close to her grief. Was there some way of creating a dialogue between these two jarring explanations or "voices"? And could this dialogue support Timo in his path to an independent existence in society? The therapy would have to include helping Timo to deal with the many anxieties with which he had been familiar since early childhood.

I asked Erik to listen to the second "voice", the one with all the questions: Is it possible that Timo's identity is faltering because so much fear and insecurity came into his life before he was three years old? Is it possible that he has focused on others his whole life and has been unable to take the steps needed for his own development? Was it this, perhaps, that led to a total collapse on the threshold to independent life? Is it possible that these fears have been present throughout his life and that they have now, driven by hard work and exhaustion and exacerbated by insecurity and smoking marijuana, precipitated a crisis? Is it possible that this crisis points not to a psychotic development but to the presence of enormous fears in his life? Should we not perhaps look at these fears within the perspective of his development?

I selected two Russian dolls, one very small and the other very large, and placed them at some distance from each other—the large doll standing with its back to the other one. If the small doll symbolised two-year-old Timo, full of fear, and the large one stood for Timo on the threshold of independent life, there was a gaping chasm between the two. It was because of this chasm, the void in his existence, that the toddler's fear continued to accompany all Timo's actions. Was it not our task to help him to bridge that gap? I took a wool thread, laid it in between the two dolls, and made the following proposal to Erik.

> What I propose is that all of us, the mother, you as the psychiatrist, I as the therapist, and his brothers and sister, draw a safe circle around Timo, and focus the therapy on encouraging the growth of his

identity and the development of his personality. That way we can help him move towards independence and to triumph over his fears. Might we then not dare to phase out the medication, since they've been causing so many adverse reactions? And could we not start off with a new paradigm: that Timo is not a patient, but someone whose development stagnated as a result of the early loss of his father, his focus on others, and his tendency to subordinate his own development to the needs of others? We could call it overdue maintenance. And can we help Timo to catch up with his development and offer him a treatment plan in which he can leave the "patient" status behind him? Might this not open up fresh prospects for his future?

Although Timo was completely unresponsive in the early part of this discussion, he gradually became more attentive, and ended up as a full participant. We decided to form ourselves into a new team to see if the new paradigm worked. Although Timo was still plagued by suicidal thoughts, he earnestly promised not to attempt suicide. His mother expressed her concern about this. Timo looked at her and promised to cooperate with the experiment, sealing his promise with an embrace. Erik would help Timo to phase out his medication responsibly and would monitor his progress critically. My role was to help Timo re-engage with his development. This strategy banished the voice that said "you are a patient" to the background. The intervention revived Timo's energy, and he gave a deep sigh of relief. From then on, he would be a full partner in his own treatment.

The first thing was to do something about Timo's sudden departure from his university town. No one there knew what had happened and all his friends were baffled. He did not dare to visit his old haunts, since he didn't know what to say. He still had no language, no story to tell. He avoided telephone calls, and outside he was always afraid of bumping into acquaintances. I therefore suggested writing a narrative about what had happened. Since Timo himself had no language for it, I dictated a story and asked Timo to write it down. When he got home he would read it through and change it where necessary, until it became his own story and he could sign it.

A message to my friends

I am writing this letter to explain what has happened to me over the past year. As you know, I had a major breakdown just before graduation. I was totally overwhelmed by the whole graduation process. Completing my thesis produced so much tension that I couldn't sleep, I became exhausted, and was paralysed by fear.

Sleeplessness, anxiety, and exhaustion, and smoking dope on top of it all, were a perfect recipe for a breakdown. At one point, after smoking a joint, I started getting weird ideas, and feeling suspicious of everyone around me. The symptoms that accompanied this breakdown were labelled psychotic. So I was given a kind of treatment that focused on these symptoms. The 'psychosis' label sent me into a deep depression and I lost all faith in the future. I started to think that I was never going to come out of it, and I didn't dare speak to any of you, out of shame. So I more or less sneaked away from my student room like a thief in the night, leaving you with all sorts of questions. You've all tried in your own way to show interest and to help me. Some of you came to visit or invited me for dinner. In many ways you tried to get me involved in the ordinary run of life again. I often failed to respond, in a way that was incomprehensible for you.

I had become afraid of ordinary life, and started avoiding you and your kind questions. With a great deal of support from my family, I managed to complete my thesis at the very last minute and get my degree. After that I left and moved back in with my mother.

It's beginning to become clear to me now why I had a breakdown at that precise moment, just before graduation. I was very afraid of embarking on life in the outside world and started to realise that this fear became part of my life when I was very young, with the sudden death of my father. My mother was left alone to care for the four of us. Those years posed a heavy existential challenge for all of us. Each one of us had to find our own way of dealing with it. As the youngest, I always tended to adapt to what others wanted. In hindsight, I had difficulties with every important transition. As a child, I used to draw a tree with only one root. The root connecting me to my father had been suddenly cut off. I never learned to stand on my own feet.

Things are going better now. I've been looking back over my life and I'm now recovering from the breakdown. I've been resting quite a bit, and have stopped all the medication I was taking. With psychotherapy, combined with the support of my mother and the rest of my family, I shall learn to be independent. I've now reached the stage that I can gradually start meeting up with you again, although I shall have to build up these contacts quite slowly, at my own pace. I've promised myself to really take the time I need to ensure that I completely recover, to be ready to take a full part in life.

I want to thank you for all your help and interest, whether expressed from close by or from further afield, and hope to be seeing you in the near future.

Timo

When he returned for his next session, having made some changes to the letter, he looked noticeably better, and was feeling more optimistic. He started engaging with the outside world again, keeping this letter in his pocket. He went to a student party and was able to explain what had happened. His friends reacted with empathy and understanding. His family helped him to pack up his things from the student room, after which he officially moved back in with his mother. He now dared to travel on his own to see friends and family, and started walking with a more erect posture again. The medication was carefully, gradually, and successfully phased out. Over a year later, Timo was doing well, had stopped all medication and was working hard. He no longer felt depressed, he was sleeping well, and with his safe home situation as base he dared to go out into the world again.

After the writing of the narrative, the therapy sessions focused on Timo's fears, the development of his identity, and the outlook for the future. We took up the thread of his childhood drawing of a tree with only one root. I asked Timo to draw a series of new trees on ever larger sheets of paper, using more and more colours: a tree with roots reaching deep down into the ground. I wanted to help him develop an inner image of "having roots". Timo found it very demanding, and also frightening, to make larger and larger trees with bright colours and to give that tree a place on a large sheet of paper. Using his drawings as a mirror, we were able to discuss his fears and the development of his identity. He started arranging to meet up with his friends again, and found the narrative, which he always kept with him, a helpful support. He started applying for jobs. I then asked him to draw a clump of trees that might symbolise his family. The tree behind him, which represents his father, has fallen out of the picture. His mother had always stood behind him, and symbolically she became a tree behind the tree that represented Timo. His brothers, sister and friends were depicted standing around him. This provided a good context for his work: he needed "a tree" behind him, someone who was in charge and whose right-hand man he could be, as befitted his loyal and devoted nature. That meant that he would not apply for jobs that would involve management or traineeships in that direction. He would present himself as a reliable second-in-command, a team player who was eager to serve. This profile helped Timo in his job applications.

At length he found a good internship. Although the position was unsalaried, it was appropriate to his aptitude and education. After a while he felt at home there, and was functioning to everyone's satisfaction. We decided that Timo, who had taken up photography as a hobby and went on frequent nature walks, would look out for a group of trees that reflected his life and could symbolise his needs.

A few months later, Timo came to see me again. He had brought a large photograph of a group of trees with him, and told the following story to accompany it. This story served as the end of the therapy:

> This photograph has several symbolic associations that mean a lot to me. The tree is still growing, it is developing. It is not finished, and that is as it is. It's fine. The tree is not alone. It's surrounded by other trees, some of them close, others further away. The tree is rooted in the soil. I realise that some trees have firm roots and others (for all sorts of reasons) have less sturdy roots. That is how it is, and it's fine. All trees carry on growing and go through a process of development. The tree also stands in a single place, and doesn't move to some other place. To me, that means that it is good not to neglect your own ego, the core of your being. I am who I am, and I do good things, and try to live according to my values and principles. I also make mistakes. That is how it is and it's fine. The path beside the tree leads somewhere unknown. That may be unnerving, but it also helps me to realise that I myself can choose the direction of my life. It also helps me to realise that my mental and physical health are of great value. And it helps me to realise that I can be grateful without feeling guilty. There is also light in the photograph. For me, the light symbolises the ray of hope that is always there, in times of difficulty. My brother or a good friend, for instance. I have framed this photograph and hung it in a prominent place on the wall of my room.
>
> Timo

This case history illustrates the various factors involved in creating a therapeutic context. First: Timo suffered a breakdown with psychotic symptoms. In quickly identifying the incipient psychosis and intervening, the psychiatric team reacted promptly and well. It had to respond to the crisis and tackle the symptoms as fast as possible. Timo himself was devastated by this crisis, and felt as if he had landed in a kind of no man's land. It was shocking for him to witness, within a short space of time, his identity being transformed from that of a promising student to that of an insecure patient. As a result, he did not participate fully in his treatment. In effect, he withdrew into his shell. He shared his concerns with his mother and brother. While the assistance provided by the psychiatric team helped him to recover, it had the unintentional side effect of affirming and sustaining his "patient" status, and it was precisely this status that precipitated him into an existential crisis.

Figure 13. Timo's Tree.

I started out as the mother's therapist, not Timo's. For a while, it was perfectly possible for the two perspectives to coexist. Eventually, however, the context ceased to be therapeutic, when Timo was back at home with his mother, with suicidal thoughts, and no longer sufficiently accessible to the care and attention of the team in his university town. It also became clear that Timo was unlikely to be returning to his student room in the foreseeable future. His mother was eager for Timo to go into therapy with me, but if this were to happen without proper consultation, the two perspectives would clash, which might have a negative impact on him. The context therefore had to be reorganised in such a way as to make it therapeutic.

Consultations were therefore held with the psychiatric team, followed by a referral to my colleague, the psychiatrist Erik de Lange, and the two "voices" defining him in different ways were articulated. It was important for the context surrounding Timo to be therapeutic, but it was just as important to create a therapeutic context within Timo himself. If the treatment were to focus on his development and future, while he continued to hear a voice saying "you're never going to get out of this", Timo would never be able to participate fully in his treatment. If all attention were to focus on the crisis with psychotic symptoms, it would block his future prospects and the treatment would foster an essential feeling of emptiness and possibly generate a depression. It is interesting to hear what the family psychiatrist Walter Oppenoorth has to say:

> A child who has fulfilled a parentified task within a family, neglecting stages in his own development in the process, will inevitably have built up certain patterns of emotions, thoughts and behaviour to achieve this. These will have formed the brain, as neural activation patterns, and will therefore partly determine future patterns of activation. Habitual responses literally form the structure of the brain—just as weight training forms the muscles—and the brain's structure in turn forms the behaviour. It is only when new neural patterns in the brain have been developed—and this will generally require a new story, and sometimes literally a new context, for instance that of a clinic or some other environment—that it becomes possible for new behaviour, which can foster his development, to start to grow. These patterns then have to become ingrained with practice. A significant framework, such as a new story, is a beginning, an "enabling mechanism". In that sense, it both is, and is *not*, a "miracle cure".
>
> In Timo's case, it became clear that he not only had to write his story but to "live" it. He had to communicate this story to his friends and start interacting with them again. This would literally "rewire" the patterns in his brain. Once he had done this, he felt liberated, and after a lot of "consolidation", his stagnated development was rebooted.
>
> In every case history, of course, once the relationship has clicked, once the story, the new interpretation, has been accepted, it will always take time to actually achieve the changes that the new story makes possible.

In any care system, it is important for the new carer to fit into the existing system, and to approach those who are working in that system in a cooperative and positive manner. The new carer must provide added value, and this necessarily includes being appreciative of the existing system. Timo's mother and I were part of his system of care, even though this was not stated explicitly. It would have been quite wrong and inappropriate for his mother and me to independently devise a regime of our own. Consulting on the context was therefore essential, and these consultations were successful in this case. All those who took part in the care system received positive affirmation, and no person or theme was excluded.

Back to Timo. A success story? Yes and no. A month after the therapy was concluded, Timo's sleeping problems returned. Thoughts and worries crowded in, and he became agitated. It became clear that the hard work he was doing in his internship had exhausted him. He had thrown himself into it, but the department was understaffed. He had built up an excellent relationship with the boss, and enjoyed his full confidence. Timo was determined not to let him down. His boss delegated a great deal to him, and his many tasks included writing speeches for the management.

The lack of a room of his own or a fixed workstation, combined with the abundance of stimuli and his predisposition to do whatever was asked of him—for boss and fellow workers alike—pushed him far beyond his limits. In consequence, he was gripped by anxiety and insecurity. He lacked a "tree" behind him, giving support, and was weathering the storms alone. Feelings of suspicion started to creep in again, but fortunately he soon recognised these thoughts as early symptoms of an impending breakdown. He decided to take some time off, and wrote a good letter to his boss, explaining his situation. However, he retreated into isolation again, sparking a sense of disorientation. Once again, the team gave him their full support: his mother, his brothers and sister, and Erik and myself in our professional roles. He felt safe with his mother. We consulted each other frequently and kept in close contact with him. When his sleep medication proved insufficient, Timo was prescribed a low dose of an antipsychotic drug, which had a rapid beneficial effect.

However, this new crisis was complicated by a number of heated emotional outbursts in the family, relating to the different stories that existed within the family regarding the father's place and position in the family and his role as a husband. As the youngest, Timo was afraid of being left alone if his mother were to die, and of having to take responsibility for managing the "inheritance". It was in this period that the anxieties from his early childhood *really* erupted. Now, for the first time, he asked his mother probing questions about his father's death, and expressed his immense sadness about the heavy burden she had had to bear. He also expressed his anger at his father's family, who had completely abandoned them. He told her how much he had always been aware of his mother's sadness and loneliness, but also of her strength. Timo's mother sent me the notes from a diary she was keeping on Timo's progress:

> You have a great many questions about your past, our past. You have been crying inside, you tell me, almost your entire life. I try to understand the theme that runs through your life, through your sadness. I see all the positive aspects of your character, your growing up and your humanity; your sense of justice, the standards and values you aspire to, and your determination never to hurt anyone. You're a lovely human being, but at the same time I realise that all this is also part of the persona you project. So let me go back for a minute to that little boy, just two and a half years old, since that's when your daddy died. Before that you were a cheerful, sweet, contented baby. You always slept well. You were clever and were quick on the uptake. You were our fourth child, and in our busy family I found it a relief that you were no problem at all.
>
> But after Daddy died, everything changed for all of us. There was a life before, and a life after, Daddy's death. That very first night after he died, you cried your heart out, and vomited all over

everything. The man from next door at our holiday address came to see what was wrong and helped me clear up the mess. You were standing up in your cot and you asked, crying: "Is this our new Daddy?" I could scarcely grasp what you had said, could not believe that a child of two and a half could say words like that. So that was what was already going around in that little head of yours! And from then on, there was one constant theme in your life. You became afraid of things, started having nightmares, didn't want to be alone any more, and insisted on a night light when you went to sleep. You got into a panic in any place where there were lots of people all together, like at Daddy's funeral. Sometimes you would start screaming in the middle of the street. Even today you feel uneasy in places where there are lots of people together, like at stations or in shops.

You didn't want me to tell people at school that your father was dead. On Father's Day you acted a part. If anyone asked about your father, you reacted with a joke or a sarcastic remark. "I never knew him, so I can't miss him." You were withdrawn and shy at primary school. After school you always wanted to sit at your table, drawing. You had lost all your faith in life and in people. Always suspicious. It was only with me and in our family that you felt safe. When you were about eight years old, you were referred to a child psychologist because of the violent emotional outbursts that were causing a problem. But you did not allow your true feelings to show through; you kept your inner pain and sadness hidden. I was the only one you allowed into your inner world, and I knew exactly how you felt. But people refused to listen to me. They regarded me as an overanxious mother, and said there was nothing wrong with you. You were able to hide it all with your amazing sense of humour and your willpower, and your good grades at school.

But all the time you were still crying inside. "I'll take care of you, Mummy. I'll make sure you have more money to spend later, and after I've graduated, I'll go into therapy." That time has come now. Today you had psychotic symptoms for the third time, and now your inner pain is coming out. You long for the old sense of security of our family. Now you've been prescribed medication; we couldn't put it off any longer, since now even I had lost you. In the past three weeks things have been gradually improving, and I am full of hope that you will come through this. You have so many talents. You will really have to get down to some serious psychotherapy now.

I shall soon be seeing Timo again. His inner world is open now. We shall go to work cautiously, and in any case hold a meeting with the entire family. It has become clear that each of the children has their own story about their father, and yet they have not yet shared these stories with each other.

## *If a context is not therapeutic*

It can certainly not be taken for granted that a particular context in which someone is offered care is therapeutic. Still, we often assume that it is, and embark on care without having a good picture of the overall context. Take the following case history, for instance, about a girl who was admitted to an epilepsy clinic to try and find out whether the tensions in the family were affecting her epileptic seizures. Although this sounds at first like a sensible intervention, little or no account was taken of the implications of her admission to the clinic for the family as a whole, and the significance that would be attached to it. Weeks turned into months, and it was impossible for the girl to return home. Let us look more closely at how all this happened.

## Annemieke and the need to be special

Annemieke had been suffering from epileptic seizures since the age of nine months, when her mother encountered her with a vacant expression, after which the entire little body was racked by spasms. She had her first grand mal seizure at around twelve months. Ever since, Annemieke had been entrusted to the care of others: a paediatric neurologist, later a psychologist, a school for children with special needs, and a life spent in care facilities. Over the years, the seizures were quite infrequent, but they were nonetheless intense and therefore serious.

A range of protective measures were taken with a view to minimising the risks. Annemieke was not allowed to go out by herself, or to take part in any sport; she was increasingly shielded from ordinary life, and thus acquired a "special position". The tensions at home became worse, since this "special position" gave Annemieke the status of royalty. At one point she received a referral for admission to a clinic to undergo further tests, initially only for a brief stay, to explore whether the family tensions were influencing her seizures. The "brief stay" of a few weeks was extended again and again, and by the point we take up this story, she had been there for over eighteen months.

Annemieke became the epicentre of a field of tension, which expressed itself in the same way as in the family. She did her utmost to secure a special position among the nurses on the ward, at school, and in the workshop. She always went the extra mile, taking on tasks that went above and beyond what was expected of her. By doing so, she acquired a very special status, until a fellow patient wanted to share a specific task, with the result that the nurses' attention too would have to be shared. Annemieke found this intolerable, and a nurse with whom she was initially on very good terms became her adversary.

Much the same happened at school and in the workshop: she tried to be "special" for someone, and ended up on the sidelines. The team became unsure of how to proceed, and became divided. Some staff tried to exert pressure on Annemieke, refusing to give her any special treatment and approaching her in the same way as other group members. Annemieke reacted resentfully to this approach: "I've been bullied all my life and I can't take it and I can't cope with what you expect of me either; surely you see that I'm being excluded as usual and bullied again." She withdrew more and more into her shell. Other staff members tried a different approach. They lavished extra care and attention on her, to encourage her to participate in the group activities. The conflicts gradually accumulated.

At some point the school asked that Annemieke be referred for therapy. It also insisted that Annemieke keep to the same rules as those imposed on the other children. If she could not keep to them, she would have to be moved to a different school. Annemieke construed this pressure as proof that she was being excluded and bullied again. This aroused sympathy among other staff members at school and on the ward, which only deepened the existing impasse. It was at this point that a consultation was requested to analyse the context. The analysis yielded the following findings:

> Annemieke's parents were relatively absent; they rarely came to visit her at the epilepsy centre and seldom called. Her father had a busy job with variable shifts, and her mother appeared pleased to have a temporary reprieve from the care and responsibility for her daughter. When

Annemieke went home for the weekend, her mother would resume her task of protector, and she appeared to breathe a sigh of relief when she brought her back to the epilepsy centre. It therefore looked as though the parents tended to delegate their parenting tasks to surrogate parents, who could care for their child better than they could. Annemieke had a sister who, though two years younger, had taken over the role as the eldest. This girl was intelligent, constantly cheerful, and successful. The two sisters had fierce quarrels, and Annemieke had recently become extremely sad because her sister had "stolen" her boyfriend.

Had Annemieke lost her "birthright"? What went through those parents' heads when they saw Annemieke lying in bed with a vacant expression, her body convulsing? How shocked they must have been! Before long, they and their young baby ended up in the neurology referral system. What can have happened after the child's birth? What happened between the parents when the illness of their first child manifested itself? Were there feelings of disappointment, guilt, worry? Were there rows? Did the father take a step back and say to his wife: you have to solve this? Did the illness send shock waves through the family, a paroxysm as a result of which the mother was no longer able to be an open, spontaneous mother and the father no longer father? What may Annemieke have gained from the special position she occupied in the family, and what may she have lost in terms of ordinary love and ordinary care? In what sense would she feel deficient?

It seemed as though her special position set Annemieke apart more and more; although placed on a pedestal, she felt cast off. She was waited on hand and foot, but meanwhile she was being outflanked by her sister, who appeared to find it so easy to win her parents' love. And whenever Annemieke arrived at the ward of a clinic, at school, at a work placement, at the GP, she always seemed to be angling for special treatment. She appeared to be asking, "Will you be my father or mother? Could I at least be special for *you*? Can I be the only one for *you*?" And the answer always seemed to be: "Yes, you are special," but followed not so long afterwards by "you're just a member of the group, you're just like all the others." Her reaction was "So I'm not special, so I'm being left out. All right then, I'll go and find some other 'parent' for whom I'll be special." Time and again, she would attach herself to a new "parent".

In this way, the same pattern of conflict within the family kept repeating itself: the sibling rivalry was mirrored by the rivalries in the group. Annemieke's loss of her position as the eldest was mirrored in her struggle to be special and to find a parent with whom she could have an exclusive relationship, and time and again, this relationship too was lost. The clinic, the team and school acquired the role of parents, and repeated the theme and the conflict in the family. Annemieke thus became more and more lost to herself and her parents as she continued her quest for that one parent to whom she could be special, repeatedly disappointed to discover that she was not the only one. Whenever she withdrew with a sense of having been wronged, it aroused contradictory responses in the team, which had divided into two camps: one camp that wanted to treat her like everyone else and another that wanted to give her extra care and attention from a sense of compassion. When the ensuing conflicts got out of hand, a different carer would be called in or another section asked to mediate. Everyone involved was full of the best of intentions.

This scenario was not a therapeutic context: all the efforts and help only led to a repetition of the theme within the family. A careful analysis was made, and a new context created.

The carers would take it upon themselves to take Annemieke home to live with her parents. Sessions would be scheduled with the parents. They would be encouraged to talk about what it had meant for them to see their first child suffering from epileptic seizures when she was so young; to discuss what it had meant for their relationship; what it had meant for each of them separately. How had they felt later, when their second child turned out to be healthy and to fulfil all their expectations? Sessions would be held with the parents, with Annemieke and with her sister about the positions each of them had within the family. These sessions would not be held at the clinic, but at the parents' home. It seemed important to help Annemieke to regain her place as the eldest sibling.

### Structuring a therapeutic context

The following example shows how a context can be structured in a therapeutic way, and how individual symptomatic behaviour can be integrated as part of the context. My supervisee Luuk Hoendervangers presented the following case history.

*Simon* (Luuk Hoendervangers and Jan Olthof)

Simon, aged five, was referred to the mental health services with an eating disorder and a range of behavioural problems. He became angry when reprimanded, he wouldn't listen, and was a little dictator at home. He frequently reverted to the behaviour of a two year old, eating only if someone fed him and wanting to be carried about. Simon's eating problems were a constant source of friction in the family. They appeared to stem from a problematic relationship between Simon and his parents. His father had subjected his mother to severe domestic abuse, and after their separation, he continued to harass her for a very long time. Simon had witnessed his father's aggressive outbursts when his parents were still living together.

Simon's birth had been difficult, and his mother had suffered from postnatal depression. He had been transferred to an incubator and fed through a tube. The mother recalled that he was constantly pulling the tubes out, and would only eat if she fed him. This became a pattern, which remained unaltered over the years. His mother assumed she was to blame for her son's lack of development, and considered herself a bad mother. She always held Simon very close to her. In the morning she would lift him out of his bed and lay him on the sofa. Since she was worried that he might eat too little, she would peel some fruit for him, squeeze some oranges, and feed him small pieces of doughnut, which he loved. Then she would carry him to the bathroom to wash him. Simon loved being taken care of like this. It seemed as though he wanted to remain a baby and always to stay with his mother.

He still spent time at his father's house, where his needs received less attention and he scarcely ate at all. This was an additional source of concern for his mother. The father often took Simon to dinner with his parents, since he was more likely to eat there. The mother had a new partner, Victor, who set rules for Simon from the moment he arrived. Simon reacted by making scenes. His mother felt she had a lot to make up for in relation to Simon, because she had rejected him at the beginning of his life, during her postnatal depression, and because he had experienced so many rows between his parents.

Outside the home Simon behaved better and acted his age, although he was a little withdrawn. As Dolto notes (Dolto, 1998), food represents the bond of love between mother and child, and a child who refuses to eat independently is stuck in an early phase of life. Breastfeeding had been disrupted, since Simon had been placed in an incubator and separated from his mother. It seemed that Simon wanted to receive his mother's love through food and being fed. This meant staying a baby. So that was what he did, when in the home. In the outside world he acted his age. This behaviour aroused considerable opposition from Victor, who encouraged Simon to act his age.

Luuk, his therapist, had already introduced a distinction between "baby Simon" and "big Simon" and the behaviour that went with each. He was helping Simon to decide when he wanted to be a big boy and when he wanted to stay a baby. The therapy was making progress.

The mother, plagued by feelings that she was not a good mother, was very frightened of voices expressing opinions and judgements from the outside world, such as that of Victor, who said that it was ridiculous that Simon acted like such a baby. Then a new voice suddenly sounded from the outside world, that of a friend who worked at a specialist orthopedagogical centre, and who exclaimed: "Hasn't Simon's eating behaviour been tested yet?" She listed the medical examinations and psychological diagnostic tests she felt to be necessary. And although the therapy was progressing well, the mother became insecure again and challenged Luuk's approach.

This new voice, that of the mother's friend, was a voice inscribed in a specific discourse, the discourse that insists: every child must undergo medical examination and psychological tests as a precondition for professional help. The friend therefore considered it essential for the therapist to be inscribed within this larger system; he must not ignore or dispute this voice from the outside world but incorporate it into his care. This meant widening the therapeutic system to accommodate this and other voices. It was important for the therapist to listen to the discourse, but also to deconstruct it. This could be done by arguing as follows.

Simon could eat well if his mother fed him, but if he had to eat by himself he could hardly swallow a bite and refused almost all foods. That implied that there was nothing wrong with his body. For it was impossible for Simon to be completely healthy one minute, when his mother fed him, and unhealthy the next, when he had to eat by himself. The "voice" advocating tests might have been very sensible if Simon was never able to eat properly, but Simon was clearly very *happy* to accept food from his mother, as if she was the only person from whom he could safely accept it. After all, in the hospital, food had been administered in a painful way, through a tube. The very word "administered" has an unpleasant sound to it. But rather than resisting this new voice, Luuk cooperated by reflecting on the friend's intentions and what they would mean, and ended up deconstructing the proposals as follows: a physical examination would be extremely taxing for Simon and trigger numerous unpleasant memories. Moreover, it was very unlikely that they would find anything, since Simon could eat perfectly well, provided his mother fed him. All this reassured Simon's mother, and she resumed her full support for Luuk's approach.

The mother's partner, Victor, was asked to come and sit beside Luuk and to listen to the story about the catching up that Simon and his mother needed to do in their relationship. For this related to a period when he was not yet in the picture. Victor agreed, which helped to create space for the therapy process. Simon was asked to go and sit on his mother's lap, after which

Luuk, Simon and his mother talked about Simon's birth, the incubator, and the first few months of the boy's life. They talked about his mother's postnatal depression, which had prevented her from taking care of him, and her eagerness to catch up. Simon listened closely and said that he wanted to be a baby and for his mother to hold him tight. As he said this, he studied his mother's reactions. His mother had experienced problems with intimacy because of her past, but said she wanted to change that.

As part of the "catching up" process, Simon was to be asked at each mealtime whether he wanted to be a baby or a big boy. Being a big boy meant feeding himself, like a real five year old. Being a baby meant that he and his mother would do some catching up, and Simon would be fed some "extra" food. This removed the conflict between the two adults, since Victor grasped the significance of the regressive behaviour; Simon's mother gave him the space they needed together, and there were no longer any losers. Victor was happy with the new framework. The change also meant that he was no longer responsible for raising Simon. The family became calmer. Simon's mother could now feed and cherish her son without any sense of unease, and could feel that she was being a good mother. Her partner was able to feel that he was being supportive by giving the two of them the space they needed, and he no longer had to "tackle" Simon. Simon was now able to decide, autonomously, what he needed. His symptomatic behaviour had been given a context and a story, and explained in a sympathetic way. Every morning, Simon's mother would ask him which Simon was going to be deciding things at home that day. Luuk asked her whether she felt capable of explaining this policy to the outside world, and she replied confidently that she did. The approach had her full support.

The symptomatic behaviour had now been inscribed in a context: the context of Simon's relationship with his mother, of his life history, and of his relationship with the new father figure at home. At this point, the discussions had not yet touched on the fact that Simon had also witnessed his father's abusive treatment of his mother. Wanting to remain a baby might also be related to this period. Simon was spending time with his father every two weeks. When the therapy had progressed a little further, Luuk wrote a letter to the family, which he read out when the three of them (Simon, his mother and Victor) were in the consulting room. This letter also referred to that early period of Simon's life. Luuk asked Simon to sit on his mother's lap and asked Victor once again to come and sit next to him. Simon sat with his back pressed firmly against his mother and looked expectantly at Luuk as he read out the letter.

> Simon, do you remember that we talked about being a baby and a big boy, about eating and not eating, about eating by yourself or Mummy feeding you? Do you think that maybe when you're eating, you have the feeling that it's right for you to be there, that it's right for you to be alive; and that if you don't eat, you have the feeling that you shouldn't be there? Then I told you that Mummy was very happy that you were there, but she wasn't completely sure. Sometimes she wants it so much, she wants it more than anything else in the world, and you are the most important person in the world for her. Then sometimes she doesn't know what to do and thinks: "Am I a good mother? Can I be a good mother? Can I take good care of Simon, and do I really want to be here at all?" For there are times that your Mummy doesn't want to be here at all, times that it doesn't seem to matter so much to her that she's alive.

Do you think, maybe, that when Mummy feels that she should be here, that she can be here, and wants to be here, that she also wants you to be here? And if she feels that she shouldn't be here, that she can't or doesn't want to be here, that she doesn't want you to be here either? If that's true, that must be very confusing for you. Do you think, maybe, that when you have the feeling that it's right for you to be here, that you can eat, it's because then you have the feeling that it's all right for you to grow up and become a big boy? And that if you have the feeling that you shouldn't be here, that you can't eat, it's because then you feel that you shouldn't grow up? After all, if you're alive you have to eat, and if you eat you will grow up. And does Mummy eat too? Or does she only eat when she has the feeling that it's all right for her to be here, and does she not eat when she has the feeling that she shouldn't be here?

When you were in Mummy's tummy, and after you were born, your Daddy and your Mummy used to shout at each other a lot, and your Daddy hurt your Mummy badly. You felt that of course, when you were a little baby. When you heard them shouting at each other, you thought: "Would it be better for me not to be here?" Or did you think: "Darn it, I'll show them that I'm here! I'm not going anywhere. I'm here and I'm staying here!"? Or did your Mummy think, perhaps, the same as you? Did she think "it would be better if he wasn't here"? Or did she think, "Darn it, he's my baby and I want my baby to be here!"? And what about your Daddy? Do you think he was sorry about all the shouting and that he thought, "maybe it would be better if my baby wasn't here!"? Was he happy that he had a little boy? Was he proud of his son? Does your Daddy think you ought to decide what to do yourself, or does he think you ought to listen and do as you're told? And who are you supposed to listen to, then? That must be very confusing for you. Should you be here, or would it be better if you were not here? Should you stay very, very quiet and stay a little boy? Or should you show them that you're there?

If you don't know if your Mummy wants to be here, does that mean you have to shake her very hard and say: "Hey, Mummy, are you still here?" Do you have to keep her alive? By being a little baby and by being a nuisance and being lots of trouble to look after, like a small, sickly little boy, you can be sure that your Mummy will stay awake and take care of you. If you don't know if it's all right for you to be here, should you be lots and lots of trouble, or should you stay very quiet and babyish? Should you eat, or should you not eat? Or sometimes eat and sometimes not? Should you be a small, sickly little baby, or should you be a big strong boy?

And then we come to you, Victor. It must be very difficult for you. What is your place here? And *where* is your place? Do they want you to be there, and who do you have to be? Do you have to be a little bit of Simon's Mummy and a little bit of his Daddy? Do you have to save everyone, be the one who watches over everyone's life? But surely it's not up to you to decide whether other people want to live? They can't place that responsibility on your shoulders, can they? So what are you supposed to do, if you love Simon and his Mummy and they don't even know if they want to be here? What should you do with all that love?

Simon, when you act up and are so difficult when the three of you are together, are you trying to say to Mummy: "Mummy, do you want Victor to be here or not?" Each one of you has to decide whether or not you want to be here. No one else can decide that for you, can they?

This letter expressed a clear connection between Simon's symptomatic behaviour and his relationship with his mother and father, as well as the relationship with Victor. It had become clear that Simon's mother had suffered from an eating disorder in the past, which sometimes recurred. It had also become clear that there were times at which Simon's mother urged Victor to be a co-parent, and other times at which she told him not to interfere. Sometimes she would delegate the parenting role to Victor and ask him to be strict with Simon; at other times she would be highly protective of her relationship with Simon and cuddle him and care for him as her little baby. It had also become clear that she suffered from depression, and sometimes had suicidal thoughts. Sometimes she had had plenty of room for Simon, and sometimes she had very little room for him, when she was tormented by traumatic memories of her childhood and her marriage.

The reading of the letter was recorded on video. Luuk watched the video afterwards, together with Victor and with Simon's mother, and together they observed Simon's reactions. It was striking that when the relationship between his mother and Victor was mentioned, Simon, who was playing with some train rails at that point, offered Victor one of the rail sections, as if he also wanted to make this connection. Mother said she recognised that this was what Simon was conveying, but Victor thought it was a coincidence. He did say, however, that he was struggling with the question of whether or not he should be "Daddy". What was really expected of him? When this question was raised during the session, Simon connected another link in the train rails in Victor's direction, and seemed to be expressing the desire for a connection between his mother and Victor. This made a big impression on Simon's mother, but Victor doubted whether it was really true that Simon wanted him to be there. He did not know how to behave in relation to his partner or to Simon. He did not know what his place was.

Simon gradually started doing better and his behaviour improved. Very slowly, his pattern of eating also started to clear up. His mother gradually found it easier to get through mealtimes without a battle. Victor now kept out of these situations altogether. It was something between the two of them; it didn't involve him. At the same time, Simon's mother worked on her own problems and started feeling better about herself. When this happened, Simon's behavioural problems disappeared. During this period, however, the relationship between the two adults became less close. Simon's mother appeared to need Victor less and less to compensate for her insecurity. Nor did she need to immediately give in all the time to avoid conflict. She expressed her own voice more and more.

At school, Simon increasingly showed his insecurity, whereas he had previously been "invisible". He also started eating better at school. The weekends with his father started going better; he was no longer completely unsettled when he came home afterwards. His father started going to watch Simon's swimming lesson every Wednesday.

### Developing a narrative

When a child is referred for therapy, the context is not automatically therapeutic. It is certainly not therapeutic when the different perspectives—that of the parents, that of the referring professional, and that of the child—all conflict. A child is often referred because of "bad behaviour", and if therapy is started without further consultation, and the child experiences the referral as an expression of blame, the context is not therapeutic. In such cases it is useful to develop a narrative for all family members, to bring the different perspectives together with a view to starting the therapy in a context of cooperation.

In all cases in which children are referred for therapy, the focus will be on the behavioural problems and the rows in the family, often without the children themselves giving their version of what is happening in the family. Some children may be deterred by feelings of loyalty from saying what is going on. Take Michael, for instance, eight years old, who was referred to our outpatient clinic.

*Prickly the hedgehog*

Michael attended a school for children with special needs, and the school referred him for therapy because of severe behavioural problems. He had a younger brother, five years old. The children's father did not live with the family. Michael had frequent temper tantrums and was constantly destroying things, at home and in the neighbourhood. At school the other children would not play with him and he scarcely had any friends. "Losing" was a key flashpoint; if Michael lost a game, he flew into a fit of rage. His mother said that she was unable to get a grip on his behaviour.

Each of the parents in succession told their stories. The mother was the youngest of eight children and had not known much love. "They just ignored me." She had felt an unwanted late arrival, and had experienced the balance of power in the family she grew up in as "seven against one." She was seen as the "black sheep" and constantly teased.

The father was born in Australia, where his parents were working on temporary contracts, and had spent the first five years of his life there. He was the middle of three children, and when the family returned to the Netherlands he had problems adjusting, triggered by language difficulties. He ended up at a school for children with special needs and was known as a child with temper tantrums. Basically, he had never really picked up the thread of his life after moving from Australia to the Netherlands. He had done a technical training course and left school early to earn some money to help his parents. He had wanted to join the army, and was devastated when his application was turned down. After that he lived what he called a "wild" life. He spent some time at a boarding school, where he met the woman who would become his wife. They became inseparable, and before long Michael was born. His father stayed at home for two weeks, devoting himself completely to the care of mother and child, after which he went back to his old "wild" life. The parents separated not long afterwards, having been married for three years.

At one point Michael had been present during a brawl in his father's favourite pub. His father was smashed over the head with a bar stool as he was leaving the pub, and sustained a fracture of the base of the skull. He fell to the ground in a pool of blood, which Michael witnessed. Ever since then, Michael had been doing badly at school.

According to his mother, he had been affected by the numerous rows between her and her husband before he was even born. She thought herself a useless mother. She had broken off contact with her parents and siblings, felt a lack of support and saw herself as having to face life alone. Since the birth of Michael she had been plagued by somatic symptoms and constant pain. Michael too had physical symptoms from an early age. He had convulsions at the age of three, and later he suffered from stomach ache, rashes, and a succession of other complaints. What was more, he suffered from unpredictable mood swings. It was also striking that Michael was very hard to wake up in the morning; he always wanted to carry on sleeping. It seemed as if he was waking from a dreamworld, and that he liked the life in the dream much more than the life that he found himself in when he woke up.

At first, Michael was reluctant to say anything about life at home. All he wanted to do was to act out his dreams with the play therapist. After the introductory sessions, he refused to come to the clinic any more. A home visit was arranged, and it became clear that the parents were living almost next door to each other. Although they were supposedly separated, they spent all day together. The father lay on the sofa downstairs, often falling asleep there, and returned to his own flat at the end of the evening. According to the parents, the children scarcely noticed that their parents were separated, since their father was always at home.

Michael put one in mind of a small hedgehog that was curled up and constantly had to stick out its spikes to protect itself. He appeared to need to distract attention from home and to carefully avoid giving any information or replying to questions about life at home. He did enjoy the positive attention he received at the clinic, and tried to find as many opportunities as possible to play. If the care were to continue in this way, without any framework, Michael would only be coming to the clinic to play, or because he had made a scene and was causing trouble. In that case, the clinic would have had to take over parental responsibility and give him room to play.

The parents too were reluctant to talk about the home situation. They took the view that their way of life was no problem whatsoever for the children. Michael didn't miss his father, they said, since he was there every day. The parents did not understand that the children were baffled by the situation at home and did not know what they ought to tell the outside world about it. A framework was needed, and the parents were offered the following framework.

It appeared that the mother still felt a certain loyalty to her own parents. She felt that she had been unwanted, and had the sense of being alone in the world. Her boyfriend, and later husband, had helped her to stand up to her parents. Her parents had never given their blessing to the marriage, and gave the family no support whatsoever. Even so, they got married. Later on they got a divorce, but only on paper. It appeared as if the mother had struck a compromise: a half-marriage, in which they were divorced and yet still together. She opposed her own parents by getting married, but remained loyal to them by getting divorced. A half-wife, a half-mother, a half-woman, half-alive, and in this way living out the script she had been given when she was born. The father was half-present: half in the home and half elsewhere. In short, the children had "half-parents", parents who had been unable to find their own path in life, who missed their own homes or had broken with them. They were only able to give their children half a home. And Michael did not know what he ought to say about his home.

We attached the significance "anger" to Michael's behaviour:

> I want a complete home, I want a whole mother and a whole father. What am I supposed to do with this situation? Sometimes it's my home and sometimes it's not. Sometimes I've got parents and sometimes I've only got a mother, but I can't tell anyone about it because my parents don't say anything about it. To the outside world they don't live together. So where do I stand? And where does my little brother stand?

It turned out that Michael fiercely defended his parents in the outside world and took care to ensure that no one came too close to their house.

The parents accepted this new interpretation of Michael's difficult behaviour and agreed to explore whether the "half" home situation could be turned into a "whole" one, and whether the half-parents could become whole parents. They gave Michael permission to talk about his home. The group leaders offered Michael the following narrative:

> Once upon a time, in a great big forest far away from here, there lived a little hedgehog who was called Prickly, because he had lots of sharp spines. He was a very handsome, sweet hedgehog, who had always lived in the forest. He was small, but very clever. He was cleverer than the other little hedgehogs in the forest. Do you know why? Because he had very special eyes, eyes on stalks! Because of those eyes, he was able to see very well, and the wonderful thing was that those eyes could turn around in all directions. Without moving, he could look round the corner, behind him, above him, and down at the ground, and he could look in all those directions almost at the same time! That's how fast his eyes could move in all directions! That was very useful, because it meant that Prickly could keep an eye on everything that happened all around him. And it was important for him to do that—but I'll tell you about that later on.
>
> There were lots of other creatures living in the forest, and Prickly sometimes played with them, but actually he was more often alone. Then he would saunter off lazily through the forest, and now and then he would creep under a bush to have a nice nap. He loved to dream under the bushes. There was one special bush under which he always had the most wonderful dreams, and if the other creatures woke him up out of one of those dreams, he would fly into such a terrible temper!
>
> There were lots of bushes under which Prickly liked to have a nap, but this one was his very favourite place. Even so, he didn't live under the bush. Actually, no one knew exactly where Prickly lived, because he was always wandering about the forest by himself, and he never took any of the creatures home with him. He did let the other creatures come and play with him at his favourite bush, but only there. When he walked home, he was afraid that the other creatures might follow him, and so he would set them on the wrong track by going off along all sorts of little paths and trails until he was quite sure that no one was following him. Only then did he go home.
>
> What no one knew was that Prickly was actually terribly tired. Once he had seen another hedgehog getting hurt and almost being squashed flat by a big black boot. That had given him such a shock that he had decided that this would never happen to him, and he would always watch out. Since then, he had practised looking with his eyes so much that they had grown stalks. By turning his eyes around, he could now see everywhere, and make sure that there was no danger anywhere. But since Prickly swivelled his eyes so much, and had to watch out so carefully all the time, he couldn't sleep peacefully at night any more. His little head felt so heavy and he hurt all over his body. Luckily he was usually very good at hiding this from the other creatures in the forest. Another thing that made Prickly so tired was that he had to walk such long distances every day to set the other creatures on the wrong track so that no one would come anywhere near his house. And you know, hedgehogs are very small and they can only walk quite slowly. Prickly always had to be absolutely sure that not one single creature was following him.
>
> What Prickly didn't know, was that the Big Friendly Bird had already followed him home a few times. With his sharp eyes, the bird had seen, from high up in the sky, all those things that Prickly had to do to lead the other creatures off the track. He had also seen that Prickly was so tired that he

had trouble dragging his feet along. When the bird had flown up into a tree and perched on one of its branches, he had seen that the house where Prickly lived kept rumbling and shaking, making the whole nest jolt up and down. Prickly's house was like a hornets' nest! The Big Friendly Bird didn't know exactly what was going on, but he saw that Prickly could hardly hold his head up any more and that he stuck out his spiky spines more and more often when the other creatures wanted to play with him. The Big Friendly Bird was very worried about Prickly and wanted to help him, but he didn't know how. He realised, of course, that Prickly must have some reason for wanting to set the other creatures on the wrong track all the time. It seemed as though he was trying to protect his family's house. Had something happened to Prickly or his family? What was going on? The bird decided to stay close to Prickly so as to help him if it turned out to be necessary.

It will be clear that this narrative could only forge an initial connection with Michael and his parents, and that it would have to be developed in the next phase of therapy. The most important thing, however, is that after this story, both Michael and his parents said "yes" to the therapy, without any reservation. The parents agreed to talk openly about their home situation. They also gave Michael permission to talk about the things that he found difficult at home. Michael loved the story and "nestled" in the clinic. He was happy to go there, and started talking more and more from then on. In the playroom, where at the beginning he had acted out his dreams and then immediately broken everything, his play now started to develop. He left everything intact and the story kept on growing. While at the beginning he was only able to lay out a false track, he was now able to create a new track.

*Little Beaver*

Leo, nine years of age, also had no story. So young, he had already been through a great deal. Not only was he without a story, he had also been diagnosed with a pervasive developmental disorder, so the mere idea of talking about himself was completely out of the question. He had already spent almost three years as an inpatient at the children's psychiatric clinic, which referred him to the outpatient clinic for therapy. Those working with Leo had learned that he would sometimes shut himself off from all contact with others. Anyone who tried to make contact with him encountered a brick wall—so often that most people eventually avoided him or gave up. Leo seldom managed to initiate contact himself. At best, he gave occasional brief signs of his presence—like an echo—but he would then withdraw again and close himself off.

Leo's parents had separated several years before. Leo had suffered from affective neglect on the part of his mother. He was neglected in other ways too: there was a lack of food and care, and he was dressed in shabby clothes. His mother entered into a string of other relationships, which prompted Leo's father to seek a divorce. After the divorce, the mother stayed living in the same neighbourhood with her three children—Leo and his two elder sisters. However, she soon became involved in a circle of drug dealers and gamblers. She gambled in an attempt to raise money to feed her drug habit. The children were frequently left to fend for themselves.

Since the mother had received threats from people to whom she owed money, she moved, from one day to the next, to another part of the country, taking the children with her. Leo and his sisters were suddenly uprooted and detached from the world they had known, as if they had been abducted and taken abroad. They were also abruptly deprived of the regular presence of their father.

Although the children still had some contact with their father, Leo became more and more isolated as time went on. He was unable to build up a world for himself in his new surroundings. Everything seemed strange to him, and he silently longed for his father. Because of his withdrawn and uncommunicative behaviour, it proved impossible to find an appropriate school for him. As a result, Leo spent eighteen months at home with his mother, who frequently left him to his own devices. Increasingly, Leo shut himself away in his own little world, and it became more and more difficult for the outside world to reach him. By the time a place was finally found for him at a school, he was a confirmed outsider. This became worse still after his admission to a psychiatric hospital, which exacerbated his isolation. In the institution too, he remained on the periphery of the group. Still, the dedicated care he received there clearly achieved a great deal.

The intensive treatment Leo had received in the hospital had given him a desire to grow up and change. He appeared to have gained enough positive experiences that he now believed in the possibility of a new world opening up for him. A new school for children with special needs had been found for him, with which the outpatient clinic would be working in close partnership. Leo had moved in with his father and was very happy there. It was clear that he had a very good relationship with his father.

We developed a therapeutic framework in the nomadic team. Questions and images surfaced, such as: what must it mean to a baby or a toddler if it cries, with or without words: "Mummy, I'm hungry," "Mummy, I'm thirsty," "Mummy, where are you? I'm cold" and hears no response except his own voice echoing back from the wall? There was no Mummy at that point in time, and Daddy was far away. Daddy was working at a factory, and as for where Mummy might be …

This situation gradually built up not only an *external* void but also an *internal* void, a hollow space inside, in which the child could hear only the echo of his own needs and his own deprivation. It seemed as though Leo had built up a world of his own in this way and was only used to the echo of his own voice and thoughts. What could a care worker do if Leo had retreated behind his wall and was locked in there? Should he leave Leo alone, reasoning "He's happy in his own world, that's all he wants, just let him be"? Or should the care worker continue to coax Leo into reacting, and try to enter his world? But how could this be done if Leo knew nothing but echoes?

What would change if Leo *did* get an answer to his question, "Where are you?" Suppose he were suddenly to hear the answer "*Here* I am!" Now that his father was there, to hold Leo in his arms and collaborate fully with the care staff, would the care workers also be allowed to hold Leo in their arms? Would Leo be able to experience that, since he was only accustomed to hearing echoes? Would it not be the case that in answering Leo's unspoken question, a care worker would also be stepping into a frightening void and would find himself in the middle of that feeling of abandonment in which Leo had become lost and in which his only option was to become attached to his own echo?

Using the method of the team as therapeutic medium, the ideas, thoughts, fantasies and associations that surfaced were collected into a theme that was addressed through the story of *Little Beaver* (MacDonald & Fox-Davies, 1993), a story in which echoes play an important role. Using this story, the team set out to respond to Leo's desire for change, as he had tried to make clear in his own way. The story is about a little beaver that goes out into the world in search of friends. It will be clear that the story only provided a framework in the early stages of therapy. The idea was that the story would invite a response of recognition, an affirmation that could help Leo set off along a path towards a therapy in which he could be an explicit, active participant.

The story was adapted and read out to Leo as the start of a therapeutic relationship. It is about Little Beaver, who was alone and lonely, although we don't know how or why.

> Little Beaver lived all alone by the edge of a big pond. … He didn't have any friends. One day, sitting by the side of the pond, he began to cry. He cried out loud. Then he cried out louder.
> 
> Suddenly he heard something very strange. On the other side of the pond, someone else was crying too. …
> 
> "Why are you crying?" asked Little Beaver.
> 
> "Why are you crying?" asked the voice from across the pond.
> 
> Little Beaver thought for a moment. "I'm lonely," he said. "I need a friend."
> 
> "I'm lonely," said the voice from across the pond. "I need a friend."
> 
> Little Beaver couldn't believe it. On the other side of the pond lived somebody else who was sad and needed a friend.
> 
> He got right into his boat and set off to find him.
> 
> It was a big pond. He paddled and paddled.
> 
> Then he saw a young duck, swimming in circles all by himself.
> 
> "I'm looking for someone who needs a friend," said Little Beaver. "Was it *you* who was crying?"
> 
> "I do need a friend," said the duck. "But it wasn't me who was crying."
> 
> "I'll be your friend," said Little Beaver. "Come with me." …
> 
> They paddled and paddled. Then they saw a young otter.
> 
> "We're looking for someone who needs a friend," said Little Beaver. "Was it *you* who was crying?"
> 
> "I do need a friend," said the otter. "But it wasn't me who was crying."
> 
> "We'll be your friends," said Little Beaver and the duck. "Come with us." …
> 
> "Were you crying for a friend?" asked Little Beaver.
> 
> "No," said the otter, "But I would like a friend, because I'm lonely."
> 
> "Well get into my boat then, come and sit with us," said Little Beaver to the otter. They paddled and paddled. Then they saw a young turtle.
> 
> "We're looking for someone who needs a friend," said Little Beaver. "Was it *you* who was crying?"
> 
> "I do need a friend," said the turtle. "But it wasn't me who was crying."
> 
> "We'll be your friends," said Little Beaver and the duck and the otter. "Come with us." …
> 
> So the turtle jumped into the boat and they paddled and paddled until they came to the end of the pond. Here lived a wise old beaver … [and Little Beaver told him that he was trying to find out who was crying.]
> 
> "It was the Echo," said the wise old beaver. …
> 
> "When you are sad, the Echo is sad … When you are happy, the Echo is happy too."

"But how can I find him and be his friend?" said Little Beaver, "He doesn't have any friends, and neither do I."
"Except for me," said the duck.
"And me," said the otter.
"And me," said the turtle.
Little Beaver looked surprised. "Yes," he said. "I have lots of friends now." …
From across the pond, a voice answered him:
"I have lots of friends now!"

That was how the adapted story of Little Beaver was read to Leo. He did not have to react, but was free to absorb it.

In the story, the beaver sets out of his own accord, and rows out across the lake. He becomes active and goes off on a quest. The beaver takes the initiative himself.

The team agreed that Leo did not necessarily have to take part in the group activities, but could stay on the periphery for the time being. The group leaders would try to act the parts of the duck or the otter or the turtle, who are invited to join him in his boat. Or the part of the wise old beaver, who leaves him alone but offers him a framework within which to understand his life. That meant that the group leaders would not appeal to Leo directly, but would use indirect techniques instead. The communication was more successful if it was oblique, rather than Leo being addressed directly. This gave Leo the opportunity to join in very gradually and circuitously. Urging him to talk to or look at the other group members directly would place too heavy a burden on him and make him recoil. Instead, he would be given an opportunity to watch from the edge, from a distance, and in this way to follow the process in the group. This gave him a leg up to help him find his way to the group.

Take the following examples. During meals, games, sports, and group discussions, the common pattern was that Leo would follow what was happening very closely, and would say to one of the group leaders, "Tell so-and-so that … ." Whereas in an earlier stage, Leo had been asked to address the person concerned directly, Leo's indirect contribution was now acknowledged appreciatively—"Thank you for your contribution, Leo"—after which the group process would continue. It was explained to the group that some children were very good at explaining and talking, and that other children were very good listeners. Leo was someone who was very good at listening and following closely what was going on. He also had valuable ideas. The group leaders would help Leo to convey whatever he found important to its destination and pass it on to the other children. The effect of this indirect approach was that Leo felt increasingly encouraged to share his observations; initially with the group leaders, and to a growing extent also expressing himself directly to the other children.

Within this framework, Leo started to talk more and more about his situation at home during individual therapy sessions. That proved easier now that his father was actively involved in the therapy. It was also easier within the safety of the story of Little Beaver. Leo was asked if he could explain how Little Beaver had built his nest, and how he ended up living on an island. He started talking about the ingenious architecture of the beaver's nest … all the little passages and doors and rooms; and rooms behind rooms behind rooms. Leo talked more and more about himself within the framework of the story of the beaver. Of course, it was never said that

Leo might be that beaver himself. His problems were never discussed directly. He produced fragments of his life history, together with his father, but within the framework of the story of Little Beaver, Leo could talk at length about his life.

## Entering the therapeutic space

Psychotherapy may be oriented towards art, literature, film, music, theatre, or poetry. Sports, too, especially team sports, may be a source of inspiration. In *You Only Start Seeing it Once You've Figured it Out*, Pieter Winsemius applies the insights gained from conversations with Johan Cruyff to cooperation processes and performance in organisations (Winsemius, 2004). In psychotherapy, this cooperation with the family focuses on seeing the *symptom as a third space* as in a team sport. After all, in a team sport too, the effort is made to achieve a common objective, to "score" and to gain a victory. In psychotherapy, the objective is to gain a "victory" together over the symptom, to alleviate the pain, help to resolve problems and conflicts.

In supervision I often use soccer metaphors to illustrate systemic thinking. Thus, the therapist and client can be described as a team in their shared construction of reality and in their partnership that is geared towards "winning" from the symptom or disorder. Within this metaphorical world, *scoring* is equivalent to reintegrating a split-off symptom to a communal story; or liberating the "identified patient" from his or her role and incorporating him or her into the team again, after a period of exclusion.

In system therapy and work with families and their networks, just getting the "ball back into play" often calls for a great deal of skill: skills such as joining in, negotiating multiple perspectives, and being capable of multiple partiality. It calls for a warm-hearted, appreciative attitude, so that clients sense that they are welcome and can feel at ease. These skills are all the more important when dealing with a family within which there are conflicting perspectives or when it is clear that the team is dealing with an "identified patient".

Once all the family members have been welcomed, all perspectives have been heard, and the severity of the disorder has received serious attention, it is important to work together to pass the ball to the midfield. For the play to have a successful build-up, it is essential to place the symptoms and complaints in a wider perspective. This calls for skills such as redefinition, textual analysis, the ability to explore the different meanings of words, and the ability to shift to a different perspective.

Midfield play requires the ability to define a theme or focus. The context has to be made therapeutic and a therapeutic framework created. Midfield play relies on possession and the ability to play within an organised structure. The lines are clear, everyone is in the right position, and the play as a whole is directed by the therapist in partnership with the client system. The ball rolls and does the work.

Starting out from structured midfield play with clear direction, the ball has to be passed into an attacking position, and this is where the development of a therapeutic framework comes in. The ultimate aim is to score; the ball has to end up in the goal, and here that means that the problem resolves, the pain subsides, and the symptoms clear up. If a "goal" is scored and the match is won, this means that everyone has won together; it is a team effort. When I am supervising therapy, I therefore always make it clear what part of the field we're playing on and which skills are needed. As supervisees progress and become more competent, it is time for "targeted attack" and "strikes on goal".

A therapeutic context and a clear therapeutic framework could be seen as a game system and a game concept. Key factors include possession, space, architecture, vision, and organisational structure—all of which are terms that Johan Cruyff used in his discussions of soccer strategy. He would say, for instance: "It's always about the place of the ball and the lines on the field. Everyone has to be in the right place. What can a player do without the ball? When you're in possession you pay attention, there's enough adrenaline, but when you're not in possession there's sometimes a loss of concentration; you have to keep moving, constantly keep moving, but you also need to know what direction to move in".

Cruyff would add that *who* has possession is not the point. The player who is not in possession will determine how things develop once his team has possession again. "What always interests me is how they're playing at the other end of the field, how they perform their tasks there. The player who's in possession has the easy job, but the real contest takes place at the other end of the field, where they're making the game" (Winsemius, 2004, p. 37; trans. BJ). If the ball is in possession at the front, the defence should already be organising itself at the back. Cruyff referred constantly to organisational structure—there must be a good distribution across the whole field; everyone must be in the right position—and to an agreed "architecture". He talked about moving in the same direction, developing a vision, and disciplined action within the agreed framework. In short, it is essential to have a plan and a shared vision.

The notion of having a good distribution across the entire field and an agreed framework corresponds to what I mean by a context that is therapeutic, with a clear therapeutic framework. If there is no plan, no vision, everyone may be performing at the top of their game and with complete dedication and conviction, but they will be playing as solo artists rather than within an organisational structure. Without a therapeutic framework that is shared by all those involved, each participant will have their own separate "frame"; there will be a lack of organisational structure in the field, and everyone will be moving without knowing where they're going. The result will be too much standing still; the defenders will be busy defending and the strikers will be busy attacking. Then gaps will open up, and the spaces will not be properly divided.

In Cruyff's words: "You always need a triangle. Then you'll constantly have two possible ways to play the ball". This corresponds to what we have described as creating a "third space". Once the third space is there, all sorts of combinations are possible, and a range of different connections can be made. In family psychiatry, for instance, it may be decided to work intensively with the parents, to give the mother individual therapy for her post-traumatic stress disorder, and/or to launch a special therapeutic programme for the children. Medication may be prescribed, and psychodiagnostic tests administered. Even so, all these concentrated efforts may not necessarily lead to effective help or a coherent framework. There may be gaps in the field; perhaps the distribution across the field is not right. This may result in a provision of care that is ill-attuned to the patient or even to care processes that are at cross purposes, to parallel processes, and consequently to complaints being "passed on" from the family to the team.

The basic skill of putting the ball in play is all about technique. You need to be able to take advantage of what occurs, to move, and to play in several different directions. You must be able to speak many different languages and to take charge in the event of conflicting processes. Simplicity is important: clear, simple language that is attuned to the language of the client, or the client's husband, wife, brother or sister in the consulting room. The next thing is that you must be able to take charge in order to pass the ball to the midfield. That calls for possession, vision, planning, and the ability to play within an organisational structure. So on that level, what matters is being able to produce a joint construction of the reality, together with the entire client system—an interpretive framework that removes the complaint as the label—personal characteristic and attribute—of the "identified patient". And it is on this level that the "third space" is created.

The creation of a therapeutic context is the work involved in passing the ball to the midfield. As soon as a therapeutic framework has been made and validated and accepted by the family, there can be said to be possession in the midfield. Once there, the key is to have the discipline to perform the task within the agreed framework—everyone must work within the agreed architecture. This means that every form of care, every session, takes place within the specified framework. A good therapeutic framework includes a path to a solution, a way of diminishing the complaint. That takes us to the attacking play.

However well the story of the birth of Jeremy (see below) is told; however cleverly the link is explained between that traumatic birth and his temper tantrums and forgetfulness, if it does not lead to any improvement in the complaint, the story is at best a great action, but one without any result. If this link *does* lead to a reduction in the temper tantrums, as did in fact happen with Jeremy, it can be viewed as attacking play. If the anger disappears altogether or is reduced to an acceptable level, you might label it "scoring a goal".

For a supervisee it is often helpful to see which part of the field we are working in together. New supervisees frequently have difficulty actually passing the ball to the midfield and arriving at a shared theme. More experienced supervisees can be helped to move from the midfield to attacking play, to sustain their discipline, to keep playing within the agreed framework, and always to keep their eye on the goal. Highly experienced supervisees will be engaged in varied and purposeful attacking play.

The key, then, is to be well prepared, well trained, and to work/play with the utmost concentration. "Chance is a question of logic", said Cruyff, "You create luck with a surplus of technique, routine, automatic reactions, and the right attitude. What initially seemed incomprehensible, what seemed such a coincidence, is perfectly easy to understand when you look back at how it happened" (Baartse, 2007, p. 10; trans. BJ).

The philosopher Peter Sloterdijk also discusses practices and the art of practice in his book *You Must Change Your Life* (Sloterdijk, 2013). He describes the appeal of the vertical to human potential—the attraction to human beings of rising above themselves. It calls for complete dedication and vertical tension to carry on practising skills so long that they become ingrained patterns. The ancient guild model of learning is an example of this. Malcolm Gladwell states in his book *Outliers* (Gladwell, 2009) that it takes 10,000 hours of intensive practice to acquire expertise in any field, and he illustrates this with examples from the worlds of sport, pop music, and classical music.

To make the best possible use of one's talents, one has to have space. Cruyff talks about organising the space, creating and using space—his terms conjure up the image of an architectural design in the field. To create space, it is essential for the consciousness to begin in an open manner and to be nomadic, that it can attune itself to what occurs and improvise, and that all its actions are informed by a vision.

*Annähern*

To create space, then, it is crucial to start with a vision and a plan. How do you enter the field? How do you fit in? German has the fine word *annähern*, which means to bring closer, and carries connotations of nearness (*Nähe*), nourishment (*Nahrung*), and the navel—the connection that brings loving nourishment. If a therapist enters a difficult context without any vision or plan, there is a danger that he or she may soon become part of a dominant problem story. It calls for immense skill and a great deal of practice to make a successful entrance in a complicated context, within a larger system, such as a family or some other organisational unit. How do you come in? Who do you speak to first? What approach do you take, and with what status? Should you approach from the left or the right? Diagonally, or face to face? How do you talk to the people who are part of this system? Standing up? Sitting next to, or opposite, the person concerned? Crouching down, or standing behind someone with your hands on their shoulders? Do you talk quietly or loud? Do you speak with authority or do you seek permission: do you mind if … ? What would you say to … ? Walking around the room, formulating thoughts out loud? Do I need the father's permission to speak to his son? Shall I move to the "identified patient" by first speaking to the father, and shall I adopt a high or low status? Should I perhaps go and sit beside the mother and talk to her about what the father would think about me talking to their son? Should I go and sit on a low chair beside the son, and talk to him about his parents' concerns about him, or about his own concerns about his parents' marriage? Should I talk to the younger sister about her elder brother, who quarrels with his father so much? Should I talk to the mother about what it is like for her that the two men in the house are constantly fighting? Should I sit beside the son who has constant rows with his father and quickly assign a different interpretation to his behaviour? Should I ask him, for instance, whether he is fighting for and on behalf of his mother, for his mother who is so full of sadness? Let's take the film *Little Miss Sunshine* as an example.

We are introduced to a family that consists of Richard and Sheryl, their fifteen-year-old son Dwayne, their seven-year-old daughter Olive and Richard's elderly father, who lives with them. At the beginning of the movie, Sheryl goes to fetch her brother Frank to stay with them after he has cut his wrists in a suicide attempt. Frank enters the house quietly and hesitantly. He makes a desolate, broken impression, with hunched shoulders. It is an unusual family with an unusual story and an unusual mode of interacting with each other. Frank is initiated into the family's culture and habits.

Grandpa is an unconventional, contrary old hippie with a drug habit, but he enjoys life and loves the company of his granddaughter, Olive, whom he helps with her favourite hobby, dancing. Olive is practising for a beauty pageant she has entered, which is to be broadcast on TV. Grandpa and Olive are enjoying practising their "moves". Dwayne, a follower of Nietzsche, has long ceased to speak and communicates only in written notes. The father comes from a commercial background and is obsessed with achievement. He loves to talk about the commissions he has raked in with his self-help books and the profits he expects to make, but is actually on the point of bankruptcy. He constantly rants about the importance of having a "winner" mentality, of dedicating yourself totally to something, of believing in yourself and in the opportunities life brings. Grandpa and Dwayne take all this with a large pinch of salt. The mother, Sheryl, does her best to mediate.

Frank is given a place to sleep in Dwayne's room, and Sheryl tells Frank that her son is quiet and that they will get on fine. Frank and Dwayne do in fact immediately hit it off, especially when it turns out that Frank is an authority on Nietzsche. When he asks Dwayne why he has stopped speaking, the boy points to a poster with a caricature of the philosopher, and Frank immediately recognises him and understands: he essentially replaces the explanation "you're quiet" with "you've taken a vow of silence because of Friedrich Nietzsche!"

Then we see the family getting ready for dinner. Sheryl is busily trying to get everyone to sit down to eat. Dwayne casually puts a few paper plates on the table and Frank takes his place, in a hesitant, diffident way. Olive and Grandpa come down in a good mood, and have clearly been enjoying their dancing routine. Richard rubs his hands in satisfaction at the profit he is hoping to make. It is a colourful bunch of characters.

Richard starts talking about Dwayne's silence. His words have a sarcastic edge, as he describes his son as someone with great perseverance. He mockingly eulogises the strong will, determination and discipline that have enabled Dwayne to remain silent for nine months. He speaks with a mix of admiration, irony and sarcasm, while Sheryl tries to shush him and to calm the situation.

Then Olive catches sight of the bandages on Frank's wrists and cries out "Uncle Frank, what happened to your arms?" Richard immediately becomes nervous, says that this is no subject for children, and tries to change the subject. Olive, disarmingly naive but also with a child's intuitive wisdom, refuses to be put off and repeats her question. Uncle Frank says that he would be happy to answer if her parents don't mind. Sheryl acquiesces, but Richard again tries to halt the conversation, and there is a harsh exchange between Richard and Grandpa. Then, however, there is finally space for the conversation between Olive and Frank.

Frank explains that while teaching at university he had been in love with a man who was a senior student. At some point his lover left him for another scholar, and Frank lost his job soon afterwards. It then turned out that the other scholar had been given his position at the university. That was too much for Frank, and he explains that he tried to end his life. "Why didn't you want to live any more?" Olive asks, with childish sincerity. Frank replies honestly that it was all too much and that he was extremely unhappy. In between the exchanges we see the silent glances that pass between Frank and Dwayne, who are seated next to each other at the table.

Imagine that this family were to call in the help of a therapist. Dwayne might be the identified patient, either because of his refusal to speak or because of the constant conflict between father and son. Or perhaps Sheryl might present herself for therapy, complaining of symptoms of depression. Olive might be troubled by nightmares or bedwetting. The entire family might be feeling the strain.

How would a family therapist approach this family? How could you even insert yourself into this situation? How many ways of doing so might not end up alienating the family? What possibilities might there be for annähern? What would happen if a male therapist were to start talking to the father about his son's problematic behaviour and if he appeared tacitly to concur with the father's view? What would happen if a young male therapist were to identify with Dwayne's behaviour, define it as a form of rebellion against the family culture, and thus enter into a coalition with the son? What would happen if a female therapist of roughly the same age as the mother were to express how difficult it must be for her to keep everyone together, how hard she tries to preserve all the connections, and what a difficult job it must be amid so much strife? What would happen if Dwayne's silence were externalised, defining silence as the "third space"? How much conflict would this not provoke, and how much of the unspoken conflict would not come into the open? How likely would it not be that the family would close ranks and fail to turn up for the next session? What would happen if the therapist were to zoom in on Grandpa and take his contrary behaviour as a primary theme?

You might see Dwayne as the "symptom carrier", and it is entirely possible that the school, youth care services, or the mother might take the boy to a therapist or a physician to find out why he refuses to speak. It seems unlikely that any therapist would succeed in getting Dwayne to speak. He will never achieve the status of Nietzsche. Only Olive, as a charming seven-year-old girl, has a positive relationship with everyone in the family; she gives pleasure to everyone and there are numerous very positive lines emanating from her. Grandpa helps her with her "moves", and her father and mother are proud of her dancing. She accepts her brother's behaviour, and Dwayne likes his little sister. Perhaps she represents what no one in the family would want to be without: something in which everyone can share: joy. It is possible that it costs her considerable energy to represent this side of the family.

A good way of entering this field, of creating space and slotting in cautiously, might be if the therapist were to go and sit next to Olive and talk to her—as an equal—about the family. A very positive tone might be adopted: "What a nice Grandpa you've got!" "Your father sure is proud of you"; "What an interesting brother you've got, so young and totally into such a great philosopher!" "Your brother has studied that difficult philosopher; and your uncle is a real expert on him!"

The therapist might talk to her about all the positive lines between her and the other family members. And then the therapist might fix on Olive rather than Dwayne as the family's "symptom carrier", since it must be a very heavy burden to stay cheerful all the time. It must surely be hard for her to see the constant conflict between her Grandpa and her father, and between her father and her brother. It must be sad for her to see her mother manoeuvring between all those parties and trying to keep everyone together. Talking about the philosopher Nietzsche might be the "third space". Nietzsche is a very striking choice of philosopher, just as her brother is a striking personality. Her uncle too is remarkable, in the honest and frank way that he shows his vulnerability and talks about how terrible it is to be rejected in love.

If the therapist were to enter the field in this way, he would connect with the little girl on the basis of equality. There are numerous possible ways of accessing the family, but a different language would be needed for each person. Grandpa speaks a different language from Richard, and Richard speaks a different language from Dwayne. The characters communicate in different linguistic domains: Grandpa and Olive in that of dance moves, Frank and Dwayne in that of philosophy, Richard in that of the business world, and Sheryl in that of connectivity. The therapist would need to be multilingual—capable of speaking to Richard in a different language than to Dwayne. The therapist would also need to adopt different positions: Grandpa would be allergic to advice and expertise; Richard, on the other hand, is a management man, who believes in taking measures and finding solutions. Dwayne would resist any attempt to speak to him; the other family members would have to go first. Only after the other family members have been heard may it be possible to gain his confidence.

It will be clear that this situation holds out a great many ways of practising, in terms of role play—of trying out all the different directions during supervision. The therapist can practise ways of seeking contact with each member of the family, using a different language and attitude and speaking from a different position.

The following example discusses ways of entering a therapeutic space that is already occupied by an explosive charge.

## Tim and his tantrums

My supervisee Leo Verleg was working with a mother and her nine-year-old son Tim, who had been admitted to a psychiatric clinic. Tim had frequent violent tantrums, during which he destroyed the furniture. The treatment within the clinical setting focused on themes relating to upbringing and behaviour management. The staff were completely at a loss as to how to deal with the boy's fits of rage. He had even been placed in a secure unit for a brief space of time, but his outbursts simply continued there. The violent tantrums had not yet been given a story. The care workers within the clinical setting attributed the fits of rage to his mother's lack of parenting skills, and asked Leo to take on the role of system therapist, to assess the mother's parenting skills in the home situation.

Leo made a home visit, after which he described the following scene: Tim, afraid that he was going to be removed from his home again, went and hid behind a stuffed bear that was almost as big as he was. His mother started talking about what their life was like. Suddenly, without any identifiable reason, the boy ran upstairs and started screaming. They could hear him ranting and raving upstairs. His mother had learned to stay calm, and said to the therapist, "This will go on for a while, and then he'll come back downstairs, run up to me to be cuddled, and tell me how sorry he is."

It was quite true. Shortly afterwards, the boy came back downstairs, ran into his mother's arms in tears, and said how sorry he was. It appeared that he had no control whatsoever over these attacks, and that he did not understand where they came from. The attacks had no story for him, and they could therefore not be attached to any categories such as reward and punishment, to any form of behaviour management. The attacks expressed a way of organising context.

Tim's mother also said that her son often cried out that he was not meant to be there. She related that her husband had raped her while they were still married and that her son had been born out of this rape.

The supervision meeting led to the following plan for "entering the field". Tim's sentence, "I shouldn't be here" evidently expressed a sense of existential insecurity. Being born from a rape leaves marks—the person concerned might well doubt whether they should have been born, or whether they should exist at all. While within the clinical setting there were doubts as to the mother's parenting abilities, Leo noted that she responded very well. The dynamics of the boy's attacks appeared to be much more complex than a simple derivative of mother–child interaction.

We posited the following story. Suppose that the boy who fell into his mother's arms after a fit of rage, full of regret, was the boy with the stuffed bear, the boy seeking comfort and protection, the boy who wanted to live and to be with his mother, safe in her arms. And suppose that the boy who had fits of rage was the boy who said to his mother and to the outside world: "I shouldn't be here at all. I doubt whether my mother wants me, and whether my father is glad that I exist. I doubt whether I have the right to exist. I'll get myself sent away. Then it will become clear whether I should really exist or not." The rape was a trauma, an event that damaged the bonding between mother and child. This damage was an obstacle that stood between them. The relationship needed to be healed.

If the therapist were to take this as the point of departure for therapy, he would first have to ensure that he had a sufficient mandate for his mode of treatment. After all, working on a parenting environment is a completely different level of operation than the existential layer on which the treatment might have been expected to take place. If the therapist were to start work on the mother–child relationship without a mandate and a crisis situation were to arise, the context would not be therapeutic. The therapist would not enjoy the necessary support of the team and might be questioned about his interventions, which would be at odds with the customary working method within the clinical setting.

Leo had gathered sufficient material to tell the staff the story of these fits of rage and to assign a different significance to them. This gave him the status of "expert" in this situation. For although he had been asked to take on this therapy as an expert, this status had not yet been formalised. The important thing was therefore to give an expert analysis and then to ask for a mandate from the treatment coordinator, a mandate for a new mode of treatment. If he received this mandate, he would also be formally recognised as the "expert" in this case. With the mandate, he could go to the mother and son and introduce the following framework:

> I've been thinking about what I saw here last time I visited. Tim, could you show me your stuffed bear again? I noticed last time that you hid yourself away almost completely behind it. I got the impression that you wanted your bear to make you safe and protect you. Your Mummy told me that you often say that you shouldn't have been born, that you shouldn't be here at all. Could you tell me where you got that idea?

This could introduce a new discourse, which would link the boy's fits of rage to his doubts about whether he should have been born. From there, a dialogue between mother and child could be initiated about the circumstances surrounding his birth. According to Dolto (Dolto, 1998), a child has a right to know all the information relating to his existence, and children have a deep knowledge, as autonomous, linguistic beings, of the existential events of their lives. The gap between that knowledge and the fact that certain things are never mentioned, or that the truth is obscured by a different story, leads to symptoms. For children have knowledge on the level of lived reality, and may lose their way if there is an incongruity between what they know and what they are told.

Symptoms arise from this in-between, this no-man's land, the land of question marks. If the therapist focuses on healing the relationship between mother and son, ensuring that the information about their lives is shared, he can help to remove the obstacles that stand between them.

### Dolls in the Attic (courtesy of Wilma Bruynen)

The following story too involves a space that is already occupied by a large story. How is the therapist to enter this field?

Mary lived with her sister in part of her family's farm. She often secluded herself away in the attic, where she had a cupboard full of dolls. She often talked loudly to these dolls—so loudly that it not only bothered her housemates but also struck passers-by and other people in the surroundings, who were prompted to ask questions about it.

Suppose that a social-psychiatric nurse or mental health therapist had come to this farm because the family had asked for help. Mary herself did not think she needed any help. She saw anyone who entered the attic by definition as an opponent. So how could a therapist become part of the story and enter the field? Were the therapist to go and stand next to the dolls and talk to them, it would probably frighten Mary. She would lose the control that she had so carefully built up. *She* was responsible for orchestrating and directing the story of, and with, her dolls. It is she who wrote the script and heard the answers. On the one hand, were the therapist to keep a distance, he or she would remain a stranger from the outside world. On the other hand, to take control and to start asking Mary questions about her life would disrupt the order she had created.

A good way of gaining access might be to get a chair and to sit down beside Mary and ask her about the various dolls and have her introduce this "family". After that, a "family conversation" might be organised, as if the dolls were people, each with her own story. In this way, Mary could retain ownership of her own story and remain in control of the conversation. It appeared clear that the therapist would have to enter this field with a lower status than Mary's own. He or she would have to ask her consent to enter her world, to ask whether she was willing to talk about her dolls, and to ask permission to sit beside her—this too implied a lower status. Not too much lower, since then the therapist would be dismissed as "insignificant", but a little lower all the same.

Once a therapeutic context has been created, there is a fertile soil for therapy. On this fertile soil, the therapist can "set up camp", by creating a therapeutic framework.

Figure 14. Setting up camp, Sinaï 2007. Photo: private collection.

CHAPTER SEVEN

# Developing a therapeutic framework

*"To get to your destination, it's not enough to leave your house, you also need to leave your outlook behind"*

—Herman de Coninck

### Introduction

A frame is something that goes around something. Once a framework has been created, you remain within the lines that have been drawn. A frame around a painting or text inset has four linked lines. Clearly, whatever is inside is more complex than these border lines. The framework serves as a boundary or protection—it keeps certain things in and others out.

A framework organises our perceptions. A camera's viewfinder sets the boundary, determines what will be seen. Some things will be inside, others outside the frame. From the vastness of the visible world, a subject is singled out and placed in relation to its surroundings. A frame organises a significant whole that is open to interpretation. A frame accentuates, highlights, plays with light and shade, places some things in the foreground and others in the background.

No frame contains "the truth", since multiple frames can be created from innumerable possibilities. Each one places a particular truth in the foreground, thus *constructing* it. All events are then viewed in this light, through this lens.

In therapy, a framework has to be made, together with the client. A sound framework will structure the interactions between carers and clients, and the client's ecology—here used to signify the client's relationship with every part of his or her social environment—in a significant whole. A framework creates perspective, indicating depth and breadth. It attaches significance to a person's behaviour and symptoms in relation to a greater whole. A framework temporarily freezes time, draws connections between flows and lines, and between forces that would not be connected without that framework.

A framework defines the setting for different stories, or may indeed serve as the plot that connects the different narrative lines. A framework helps to convert unarticulated reality into narrated reality. Like a camera, it adopts a particular vantage point and perspective in relation to reality. A framework shows how the story links up to the future and the past, and attaches significance, retroactively, to facts and events that they did not have before. Reviewing the past, it reorganises interactions, enabling them to be imbued with fresh significance. Looking to future interactions, it creates new perspectives.

A painting has a frame around it, and a vanishing point within: a point at which the parallel lines vanish out of the painting, into the distance. A therapeutic framework also has what Deleuze calls lines of flight, along which symptoms can resolve or vanish, or create new a perspective.

Symptoms are often seen as separate dance steps, steps that disrupt or derail a dance. Or possibly steps that have originated from the dance but escaped from it. So once significance is attached to symptoms, they are placed in a dance and become part of a story, a text, and hence a framework—part of the wider context of the choreography of a nuclear or extended family. The entire ecology then becomes the con/text, the larger story around the text of the symptom.

The therapeutic framework must offer a safe boundary enclosing a symptom or an individual. Alternatively, the therapeutic framework might be seen as a harbour that offers ships a place to moor, and from which they can set sail again. The quayside offers a temporary home and the prospect of a new voyage. The quayside is part of the harbour, which itself makes up part of the framework.

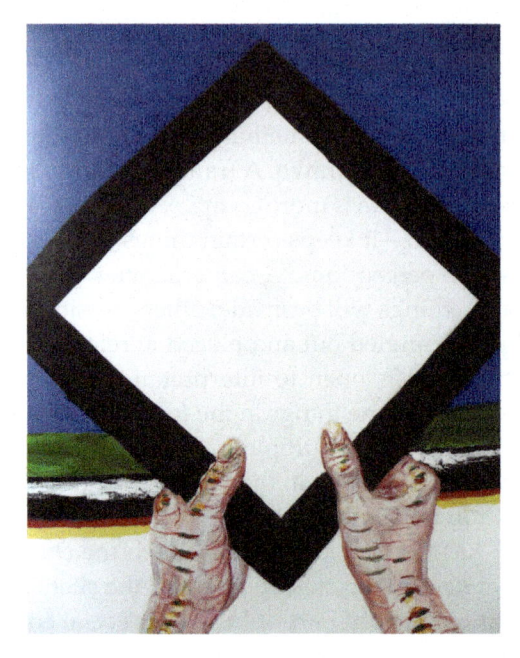

Figure 15. © Roger Raveel. *Een Sacraal Vierkant (A Sacred Square)* 1966, oil on canvas, 100 × 84 cm. Private collection. c/o Pictoright Amsterdam 2016.

Let us consider the process of constructing a therapeutic framework by looking at some examples. The aim is to make the framework as simple as possible, one that holds out the prospect of a solution, and that is sufficiently relevant to the symptoms, and significant enough to the patient and all those concerned. This means that everyone must be inscribed in this framework, including the therapist—and the institution, where appropriate—as part of the therapeutic system.

Nomadic thought needs to find a home base at some point, a settlement in which to dwell for a time. Developing a therapeutic context provides such a settlement, in which family members and everyone involved in the therapeutic process can reside. Since they will all be staying there, they must all be accommodated—all voices must be able to make themselves heard. The underlying assumption is: in this place, our interpretation, we have created a particular definition of reality.

Once the home base has been agreed, the next step is to develop a therapeutic framework—an organising principle at meta-level that will guide all therapeutic choices for all those concerned, regardless of discipline. Without a framework, it happens all too often that different parts of the care system offer well-intentioned help with great commitment but separately, and are therefore frequently at cross purposes. Such meetings are not so much consultations as polite enquiries as to what everyone is doing. It is essential to have an overall plan, an organisational structure within which everyone's actions make sense. Each person needs to know what they are doing and what their position is. We often see two different paths being followed: one for the child and a different one for the parents. Certainly when it comes to complex dynamic systems, there is often a clash of influences leading in different directions. The specific approach to context and framework does not depend on any particular school of psychotherapy: it is a meta-level for all therapy.

The therapeutic context may be visualised as a circle. The framework, then, is a square—which consists of four connected lines—inscribed within that circle.

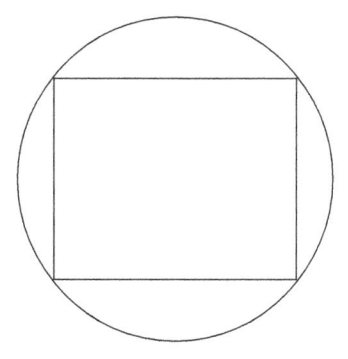

So when asked to explain why it is so essential to create a framework for therapeutic treatment, we may reply that care is too often provided within frames made up of disconnected elements. The result is not just a lot of wasted energy, but—more importantly—a lot of wasted significance, with rival interpretations clashing in the air. The Dutch psychiatrist Maarten Dormaar conducted an interesting study to find out whether care workers and their clients had the same ideas about the substance of the therapy (Dormaar, 1989). He asked therapists to name the theme and subject they were focusing on in their treatment, and then asked their clients the same question. Remarkably, the answers were very different. When a framework is developed within the therapeutic context, the significance is defined together. Each carer or therapist acts within that agreed context, and each intervention or medication has the same context.

Consider the following example, to illustrate the consequences of the absence of an agreed framework. A child admitted to a clinical child psychiatry unit is prescribed medication and placed in a group. The parents are given counselling, and psychological and psychodiagnostic tests are carried out. The child receives individual therapy and play therapy, and the school makes an important contribution to the child's treatment. What is the connection between all these efforts? What are all these individuals trying to achieve? What does the child think of the therapy? How do the parents (assuming they are in the picture) define what is going on? What is the pattern that connects all this activity?

As we saw in Chapter One, symptoms that occur within a family are often replicated in a derivative form within the team. This may lead to conflict between group leaders and parental counsellors, between psychologist and psychiatrist, between different sections of the same team. There is often insufficient recognition for these processes of replication. What is needed is a *team as therapeutic medium*, which is able to "live through" the phenomenology of the problems concerned—a team that defines a connecting pattern. A framework is an example of a connecting pattern. If there is a clearly defined framework, everyone knows his or her role, has a place and a voice. Every intervention fits within the given framework—it has a clear context on a meta-level: a context that is explicit for client and therapist alike. At the end of every session—whatever kind of session it may be, and whoever may be involved—the question can be answered as to the degree to which this activity has helped *within the given framework*. A psychomotor therapist who has been working with a child in the gym, a creative therapist who has just finished making a painting together with a child, a play therapist who has acted out a scene of medieval chivalry with a child in the sandpit, the psychiatrist who has been prescribing medication, a systems therapist in consultation with a single mother—how are all these activities connected?

In narrative psychotherapy, the therapeutic framework is developed in the initial dialogue with all those concerned. Therapy does not commence until a communal definition of the problem has been found, the context for cooperation, a joint definition of the significance and the purpose pursued by therapy. The struggle to develop a framework is itself part of the process. A clear framework helps to prevent methodological and other conflicts, which undermine therapy. A framework developed together can help to move beyond the friction that may arise between young and old, experienced and less experienced, men and women, individual and systems-based approaches. A framework explicitly embraces all approaches: it organises care at a meta-level. A good framework serves as a beacon to guide all those taking part in the process of helping a client.

A framework also gives a client a text—if possible, a new text. That means that the framework has to be articulated. It also means that the client and his or her relatives—the larger system—must be able to recognise themselves in the framework: only an affirmative response from them will make the framework viable. The team offers this viable text, this narrative, to the client. The narrative may be communicated in the form of a poem, a song, a symbol, part of a comic strip, a slogan, or a story. Once the client has signalled his or her recognition of this narrative, there is a shared home base. Then the cycle—what I call the narrative cycle—is complete, and the lines of the frame will meet.

Making this framework is a therapeutic skill, which is not linked to any specific school of psychotherapy.

### Developing a therapeutic framework: basic principles

In devising a therapeutic framework, a number of practical principles may be distinguished.

### The principle of the team as therapeutic medium: multiple stories about reality

The patient's complaint makes its way into therapeutic teams by way of the individual team members: each team member will be sensitive to certain aspects of the patient's complaint because of their own life history. Each team member will link a story of their own to the patient's story. This linked story is a "small truth" (Lyotard, 1984). In most therapy teams, the story with the largest number of "votes", the strongest story, is elevated to the "big truth". The result is that the patient's complaint is replicated in the different positions adopted by the team members and as such is recreated.

This process of replication can be illuminated using the metaphor of a viral infection. A virus invades a host organism and forces it to replicate its material. In this case, the patient's complaint, a particular array of symptoms, "blows over", as it were, to the group of carers and, finding a seedbed there, takes root. It introduces a code into the team that makes the phenomena tangible: the team, or individual therapists, also become "sick", develop the same "symptoms". The atmosphere surrounding the symptoms and the language and text used to talk about it are all reinscribed and replicated, producing a chorus of voices, a multiplicity of positions, a mix of emotions. Experience teaches us that after a certain incubation time, the patient's symptoms communicate themselves with great precision, manifesting themselves in the form of depression, psychosomatic ailments, secrets, taboos, fears, and quarrels. The team, which does not, in the manner of an immune system, recognise the virus, becomes "sick". The sickness may be expressed in protracted, destructive team conflicts, in struggles between different schools or approaches, in coalition-forming with the development of majority and minority views, dominant and dissenting stories, or even more literally, in the form of sickness absenteeism.

When this sickness arises within the team, it is often tackled using the same medicine as that used on the patient! That is, certain team members are put under pressure and certain themes suppressed, people are silenced, requests are issued for supervision or peer review, procedures and rules are put in place, and so on. The bottom line here is the denial of the right of difference, the right to allow a different voice to be heard, one that is not in harmony with the tone of the moment. Just as in the patient's family a dominant story has arisen, from which the family suffers, a dominant story arises in the team, which becomes a source of suffering for the team. The malaise is often blamed on the way a particular team member functions, or the way the team as a whole functions. If this process is analysed using the metaphor of the viral infection, the replication process can instead become illuminating and actually facilitate progress. It can enable an in-depth, lively, sensitive contact with what takes place in the family—empathic contact that resonates physically.

*The principle of slowness*

The writer Milan Kundera writes in his novel *Slowness* about the wisdom of slowness and the technique of retardation: imposing form on a period of time is essential not just to beauty, but also to memory. "For what is formless cannot be grasped, or committed to memory". Kundera adds "There is a secret bond between slowness and memory, between speed and forgetting…. The degree of slowness is directly proportional to the intensity of memory; the degree of speed is directly proportional to the intensity of forgetting" (Kundera, 1996, pp. 38–39).

It will be clear that nomadic thought processes in a team also call for a certain slowing down. Unconscious thought processes do not proceed slowly by definition, but they do require more time than rational thought. Slow does not necessarily mean ponderous—on the contrary, a certain light-footedness may be apt. Still, there needs to be time to roam, time perhaps for serendipitous discoveries—time for the undirected, creative mental activity that can culminate in a form, a theme, a narrative.

Kundera again:

> Time became a mere obstacle to life, an obstacle that had to be overcome by ever greater speed. … In the world of highways, a beautiful landscape means: an island of beauty connected by a long line with other islands of beauty. In the world of paths, beauty is continuous and constantly changing: it tells us at every step: "Stop". (Kundera, 1991, p. 223)

The team too may take this message to heart: "Stop! Slow down, and wait for the associative ideas, the details from the landscape of the text and the images that surface, the language of the body, the wisdom of the now". This is very different from a route that is wholly determined by the destination. In that case, the journey is defined in relation to that goal, and the journey's value is a derivative of the value of the destination. This is a linear mode of thought like Toon Tellegen's swan, "whose thoughts were always majestic, as if striding down long avenues, with occasional, scheduled nods at old memories" (Tellegen, 1990). The swan wants to learn how to flap its wings, and asks the butterfly to explain, since it has no idea how the thing is done:

> "But it's quite simple," said the butterfly.
> He fluttered around the swan a little before coming to rest atop a blade of grass.
> The swan's head sank into his feathers, and he looked gloomily down at the ground.
> "You have to start by letting your thoughts flutter about, swan," said the butterfly. "Only then can you do it yourself."
> The swan fell silent, unsure whether he was going to be angry or sad or cold.
> "Look," said the butterfly, "you think of honey, mmmm yummy honey, and from there you think of the bark of a tree, and then of a hippo, and duckweed, sand, scissors, roses, it doesn't

matter what you think of, as long as you think of something else straight away when you think of something."

And as the swan practises, gaps open up in his thoughts.

In the team as therapeutic medium, slowness is valued. However, the truth of the proverb "more haste, less speed" is often borne out: a slow beginning may well expedite and deepen the process further down the line. So during the initial discussions of the patient's factual details, the team takes its time. The aim is to create ample room for spontaneous ideas, unfocused thought, and contemplation, in order to widen the gaze. This period may vary in length, depending on the circumstances, but the process is never rushed.

### *The principle of reality as narrated reality*

There is room to value multiple stories about reality, including making room for, and appreciating, narrative knowledge—that is, physical sensations, associations, fantasies, daydreams, and whatever images may come to the fore. The atmosphere that arises in the team discussions also receives attention. It may be oppressive or light-hearted, grave or humorous. Sometimes people find themselves laughing at moments that seem inappropriate, jokes are told that arouse resistance in others. All this is part of the process and is taken on board as information about what takes place in the patient's system. The atmosphere is not declared taboo, but allowed to be present.

### *The principle of losing one's way*

Susanna Tamaro says that when telling a story she often strays from the main path, taking small side paths and giving the impression that she has lost her way. Or not an impression, she *does* lose her way, but it is precisely in doing so that she finds the centre of things:

> And later on, when so many roads open up before you, you don't know which to take, don't pick one at random; sit down and wait. Breathe deeply, trustingly, the way you breathed on the day when you came into the world, don't let anything distract you, wait and wait some more. Stay still, be quiet, and listen to your heart. Then, when it speaks, get up and go where it takes you. (Tamaro, 1995, p. 204)

Losing one's way forges new interfaces and connections. During that straying, that hopeful waiting, we become receptive to details and to "the aesthetics of serendipity" (Okri, 1997). Losing one's way, then, is a consciousness with which we can open ourselves up, so that we are receptive to other impulses that swim up from the depths to the surface.

### *The principle of humility*

There is an old Indian saying: "Do not judge a man until you have walked a mile in his moccasins". This principle militates against accepting an all-powerful signifier. Rather than allowing some impersonal agency to judge and diagnose from a distance, therapists need to listen to the story related by the patient and attune themselves to it.

> Seen from the outside, many people's lives seem flawed, irrational, even mad. If we look no deeper than the surface, it is easy to misunderstand people and their relationships. Only by looking below the surface, by walking in their moccasins for three months, can we hope to understand their motives, their feelings, what makes them act one way rather than another. Understanding comes from humility, not the pride of knowledge. (Tamaro, 1995, p. 141)

### The principle of waiting

In a speech given by Václav Havel in 1992, as president of the Czech Republic, Havel discusses different kinds of waiting. He begins with Samuel Beckett's play *Waiting for Godot*, symbolic of a waiting without hope, since those who wait endlessly for Godot are bound to be disappointed; Godot will not come, because he does not exist. Here, waiting acquires an absurdist quality. Godot is a mere surrogate of hope. Conjured up by our impotence, he embodies not hope but an illusion—the expectations of people without hope. The characters cannot jettison their expectations, "because without hope a meaningful life is impossible". So they wait for Godot, from whom they expect some ill-defined form of salvation.

Havel's second category is waiting for time to pass: waiting for a bus or train, or a delayed plane, or being caught in a traffic jam. Waiting for a shift to end, a shop to open, an alarm clock to go off, or for a lover's return. Waiting in patience that may eventually wear thin. Minutes, hours, days dissolve in time. This waiting for a specific purpose, the fulfilment of a desire, is ruled by Chronos, the Greek god of time. It refers to linear time, a path from A to B. Waiting can lead to the frustration born of powerlessness. Those who are waiting—in captivity—are expected to resign themselves to the dominion of waiting, whether they are in a draughty bus shelter, standing in line, or waiting for a promised telephone call or the verdict that will change their life.

Then there is the kind of waiting that is expectation, as in a pregnancy. This rests on the knowledge that the waiting will result, if all goes well, in the birth of a living child: a hope and waiting outside time and space, in the knowledge that the process is intrinsic and inherently good. This waiting, the waiting of expectation, is governed by Kairos, the Greek god of the right or opportune moment. It is an exercise in patience.

Havel also refers in his speech to life in a totalitarian system, in which speech and writing are censored, and people are "surrounded, enclosed, colonised from within"—what he calls a "dissident's kind of waiting"—and he recalls:

> [This kind of waiting was] based on the knowledge that it made sense to resist on principle by speaking the truth simply because it was the right thing to do, without speculating whether it would lead somewhere tomorrow, or the day after, or ever. This kind of waiting grew out of the faith that repeating this defiant truth made sense in itself, regardless of whether it was ever appreciated … [A] seed once sown would one day take root and send forth a shoot. No one knew when. But it would happen someday, perhaps for future generations. (Havel, 1992)

Unlike waiting for Godot, which is delusional and time-wasting, this other kind of waiting is "a state of hope" that *does* have meaning.

*Hope*

Deep in ourselves we carry hope;
if that is not the case,
there is no hope.

Hope is a quality of the soul,
and does not depend
on what happens in the world.
Hope is not to foretell or foresee.
It is a directedness of the mind,
a directedness of the heart,
anchored beyond the horizon.

Hope
in this deep and powerful meaning
is not the same as happiness
because all goes well,
or readiness to devote yourself
to that which has success.

Hope is to work for something
because it is good,
and not only because it has a chance to succeed.
Hope is not the same as optimism
neither is it the conviction
that something will end well.
Rather it is the certainty that something is meaningful,
irrespective of the outcome,
the result.

*Václav Havel*

Waiting/expectation takes place in the *subject–object–free space*. In this space, the depth of the therapeutic relationship is created. It is in this space that creative ideas and serendipitous discoveries may come to light.

## The principle of aesthetic standards

A therapeutic framework must comply with aesthetic standards; it needs to possess a certain elegance. This means it has to have a certain air of excitement about it, an invitation to join a quest. The framework must also be geared towards empathic sharing, cooperation, and love. Rejecting any combative or competitive gambits, the framework will focus on preserving peace within a disrupted context.

The framework organises the therapy at a meta-level: it connects different disciplines and gives actions direction and meaning. This means that any rivalry between disciplines is transcended—or exploited as mimesis. Diverse care workers can operate in different contexts and places in multidisciplinary teams within a single cohesive framework.

### *Developing a therapeutic framework: methodology*

Let us discuss the construction of a framework by looking at some examples. We shall see how team members can draw on a wealth of information and on different narrative lines and significances to construct a viable theme, a home base for nomadic thought. They move in the zigzag patterns of narrative thought, going back and forth between the imaginative, nomadic processing of the material and the order and structure of the thematic home base. While nomadic thought is free to travel, finding space, freedom and pleasure, passion and adventure, the framework provides a temporary home base, leading to a "game plan". Adopting a sporting metaphor, the therapeutic context is the team formation and the framework sets out the game plan in terms of strategy and tactics: all directed at a "vanishing point", which is winning the match.

Some readers may wonder where the subject of diagnostics fits into the framework. The fact that they have not been mentioned yet should certainly not be taken to imply that diagnostics are unimportant; quite the contrary. In the framework, diagnostics are inscribed by the team working as a therapeutic medium, and each diagnosis essentially becomes a diagnosis with a different story. If the term narcissism is mentioned, the team members embark on a "journey" through narcissism, complete with travel journal. Narcissism leads to the story of Narcissus, and from there to a mirror, to water, a flower, reflection, and emptiness: in this way, this is thought undertaking a journey. The team proceeds on the assumption that every depression will have similarities to other depressions, but will nonetheless have its own story to tell.

Looking at the four linear segments that make up a frame, the first—let us say the left-hand segment—is the world of the narrated facts:

> The narrative of the facts develops at registration and in the initial intake sessions. Here, the therapist needs the skill of "joining", of incorporating the client's use of language, moving within the same linguistic domain. This includes picking up and echoing keywords, sayings, key metaphors, and so on. It means paying attention to details and what appear to be chance events: the adventure of meeting and discovery. In football terms, we may say that the work in this segment involves the skills required to "put the ball into play".

Once the ball has been put in play, it has to be passed to the midfield. In therapy, this means attaching apt significance to the patient's symptoms. Apt significance possesses added value. After all, the mere adoption of the narrated facts is a repetition of the dominant problem story. So at this stage, a therapist needs the skills to place the symptoms in a significant context, to make them part of a story. The diagnostics that occur here also need to be part of a story. This is the transitional work of moving from the first to the second segment of the frame. They are linked by words of causality, such as "consequently", and "therefore". When these connections have been established, together with the patient, the ball has moved towards the midfield.

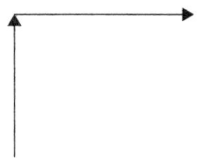

In this second segment, the work focuses on organising the perspectives, which naturally differ and often conflict. The facts acquire a different significance: for instance, they are revealed as solutions that were once crucial to survival. The midfield play is about possession, a game plan. Everyone needs to be in the right position, to avoid obstructions.

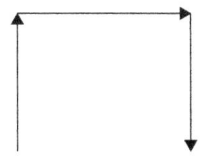

Then comes the work of going from the second to the third segment. In this midfield section, the group's structure and organisation are crucial. Everyone must have a plan. The interpretation, which must provide added value and open up new perspectives, leads to the third segment: the proposal for treatment. This connection is made with words such as "and so we are going to" and "so it is necessary for you to" and "therefore the treatment will focus on", and "therefore everyone will need to contribute to". At the end of the third segment, once the patient has agreed to the interpretation, the focus shifts to the fourth segment and the start of therapy. In football terms, play shifts from a well-organised midfield to the "attack".

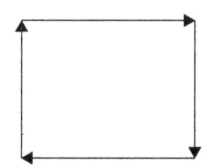

As treatment gets under way, each person plays a role within the organisation, and all activities take place within the agreed framework or contract. The aim now is to move in the direction of the "vanishing point". This is expressed with words such as "when we have achieved that".

The next stage is to discuss the line along which the symptoms will disappear. We can imagine this line as leading from the bottom left into the distance. "Scoring a goal" is a metaphor for the reduction of the complaints, and "winning the match" for the successful completion of therapy: there are only winners here: it is the symptoms or complaints that have been defeated.

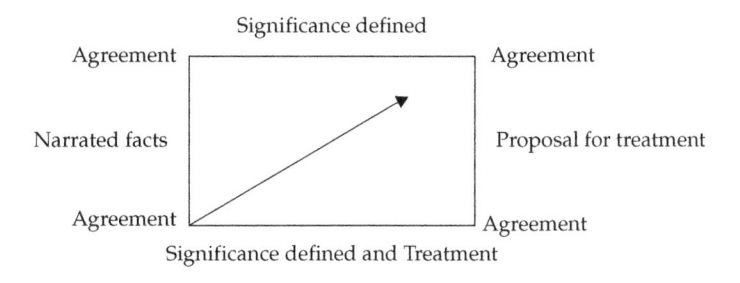

```
                    Significance defined
        Agreement ┌──────────────────────┐ Agreement
                  │                      │
                  │                   ↗  │
   Narrated facts │                ↗     │ Proposal for treatment
                  │             ↗        │
                  │          ↗           │
        Agreement └──────────────────────┘ Agreement
                  Significance defined and Treatment
```

This is the basic structure of a therapeutic framework. It will be clear that working within a framework will not always involve linear, forward movement. Just as the ball may be played back from strikers to midfield or from midfield to defence or the goalkeeper to allow for repositioning, care professionals too will sometimes need to regroup. It may be necessary to modify the interpretation, or the proposed treatment on the basis of new information or experience. Ideally, it should still always be clear what stage of the process one is in, and in which segment. Turning the corner, transitioning to the next segment of the frame, needs the agreement of everyone involved.

The following pages will examine the method on the basis of an example. This case history shows the making of a framework in action, and clarifies the method of organising the context so as to make it therapeutic. My thanks are due here to the care professionals who were involved: the systems therapist Carla Snethorst, the child psychiatrist Yves Serdobbel, the care workers at the outpatient clinic, and the staff of the counselling services, whose tasks included keeping in contact with the patient's school.

*Jeremy: healing a relationship*

A consultation was requested to discuss the stagnation in the therapy provided to seven-year-old Jeremy and his mother, Surina. Jeremy was referred for attachment disorder, behavioural problems, temper tantrums, and absentmindedness—wool-gathering and forgetfulness. His mother said: "I say something to him, and two seconds later he has forgotten what I said."

The mother related the family's history. Jeremy's birth had been traumatic and the connection with the father tenuous. The parents had met in Africa, while Surina was employed as an aid worker, and the father had since returned to the African country of his origin, and was living there with his new family. The care workers knew little more than this about the family's history. The care workers' attempts to provide help in the home situation were floundering, since they had been unable to forge a constructive therapeutic relationship with the mother. The treatment at the outpatient clinic had also stagnated. The child psychiatrists were unable to make a clear diagnosis of Jeremy's problem. We therefore decided as a team to start the consultation by focusing on forging a relationship with the mother, Surina. We asked her to tell us a little more about the history of her family and her relationship with Africa.

Surina started by giving more details about Jeremy's traumatic birth, which had been by caesarean section. The newborn baby could not breathe independently and was placed on a ventilator. Jeremy was born with a life-threatening transposition of the great arteries. He was immediately transferred to a paediatric unit, and a few hours later he underwent surgery for the first time to save his life. Surina too was ill, and was also transferred to hospital. She did not even see her son for the first twelve hours, and even then it was a moment of possible farewell, surrounded by medics waiting to operate; the baby's breathing was laboured and his life hung in the balance. "Lying there in bed, with him beside me: our contact lasted just thirty seconds." A second operation followed, and then a third, with open heart surgery: without intervention he would certainly die. He eventually came round and started breathing for himself, but the prolonged separation between mother and child was a gaping hole at the centre of their relationship.

They had brought a photograph album documenting Jeremy's life. Many of the photos showed a tiny baby in intensive care, linked up to a mass of tubes. Surina spoke of the terrible pain Jeremy had suffered, and the possible brain damage. Attentively, they leafed through the album. Jeremy pointed to significant relatives: grandparents, uncles and aunts, cousins, who all visited him in hospital.

Summing up, Jeremy had been born by caesarean section, and mother and child had been separated immediately, since Surina too was very ill. We define this separation as a gap in the centre of the relationship—a gaping hole between mother and child, who was unreachable, submerged beneath tubes and instruments.

The subject shifted to African cultures and traditions. Surina explained that Jeremy was born in a country where the care of infants was always women's work; babies were carried on the back of the mother or grandmother, a sister, aunt, or cousin. Fathers played no role until it was clear that the child was completely healthy. This explained why Jeremy's father seldom saw his son and did not play a significant role while the child was in hospital. Furthermore, a sick child was not seen as a source of pride in that culture, which tended to blame the sickness on the mother. So there was also a gap in the relationship between Jeremy and his father.

Surina dwelt on Jeremy's sensory deprivation. From birth, he had smelled people before deciding whether to trust them. Surina explained this by pointing out that he had never had the familiar scent of his parents, his home. Although he received excellent care, the nurses handled him with strange hands and could not help hurting him, with the plethora of injections and drips.

We took the first steps towards developing a framework. Besides photos, Surina had brought cards sent by well-wishers after Jeremy's birth. I asked them to together select a card that went with the image of that tiny sleeping baby. Finding a card with a sleeping baby, they looked at it together. The next thing was to find the third element that could bind them. At seven, Jeremy felt secure in the knowledge of who his parents were. The mother of seven years ago and her tiny baby had lost each other. The little baby depicted on the card and in the photos had lost his way in his sleep. Searching in vain for his mother, he lived in a no-man's land, a hole in his existence—a hole into which everything disappeared.

We placed the card on a chair in a corner in the room, with the chair facing away from Surina and Jeremy. The distance was vast. All the way over there, almost invisible, was that tiny baby. That child had to be brought home; he needed to feel his mother's hands and to smell her body. The father's smell and his departure from the family would need to be discussed in later sessions. First, mother and son. Together they fetched the card, and I asked them to place it in between their bellies. This third element could now speak, and bridge the gap in their relationship. I lowered my voice and carried them along in a story:

> If you rock gently back and forth together, perhaps quietly humming a little tune, you can imagine yourselves, mother and son, very carefully closing that gap, weaving it shut. The gap between that tiny baby and the Jeremy of today, and the gap between the mother of the past and the mother of today, and the gap between the two of you.

In an atmosphere full of intense emotion, the two sat in silence, gently rocking back and forth. I asked them to repeat this ritual at bedtime for the time being: "this will weave threads from one belly to the other, closing the gap".

Surina also talked about Jeremy's insomnia, and the daily struggle she waged to get him to sleep in his own bed. When she mentioned that African children sleep with their mother until they feel ready to sleep alone, we decided that it might be important to preserve this ritual for now. If Jeremy slept in his mother's bed, it could help to redress his mother's absence at the beginning of his life. This meant that sleeping acquired new significance: an African ritual to make up for past deprivation and to help him grow. When he was ready, he would move to his own bed of his own accord.

To place this story in a frame with four segments and a vanishing point, we proceeded as follows: the first segment, containing the world of the narrated facts, carefully preserved the words and expressions used. For Jeremy these were:

- he had been born by caesarean section;
- he had had three operations as a baby;
- he had been ventilated in intensive care. His life had been saved by numerous medical interventions that had been extremely painful;
- he had been separated from his mother in a period of crucial importance to mother–child bonding;
- his father was also absent in that period.

The second segment, organising the perspectives and defining significance, in this case highlighted the gap in the mother–son relationship. It was reached by the following logic (turning the corner from the first to second segments):

- it was *because of* the early hospitalisation and painful procedures that a gap had arisen;
- Jeremy was forgetful *because* he lost his way as a baby in a no-man's land; *because* that baby got lost;
- it was *because* he had so missed his mother in that crucial early period that he now wanted to sleep beside her;
- he had gone through so much pain that every problem he encountered in life reminded him of that pain. He experienced a rising rage that he was unable to restrain;
- this mechanism *explained* his temper tantrums.

Once both Jeremy and Surina had agreed to this significance, we had turned the corner to the second segment.

The second segment involved the story of attaching significance to the gap in the relationship that would help to shape a proposal for treatment. A gap had arisen between Jeremy and his mother, between the mother then and the mother now, between the baby then and the seven-year-old son now. *Therefore* this gap had to be closed. I explained:

*That is why* we propose that you go through this ritual every evening at bed time. You place the card between your bellies. Jeremy, you sit on your mother's lap, and the two of you will rock gently back and forth, softly humming a lullaby. Then you will go to sleep in your mother's bed. You will feel at home there and will be aware of your mother's familiar smell. That tiny child will know that he is totally safe at night and will feel at home. In this way, that child will gradually find "his way home", a little more each night, and the gap will slowly be woven over and closed.

Once both had agreed, we turned the corner to the third segment, on the way to the fourth. I said:

And if you carry on doing this for a while, the gap will get smaller and smaller. Then you, Jeremy, will feel more and more at home and will not need to wander about any more. When that happens, you will no longer need to forget, because you will know where you are. That tiny child who got stuck in time can start growing again and be part of you again. Then, as you work together, the symptoms will disappear by themselves. When you're ready for it, you'll go and sleep in your own bed again.

We used nesting dolls to depict the gap between the baby, a tiny doll, and seven-year-old Jeremy, represented by a larger doll. And the dolls in between illustrated the process of growth. We also chose two chairs: one for the seven year old, and one for little Jeremy, who often behaved like a child of three or four—midway between birth and seven.

I asked Jeremy when he thought the gap would be closed and he could sit on the big chair.

"When I'm nine," he said.

That was about fifteen months away, and sounded realistic.

In this way we turned the corner to the fourth segment, treatment. The vanishing point was "When I'm nine." This phrase and "the gap will be closed" acquired magnetic appeal. From then on, all assistance and therapy would take place in this framework.

I occasionally saw Jeremy over the next eighteen months and was struck by his growth. Although there was a temporary regression when he had to deal with his disappointment at his father's indifference, the therapy, within the framework described above, enabled him to heal the damage done when he was a baby, and I was pleased to see him as a nine year old confidently sitting on the big chair.

It will be clear that many hurdles had to be overcome and many knots untied in providing help to this family. Several staff members worked hard: reacting to crisis situations, meeting with teachers at Jeremy's school, and dealing with the painful contacts with the father, who disappointed Jeremy again and again, constantly failing to keep his promises. Jeremy often waited in anxious anticipation for a phone call that never came. He spent months looking forward to his father's visit, which was cancelled at the last minute.

When his father happened to be in the Netherlands, we set up a meeting at which Jeremy had a chance to ask his burning questions, which he had prepared carefully beforehand. He decided to meet his father without his mother's supportive presence; he was older and more emotionally mature by then. At this meeting, the father said that he could not, and did not want to, play any significant role in Jeremy's life. He had a new family. So there was another gap, between Jeremy here and his father in Africa.

Jeremy was deeply disappointed in his father and went through a severe relapse in the period after this meeting. He vented his frustration on his mother, who found him unmanageable. At the same time, he allowed his mother to hold him lovingly in this period. His father had told Jeremy emphatically that he was glad that his mother took good care of him.

With a great deal of help, Jeremy managed to overcome his relapse, and by nine years of age he had become an integrated individual. When the above report was presented to Surina for her approval, she wrote:

Going through this therapy was a very positive but intense period. The gap was not just on Jeremy's side, but on mine too. As I sat cuddling and comforting the "lonely baby", I was able to really enjoy our closeness together, a closeness untainted by fear of losing him or anger at his behaviour. Those were very pure moments, in all their simplicity. During the day I would look forward to those bedtimes, to those times of real intimacy. A little boy who is seven or eight years old, and is aware of what he missed and who is now making up for it by drinking it in, that closeness. It gave me the feeling—for the first time—that I could do something constructive to help towards his recovery. All the parental advice I'd received seemed beside the point. The cuddling was not just pleasurable in itself, but it also gave me a better understanding of the situation that had developed, which helped me to understand his behaviour and to deal with it better. You react differently to a child of three from one of seven. Now that I could treat him like a three-year-old, he was more open to me, I had more patience, and at the same time I had the opportunity to help the seven year old to grow. It was wonderful to gain insight into all that, with the aid of the nesting dolls.

Recapitulating: in the therapeutic framework, the first segment of the frame contains the narrated facts; the second segment consists of attributing new significance, with added value and new possibilities; the third segment is the proposal for treatment; the fourth segment is the treatment itself, which leads to a vanishing point.

### *Eduard and the erased memory (in collaboration with Rudolf Ponds)*

Eduard, a forty-five-year-old former truck driver, was referred to the outpatients' memory clinic at a teaching hospital, having developed a severe memory disorder after a relatively minor cerebral haemorrhage. Extensive neurological and neuropsychological tests had failed to identify the cause. Eduard had forgotten *everything*: he only remembered the events of the past two days, and all elementary skills—from how to swim and ride a bike to how to count past three—had evaporated, as if his entire memory disk had been formatted. The cerebral haemorrhage could not be the cause. Eduard could no longer find his way, literally or figuratively. He got lost in his own village, unable to recognise once-familiar landmarks; he had lost all sense of direction, and his identity seemed to have been almost obliterated.

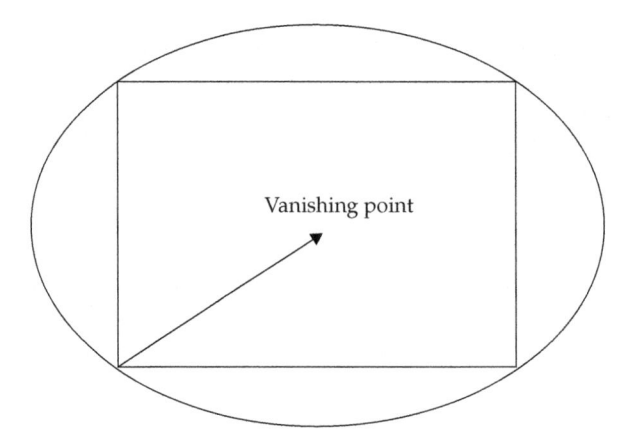

Figure 16. The circle around the framework is the therapeutic context.

Yet tests revealed a strange anomaly: in answering questions with only two possible answers, almost all Eduard's answers were wrong. Someone with memory loss might be expected to choose equal numbers of right and wrong answers. Only someone who knows the right answers can get all the answers wrong. The attending psychologist, Rudolf Ponds, provisionally diagnosed a dissociative disorder or an extremely rare condition known as a conversion disorder: neurological symptoms without a definable organic cause.

Asked to attend as a consultant, I reflected on the possible causes and story underlying this puzzle. At first, no causative factors suggested themselves. The case history described the traumatic stress suffered by Eduard and his wife in the period surrounding his cerebral haemorrhage. The initial symptoms had terrified Eduard. Taken to A & E, he was forced to wait for hours while more urgent cases were dealt with. He felt abandoned, afflicted by pain, physical sensations, and numbness that filled him with dread. In spite of his wife's repeated entreaties, it was a long time before he received the necessary care and attention.

By the time I saw him, Eduard had lived with this memory loss for a year. His wife, children and friends had acclimatised, and had become his essential support system—his compass and his map. All the voices in the family rejected the diagnosis "conversion disorder": everyone remained convinced of a somatic cause. They urged further neurological tests, which were therefore repeated in minute detail.

I reached the conclusion that any possible framework must provide an elegant solution: one that inscribed the conversion disorder without leading to a loss of face. At length, I spoke to Eduard and his wife about the scope for drawing up a framework for therapy. The following is a brief summary of this initial proposal.

> You went through a terrifying experience. Your subconscious might well have been forced to eradicate all recollection of this terrifying event, and ended up erasing your identity, to prevent all recollection of that dark night. Still, your identity was not completely erased: tiny fragments occasionally appear and disappear. It seems to have remained intact, under a bell jar, like information saved on a hard disk without the necessary software to access it. A living identity is still there, beneath the bell jar.

I then said that treatment meant going back through that dark night. Given the existential terrors associated with it, the subconscious would understandably resist any attempt to relive that terror. I said:

> Only one motive might be strong enough: your love for your wife and children. It would require a heroic effort to relive that dark night, and this is a hard thing to contemplate. Truly, only the courage and determination of a hero could suffice. Then, if pieces of your memory were to return, it would constitute the proof for your wife and children, your friends and relatives, that you have displayed that heroic bravery. It is therefore essential to think things through carefully, together and with the children, to decide whether it is right for you to be encouraged to make this extreme, heroic effort.

I explained that for me, as the therapist, this was what needed to happen if there was to be an opening for treatment. I added that I was very hesitant to make this proposal. I urged them to think and discuss the matter carefully before making a decision, and then to call me.

This narrative suggested an interpretation and new significance for the erased memory. Given the absence of any neurological explanation, Eduard would not be able to spontaneously regain his memory without such a shift in significance.

*First segment of frame: the narrated facts*

- The cerebral haemorrhage
- The frightening wait at the hospital
- The lack of empathy of hospital staff
- The pain and fear

*Second segment*

The second segment consisted of the interpretation that the loss of memory was a protective measure undertaken by the subconscious in response to mortal terror. The subconscious had erased everything, starting with the terrifying experience, but leaving Eduard's identity intact under a "bell jar". The bell was a new element in the story. An organic image of a method for preserving food, it served as a metaphor for the preservation of Eduard's memory somewhere in his subconscious.

*Third segment*

To turn the corner to the third segment, a proposal for therapy was needed. This would involve revisiting that terror—a daunting proposal that was not easy to contemplate. The only legitimate motive to go through that experience would be to do it for love of his wife and children. To choose this path would be truly heroic; it would be perfectly understandable if he did not feel able to undertake such a hazardous journey.

Once Eduard and his wife subscribed to this interpretation, we had arrived in the third segment. Their explicit endorsement was vital. Many voices in their surroundings continued to urge further tests, and there was considerable dissatisfaction with the lack of concrete findings. Now, each new piece of memory that resurfaced in the course of therapy would prove Eduard's heroism. This provided an elegant solution, making improvement possible. The framework also provided significance retroactively, explaining the "point" of erasing the memory. To make the context therapeutic, all those involved were invited to the consultations and asked to cooperate.

Two weeks later, Eduard's wife called to say that they wanted to pursue this path. When I asked them to summarise the proposed framework, they were able to express it well. Given the great discrepancies in the ecology of voices, and the importance of agreeing a common definition of the problem and the road towards the solution, and placing every improvement in the perspective of the "hero's path", the framework was described in detail on paper, together with Eduard and his wife. This description became a document for the entire family, and the therapy could begin: the hero's path.

*Fourth segment*

Once the family was on board, we had arrived in the fourth segment of the frame. Hypnosis and EMDR (eye movement desensitisation and reprocessing) were proposed, such that Eduard's conscious mind would not have to take part in this journey through the dark night. Using hypnosis and EMDR, the subconscious was encouraged to gradually clear a path through the darkness, taking over pieces of empty space, so that the memory would be able to return, one piece at a time. When we started with the eye movements, his eyes flickered some six times before closing. Behind his closed eyelids, the eyeballs rotated at immense speed. This response was defined out loud as a massive exertion on the part of the subconscious, to get through the dark night at breakneck speed. The suggestion was made to the subconscious that the eyes would eventually come to rest and open of their own accord.

The reaction was positive: Eduard's eyes came to rest and opened after a few minutes. He was tired and dizzy. It was suggested to him that his immense effort had perhaps won back pieces of his memory; time would tell.

Ten sessions later, Eduard's wife informed me that he was more cheerful, his mood had lifted, and the weekly headaches, which caused bodily malfunctions and dizziness, appeared to have ceased. She stated that Eduard was showing a greater interest in his surroundings, talking to his children, asking questions, and becoming once again the warm and affectionate father he had been before.

Eduard's memory returned one small piece at a time, almost imperceptibly. His everyday skills also started to return, and Eduard learned to use household aids, thanks to the constant presence of home help. At the moment of writing this book, Eduard had recovered parts of his memory and his independence. The therapy was still in progress.

## The vanishing point and the magnet or "attractor"

A good therapeutic framework has lines of flight leading to a vanishing point, where the symptoms may disappear. Once this point—a moment in the future—has been defined, it serves as a magnet for all subsequent actions. Once the subconscious has formed an image of this point, it has a vision of the future towards which all actions can be directed. All that remains is to organise all therapeutic activities in the direction of this magnet.

*The boy with the blue heart*

Kuipers and Olthof (Kuipers & Olthof, 2005) give an example of an effective therapeutic framework with a clear vanishing point in the treatment of a nine-year-old boy struck by insuperable grief following his mother's sudden death, a few years earlier. He seldom spoke, and when he did his voice was almost inaudible. The therapist, Paulien Kuipers, asked the boy where his grief lived. He drew a black heart in his body. When they enlarged the heart together, he drew a red heart with a large black blot in the middle, symbolising the grief-that-could-not-be spoken.

Together they formulated a framework for therapy: once he could speak about his sadness and was able to cry, the black would vanish from his heart, his voice would grow in strength, and he would be able to feel his mother's love—which was given the colour sky blue—in his heart. After each session in which he was able to speak about his life and his mother, could allow his sadness to express itself and make drawings about his former life, he would be able to add more blue to his heart; the black would gradually disappear. The vanishing point, the goal in the healing process, was clearly defined: the complaint would vanish once his whole heart was coloured blue. Then, his mother's love would live in his heart forever, and he would regain his voice.

Each session worked towards "making the heart blue". Sometimes the boy talked a great deal, but the therapist was surprised to see that little had changed: there was only a tiny bit more blue. At other times he said little, but the session acquired great significance for him and he coloured in a large section of blue in the heart. The boy was a full participant in the therapy, with autonomy and his own judgement as to how much black had been erased and how much blue added. He possessed expertise in this respect. The framework implied collaboration towards a common goal, coordinated movement in action. "Winning the match" would mean that he would regain his voice. Through this close partnership, the problem was defeated: in this "match", all participants were winners!

### Off-screen

When reflecting on frameworks for therapy, film too can prove an inspiration. Joost Raessens (Raessens, 2001) discusses the work of Deleuze in the realm of film, which has terminology such as editing or "montage", "framing", and "off-screen".

Films are edited: from the multiplicity of images and shots, a certain sequence is chosen. Images are placed one after another in a particular order: perspective and narrative lines converge in the arrangement that has been created. Editing is an art, and numerous arrangements can be made from the same multiple images. In the same way, a psychotherapist chooses certain images, stylises a logical context or "montage" from the multiple narratives. Many images and stories are omitted, and end up outside the film.

Following Deleuze, Raessens explains "framing" as defining a relatively closed system that contains everything that is present in the image, in terms of setting, characters, and props. Only "relatively" closed because it stands in relation to what is "off-screen"—elements that are not in that system but are present and belong to the filmic space (Raessens, 2001, p. 61). This gives rise to a split between the world within the frame and the world outside it—the wider field connects them. Whatever falls outside the frame is not seen, but is nonetheless present. It represents the trans-spatial, in which the spirit of the large whole is present.

Another concept that Deleuze uses, and that may be useful in relation to frameworks for therapy, is that of an assemblage—a collection. A framework too can be seen as an assemblage—a collection of heterogeneous stories in a framework that has been edited and combined. An assemblage is useful for a particular period, in a certain period, and for a specified purpose.

In an assemblage, items are ordered, organised, juxtaposed. A therapeutic framework too involves ordering and arranging in an organisational structure—an active management process. But this "management" comes from within; it is not imposed from outside. The stories and symptoms that come from the wider family system make up the internal workings of the assemblage. Each assemblage has its own dynamic, a self-organising activity that cannot be reduced to its constituent parts, but comprises the relationships between them (Romein, Schuilenberg & Van Tuinen, 2009). Each link in one of these relationships creates something new.

Romein remarks that when an element is mediated by relationships linking it to others, that element can no longer be said to have a fixed significance (Romein, Schuilenberg & Van Tuinen, 2009, p. 207). Significance is not a fixed entity, but shifts in response to the links that are made between elements. These relationships determine the significance, and the relationships are linked to the context. The properties of the relationship, the elements, do not determine the relationship. The significance shifts with each change of context.

A framework for therapy is not repeatable, and has no permanent form or substance. It is constantly being opened up again by internal or external forces. A framework is a temporary settlement—it proves fruitful for a time, after which a new assemblage is needed. A framework is situated at the boundary between inside and outside, between what is seen and discussed within this framework and what might have been seen and discussed outside it. This means that drawing the four lines of this framework is a creative process, a constant re-creation.

*Health resort*

Elsie faced me, exhausted. I was familiar with her story, since I had been involved with the family's supervision for some time, and had treated her daughter for her severe borderline disorder. By now, her daughter had been an inpatient in a clinic for six months. The time that led up to this admission had been extremely stressful for Elsie, who had been the main butt of her daughter's confrontational behaviour. Still, together with her husband, she had weathered the storm. When her daughter was admitted she could not establish any kind of contact with the care professionals and was not permitted to take any part in the therapy. The daughter avoided all contact with her parents, who often made a long journey for a family session, only to find that their daughter refused to take part or walked out after a few minutes. The therapist did not intervene. This was an exhausting time; Elsie and her husband felt that they were treated with a total lack of respect and decency.

Since then, their daughter had been transferred to a supervised accommodation project. Elsie reported: "She feels at home there. She's doing well now. The care professionals work with us; they consult us about everything and we feel totally involved. Plus they're really helping our daughter to deal with everyday life. Although this is an enormous relief, I feel totally shattered. I can't get myself to do anything. I'm terribly depressed and spend all day crying."

It was clear that given Elsie's depression, the conversation could be organised around the status of "patient": Elsie could be prescribed antidepressants in consultation with the GP and remain on sick leave. But I saw that it would take a long time for her to climb back up again, especially if she was defined as a patient and given medication. I thought Elsie deserved something different, and I had the idea of a health resort.

I put the idea to Elsie. I reminded her that she and her husband, consumed by fear and worry, had exerted themselves to the utmost to keep the family together, and she was only now feeling the devastating effects and exhaustion. At Christmas she had received the best possible gift—a wonderful letter of apology and thanks from her daughter, honouring her for all her efforts.

Now it was her turn. *She* was the one who now needed rest, and the care of others, somewhere good for her body and spirit. Unfortunately, the Dutch health insurance would not pay for such a solution. Still, it would do her the world of good to go away for a while and to be taken care of—with hot baths, good food, walks, swimming, a little sport.

We agreed that I would ask her husband to seek sponsors for this well-deserved holiday. I persuaded her that it was right for her to accept, since she deserved it—a break for a few weeks, in which to acknowledge what a difficult period she had been through.

Elsie was taken aback, but rather pleased, and agreed to the plan. Her husband too reacted with enthusiasm. Within just a few days he had found enough sponsors. He would take her to the health resort they had chosen, in the Czech Republic, and go and fetch her at the end.

When I spoke to Elsie on the phone a few months later, she was elated. Six weeks of the health resort had done her the world of good.

So the framework she had been offered was: "I'm going to ask your husband to get sponsors to ensure that you can spend some time in a health resort."

The significance attached in the second segment of the frame was crucial here. Instead of labelling Elsie as a patient suffering from depression, thus confirming her sense of inadequacy, Elsie was characterised as someone who had done her best and kept afloat in spite of the difficulties and her daughter's accusations—someone who now deserved to be fussed over.

Elsie's agreement to the plan took us to the third segment, within which it made sense for me to ask her husband to organise a fundraising effort. After all, a stay in a health resort is not something the person herself should have to request; it is something offered by others.

Since the family was not well-off, sponsors would have to be found. The hierarchy of significances was respected: as a care professional, I explained my view to Elsie's husband and asked him to organise something special for her.

Once the money had been raised, we had rounded the corner to the fourth segment, and treatment could begin. The context had been made therapeutic, with everyone working in the same direction.

My advice was to ensure that the stay lasted more than a week. Her symptoms were too severe for a short stay. The implicit suggestion was that a few weeks' stay in a health resort—which thus constituted the "treatment" in this case—would reduce or even eliminate her symptoms.

### A fat lot of guilt

The twenty-one-year-old student Tessa came to see me. The young woman sitting before me scarcely fitted in the chair. Her skin looked layered, almost rubbery, and in that rubbery face I saw a frightened little girl, close to despair. She was eligible for gastric bypass surgery, and the hospital had referred her for therapy for morbid obesity and family troubles related to this obesity, which complicated the planned operation.

She told me that she had started gaining weight in puberty, at about fourteen years of age. She believed that her weight had less to do with food than with the constant fierce rows at home. Her parents fought in the bedroom at night, unaware that she was listening, and in the morning she would see her mother's bruises. When she finally dared to tell her mother that she had heard all the rows, her mother started enlisting her support as a witness: from then on, she was in her mother's camp. Her father started ignoring her, just as he ignored her mother, and in order to break the unbearable tension, her mother would eventually insist that Tessa apologise to her father: for what, she did not know. When she eventually did so, having incurred both her parents' wrath, she experienced the apology as a humiliation. By the time she was preparing to go to college, her body had ballooned. She had now been living in a rented room for two years, and things had only got worse.

As I listened to her, I thought of all the expressions that exist containing the words "fat" and "thick": "fat profit", "through thick and thin", "laid on thick", and "thick-skinned", for instance. The Dutch language also has the interesting expression *zich dik maken* (to wind oneself up with excitement or worry, but literally "to make oneself fat").

I pondered this last expression, since Tessa had said that she had begun to gain weight amid extreme family tension. The Dutch linguist Heidi Aalbrecht, reflecting on this expression, remarks (in Aalbrecht, 2008) that feelings such as anger are symbolised by increased body weight, as though these feelings and the behaviour associated with them make the person fatter.

It was clear what Tessa had "made herself fat" about: having been placed in a highly tainted, parentified position, she had tried to help her mother, earning both parents' disapproval as a result.

I made some suggestions concerning when and why she might have "made herself fat":

- As a frightened young girl feeling unsafe at home, hearing such violent rows that her mother was covered in bruises the next day.
- Later, compelled to be strong enough to protect her mother, carrying her, as it were, on her own back.
- When she was forced to act as a buffer, to defuse tension and accept the aggression herself.
- When she had to protect herself.

Through her tears, Tessa said that when I suggested that her obesity might not be wholly attributable to food, it lessened her feelings of guilt. Her father always blamed her, saying she simply ate too much.

"Have the blame and guilt made you fat, then?" I asked. "And if I were to say that it might be about something other than food, would that be a relief?"

She cried, and said that she was crying tears of relief.

Then I said, "Do you know what it means if you can 'make yourself fat'?"

After a few moments of silence, she suggested, "That you can also make yourself thin? Is that possible?" She gazed at me in disbelief.

"If the main problem was not a pattern of unbridled overeating, it might well be possible," I replied.

I had a plan, but before suggesting it I needed more information, I explained, to be sure it was a good idea. Tessa had told me that she was in contact with her grandfather, but not her parents, who wanted her admitted to a psychiatric institution if she continued to avoid contact with them. Although initially torn, after listening to Tessa's side of the story he had decided to protect her and to advise her parents not to seek contact with her for a time. In other words, it appeared that he had adopted her old role as buffer in the family.

I described a situation in which Tessa would be surrounded by people helping her—the doctors, her grandfather, and myself. And when I asked her what it would mean to her if it was suggested that her obesity was not mainly due to unbridled overeating, she said it would mean that more people had confidence in her abilities, and believed in her.

Once the context was clear—a psychotherapist who believed in Tessa, and a grandfather who had taken on the role of buffer, so that Tessa no longer needed to have any contact with her parents—it was time to present my plan. This plan was to be kept "secret" from her parents. Only the helpers I had mentioned and her boyfriend would know about it. The plan was as follows: since she had "made herself fat" in response to conditions that were enormously stressful, she could "make herself thin" in these new improved conditions. Her grandfather would ensure that there was no contact with her parents; there were several other people who believed in her, and the stress factors had been removed. In the six months before the gastric bypass surgery, she would work on this "secret plan" to banish the feelings of guilt as she continued with the diet and fitness programme she had taken up. All this might help her to "make herself thin", and everyone would be amazed. She agreed that it was a good plan, and was sure that her boyfriend would agree.

By the end of the first session, a framework had emerged: Tessa had "made herself fat" with blame and guilt, and she could now "make herself thin" through her own efforts and the assistance of a therapist. This also meant that Tessa would take an active role in the process, rather than being at the mercy of a field of forces that were too great for her.

It was clear that the session had created a solid, clear therapeutic relationship. The context had also been therapeutically organised. The cooperation with the hospital was good. Tessa was on the waiting list for surgery, and would continue making the necessary preparation. Her overweight had been invested with new significance, and there was a new story: the "narrativity of the body". Everyone taking part in the care process shared a common goal. The medical voice—"obesity is a serious health hazard"—and the psychological voice—"the fat was produced by guilt and blame"—harmonised.

The "secret plan" was an attempt to change what was essentially a paradoxical context. As things stood, undergoing surgery would confirm her father's view, and the old feelings of guilt and blame would still be there afterwards. Because of the health risks associated with her obesity, her whole family wanted her to undergo surgery as soon as possible, and any demurral on her part would be taken as proof of her pigheadedness, and the fact that the whole situation was her own fault.

Over the following months, Tessa became stronger, and the operation acquired a different significance for her: as a great help, a useful helping hand to alleviate the conditions of her life. She also now felt that she "owned" the decision to undergo surgery.

Less than twelve months after the operation, Tessa had lost eighty kilos. She was immensely proud of herself. She felt she had got her own life back, and she had given birth to her first child.

### Developmental psychology

Developmental psychology, the psychological age, and the tasks involved in psychological development, provide elegant possibilities for making a constructive therapeutic framework.

Russian nesting dolls or matryoshka dolls are excellent symbols in this context. They stand for the female principle, in that we are all born from a woman: women pass on life. The dolls ascend in size, with each one fitting into the one above. The larger one can be seen as the "meta-level" for the smaller one, so that together they depict the gradual maturing of a human being—growth, maturing, and unfolding. They all have the same basic, expanding structure, and together they form a cohesive whole.

A person's development into a mature, cohesive individual is not a given but a fortunate result. We consist of numerous elements: we are chaotic, polymorphous, polyphonous. Harmony is therefore a resulting state—the "I" is a multiple self (Sermijn, 2008). All the different parts and voices can acquire a place, can be represented, using the nesting dolls. Symptoms can be linked to a particular voice or a certain part of the personality. The dolls can represent different phases of life, from birth and childhood to adulthood and old age. If cohesiveness is the end result, each phase of development can be linked to a particular task. If one of these developmental tasks stalls or falters, if some part is poorly developed, the resulting stagnation may give rise to complaints. Working backwards, a symptom can therefore be traced to a particular time and phase of life; qualities too can be connected to specific phases of life.

The Dutch children's writer Annie M. G. Schmidt once said, "I have an eight-year-old child inside me, and I always remain in contact with her. That little girl from Zeeland grew up in a silent, rigid world. She yearned to read, but her father—the vicar—had bookshelves full of theology and nothing else." It was for that little girl that she wrote her books. (*KRO Magazine*, 20 May 2011, published to mark the 100th anniversary of Annie M. G. Schmidt's birth).

The notion that a person may pass through all developmental phases organically is clearly an ideal. Every existential event disrupts development. Each such event forces us to adjust in ways that may make us stronger, or force us to leave other developmental tasks unfinished.

The following examples illustrate ways of working with themes from developmental psychology, of highlighting stagnation in a person's development and identifying developmental "tasks". The nesting dolls can be an invaluable aid here.

### Madelon

Madelon, aged thirty, sought therapy for severe panic attacks and chronic fatigue syndrome. She told me her story. Although she came from a happy family, her sister, who was disabled, in a vegetative state after medical incompetence, required round-the-clock care. Her parents, consumed by guilt and anger, frequently visited the sister. Madelon accompanied them and helped care for her sister, whom she loved. The family had remained close. Still, the sacrifice had taken its toll on Madelon, who began to experience panic attacks when she went to college. Madelon had set aside her own identity and her own story for her sister's essential care. Using an arrangement of nesting dolls, it became clear which of the dolls—which of the phases in her development—had been left out. The problem was linked to the age of nineteen, when she did not dare to tell her parents that she was floundering and needed their care. Using the dolls, she was able to identify the gap in her development. This was crucial to drawing up a framework for therapy.

### William

When William was twelve, his parents were divorced. His father left, and William became the sole mainstay for his desolate mother. However, at about seventeen years of age, William rebelled. The change in her dear son baffled his mother. William had developed problems with his identity, which become clear only when we see the heavy burden he took on as a young boy. Besides the lack of a happy-go-lucky period of boyhood, he had cut off contact with his father out of loyalty to his mother. Arranging the nesting dolls, he chose a very large doll for the twelve-year-old boy. When I asked him which doll was appropriate for a boy of twelve, he chose a far smaller one. This drove home the distance that needed to be bridged between this smaller doll and the large one.

### Roxanne

Roxanne, age fifteen, was referred for therapy by her GP. So great was her anxiety for surrendering control that by dinner time she was unable to eat, having felt her stomach churning with tension all day. The tension also prevented her from falling asleep at night. Exclusion from her group of friends had exacerbated existing feelings of extreme loneliness. Some of her peers carried out acts of vandalism and burglaries. Although Roxanne did not approve of such activities, she enjoyed the excitement of sneaking out of the house at night and standing guard. The group had eventually kicked her out because of her refusal to drink alcohol or take drugs, which she was afraid would make her sick.

Roxanne's mother accompanied her to the first session. They told the story that was associated with Roxanne's problem. The youngest of three girls, Roxanne had lost her father, to whom she was very close, when she was seven. Her mother had a job, and her father, who was sick and unable to work, had taken care of the children and the household. Roxanne was distraught when her father died. Her mother was always busy: she had to earn enough money to raise the girls. Roxanne had often been left alone, and missed her mother. She was sometimes left with her grandma or the neighbours, or sent to play with friends. Roxanne evidently decided to grow up quickly and take care of herself to help her mother. By the time she was twelve, she did whatever she wanted; her mother no longer had any authority over her. Her mother said that she had always had faith in her daughter. The two still had an open, honest relationship, and Roxanne always spoke frankly to her. The lines of trust had remained open, whatever she got up to.

Roxanne's complaints could be placed in the context of "growing up too fast". I suggested to her that there was still a little girl of seven inside her, who had been unable to keep up with the pace of suddenly having to grow up. The new group that had seemed to offer a new home only made her feel frightened and more alone. Not only did she miss her father, but her elder sisters also moved away. The entire process of growing up was going much too fast, making her feel nauseous from anxiety; she really needed her mother! They related that Roxanne's mother had started taking her daughter to bed with her, stroking her head and belly and doing yoga exercises together. This helped Roxanne to fall into a peaceful sleep.

We worked with the little girl that was symbolised by the teddy bear she always brought with her. Talking to the teddy bear, we bridged the gap that had arisen between the lonely little girl inside and the tough exterior, the Roxanne who had grown up too fast. We talked to the mother and one of the sisters about the rapid changes that had overtaken the family. Roxanne's anxiety gradually diminished.

*The lost place*

Jonathan, a man aged forty-two who had great difficulty committing himself to someone in a relationship, described a period during which he had been seriously ill, at three years of age, and had been admitted to hospital. He still remembered it vividly. No one explained anything and he was utterly confused. He was separated from his parents, who were not allowed to visit him very often, and he felt abandoned. When he returned home, he found that a new baby had been born, who consumed all the family's care and attention. Instead of a warm welcome home after his ordeal, he felt that this new brother had taken his place, and he had lost his close relationship with his parents. That pain and sadness belonging to the three-year-old boy had stayed with him all that time. The little boy had withdrawn and decided not to attach himself to anyone ever again.

His developmental task would be to recapture his place among his siblings. The opportunity arose when his mother fell ill. The children gathered around her, and Jonathan contacted them, re-establishing his place in the family. This enabled him to repair the disrupted attachment he had suffered as a boy. The part of him that had been suspended in time, with its untold story, could now move forward, could develop and flourish.

*Second-rate*

A thirty-year-old man, Frank, came to me for therapy some time after his wife Beth's successful completion of her own therapy. He came to see me because his wife's reinvigoration had renewed her desire for children. They had delayed this unspoken question for a long time, parking it in the domain of not knowing.

Before dealing with his treatment, we need to tell Beth's story. Beth had imbibed the idea, as a child, that she would always be "second-rate". She had loving parents, but as unskilled workers they had trouble understanding her, from the time she went to secondary school. By then she was already feeling stronger than her parents, and she took the decision to make herself smaller, by not using all her powers. She did not want to eclipse her parents. Although she completed grammar school and later graduated from university, she always felt anxious and insecure. She often felt listless and suffered from depression—something that continued in her marriage.

The girl who had decided at the age of twelve to remain "second-rate" was a part of her that had been suspended in time. At work, she did not achieve her full potential. Her relationships with her family and her husband stagnated. Her life was not flourishing; there was no colour in her home. The decision she had made at age twelve had become an organisational principle: "I'm always going to be second-rate". This imposed a form of permanent self-restraint, and ensured that she could never live her life to the full.

The framework for therapy became whether this decision could be reversed; whether she could obtain permission to flourish, to become "first class". The process started with a session interview with her husband. He was asked how he would react if his wife were to flourish, achieve her full potential. What consequences would this have for him? Could he follow her? Would he enjoy it?

Frank gave his full consent and said that he would be pleased if his wife were to fulfil her potential. Then came sessions with her mother and brother (her father was deceased) that also broached the theme of "flourishing". They too replied that they understood Beth's predicament (the same theme having dogged their own lives) and would be glad if she forged ahead and reached her full potential in this process. And so she did! The change in Beth was very rapid. She grew in her work and was soon promoted. The house was suddenly full of flowers, and there was "music" in her life again. The process unfolded quite rapidly, and her husband noticed that he could not keep up: that was why he himself came to seek therapy.

The theme of remaining "second-rate" had played a role in Frank's life too. He was enjoying his wife's rebirth and had no desire to retard it, but he noticed that he himself was now constantly feeling inhibited. In Frank's case too, part of him had remained behind, suspended in time. Using the nesting dolls, he depicted this by taking the doll belonging to the neglected part, and removing it from the row. This produced a hole, a blank space, and it was clear what his developmental task must be. After all, each phase of development has its own task in terms of psychological development. Milton Erickson (Haley, 1973; Rosen, 1982) makes this part of his therapy. The part that is left behind acquires its own personality, and the therapist addresses it directly. In the main, this neglected part has a protective function for other family members. This certainly applied in the present case. When he was three, Frank's younger brother was born. Soon afterwards, this baby brother became seriously ill and had to spend a long time in hospital, where he needed all the care and attention of his parents. Just when Frank's ego was being born, you might say, he had to take a step back because of his brother's needs. Relinquishing the existential cry "I'm here too", he made a sacrifice that would become, for him too, an organising principle. In fact "taking a step back" would become a key metaphor in his life. Whenever things came to a head, he took a step back and did not dare to go forwards.

With Frank too, a framework was developed that would involve him taking a step forwards and acquiring permission from those around him to take up the entire space he needed and to live his life to the full. Actually asking for this permission was an important step in this process. For instance, he broached the subject with his father. His father was pleased, and interpreted it as a reinvigoration of ties with his son. Frank also raised the subject with his brother, who replied that he would feel nothing but pride if Frank were to achieve his full potential.

Then there was Frank's cycling club, friends who rode fast for sheer enjoyment. Although Frank was a good cyclist and liked keeping up a good speed, he had never tested his limits. He did not dare to stretch himself to the utmost, partly for fear of embarrassing the others. I asked him if he could pull away from the rest if he were to do his best, and he thought that he could. At my suggestion, he asked his friends what they thought of his trying to take the next mountain as fast as possible. They replied positively: they would simply see it as a challenge and do their best to follow him. This created a context in which he dared to give his utmost. He extended his limit, reached the peak first, and pulled ahead of the rest.

The same theme cropped up at work. Frank was the manager of a small unit at a research institute and felt he could achieve more than he had done thus far. He went to see his superior, and asked his permission to push his team harder, since he felt it could achieve more than it had in the past. His superior was pleased and promised his full support, even if certain team members started to complain. Some time later, the therapy was concluded: Frank was achieving far more, enjoyed his work, had renewed contact with his father, and had reinvigorated the relationship with his wife. He was evidently ready to become a father, now that his wife had clearly decided that she wanted to have a child.

### Chorus and territory

Another concept that is useful in approaching context and building a framework is Deleuze's term *ritournelle*, meaning "refrain" or "chorus". Ritournelle means a repeated theme. Its Latin root, *refrangere*, from which the English word "refrain" derives, means "to break up".

Deleuze uses the concept of "refrain" together with that of "territory". As we have seen, nomadic thought calls for the creation of a home base, a temporary settlement that breaks up the journey of the travelling mind. After the initial decontextualisation or what Deleuze calls "deterritorialisation", there is a need for a new territory, a new refrain. In Deleuze's view, the refrain functions as a reference point, a recurrent theme that generates structure and recognisability. A musical chorus shares certain common features with territorialisation: the definition and outlining of a specific area. It has been said (in Romein, Schuilenberg & Van Tuinen, 2009, p. 254) that every demarcation of territory can be defined in terms of a refrain.

According to Deleuze and Guattari, defining a territory has two key effects: it reorganises functions and regroups forces. Each creation of a territory leads to a restructuring of time and/or space, as a result of which the chaotic forces (interference, white noise) must be excluded as far as possible. While the *infra-assemblage* stands for a circle drawn around a fragile centre, defining the territory that is thus enclosed is an *intra-assemblage* (Romein, Schuilenberg & Van Tuinen, 2009, p. 255).

The transformation process that takes place in territorialisation can be said to consist of two components: the de-territorialisation or decoding of the old structure and the re-territorialisation and re-coding of a new one. The former must occur to make the latter possible. This means that the refrain essentially consists of two opposing forces.

Deleuze and Guattari also refer to the process of de-territorialisation or decoding as the *inter-assemblage*, or line of flight. The role of the refrain is to define a territory; so three different assemblages can be distinguished here: an *infra-assemblage* creates order from chaos, an *intra-assemblage* regulates a territory's internal organisation, and an *inter-assemblage* makes it possible for one assemblage to be transformed into another (Romein, Schuilenberg & Van Tuinen, 2009, p. 255).

Thanks to the lines of flight, creative processes are generated, and external influences are admitted. Thus, gestational processes are generated that forge paths between territories. Here too we encounter the zigzag movement of narrative thinking, the movement between structure on the one hand and imagination on the other.

Thus Deleuze enters the world of music, and associates the refrain with birds that enter a territory and organise it with their song: an auditory demarcation of territory. Once a bird has demarcated its territory, a harmony is created with other birds. No bird sings alone, for itself;

each bird wants to be heard, to seduce, and to impress. For instance, a jay warns other birds in their shared territory of outsiders that might disturb the existing order. Animals often demarcate their territory with traces of urine. Human beings often choose the same chair or corner when we return to the same place: the chosen spot has become part of that person's "territory". Thus, members of the same group acquire fixed places and positions, in the manner of a "seating arrangement".

A framework for therapy can be seen as a refrain, a home base for thinking, a repetitive theme at the end of each verse. The music returns to its home base. A context is not therapeutic until there is a collaborative effort on the part of different participants working from different positions; when the music sounds in all its diversity, but constantly returns to the familiar words of the refrain. All the participants in the therapy join in this refrain, know the text that is "sung" in it. When this happens, the framework creates order in chaos and demarcates a territory; it places four linked segments around the space as a refrain for the therapy. A refrain is a familiar, recognisable melody, a home base for therapy. From this home base, the music can become a counterpoint, in which two or more voices sound together, becoming a polyphony. There are no gaps between the four segments: they dovetail smoothly. There is concord and harmony, a co-creation in which each participant has a voice and every voice is subsumed into a melody.

This set of concepts provides the linguistic domain of music as a possible reference for therapy. Using the framework and the refrain, external influences can be admitted without disrupting the order. The large number of changes and influences make it hard to keep to the framework. Defining a framework requires a creative process, since lines of flight first have to be drawn from the existing, dominant discourse attaching significance to the problem. A path needs to be created between two territories. Creation means abandoning the existing lines and drawing new ones. These come together in the four segments of the frame. The frame organises perception like a viewfinder: a photographer too can shoot a scene from a different angle or position, or using a different lens. The frame is a cooperative effort, and always requires the full endorsement of all concerned.

*Seven missing months*

Take the following example. In our hospital unit for family psychiatry, we devised an excellent framework with a refrain for a complex family system consisting of grandma, mother and four grandchildren, three of whom had been placed in care. Grandma, a refugee from Eastern Europe, started off by explaining that she had been five months pregnant when she first realised she was going to have a baby, and the child was born two months later. She felt that she had "only been pregnant for two months!"

Following the logic of abduction, the key to the necessary framework was the concept of "seven missing months" and the need to catch up. This concept turned out to apply to the family's entire complex system. Grandma had tried to make up for her seven missing months by taking on the care for her grandchildren. Her daughter, the children's mother, had made up for her own seven missing months by taking good care of her fourth and youngest child, which she had failed to do with her other children. These other children too had "seven missing months". Now, the two women could start making up for the seven months they had missed together. While the care for the children had led to repeated flare-ups between them, the new focus created an atmosphere of partnership to catch up with the lost seven months.

The theme made it possible to create a framework for help to all those concerned. Clearly, providing assistance here was highly complex. Three children were in care, Grandma had been given parental authority over the children, the children had different fathers, both women had histories of abuse, and they had constant battles about the children's care. Completely dependent on each other, they were also locked into constant warfare. Where should the care professionals start? How could a home base be created? What might the "refrain" be?

Until the consultation, the communication had been a constant slanging match. When communication was established temporarily with one member of the system, the other fiercely attacked it. Care was being provided without any framework—or with a framework that did not connect or "hang together". The concept of "seven missing months" and the need to make up for them did justice to all those concerned and helped to stem the quarrelling. Now it was possible to start offering help: different therapists could work with different parts of the family—children, Grandma, mother—in the context of this key phrase, the refrain "making up for the lost seven months". Every intervention and every session could be assessed for its contribution to this goal. A time frame was also established, with a vanishing point: after about *nine months*, there would be a birth, and new life would begin.

Even so, in practice it remained difficult to keep to the framework amid changing conditions and the free play of forces. Quite soon, help was being provided outside the agreed framework, and well-intentioned efforts were sucked into a vacuum. This gave rise to frustrations and feelings of powerlessness in the team, which sometimes degenerated into accusations. The team's immune system became weaker, making it susceptible to a "viral infection". After a period of hard work, everyone had to start again, with a number of questions: was the agreed framework being neglected or was a new one needed? Had the refrain been forgotten?

# PART II

NARRATIVITY IN ACTION

Figure 12. Jeroen Olthof, *Transformation 2011*, corten steel, aluminium bronze and concrete Ø 3.25 m. Photo © Jeroen Olthof, www.jeroenolthof.net

The statue *Transformation* by the artist Jeroen Olthof stands in the landscaped park of the Steenwijk estate in Vught, the Netherlands. The artwork connects the main building, in the manner of a magnifying window, to the cemetery that lies at some distance from it, hence linking past and present. With its open form, the broken circle is caught up in a technical play with gravity. The work is shaped like a huge letter C, one section of which is made of corten steel supplemented with concrete, which merges seamlessly into a section made of solid, highly polished aluminium bronze that shines like gold. The work thus symbolises the individual transformation process experienced by each human being.

CHAPTER EIGHT

# Finding a therapeutic script

*"It takes two to know one"*

—Gregory Bateson

## Introduction

Psychiatric symptoms can be seen as coagulated stories that are repeatedly told—and frequently heard—in the same way. They constantly organise the same context. It is as if the patient has ended up completely synonymous with the symptom, leaving no room to speak about other aspects of his or her life; the symptom has become the sole communication channel. The case of Mrs Peters provides a good example.

### Mrs Peters (with thanks to Ger Zwartjes)

Mrs Peters, a slight woman aged around sixty who had raised five children, was admitted to a ward for patients with serious psychiatric problems and frequently baffling symptoms. She tended to haunt the corridors, chatting cheerfully to other patients and chain-smoking—that was allowed in those days.

Sometimes she stood at the window, gazing out over the large square that led to the hospital entrance. Whenever she saw her husband approaching over the square, the same scene played out, again and again: just before her husband emerged from the lift, Mrs Peters fainted and lay motionless on the ground, seemingly unconscious.

Bystanders would rush to help, a doctor would be called, and Mrs Peters would be the focus of caring attention. Once she had "come to", life resumed as normal. When she lived at home, she had also frequently been found "unconscious" either in the house or in the neighbourhood, culminating in numerous ambulance trips and extensive hospital tests without any medical cause being identified. Each test had been repeated umpteen times, and Mrs Peters's frequent hospital admissions—someone would always call an ambulance—had started to cause irritation. Staff tended to avoid her.

Repetitive symptomatic and almost ritualistic behaviour of this kind generally elicits an equally unvarying pattern of interaction with care workers. The same words are used by all those involved, and the patient's care ends up in an impasse. The symptomatic behaviour demands an answer, an audience. It always succeeds: there is always someone who is startled and assumes that it is an emergency. Conflict also arises within the team. Some members will remain concerned while others wish to ignore the person, which is hard to do when someone is lying ostensibly unconscious on the floor. When someone attracts so much attention, the situation is sometimes labelled "secondary disease profit". This is an unfortunate term, since it glosses over the "primary disease loss" that must underlie it. The stories related to the "disease loss" can no longer be told, it seems. Either that or they are not heard, because of the compelling way in which such "fits" impose meaning and prescribe action: "something serious is going on: examine me, I need a doctor." If neither ignoring the person nor taking firm action helps, the relationship with the care team can only be held together with willpower: staff "put up with" the patient until the generally brief admission is over and the cycle repeats itself at home.

Mrs Peters's husband visited her faithfully. Three of her children had distanced themselves from her and avoided all contact, while the other two were fully involved in the care programme. The situation provoked frustration and at times outbursts of anger. A different approach was clearly needed, but how? Mrs Peters was not willing to discuss her "fits". After consultation in the team, the psychiatrist Ger Zwartjes and I decided to stage a dialogue about the situation in her presence in the manner of a Greek chorus. This provided an opportunity to allow diverse voices from Mrs Peters's world—her internal world and the world around her—to be heard, voices that had not yet been able to speak and which we furnished with a text in the hope that it might prove apt.

Mrs Peters lay in bed after one of her "fits", and we appeared at her bed, one on each side, and had the following conversation:

*Any idea what the problem could be, doctor?*
No idea at all, but I'm very concerned.
*I've noticed that she often faints when she sees her husband coming. She looks forward to the visits, literally stands on the lookout for him, and then faints, as if it is all too much for her.*
Yes, and in the ward she often talks to people who are having a really difficult time, as if she takes other people's suffering to heart. Anyone who is depressed can count on her.
*A sensitive heart, you might say, that is open to other people's suffering and then finds all that suffering unbearable.*
As if she demands too much of herself, takes on far more than she can bear.
*Exactly, and then it causes a sort of short circuit. Her body says "this is too much for me." Maybe Mrs Peters doesn't hear her body's message, or doesn't take it seriously.*
She's just weighed down by too many demands, she goes much too far!
*She seems to need protection; we have to protect her body.*

Although we kept our eyes on each other, we could see that Mrs Peters was listening intently. We carried on:

*What sort of protection are you thinking of, doctor?*
Bed rest, in any case bed rest and no visitors! Ab-so-lute-ly no visitors!
*But surely she can go home for the weekends?*
Certainly not! The same thing happens again and again at home; you know how often Mrs Peters has arrived here in an ambulance. First we must find out what is overburdening her heart, her oversensitive heart; we have to help her heart.
*And how do you plan to do that, doctor?*

Consulting the case file with a serious expression, the doctor fell silent.

*You're thinking of pills, aren't you, doctor?*
Oh yes, definitely pills.
*Not those big pink ones, surely?*
I think so.
*But those are almost the strongest pills you have!*
Can't be helped ... her heart really needs firm support!

Obliquely, we noticed Mrs Peters taking all this in. She seemed rather impressed that she needed these strong pills, "almost the strongest" ones. Zwartjes gave strict instructions about tests and frequent blood pressure measurements and remarked to me on the seriousness of the case, before slamming the case file shut, marching out of the room, and closing the door just a little harder than necessary. Mrs Peters and I were left to digest it together. A hierarchy had been created, with the doctor at the top, while I was aligned with the patient. She and I had almost become allies.

"The doctor's really serious about this," I said. Mrs Peters was clearly impressed by all the good care she was receiving and by the doctor's sternness. We were creating a therapeutic context.

Although Mrs Peters was not forced to stay in bed, whenever nurses met her in the sitting room or the corridors, they followed the new treatment plan by asking her if she was all right and not straining her heart too much. Mrs Peters replied that she would be careful, and if a nurse said, "the doctor said that you don't know your own body and it might be too much for you," she replied, "No, I'll pay attention, it's really not too much!"

The atmosphere became more relaxed and friendlier; the nurses now knew how to treat Mrs Peters. Having another fit now became an unappealing alternative for her. She did not want to create the impression that she had not been following the doctor's advice!

Mrs Peters spent a fair amount of time in bed, but also roamed around the ward. She entered into a more constructive relationship with her surroundings. At this point, Zwartjes and I set up another bedside dialogue:

"Doctor, Mrs Peters has been doing so much better. She is examined every morning, rests a good deal, and hasn't had any more fits. She would really like to go home for the weekend, since she misses her family."

"Absolutely not!" exploded Zwartjes, saying that it was far too soon, reminding me sternly of all the many fainting fits in the past.

I pleaded meekly on Mrs Peters's behalf, while Zwartjes continued to object that Mrs Peters's heart was not yet strong enough. After I had persisted for a while, Zwartjes consulted the case file with an eagle eye and then turned to me, warning again that Mrs Peters did not know her own body and he thought a weekend at home ill-advised. He would be blamed if it went wrong, he added grimly.

Mrs Peters had told me of her desire to go home, and now she beseeched me with her eyes. I tried again. "Couldn't we try, doctor, please? She's doing so much better!"

The doctor raised his voice in feigned irritation, saying: "Right then. If you think you know best, you are to blame if it goes wrong!"

He turned around and left the room, again shutting the door a little louder than necessary.

Now Mrs Peters and I were true allies. We would share the responsibility if the experiment failed. Mrs Peters had become "part owner" of the problem, making the context therapeutic.

The weekend at home went well, and Mrs Peters returned with cheerful stories of her exploits. Subsequent weekends at home also went well. A close therapeutic relationship had been created, in which I remained Mrs Peters's advocate and the doctor was our pessimistic antagonist. "One swallow does not make a summer," he liked to say. His attitude kept up the pressure, which supported the therapeutic relationship. Mrs Peters started to talk more, including stories relating to the "primary loss" of her illness.

Her situation resembled that of Mrs Johnson in the Prelude. Her children too had flown the nest, and she too had been overwhelmed by the abrupt transition. In the ensuing vacuum, stories from her own childhood, in which she had suffered abuse, had welled up. Once she was able to tell these stories, her relief enabled her to return home. With the revised significance attached to her complaint, further care could be left to outpatient services.

The opposing roles adopted by the doctor and the therapist here reflected the impasse of the symptomatic behaviour. One voice said, "see how burdened I am, please take care of me," while another said "something else is going on here; let's look further." These two voices remained in equilibrium for a while, but eventually the process tipped in favour of the caring mother who was suffering from untold stories. The dialogue between these voices was played out in Mrs Peters's presence. She became the audience of her own story, and we, as care workers, together succeeded in attaching significance to the symptom, and in creating space for the congealed story to become "unstuck" and take a new turn.

The intervention disrupted the existing pattern, in a manner proposed most notably by Milton Erickson (Erickson, 1967; Erickson & Rossi, 1979). Erickson advocates this "utilisation approach", as it is sometimes called, in the context of hypnotherapy. The approach involves not just accepting—without any kind of judgement—everything the patient offers, in terms of language, behaviour, significance, and symptoms, but also harnessing all that is offered in the service of changing the symptom. It is also sometimes called a "naturalistic approach", in which everything that is naturally present in the patient's life and context can be harnessed as a resource. Motives and interests, strengths and qualities, are also resources.

Mrs Peters's symptom was reclassified: instead of being called an "unknown disease" or "manipulative behaviour", it was assigned to the class of "people with a sensitive heart". This was a benign description to which Mrs Peters could not object. Such strategic interventions in existing patterns are part of the utilisation approach. Since neither fighting nor ignoring the symptom is effective, the key is to offer treatment geared towards *cooperating* with the symptom.

The inspiration for this approach comes from the fairy tale *Stone Soup*, from Eastern Europe:

A poor, hungry tramp came to a cottage in the woods hoping for something to eat. But this was Mrs Miser's house. She had cupboards full of delicious food, but hoarded it. She didn't even eat it herself! She saved everything up, even the vegetables in her garden. After all, she reasoned, "You never know when it might be needed."
When the tramp knocked at the door, Mrs Miser cracked it open and shouted: "Who are you and what do you want? Something for nothing I'll be bound!"
The tramp looked past her shoulder to the kitchen, and saw onions hanging from the ceiling, piles of canned goods and rows of bottles everywhere. He was famished.
"Go away! I never give anything away!" shouted Mrs Miser.
Seeing how thin Mrs Miser was, the tramp decided it was time for his Stone Soup story.
"I only need a little water," he said, "to make some stone soup."
Curious, the old woman said, "Stone soup?"
"Yes," said the tramp. "My magic stone makes delicious soup!"
The old woman hesitated, then fetched a bucket of water.
"Thank you!" said the tramp. "Would you like some, when it's ready? I make the best stone soup in the world!"
Mrs Miser snorted and went back inside. But she watched sneakily from behind the curtains as the tramp made a fire beyond her garden fence, took out a little pan and a stone, filled the pan with water, and waited for it to boil.
She came out to look, and wrinkled her nose.
"You're going to eat that?" she said in disgust.
"Well, you're right. Stone soup is better with an onion, but I don't have one." Mrs Miser harrumphed and went off to get a tiny onion, handing it over with a sour face.
The tramp thanked her brightly, and as he stirred, he said that the soup was getting really tasty. She looked astonished.
"Of course," he mused, "brown beans would make it even better, but sadly I don't have any."
"I might have some," said Mrs Miser. She went back inside and returned with a can of brown beans.
"Well! You must certainly share this soup with me!" said the tramp, emptying the beans into the pan.
Mrs Miser sniffed and still looked suspicious.
"Oh, I know what you're thinking," said the tramp. "Ladies like stone soup best with mushrooms, but I'm sure you'll like it with just onions and beans!"
"I've got mushrooms!" shouted Mrs Miser and rushed off to get them.
The tramp continued in this way. Eventually he enticed the old lady to add beef, potatoes, turnips, and cabbage.

"Doesn't it need salt?" asked Mrs Miser.

"Good idea!" said the tramp.

Later, when they sat down to eat the delicious soup, the tramp suggested that bread and cheese might be nice, and Mrs Miser, in a cheerful mood now, opened a bottle of wine. Afterwards they feasted on apple pie.

"That was the best meal I ever had. That magic stone is amazing!" said Mrs Miser.

"You can have it, dear Mrs Miser," said the tramp.

"Really? What a wonderful gift! Now I'll be able to invite people to dinner!" she cried, delighted. "And it won't cost me a thing!"

"Don't forget to flavour it with onions, beans and mushrooms," said the tramp, getting ready to leave.

"I won't forget!" said Mrs Miser.

"And some beef, potatoes and turnips, of course," added the tramp.

"I'll remember it all!" she said.

"That will be fine then, since everyone loves stone soup when it's cooked like that!" said the tramp, and went off into the woods.

The tramp in the fairy tale sees that Mrs Miser is suffering from her own behaviour. It is stronger than she is, and does something with her that she doesn't want. He sees how thin she is. Although he is hungry, and sees that Mrs Miser has food, he knows that asking within the existing order would lead to a rejection and would preserve Mrs Miser's usual script. So the tramp uses her "symptom", suspecting that Mrs Miser would be enchanted by the idea of making something out of nothing.

The tramp is not just concerned to still his own hunger; he also wants to help Mrs Miser to enjoy what she has. He sets out to cure her of her miserliness by *using* it, and only adding a small element. This strategy allows space in which to attach significance to the symptom (a significance that Keeney calls "meaningful Rorschach" (in Keeney, 1983; Keeney & Ross, 1992)), thus giving it a context that speaks to her. What seems at first sight to be an inconsequential stone proves to be a "meaningful Rorschach" to Mrs Miser. Stones are freely available everywhere. If they can be turned into a filling, delicious soup, that is naturally grist to her mill.

The tramp successfully distracts Mrs Miser's attention from her suspicious tendencies by focusing so intently on the "stock" he is making from the stone. Adding the stone creates an entirely new framework; the stone soup provides the logic she requires to supply ingredients that she possesses in abundance. The stone helps her to bring her own resources into play. Since she gives the ingredients to the soup, rather than the tramp, she is able to forget herself and her own symptom. As the tramp invites her to share in the meal, it induces a rare festive mood in Mrs Miser. Together they enjoy a feast. The tramp leaves the stone with Mrs Miser, as an added value with which to make her own stone soup. She is "cured", and is already planning to invite people to dinner. After all, it won't cost anything!

The stone is part of a strategic approach that lends itself to a wide range of complaints, provided it adds something to the existing story. The tramp is not intrusive. He does not disrupt Mrs Miser's order, but encourages her to change it herself. He makes the soup beyond the fence, outside her territory. He makes no demands, and does not invoke the moral imperative of helping the poor and hungry. His actions are all oblique. He knows, from one glance at her kitchen, that he can use the material there as an aid.

Just as the Mrs Miser of this fairy tale takes part in her own story, Mrs Peters too became a participant in her own treatment. She too was "cured" in a change that took place at the level of the unconscious mind. The treatment of Mrs Peters was likewise non-intrusive and non-coercive. She was given advice, but was free to ignore it. Her "fits" were invested with the new significance of a concerned, fragile woman who cannot bear the burden of her past, or of other people's emotions. The new significance enabled Mrs Peters to develop more positive relationships with those around her, and created space within which the coagulated story could become "fluid". She started talking about the world behind the fits, the world of the primary disease loss, about her *real* suffering for which she had hitherto been unable to find the words.

## Enactments

"How can we know the dancer from the dance?" With this line from a poem by W. B. Yeats, Minuchin begins his chapter on enactments in his book about techniques in family therapy (Minuchin & Fishmann, 1981). The dance and the dancer are one: they form an integrated whole, and belong to the same context. When families come to a therapy session, it is as if they stop the music and the dance in order to talk *about* the dance. They come to therapy to talk *about* the interactions that take place at home. Enactment, on the other hand, is an approach or technique in which the family is invited to "make music and dance" with the therapist.

The aim is that the session acquires such a level of intensity that it becomes a significant, lived-through, bodily-felt experience for all those involved, including the therapist. If we as therapists adopt the position of observing our clients and gathering information, we are really talking *about* what happens elsewhere. We are proceeding on the basis of a theory that is laid *over* the experience, as a result of which the experience itself can no longer be felt. Therapy effectively begins in the very first second in which client and therapist meet. People sometimes come in at the same time as the postman, leading to a brief exchange. Sometimes people arrive feeling guilty because they are late for their appointment, and the first sentence they utter is full of significance.

> The first sentence spoken by a six-year-old girl who came in with her grandma was "This is my Mummy!" The little girl was fully aware that grandma was not her mother, but grandma is bringing her up and the child feels good with her. The mother had been divested of parental authority because of addiction problems, but had now submitted an application for the child's return. The visit to the psychologist was fraught with the tension of this context. (Story with thanks to Paulien Kuipers)

> A woman came in panting and stumbling over the threshold. She said: "It's just like me, I'm always making stupid mistakes." In this way, the theme of "making mistakes" accompanied her into the consulting room.

The spontaneous opening sentences that are picked up, as it were, in a continuous process, are the beginning of the dance. Alternatively, they sound the referee's whistle for the kick-off; present the opening scene of the film or of a play at the theatre; they articulate the first sentence of a book or provide the opening notes in a melody. The opening sentence is immediately a central part of the whole.

We have already discussed voice and the multivocal self, the concept of having and acquiring a voice, the right to speak. All this refers to the auditory channel and speech itself. But language is also a physical, bodily phenomenon. You might even say that it is also visual. Language is experienced in a kinaesthetic way in the body. So if a therapy session is compared to a dance—with movement, space, and choreography—it means that an appeal is also made to other senses to make the experience as intense as possible, to create an opportunity for change and to allow a new equilibrium, with greater flexibility, to come into being.

Minuchin says "Make it happen". Erickson says "Show me". Both refer in this connection to *narrativity in action*: allowing things to happen, allowing things to be seen, to come into existence. The aim is to indicate that the therapeutic process focuses less on content than on process and form. If there is a secret in a family, it may be necessary to know the substance of that secret. Still, it is often more important to explore the significance of this secret in the family. The secret dances with and within the family, is part of its choreography. The secret is *itself* a dancer. The secret may be given a place in space, for instance in the form of a cushion, or as a newspaper on an empty chair with a coat laid across it.

Enactment is about being inventive with evocation.

### Organising space

We could also see a psychotherapy session as a particular organisation of space. Organising space has to do with who sits where, and in what position.

A little boy sits on his mother's right;
his father sits on the other side of the table, far away from them.

In a different family, a six-year-old boy sits in between his parents,
with one leg on his mother's lap.

Different positions organise the discussion and the space in different ways. They lead to different "formations"—to use another soccer term. The ways in which people sit, the positions they occupy in space, do not have any fixed significance; each organises the therapeutic meeting in its own way. "Meeting" is used here as a noun, and here we run up against the limitations of denotative language use, which refers to objects, things. It would be better to see it here as a verb, given that significance is not a fixed *thing*, divorced from the process in which those concerned meet.

Karl Weick uses the term *sensemaking* (Weick, 1995) for the constant process of giving meaning to experience. As we saw in Chapter Two, language itself creates, sets things in motion, triggers events: language is action. Naming is a self-fulfilling prophecy: the name becomes part of what is named. We refer to *narrativity in action*, since the space may be reorganised in the course of the therapy session.

In the first example given above, the therapist might sit down beside the little boy, in between him and his mother. In that case, the therapist would be sitting roughly opposite the boy's father and almost taking over his role. Alternatively, he might sit beside the father, facing the mother and child. Such decisions involve occupying a position in space. The therapist might choose to place his chair in the "midfield", observe events, and focus on the space that has arisen between the mother and son on one side and the father on the other. Yet another choice might be to sit on the other side, in a "connecting" place between the two parents.

Each of these arrangements leads to a different organisation of the space. As part of the context, the therapist can help to ensure that certain things happen and others do not. Context can facilitate and it can restrict, producing certain patterns of interaction. The space can constantly be divided up differently, by moving chairs and changing places. If the therapist asks the child to come and sit beside him, for instance, this may be a more helpful arrangement in which to talk to him about his parents.

A couple who sit side by side are making it clear to the therapist, who is sitting on the other side of the table, how things are at home. The enactment changes instantly when the therapist stands up, walks over to them, and asks them to rotate the chairs until they face each other, to look at each other, and then to repeat the sentence they have just said: "I don't want to lose you." There is a fundamental difference in experience between the man saying to the therapist that he doesn't want to lose his wife and the man looking into his wife's eyes and saying to her "I don't want to lose you." Directly addressing another person is therapy in action, dancing: that is when things "happen", when therapy is "done".

A man who says to his wife, "I'm right behind you" to signify his support for her in the difficult process she's going through may be asked to get up and *physically* stand behind his wife. How will he do it? Will he stand several feet away from her? Or will he place his arm around her shoulders or her waist, or with his hand on her back? With these actions, his support becomes a tangible experience, and this in turn helps the therapist in the process of diagnosis.

A woman who is very anxious because of childhood experiences of witnessing her father's frequent abuse of her mother may derive enormous support from a husband who says, "I'm right behind you." If the man goes over and stands behind his wife but scarcely dares to touch her, evidently filled with fear by his wife reliving her experiences, his actions belie his words. If he then goes on to tell her about the abuse that he himself suffered as a boy, his fear will become an oppressive, tangible presence. His own abuse will enter the space.

A son who tells his therapist that he is sorry for the way he has behaved to his mother could be invited to move his chair so as to face her and to say, "I'm sorry, Mum." Then the dance begins, the dance partners start to move together.

Space can be organised in many different ways. The following paragraphs describe a few possible scenarios and a few approaches to them, using the organisation of space.

### The visualisation of the family history

In a family consisting of father, mother, and three children, the children are locked into perpetual conflict. There is only room for two: one is always left out.

We divide the space in the consulting room as follows: the three children sit on a rug on one side of the room. The rug symbolises the time before their birth. On the other side of the room, father and mother walk towards one another; they meet and fall in love. Then they stand shoulder to shoulder and hand in hand, as lovers, and their first child is called. The eldest rises from the rug and finds a comfortable place to sit with her parents. It makes a nice picture, a good-looking threesome. Then it is time for the second child to be born. The little girl goes over and finds a place to sit beside her elder sister. Once again, bodies shift and make room; there is ample space for four: the eldest girl sits with their mother and her younger sibling with their father. The picture looks harmonious. Then the third child is born. She runs over to the other family members, jumps on top of them, and wriggles in between the parents. She pushes her sisters to one side and the beginnings of the struggle are apparent straight away: elbow-digging, pushing and shoving. The harmony is disrupted immediately. So the theme is clear: how to make space for five? There is a conversation, in which everyone takes part, about the history of the family and the conditions in which the children were born. At the end of the session, there is space for all five.

In the case of a couple caught up in endless arguing, the therapist may choose to visualise the way in which they first met. When were their best times as a couple? If the woman says, "I wish we could get closer," the therapist could ask her how far apart they are at this present moment. Then he can invite them to stand up and to occupy a place in the room and to determine their distance to one another; then he asks which of the two wants to come closer.

"How close? Get up and go closer: show what you mean."

The woman walks towards her husband. This provides an opportunity for process diagnosis: does she run into her husband's arms? Is it almost impossible for her to move at all? Is sweat breaking out on her forehead as she comes closer? Is there a noticeable struggle taking place with the different voices and forces within her? Is she actually *able* to get any closer?

At the same time, the therapist may observe the place that her husband occupies in the space. Does he open his arms? Does he start moving too, helping his wife to shorten the distance between them? Or does his body express a barrier? The dance cannot start until there is actual movement: when the sentence "I want to come closer" is actually experienced as reality.

### *The positioning of chairs in space and the use of objects*

A man who says "I tend to withdraw into myself" could be asked to demonstrate this behaviour in the room. What does this withdrawal mean, exactly? Does he place his chair in the corner? Does he turn his chair around? Does he pull his coat over his head? Does he crawl into a corner on hands and knees as if to make himself invisible?

### *Breaking the impasse*

A couple who have been together for eighteen years are now thinking of going their separate ways. They sit in the therapist's consulting room in silence. Then the woman says that she feels no more contact with her body, in any case not with her belly. The man says that he is only capable of thinking, and that he is only in contact with his head, and not with the rest of his body. If their relationship is to have another chance, they say, other layers in themselves and in their relationship would have to be engaged. It will have to tip either one way or the other: either to the side of breaking up or to the side of coming together in a new way. Their fears are paralysing them, holding them both captive in an impasse.

I ask them to turn their chairs to face one another and ask the woman up to what point she feels in contact with her body. I ask her to indicate this as precisely as possible. The area from the lower abdomen up to the region of her heart is for her a "lost area". The man says that he feels nothing from his head downwards. I ask their permission to visualise the situation together with them.

The woman chooses a cushion that exactly covers the "empty space" in her body. She calls this cushion her "obstruction". It is big and solid. The man has a small cushion, which he holds near his throat. From then on down, he has lost all contact with the rest of his body. He is only able to think.

The man now sees his wife—once they have turned their chairs to face each other—with the cushion that symbolises her obstruction. The woman sees her husband with the cushion that symbolises the split between his head and his body. It becomes clear that the man can only feel a connection with his wife through his own body, through the act of intimacy with her.

What he says is effectively: "Please, you take care of the contact with my body; lend me your body."

He sees the cushion that symbolises the obstruction and does not know what to do. His thoughts are full of panic—his head is chaos, the world is no longer what it was. The woman appears to be saying to her husband: "Please, you get rid of my obstruction so that I can feel my own body again."

The impasse that holds them captive has now been depicted, acted out in space. This is *therapy in action*: the process is ongoing, and its course cannot be orchestrated one-sidedly. The tension rises. Then the woman removes the cushion from her lap and places it beside her chair. She gently lays her hand on the cushion and says: "I'll keep it close to me, but I'm going to put it down here beside me for now."

The man keeps holding the cushion next to his throat and continues to maintain that he does not know how to make contact with his own body. An only child, he has never learnt this, nor has anyone ever called him out on it. His parents are no longer alive. He does not have any story about his life, and his wife and daughter know almost nothing about his past. He has boxes full of photographs, and he may well have shown some of them to his wife, but when looking at them he can only add a few facts—no stories.

To help him regain contact with his own body, we organise the process as follows.

He will look at the photographs and make scrapbooks out of them, in order to arrange the story of his life. He will make a selection to show his wife, to tell her about his life and to fill in the blank spaces in his existence. He will speak himself, rather than merely answering questions. This breaks the impasse.

### Selecting chairs for different voices within one person or for persons who are absent

- For the child that wants to remain small and close to Mummy or Daddy, a small chair can be chosen. A larger chair may represent his or her age at that moment in time.
- A chair can be placed in the room for the voice that says "I want a divorce" and another one for the voice that says "I'd like to be closer to my wife."
- A chair can be placed in the room for the deceased father or for the father who is absent after a divorce. So where should this chair be placed?

A chair can be placed in the room for each person who cannot be present at a family conversation, but who is nonetheless important to the family. This does mean that the space and the "positions in the field" must be organised differently. The therapist can ask the family to choose where to put the chair for the absent person and the chair for the therapist.

In a supervision meeting, a trainee presented the following situation. He had walked into a room in which a mother and father and their three children were waiting for him, and saw the following scene. The mother and the middle daughter were seated on one side, while the father and the eldest daughter were seated on the other side of the large room. In the middle of the room, in between her parents, sat the youngest child, a boy, rocking and bouncing back and forth.

The family had been referred for therapy because of the severe abdominal pains suffered by the middle child and the overexcitable behaviour of the youngest. Extensive hospital tests had failed to suggest any physical cause of the abdominal pain. When the conversation began, the youngest child was extremely agitated. His parents corrected him, but only from a distance and to no avail: the boy continued to cavort around the room. The parents gave the clear impression of powerlessness, and waited to see what the therapist would do.

If the space was not organised differently, the therapist would run the risk of finding himself in the place of the parents and having to correct the boy himself. Alternatively, he might have to ignore the boy's behaviour, as a result of which the home situation would simply repeat itself in the consulting room. The boy gave the impression of drowning in the space. So where could the therapist decide to sit? Sitting in the middle, with the mother and the middle daughter on the left and the father with the eldest daughter on the right, he might be able to calm the family system and provide an anchor on which all family members could concentrate. However, he would also run the risk of getting stuck in this position, and of becoming immovable. It was essential for the space to be organised differently, to allow a different dance to begin. For instance, the therapist might ask the little boy what it was like to be sitting by himself there. He could ask the boy if he would rather sit somewhere else, and then invite him to actually go and sit there. Suppose the boy were to say that he would like to sit with his father—in that case, the eldest child could be asked to change places with him for a while. After that, the daughter could be asked how it felt to be sitting in this new place. In this way, the family members could keep changing their places and positions.

The therapist could also place his chair next to the little boy's and talk to him about the family. "What do you think it's like for your sister to be sitting next to Mummy? And for your other sister to be sitting with Daddy? What do you think about your sister's tummy ache? Where do you think it comes from? Do you ever have a tummy ache? Does your other sister sometimes have a tummy ache? What about Mummy and Daddy? What do you think tummy ache tells us?"

So the space is organised differently and the therapist adopts a different position, or asks the children to keep changing places and to sit somewhere else. At some point during the conversation it becomes clear that the parents have difficulty making a decision together. When the girl with tummy ache asks her mother if something is allowed and Mummy says yes, after which Daddy says that it's *not* allowed, she gets confused. Could her tummy ache have something to do with this? It turns out that when this situation arises, the girl bursts into tears and goes back to her mother, who comforts and protects her. Could this be a "tummy ache" position?

Next, a specific subject came up in the family: whether or not to get a dog. They already had a basket, a leash, and other attributes. But they still didn't have a dog, since Father had put his foot down. A concrete subject like this can be magnified and extrapolated by asking the parents to negotiate this subject together, in the children's presence, to arrive at a joint decision. The children, seated on the other side of the room, can hear and witness their parents negotiating, with the therapist's help. The therapist can move through the space, and stand behind the children if the tension starts to rise. Then he can say out loud how tense this situation must be for them, and ask the middle daughter if it gives her a tummy ache. Alternatively he might choose to stand with the parents and actually help them to reach a decision, to reach a tipping point. Whatever "dance steps" the therapist may choose, he will organise the space consciously, to allow other stories to be told.

It is self-evident that such enactment must always be done on the basis of support and a strong therapeutic relationship. Identifying tensions and trying to achieve a tipping point are things that require a safe environment.

If we use the metaphor of a soccer match, this staging is part of the midfield game—it is part of organising space in the midfield. Very occasionally, it may belong to the very beginning, when the ball is brought into play—to the first moments of therapy. Even at that stage, however, the therapist must be able to make the client feel safe. This can be achieved with posture and gestures, intonation and the sound of the therapist's voice, with a smile and an attitude of friendliness and warmth. It can be done with what Ricoeur calls the "second naïveté" (Ricoeur, 1969, p. 351).

Ricoeur draws a distinction between the first and second naïveté. The former is the innocence and ignorance of a child who has not yet been burdened by life—a child who has not yet been wounded, and who looks upon the world with trusting eyes. The "second naïveté" is linked to a later age, once life has left its traces, when our biography can be read from our faces and our facial features tell stories. Then we can look again with eyes of innocence, but this time it is a knowing innocence. Looking with the eyes of knowledge, the eyes of mildness, which do not judge, but which know what life can do to people. It is an attitude that combines the wisdom of naïveté with the naïveté of wisdom.

Narrativity in action starts with someone urging: show me, demonstrate what that looks like, make it visible. This is the way in which *sensemaking* arises, and it is very different from interpreting or assigning significance. *Sensemaking* has to do with vision. *Sense* refers both to the senses and to *significance*. This also means that it involves all the senses, not just our cognitive responses.

Let's illustrate this with a few examples.

*No one must know*

In a supervision meeting, a trainee described the following situation and asked for advice.

A twenty-two-year-old man had come to a crisis centre. He had realised that he was homosexual, and the discovery had precipitated him into a state of confusion. He said that he found it impossible to accept that this was his real nature, and that he considered it vital that no one find out about it. This closed story did not leave much room for the psychotherapist: it did not give him any point of access. Predictably then, after the first two conversations, the therapist found his efforts getting stuck, paralysed. In supervision, some preliminary work was done for a possible framework, based on the client's literal words:

"I can't accept that this is how I am; I don't want anyone to know."

The supervisor and supervisee analysed the client's words and concluded that the assertion refers to a "this" and to "how I am". It implies a shadowy part that is not allowed, a separate part that had suddenly popped up, quite recently, to the client's own astonishment. This part had become present, and was therefore no longer absent. So how could this present absence or absent presence be depicted? It might be represented, for instance, by placing an empty chair behind the client's back. The client might turn his back to the chair, as if to symbolise what was not allowed to be present and what he did not want to know. Of course, it was essential that the client was willing to depict the situation.

The sentence "no one must know about it" implies the existence of a secret. If this part cannot belong, if the client turns his back to this part, and that part must remain a secret to the outside world, a coat or blanket might be thrown over the empty chair, for instance, as an image and symbol of what must remain concealed. An invisible secret. Since that part had surfaced and suddenly asserted its presence, the client was very shocked and his equilibrium had been completely disrupted. And since that part must remain concealed from the outside world, despite the fact that it is there, he would have to keep the chair behind his back and ensure that it stayed out of sight. This would involve keeping a careful eye on his surroundings and watching to make sure that no one slipped past him, behind his back, where they might catch sight of that concealed part, his shadow—a watchfulness that would naturally make huge demands on his energy. To depict that life, the therapist might keep shifting the chair, which symbolises the shadow. These movements would symbolise the impact of this life on him.

Once the framework had been presented in this way, and visualised with the aid of the chairs, the client could be asked whether this representation gave a good picture of the situation in which he found himself. Then the therapist and the client could look at the two chairs from a distance, together. They could walk around them and explore all the diverse facets of this way of life. They could look to see whether the story might be turned in any other direction. This approach would ensure that the client retained ownership of the problem.

*Grumpy and the china shop*

Two patients appeared in my consulting room: a man and a woman, John and Susan, who loved each other deeply and had a shared history going back thirty years. John had been undergoing therapy, and had already achieved a great deal. His mother had claimed him possessively when he was a small boy. John's desperate overtures to his mother were frequently ignored, while he was often picked up at moments that felt completely wrong. A voice developed—"No!"—inside him, a deeply entrenched, deep-rooted voice: "No!"

John's father was often away at work, and was hardly part of their family life. He left his son with his wife. This meant that John came to belong to the world of his mother and her female friends, who often came to visit. He did not lack attention, but he also wanted his mother for himself.

At one point we found ourselves talking about *Snow White and the Seven Dwarfs*. John had seen the Disney version, and identified with Grumpy. When the dwarfs go off to work in the morning, each one kisses Snow White goodbye except for Grumpy, who really wants a kiss, but is unable to ask for one. He just walks past Snow White as if he doesn't care, feigning "No" while feeling a yearning "Yes".

John enjoyed the Grumpy part of himself, and yet he also identified with Happy. To Happy, the whole world is a good, jolly place. John yearned for his wife to be his very own Snow White. If the world was not "happy", if his life was disrupted, he would feel a "No" rising up in him, and Grumpy would come to the fore. But Susan could no longer bear having to be Snow White all the time for her husband, and having to smooth out every trace of discord.

To depict their relationship, we invited Susan to sit on one chair and to look in front of her, while John seated himself diagonally behind her, with his back to her. I took a sheet of paper, wrote "NO" on it in big letters, and placed it on his lap. Seated in this way, facing away from his wife and with a big "NO" in his lap, John became fully conscious of his immature attitude within their relationship and the non-stop pressure he exerted on his wife. Tears rolled down his cheeks. The deeply rooted "NO" took on real, bodily felt significance. For a while there was silence; for both John and Susan, the situation visualised in the space was very confrontational and at the same time healing. Then John picked up his chair, turned it round, and sat down beside his wife, shoulder to shoulder.

"This is how I'd like it to be!" he said.

## Language is action

Lively sentences, sentences that can be articulated with vitality and energy, can come to life in the consulting room, and these sentences can be listened to with the logic of abduction. Then they can take shape and be assigned a place within the space.

### You are my life

A couple, Milly and Nick, were locked into perpetual conflict. Milly said that she had the feeling that Nick was draining all the life out of her. In the consulting room stood a basket with balls of wool in different colours. I asked them each to choose a "thread of life" and to attach it to each other and to their own past. Nick attached his own thread to Milly's waist, with the knot at her navel. After that the thread passed around his head to his other hand. He appeared to be asking "the other" in the outside world to take his "thread of life" and hold it.

Nick stood with his back to Milly. The woollen thread around his head represented being no longer able to think. Nick was someone who took great risks in everyday life, while driving his car and on the stock market.

Milly attached her thread to Nick's thread, and also wound it around her waist and attached it to the knot at her navel. Then the thread passed around her throat and led to the world behind her. This thread attached her to her mother. Searching for words for these threads, the thread attaching her to her mother and depriving her of breath said to her: "You are my death." When Milly's mother was carrying her, she had made a failed attempt to have an abortion.

Nick's thread said, "You are my life."

Both ends of the thread were being pulled. Milly felt torn, all the more so since there was another thread, connecting her to her father. This thread too told her, "You are my life."

With these three threads, Milly became entangled. A father who says "You are my life," a mother who says, "You are my death," and her husband who says, "You are my life." It is easy to imagine how confusing this must feel.

## *The mole hole*

Yolanda came for a psychotherapy session with her son, Ian, aged twenty-one. According to Yolanda, Ian was living in a cave, a sort of hole—a mole hole. She said that Ian rarely went out and suffered from chronic anxiety. I asked Ian whether the words *mole* and *mole hole* sounded right to him. He said they did, adding that the cave was his protection while at the same time he was suffocating in it. This brought the sentence "I live in a mole hole" to life. I asked Ian what part of the room might represent that mole hole. He pointed at the table, and I asked him to go and sit underneath the table and to look at the room from that perspective. Even then, he experienced the space as too wide open. So I moved chairs, coats, and bags closer and grouped them around him until he was almost completely hidden from sight.

In this way the mole hole was made present in the room so that it became an experienced reality. We did not talk about his life in the hole; instead, his life in a hole was made tangible in the here and now. His mother's sentence was brought to life and "enacted". Ian was able to explain what it was like from *within* the experience. I went and sat down on the floor beside him and talked to him about his life in the hole. Yolanda could hardly bear to see her son sitting under the table like that, and wept. For Ian, this space under the table initially represented safety, but soon afterwards he started to sweat and said that the space also symbolised his fear.

Enactment involves a quest for tipping points. The aim is to set the process in motion and to push it over its limits, over the existing equilibrium. If Ian could be persuaded to leave this space within the "as if" of the therapeutic situation, this movement could be translated into everyday life. This enactment also gave him an opportunity to truly confront his fear: seated on the floor, he was trembling with anxiety. I could feel how devastating the experience was for him. At that moment, in this place, what he needed in order to be able to move became a truly physical reality.

When Yolanda was asked for her consent to publish her family's story here, she recalled:

The "mole hole game", on which Ian embarked in a rather nervous, giggly way, became a reality that we all experienced. It was very hard for me to watch, as his mother; feeling his real anxiety, pain, with such intensity. But it created (finally!) an opening, literally and figuratively. Not long afterwards, Ian passed his driving test. It was the first time in many years that he had finished something—a positive experience that he had badly needed.

Sentences pronounced literally can come to life and be enacted. This enactment is achieved through the "as if" of the sentences and makes them into metaphors. The "as if" is then translated literally into everyday life again—beyond the consulting room. So the sequence is as follows: the sentences are spoken as a metaphor and become an "as if". Then the sentences are enacted in a literal sense, at which point the literal enactment becomes "as if" again; for there is not, of course, an actual mole hole in the consulting room. This new "as if", then, produces an existential experience that is lived through in a physical sense, anchored in the person's body and represented in all his senses. This experience is then translated, often literally, to everyday life.

## *The use of drawings and objects*

Narrativity in action can also include inviting clients to make drawings or objects: clay modelling, painting, and making three-dimensional objects. A child troubled by constant tummy ache, for instance, can be encouraged to draw the tummy ache and to make a sketch of its presence in the body. By drawing the tummy ache and choosing a colour for the pain, the tummy ache is made present in the consulting room and becomes tangible in that space. Or a client may produce a painting that imparts a physical structure to the process of therapy. A drawing might be made of the desired final state—once the drawing has been created, turned into a real image, that image is present in the client's consciousness and acts as an attractor. The unconscious mind can tune into it; the image is clear and unequivocal.

A client named Petra made a styrofoam ball and covered it with moss. She filled the styrofoam ball with pieces of hard cardboard painted black, which she cut into specific shapes using a box cutter. She spent months making this object. For every piece of cardboard she painted, she said that she experienced a little sense of release, liberation, in her body.

A man who struggled with his male identity, his place among his brothers, and his place in relation to his past female lovers, underwent a rapid process of development, of growing self-confidence. For his training course in personal leadership, he decided to forge his own sword. This was a very time-consuming project, and at length he proudly brought the sword with him to the session. His mission was accomplished.

A woman suffering from multiple sclerosis spoke about the sources of poison in her body. There were twenty in total, each one relating to periods in her early childhood, when she was frequently abused, fell ill, and had multiple operations. In the course of her therapy the sources of poison were cleansed. The woman travelled through her body under hypnosis, cleansed the places in her body that were linked to these periods, which enabled her to process her experiences. She made these twenty periods present in the form of objects she placed on a canvas, which she then burned in a ritual. This canvas with the objects attached to it became the third space, the externalisation of all pain, illness, and hospitalisations. She was able to look at it, and the knowledge that she had triumphed over all that gave her a great sense of satisfaction.

A client made this photograph of a flight of steps in Zeeland. She entered a hypnotic state by visualising herself going down them, one step at a time, from the dunes to the beach. Once she was on the beach, she was in a deep trance, and the journey through her body could begin.

Figure 17. Flight of steps in the dunes.

## Rituals

Rituals can help us in the transitions we go through in our lives. They are enactments that can help us to pass through a threshold or to overcome an obstacle that lies in our path. School-leavers have a variety of ways of marking their transition to adulthood. In one case, the parents may take their teenager to his or her new rented room as a ritual form of departure; in another, a young man or woman may go on a trip around Asia before starting university. Some transition rituals help us become acclimatised to a new place or phase of life. Mismanaged transitions take their toll. A past phase that was not completed carries on sapping our energy. Rituals help to complete phases in life.

### Meryl's ritual

One of Meryl's twins died at a very young age. The child had fallen ill and died in hospital. Years had passed, and the possible role of medical negligence in the child's death had never been clarified. Meryl remained fixated on "the medical file" all that time. The story was not finished. Not knowing exactly what had happened, she was unable to move on to the next phase of her life. The loss of her child was too traumatic.

We drew up the following framework together. We would ask Meryl's GP to request the case file from the hospital and study it carefully. His study was unlikely to reveal a definitive answer, but the ritual would function as a process in action. Meryl agreed to make this final attempt to clarify her child's death, with the GP's assistance, and said that she would then be satisfied with the findings.

The GP cooperated with this plan. He requested the file, called specialists, and studied the entire case thoroughly. As expected, he could not give a firm answer, but he concluded that the child had most probably died from natural causes. Now that she had done everything possible to discover the truth, Meryl found that she could live with this answer, and pass the threshold to the next phase of life.

She decided to go to a place she loved in the woods, together with a dear friend, and to burn the entire case file there. The ritual was accompanied by many tears, as the powerless anger she had kept within her for so long was released: tears of her long and lonely fight with institutions, tears of loss and grief, but also tears of relief, that she would finally be able to leave this phase of her life behind her and keep her child close in her heart. The burning of the file created space for a new beginning. Meryl enrolled for a university course and her new life could really begin.

### The hands that receive

In the consulting room I have a beautiful ceramic object depicting two open hands. What the hands express is: "Give it to me." (See Figure 18 on next page.)

A ritual that is frequently enacted in my consulting room is the burning of letters written to people who have passed away, to former lovers, to unresolved situations. Letters of thanks and apologies, angry letters, letters seeking redress. By writing these letters, bringing them to a session, reading them out loud and then—at the right time—tearing them up and surrendering them to the hands to be burned creates actual, physical space.

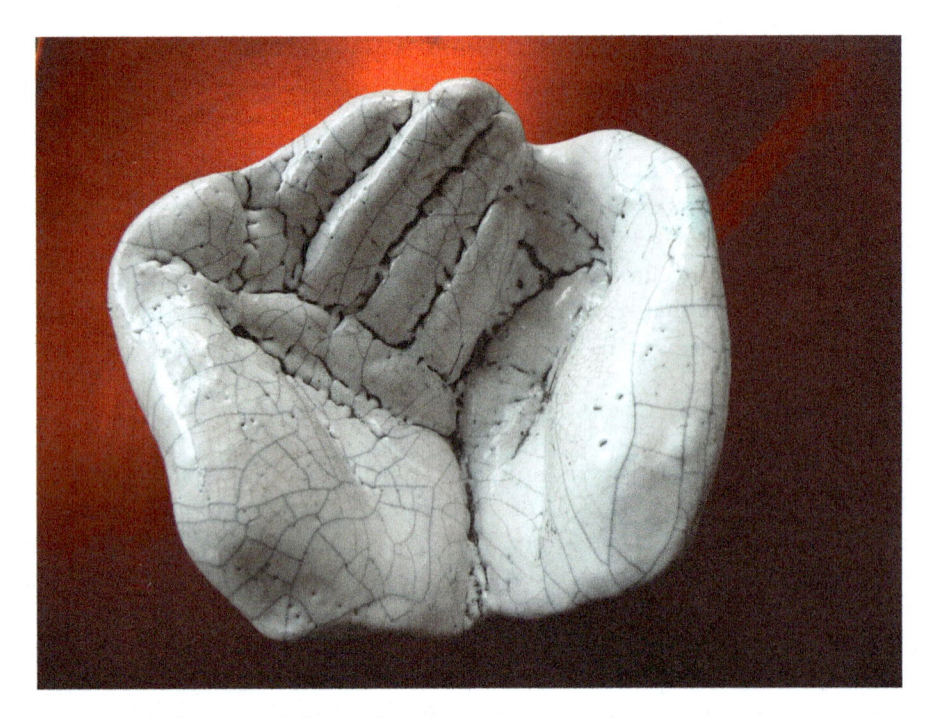

Figure 18. *The hands that receive* by José Aerts.

Numerous rituals can be devised and tailored to a particular situation. For instance, a client may write a letter to be taken to their loved one's grave, using the written word to make amends, to say something that had remained unsaid. Perhaps the letter may be read out loud beside the grave, together with other close friends or relatives. That is narrativity in action: the act of reading the words they have written out loud creates space and makes change possible. *Sensemaking* requires action of some kind.

A client was burdened by a lie she had spread among her entire circle of friends, relatives, and acquaintances. The person about whom she had lied had moved away and could no longer be traced. The situation was in the past, but the lie lived on in her body. Once she had written down the lie and spoken it out loud in the consulting room, we were able to relinquish the letter to "the hands" and burn it together. The smoke circling up to the ceiling produced visible relief.

*The merger ritual*

I worked for a time at Boddaert outpatient centre in the south of the Netherlands. When it became known that the government was going to impose a merger with another, larger institution, the entire team was full of grief and anger. Proud of our hard work and achievements, we were determined to fight to preserve our centre. Some team members said they felt as if they were being taken over and gobbled up. For months we did our utmost to preserve the small centre's independence. When it became clear that our funding would be stopped if we continued to block the merger, we reviewed the options. How best to preserve the spirit of the centre in the new situation of the merger? How could we find a constructive way of moving on to this new phase?

We concluded that a farewell and transition ritual was needed. We needed to say goodbye to our existence as a small-scale, independent clinic and make the transition to a larger organisation. We decided to go into a group retreat in the woods for a day. All the team members had agreed to work on a ritual transition, and individuals or small groups would contribute something by way of farewell. Some wrote songs, some cooked dishes, and some related their memories. We also produced a tangible memorial: a totem pole on which the centre's history was inscribed, with an image of its good spirit. The totem pole was unveiled during the day in the woods, and stood in the new meeting room for many years afterwards, to commemorate the good times and the spirit in which people wanted to continue to provide care.

We also staged a small play, which demonstrated the useful, cathartic role of humour—even farcical humour—in a painful situation. The play unfolded as follows:

> The director sits at a huge, empty table, wearing a smart suit but a clown's nose. Enter a second clown, his overalls bulging with carpenter's tools and a large bunch of keys dangling from one hand. He too has a clown's nose. The second clown is clearly a real workman, who has been summoned by the director. He shuffles into the room, patently disconcerted by the director's imposing presence. Neither man speaks. The director gestures for the workman to approach, without offering him a chair; it must be clear who is the boss here! The workman-clown looks towards the audience—the other employees—in an appeal to their sympathy. Everyone is naturally on his side.
>
> The big boss gestures to the workman to hand over his tools. Reluctantly he hands over his carpenter's pencil, exchanging glances with the audience. The big boss stares at the pencil and then at the workman's bulging overalls, and then gestures for him to hand over each tool, one by one. To the sadness of the workman and the audience, the workman is gradually "undressed" in this way, parting slowly and lovingly with each of his tools. Finally, the boss demands the keys to the workman's house! The audience holds its breath—surely not? But yes, this too must be handed over.
>
> The workman-clown slinks away, looking back fondly at his tools until he has left the room. The "big boss" is left sitting at a table covered with pieces of equipment he cannot use.

The play expressed the staff's sorrow, the feeling of having been "undressed", their sense of injustice and of the inevitability of events. Once this farce had been played out, the air cleared and everyone was able to sing, laugh, eat, and dance: they made their peace with the new order, and the healing started.

## *Russian nesting dolls*

Working with the Russian nesting dolls is another form of enactment, and of organising space. The arrangement that is made with the dolls can make people who are important in the client's life—the client's long-gone father, for instance—present in the room, but they can also represent the client's own inner voices. A very small voice within the client can be made present through a very small doll.

Figure 19. Russian nesting dolls.

The Russian dolls have a female appearance—they are "matryoshkas", meaning grandmothers, and tell of the female life principle; there are no male variants. Some boys and men have difficulty at the beginning identifying with a female doll, but in most cases they are soon persuaded when reminded that everyone is born from a woman, and that the dolls tell of this female life principle. I have used the nesting dolls for many years, and gender has never been a problem.

The Russian nesting dolls can tell the story of the family's "ecology". A doll can be assigned to every member of the family or to anyone in the ecology beyond: the office, school, the soccer coach, the company doctor, the mayor. It is possible to assign a doll to a theme: "the secret", fear, anger, hurt, pain. A place can be created for those who are not present, the deceased, or for a child who was stillborn or aborted. Instead of discussing the loss of a child, the child's presence can be conjured up existentially in the form of a doll on the table. The completely absent father can be made present in the form of the smallest doll—placed under the table. Past, present and future can all be given a place. How will things look when all these problems have been resolved? Where will everyone be standing then?

An arrangement of dolls provides a framework that clearly visualises each person's influence and relationships of dependency. Working with nesting dolls ensures that everyone has a place: young and old, the present and the absent, regardless of class, skin colour, gender, and origin. In the case of people from another country, their homeland can also be represented in this way.

The nesting dolls organise space through the places assigned to each one. The arrangement is language in action: once it has been made, it comes to life in this "third space", becoming a truth that focuses everyone's attention. Changes that are made in the arrangement are translated into changes in everyday life. Distances that are hard to bridge are represented by the big gap between two dolls. Once the client, as the owner of the arrangement, moves a doll in the direction of the other, the tension in the space increases. The client starts sweating and breathing heavily. It is an actual physical change: this is narrativity in action.

I use dolls to depict the different positions in the family. An entire tray full of dolls of all kinds, sizes, colours and textures is brought out, and each family member is invited to choose one to represent him or her.

A six-year-old girl chooses a large doll for herself and two smaller ones for her parents. Then she places herself in between her parents.

A mother places dolls for her two sons very close to herself and a doll representing her husband.

Following a divorce, the father has ceased to play a role in his son's life. The boy, who is twelve years old, chooses for himself a doll that is larger than his mother's. For his father, he chooses the smallest possible doll, and places it at the other end of the table.

A girl aged sixteen, the eldest of six, chooses a smaller doll for herself than for her five brothers and sisters.

Once the arrangement has been made, the nesting dolls tell their stories in a natural, simple language. They have a friendly, benign expression, and are scarcely figurative. This distinguishes them from Duplo dolls, for instance, which are explicitly made to look like a doctor, a fireman, or a police officer. Their significance is already given and encoded: a child is unlikely to choose a "nurse" to represent his father.

Children, in particular, love working with the dolls, and even the youngest are able to indicate the relations within the family with great precision, for instance in terms of relative size, and who is close to whom. They know which place is the most difficult, who looks at each other and who looks away. Each arrangement of nesting dolls presents a clear picture and conveys a unique experience. It is a prelinguistic image, a picture that is independent of education and intelligence. The nesting dolls speak for themselves and represent universal and narrative knowledge.

*Vanished into a black hole*

Sandra, aged thirty-five, sought psychotherapy because of her sense of guilt. She found that she had no feelings for her children, a daughter of five and a son of eight. She took good care of them and in many ways everything at home was going well, but her lack of feelings for her children gave Sandra the conviction that she was a bad mother. She spent much of the time in her own private world, and that is what had precipitated the break-up with the children's father.

Sandra's eldest child had been admitted to hospital and died, when just a few months old. Sandra recalled, "When he was ill, when he was dying, and in the time after that, I was completely present, and my mother was totally there for me. My mother was also extremely supportive during my divorce."

Sandra said that she had a lot of conflict with her little daughter, and we explored her life history. We started by calling her withdrawal "vanishing into a black hole", a hole in which she felt depressed. Gradually it became clear that it was not in fact a black hole, but a state of absence, of present absence, of being somewhere else, in a world of her own. This world turned out to have originated around the time of her fifth birthday. It was then that her father fell in love with another woman and withdrew into a world of his own. A few years later, her parents were divorced. "I felt that my mother had her hands full taking care of my younger brother and sister and dealing with her grief at the divorce. Although I was very young, I decided that the best solution was for me to make myself invisible. I loved going to primary school and learning to read. Ever since then I have lived in books. In a book you are never alone, and you can completely immerse yourself in your own world."

Her little daughter had now reached the same age at which she herself had retreated from her own mother and made herself invisible. Her daughter was constantly circling around her and often asked literally, "Can you see me?" And when Sandra confirmed that she could see her, her little daughter would nonetheless ask again a little later. It was as if she felt she had to keep her mother awake all the time, and that she was taking care of her in this way.

When this care became visible in an arrangement of Russian dolls, Sandra started to cry—something that felt quite unnatural to her. What happened here was that the five-year-old daughter was encountering the five-year-old child in her mother. That little girl in the mother had decided long ago not to be present, and this decision was still making itself felt so many years later.

The result was a struggle between Sandra as mother and the five-year-old child inside her—a struggle between the two five-year-old children, and between mother and daughter. The doll arrangement made this clear.

Figure 20. Russian doll arrangement of Sandra.

Then Sandra chose the same colourful doll for her mother as she had chosen for her daughter. She said that her mother was now behind her; as if her mother was now saying: "I'll take over, you're having such a difficult time." In the new arrangement, she was not just *behind* her daughter, but also *facing* her, as if she was saying: "I see you! Wake up! Where are you?" It was an appeal, urging Sandra to manifest herself, to be present. For this therapy session Sandra had taken her children to her mother's house, but she had not answered when her mother asked where she was going. She did not yet dare to make it clear and visible that she had sought the help of a psychotherapist. Some time later, however, she did make this clear, and her mother accompanied her to the session. The therapy enabled Sandra to speak about the sadness she had experienced as a little girl. Her mother listened attentively and *saw* her daughter. When Sandra was able to lay her head on her mother's shoulder, weeping, her inner and outer worlds flowed together harmoniously, and something in her inner world was healed.

# CHAPTER NINE

# Stories from beyond the horizon: on dissociative attacks and on stories-as-yet-untold

*"Only by restoring the broken connections can we be healed. Connection is health"*

—Wendell Berry

## Introduction

This chapter starts with a discussion of the project on patients with non-epileptic fits at the epilepsy centre Kempenhaeghe in Heeze. A new approach was tried with these patients, given the lack of success in diagnosis and treatment up to then. Many had tried numerous hospitals, clinics and mental health services to no avail. In each case, diagnostic and neurological tests were requested to exclude the possibility of epilepsy. In one group of patients, it proved impossible, again and again, to find any somatic cause. It was decided to devise a new treatment for these individuals (some clinically, others on an outpatient basis) and a group was set up to build up expertise on fits of non-epileptic origin.

The first difficulty was finding a suitable name for this syndrome. Previous names such as pseudo-epilepsy or psychogenic, dissociative or non-epileptic fits highlighted something—epilepsy—which had not in fact been diagnosed at all. In the absence of a better term, we decided (in consultation with the patients) to call them "somatic fits".

We discovered that the fits were linked to multiple physical and psychological traumas, to stories that had proven impossible to tell in any way other than through fits of the body—to stories that were untold, parked and banished or detached from consciousness because of their unbearably painful content. Coagulated stories, stories that could not be told in any way other than through violent physical movements, but that kept falling on deaf ears.

The therapeutic context was carefully structured. The neurologist remained the primary practitioner. For peer review, a psychiatrist attached to the project group was consulted. The fits were filmed and then watched and discussed with the patient. We saw patients who crawled under their beds and covered their heads protectively with their arms during a fit. We saw their bodies telling unarticulated stories of abuse and traumatisation. Most of the patients found it highly confrontational to watch the video clips, but the experience nonetheless helped to provide a starting point for an appropriate, highly specific, course of therapy. The trauma-linked stories surfaced. That was the moment at which a patient would be referred for psychotherapy with the aid of hypnosis, since this is an excellent way of inducing cooperation between the conscious and unconscious mind.

The psychotherapy was set up under the supervision of a trusted doctor who followed the patient's progress with interest. The psychotherapy team reported back to the neurologist, who in turn kept the referring practitioner informed. A good deal of preliminary work had already been done before a patient arrived at the clinic for hypnosis, including setting up a sound therapeutic context.

Tracking down the story behind the fits was in itself a nomadic journey. No two journeys were the same, and the incidents that could be broadly classified as loss of, or diminished, consciousness were extremely diverse: it was impossible to find a single common denominator. Within the safe setting of an epilepsy centre, a secure therapeutic context under the neurologist's medical supervision, each journey could be undertaken in an atmosphere of trust. In most cases, the approach was successful. A few case histories have been selected from this varied collection to discuss here.

*Petra and the beatings*

Petra, forty-seven years old, was referred to the outpatient clinic of the epilepsy centre because of severe recurrent fits that greatly resembled epileptic seizures. During these fits she would lose consciousness. The episodes occurred roughly once every nine days, after which she was "out like a light" for a day or a day and a half. She would sense the fit coming a few hours in advance. Each one started with pain on the right at the back of her head, a pain that gradually "rolled" forwards over the following few hours. About twenty minutes before the fit "struck", she would get gooseflesh: a sign that she must quickly take to her bed. Spasms would surge up and down her head, after which she would lose consciousness. Twenty-four hours—sometimes thirty-six hours—later, she would wake up. She was generally woken by a particular friend, whom she always called when she felt an attack coming on. The friend would then come to visit a day later, and would often have to work hard to bring Petra round. On waking she was always highly disoriented and anxious. These fits had been a feature of her life for over thirty years, although in varying degrees of severity. Petra had always allowed the fits to "happen". Her friends and relatives were used to them, and reacted by calling a doctor. She had been subjected to countless tests in hospital, but no medical cause had ever been found. The frequency and severity of her fits had increased after her hysterectomy and her mother's death. Since then they had remained at the pitch described above.

Since Petra felt attacks coming on beforehand, the attending neurologist suggested to Petra that she call him the next time she felt one approaching. The neurologist would film her and monitor her EEG for twenty-four hours, and afterwards he and Petra would watch the video together and analyse it.

When the next fit occurred and was monitored in this way, the EEG revealed that there was no epileptic activity. However, the video images showed Petra's terror: during the fit she crept away into a corner, shielding her head with her arms as if from an external threat. She was referred for psychotherapy. Eventually, in these sessions, the story about the beatings she had suffered as a child gradually emerged, one piece at a time.

Petra's father had beaten her with a stick throughout her childhood, starting when she was "still in the cradle". The sticks he used were all around the house and she was expected to fetch them. If she made the slightest sound, the beating would last longer.

Petra was the eldest daughter in a family of seven children. Her elder brother, the family's pride and joy, had left home early to train for the priesthood. One of her other brothers was also severely abused, while her youngest sister was the apple of her father's eye. The family was well regarded in the community. Within the home, however, a dramatically different scenario was played out.

Her mother had always tried to protect her and did her best to prevent the beatings. However, she found it impossible to oppose him and was accustomed to taking her cue from "the man of the house". Her father always maintained, even on his deathbed, that Petra had deserved her beatings, and he "died with a grin on his face". She still saw his menacing eyes every day and shrank from the image in fear. She imagined him suddenly entering her living room or bedroom, and it seemed as if the abuse was still going on. When her hysterectomy coincided with her mother's death, it was as if her only vestige of protection had gone, and the fits became worse. During the fits she experienced her father's abuse again, in a dissociated consciousness. Her friend told Petra that she had once found her under the bed and heard a voice strangled with fear shouting: "Stop!" or "Don't!" From then on, Petra involved her friend in her life story.

When Petra heard that her fits were not epileptic in origin, it became completely clear to her that they derived from the childhood abuse. They were now reclassified as "dissociated fits arising from severe and protracted abuse". For years she had concealed the abuse from the outside world, finding it shameful and humiliating. She also acknowledged that she relived the beatings during every fit and that her fear of her father still oppressed her after all those years.

At this point it was possible to start therapy. We started by trying to ascertain how Petra's mother had acknowledged the abuse that her daughter had suffered. Petra related that when her mother was dying she had spoken clearly of the torment she had suffered from the beatings meted out to her daughter. She apologised for not having been able to prevent them.

"My mother did not want to die, she held my hand tight up to the very last moment, as if she wanted to carry on caring for me. So I said: 'you can go, mother, it's all right!'"

To create a therapeutic context and to ensure that the means and ends were congruent, without creating any conflicting loyalties, I asked Petra if her mother would give her blessing to the therapy. Petra replied unhesitatingly:

"Oh yes! She would like nothing better than for me to do well. Mother acknowledged the beatings and I am sure that she is taking good care of me from where she is now."

Picking up the phrase "where she is now", I asked Petra to write her mother a letter requesting help and support in working through her traumas and reducing the role of fits in her life. Petra wrote a moving letter to her mother and pasted it into a large white exercise book that she called her "therapy book". She also pasted a large photo of her mother on the inside cover. In this exercise book she would write about the therapy, address her father, include diverse reflections and paste all the encouraging cards she received in support of her therapy. It gradually became a real workbook, a book about "the right to speak".

I had placed Petra's mother high in the significance hierarchy and I myself adopted a position next to Petra. Mother was unable to protect Petra effectively during her lifetime, but she nonetheless had the intention of doing so. For the time being it was the father, with his terrifying menace, who ranked highest in the hierarchy.

The next stage was to find a safe place amid all this fear and menace. This began with hypnotherapy, as practised at the outpatient clinic with persons afflicted by dissociated fits, and we went in search of a safe place for Petra. She succeeded in entering a deep trance and travelled to her favourite place, the sea. She experienced the atmosphere of the sea intensively, with all her senses. She heard the waves and the birds, the children playing; she felt her footsteps in the sand and enjoyed the view towards the horizon. She was able to relax and feel safe.

I then asked her to conjure up the image of a little girl playing on the beach in carefree abandon. This little girl symbolised a new world of untroubled childhood, and we called her "little Petra". She played on the beach and knew nothing of beatings. Hopefully this strategy might help to create a new, parallel identity: what Milton Erickson calls the "my friend John" strategy (Erickson & Rossi, 1980).

In the subsequent sessions, Petra returned to the beach each time she was hypnotised. Initially the little girl still clutched her tightly or stayed close. Gradually, however, she became more relaxed and dared to play freely. Petra was able to give her space in which to do so, to observe her and enjoy her play, her pleasure and carefree attitude. Little Petra went through a second childhood, as it were, and she also surfaced spontaneously at safe moments in her everyday life. Once the therapy had been started along these lines, Petra was able to spend Christmas and New Year's Eve alone. This was something she had longed to do for many years, but up to then she had always given in to the expectations of the outside world. She enjoyed herself tremendously on these days and had the feeling that little Petra was with her. She experienced this as the initial result of her therapy.

When Petra went to the beach under hypnosis, she had the space and time to think about her life. She started sharing recollections and often experienced beautiful images or sensations, such as a bright light swimming into view or a warm physical sensation, and her self-confidence gradually increased. She recorded the frequency and duration of her fits in a graph in her exercise book, indicating the progress with colours. Quite quickly she noticed that the fits had become less frequent, from once every nine days to once every fourteen days.

Petra started addressing her father directly, writing: "I want you to leave, I never want to see you again". She experienced every word she wrote down as a victory and increasing "degrees of freedom". When I noticed her growing in strength, I decided to adopt a provocative stance. Since Petra was still paralysed with fear, I wanted to help her to develop an opposing force. Adopting a provocative, oppositional attitude can be a successful strategy in such situations.

Van de Ven has called it a "friend as foe" strategy and has coined the word "ludagogy" for it (Van de Ven, 1975, 1982).

If the therapeutic working relationship is sufficiently close, telling provocative stories, against the grain, can help to arouse an opposing force and a decisive shift in the story. In Petra's situation, the aim was to help her claim the right to speak. The provocations were designed to reduce the fits precisely by magnifying their influence in space. By emphasising the presence of the fits, I tried to help Petra to reduce them herself. I put two chairs near Petra: one beside her symbolising the help she was receiving from me as a therapist, intended to help her develop her own strength to resist. The other chair was placed opposite her, and this was the chair of the fits. The fits acquired their own voice and identity; they acquired intentionality and "lectured Petra on how to behave", as her father had done. It was a homoeopathic process in which the pathogen or toxic matter was present in diluted form. In this process of mimesis, imitation, it was the therapist's responsibility to carefully monitor Petra's ability to cope.

I went and stood behind the "fits" chair, but we agreed that Petra could always make a sign at which I would immediately move and stand beside her. When I was sitting in the chair next to her, I would encourage her to say "I want to be free". It was a very long time before she dared to articulate that sentence, and even then she could only mutter it, with sweat breaking out on her forehead. As soon as she had articulated that sentence, I went and stood behind the "fits" chair and said, "Next year perhaps, or in a few years' time." In a trembling voice, tears coursing over her cheeks, Petra was finally able to say: "Now!" From this point onwards she gradually gathered strength, supported by me as the therapist, seated on the chair beside her.

I encouraged Petra to express herself further. Within a safe therapeutic relationship, my opposition provoked resistance: "I don't want to have fits any more, I want them to stop, I'm going to banish them from my life." This resistance was gradually developed, and the fits acquired an even more emphatic voice of their own, the voice of "the father's power". Petra succeeded in distinguishing between me, as the therapist, and her father, as a result of which I could further develop my provocative stance.

"I'm going to take your freedom back. Your progress is going much too fast. Any progress you gain is thanks to me anyway, and not to yourself. I merely allowed you to think you were free, to maintain that illusion. I allowed you to get stronger, day by day, and now you think, since I'm only there every twenty-five days now, that you've done this by yourself. But you really shouldn't think you've got anywhere, because I'm going to claim my space back from now on. I won't let you go. I'm going to make the fits last longer."

Petra shrank back and cringed with fear, but she managed to resist and to mark out her own territory. Then I switched again:

"How long have you been having those fits?" I asked provocatively, "thirty-two years? Tell you what: I'll leave when we celebrate my fiftieth anniversary."

"No way!" said Petra.

I backtracked a little:

"Well all right then, how about my fortieth anniversary … You can keep it up for another eight years."

"Absolutely not!" said Petra.

"You're so ungrateful! I've given you so much space and it's still not enough. You never amounted to anything anyway! You even have some foolish idea that you've got somewhere under your own steam."

For the first time Petra was able to say, "Yes, I did it under my own steam, and I'm going to get much stronger now!"

"No you aren't! You'll see … The next fit will be a few days earlier and then you'll know how much power I have."

"No I won't!" said Petra. She squeezed the words reflecting her fighting spirit out of her body.

Her head shook back and forth, she wept continuously and sat there with clenched fists. Still, she succeeded in claiming the right to speak. The session ended with her words: "I'm kicking you out. I never want to see you again!"

She then picked up the "fits" chair and put it outside the door in the corridor. It was an amusing sight, after the session, to see that chair standing there in the corridor. My colleagues must have wondered what it was doing there.

This method gradually succeeded in reducing the length and frequency of the fits. The time in between fits increased one day at a time. It was a slow, difficult process, but after eighteen months of therapy, the frequency had decreased from once a fortnight to once a month. Twice Petra had to make a new graph, since she had "fought her way out of the old one." The duration of the fits had been reduced to sixteen hours.

Gradually Petra's physical resistance also increased. When I stood behind the "fits chair", I slowly slid the chair in Petra's direction to express that the fits were gaining in influence. This inspired Petra to use her strength to push the chair back, engaging in a power struggle. It still took an enormous emotional toll on her. She wept, sighed, and groaned, but her strength was released, and grew.

Petra's inner energy was also released when she concentrated on her body in a different way. She felt trapped in her body, so stifled and cramped that at one point she cried out "I'm full of hard cardboard." This was a key metaphor for her situation, in which cardboard represented frozen emotions. Petra was initially incapable to feel any anger in relation to her father. She was gripped by an all-encompassing, crippling terror. Even sorrow was only possible in small doses.

When Petra was under hypnosis on the beach, she imagined herself walking into the sea, and the seawater saturating and softening the cardboard. This was a form of trance logic, in which an "as if" was translated literally into the reality of the physical body. Once the cardboard was totally saturated with water, she experienced it gradually leaving her body in thin threads. This went one thread at a time, and each one was painful. Sometimes larger chunks of cardboard would break loose and were almost impossible to remove, but gradually more space began to open up in her body, in her hands and legs and her pelvis.

In the space that developed, new emotions became possible: not just sadness, but also joy. When she was out walking in the street, she had the feeling of being able to stand up straighter than in the past, of daring to look into the world. She saw more colours and brightness. She also created space for herself by externalising her trauma. She divided a large foam rubber ball into two pieces. In one half she inserted a whole pile of notes inscribed with negative messages imparted to her over the years: "you're stupid", "you're worthless", "you deserve to be treated like this", "you'll never learn anything". The inside surface of the ball was black and the negative notes were also black. All the notes were written on pieces of stiff cardboard. In the other half she made room for new, positive experiences. She said:

"One day I'll be able to attach the two halves. Then I will have conquered my trauma and I'll have put it all inside this ball."

For the time being, however, her father continued to return to her home in some form or other, every day. It became clear that there was an unconscious factor blocking Petra's efforts to become stronger:

"When I use force to push the chair back, I see my mother standing beside my father, and it feels as if I am pushing her away too. So apparently I want to protect my mother by accepting my father's beatings. I don't want to push my mother aside, I don't want to lose her—but she stands beside my father, because in spite of everything, she loved him."

Once she realised this, Petra was able to make space between father and mother, and she felt her mother giving her permission to oppose her father. She obtained that permission by writing her mother another letter about the progress of her therapy and about her discovery. She wrote, "Mum, I'm sure that you will approve of me kicking Dad out."

Once there was space between her mother and father, space also opened up between Petra and her father. We then looked at the father's history.

> Father came from a family in which many of the children had been stillborn. Two of his elder brothers had become priests and were placed on a pedestal in the family. Granddad was a man with hard eyes and I'm sure that he beat my father. A story was told in the family about something that happened when my father was supposed to be taking care of his youngest sister. He forgot about her while playing with friends, and she had an accident after which she was permanently bedridden. This sister was "canonised" in the community: she was very pious and had a large circle of correspondents. My father was the only one of the siblings who had to go out to work; he was overshadowed by his brothers and also by his sister.

When Petra was born, her father registered her as a son at the population register! Later, returning to correct his mistake, he named her "Petra" after his "saintly" sister. Petra posited the theory that her father had conceived hatred for his sister, along with a lifelong sense of guilt for the accident, and that he projected them both onto her, seeing her as his sister rather than his daughter: "I became the one onto whom he offloaded all the pain he had been unable to deal with."

Petra was now able to distinguish between her own identity and the identity superimposed on her. Instead of saying "I'm stupid" she was now able to say, "I was called stupid, but I'm not. I'm someone who has potential for growth!"

All in all, the therapy continued for about seven years, with long gaps in between sessions. Eventually Petra won a complete victory over her fits. She sealed the foam rubber ball shut and covered it with moss. She developed a cheerful, optimistic attitude to life and was much admired within her large circle of friends. Her best friend stood by her throughout all those

240   HANDBOOK OF NARRATIVE PSYCHOTHERAPY FOR CHILDREN, ADULTS, AND FAMILIES

years of therapy, and was closely involved in it. She took a photograph of the moss-covered ball, with the following verse inscription:

> The true me hides behind trees
> The true me hides behind leaves
> under the fruits of nature.
> But I shall find the true me,
> pick her up, caress and hold her,
> and never let her go.
> Petra

Some time after the therapy was concluded, Petra came to say goodbye. She brought her film material with her, consisting of an interview that one of my colleagues recorded with her about every aspect of the therapy. She had thrown away her therapy notebooks, because she wanted to leave the entire period behind her and did not want to preserve any part of it.

Every year Petra would send a New Year's card and a brief note on how she had been doing. Each one reflected her new zest for life and the affection she shared with her warm circle of friends, and included references to her holidays—often spent, naturally enough, at the seaside.

Petra became ill two years ago. She conducted herself with optimism and dignity, but sadly passed away not long afterwards. In approving the above story for publication, Petra's friend wrote:

Figure 21. The foam rubber ball of Petra.

I think the story rings true, although I found it a confrontational, emotional experience to read it. As Petra's friend I sometimes had to answer questions about her, and the therapist's openness was extremely helpful. That openness gave me the strength I needed to support her. I continued to say that I believed in her and admired the way she was responding to the therapy. Her self-image and her self-confidence grew one small step at a time. Eventually she dared to go on holiday again, for the first time in many years, and had a wonderful time: she loved life so much!

*Smart strength and brute force*

Steven was sixteen years old when he was referred to the epilepsy centre's outpatient clinic. About a year earlier, he had lost consciousness at a school camp in the Ardennes, Belgium, during a difficult rope-climbing exercise. Not daring to climb up, he fell down, unconscious. After this episode, Steven suffered renewed fits at school and elsewhere when he faced tasks that made him fearful. He would suddenly fall down, forwards or backwards, trembling all over and thrashing his arms and legs against the ground. Friends and acquaintances learned to deal with these fits and tried to help Steven to reduce or regulate the stress in his life.

At school Steven was afraid of tests of all kinds, and often fainted in class. Teachers were at a loss as to how to assess him. Steven, his parents and the school were all unsure as to how much pressure he could be put under, and whether it was better to challenge or to spare him. Alongside all his anxieties concerning achievements, Steven was brash in his interaction with others: he often quarrelled, and fist fights were not uncommon. He usually won these fights, since he hit out without hesitation. His life came to be dominated by rows: rows at school, with fellow pupils and teachers, and rows at home with his parents.

After neurological tests revealed no EEG anomalies and the boy did not appear to have epilepsy, Steven was referred to me for therapy. He expressed strong resistance from the outset: "Here we go again. Another psychologist or one of those characters who wants to test me. Fat chance!" I felt the fear underlying that resistance. I had read that Steven was crazy about trucks and wanted to be a truck driver. His father had an important job in transport and several other relatives worked in the same sector. Steven greatly admired his father. I decided to organise the session with Stephen around the theme of trucks to see whether I could attach any significance to his symptoms within the framework of the world of trucks.

Milton Erickson's "utilisation approach" (Erickson, 1967; Erickson & Rossi, 1979, 1980) involves enlisting resources from the client's world to achieve positive change. The categories listed by Jeffrey Zeig (Zeig, 1980) help the therapist to connect with the client's world. With this in mind, I started talking to Steven about trucks, and before long his cheeks reddened with excitement and enthusiasm. He talked about his favourite trucks, his father and his brothers, about trips on which he had gone along as driver's mate, and about engines. This soon established a working relationship. I also noted the message projected by his body: "See how strong I am! I'm perfectly friendly as long as you don't cross me! If you don't get in my way I won't hurt you. But watch out, I'm fast and alert". I told Stephen that he looked impressive for a boy of sixteen and asked him to stand beside me.

He was clearly already taller than me and broad-shouldered. I spoke admiringly of his physique and the powerful image he projected. It is important for the therapist to adopt a lower "status" here.

"If we translate your physical strength to the world of trucks, I'd say that you have a pretty powerful engine."

I tried to add different words. "What do you call that sort of power?"

I paused and invited Steven to name it. He suggested calling it "brute force". This became the first serviceable element for a framework: Steven possessed "brute force". The advantage of brute force was that it made an impression; the disadvantage was that it often led to fights, which fuelled the tension in his body. That body, so full of strength and bravura, was also full of tension and fear.

I added: "A truck driver needs smart strength as well as brute force. For instance when waiting in a traffic jam or at a border crossing. When driving down narrow roads or making sure that the load doesn't slide about; manoeuvring around a new city or reversing down a lane. Turning the truck around. Responding when other people try to rush you or get angry because they think you're blocking the road. A truck driver needs to be able to apply the brakes just as well as to accelerate."

Steven apparently had a lot to learn about smart strength, and perhaps I could help him. As for that other strength, he had much to teach *me*. By this point, Steven had become interested in the therapy. So I asked him: "Thinking about what we've discussed up to now, Steven, do you have any idea what your fits might mean?"

Steven replied: "My body is full of tension and it goes to my head. Then everything goes black and I pass out."

So in order to develop smart strength, it was essential to release the tension from his body. I added: "If we can get your body to release that tension, your head will be clear and calmer, and things may go better at school. After all, you need smart strength there too."

Steven agreed that we would do some exercises to help release the tension in his body. I started by asking him to concentrate on a place or time that he associated with feeling good and peaceful. He described a horse in a meadow in his village that he regarded as his very good friend.

"Whenever I visit that horse, I get really calm. He seems to understand me. Once, when someone got mad at me and I nearly got into a fight, he protected me." As Steven talked about the horse I noticed him softening, relaxing. We decided to use this experience with the horse as one of our resources. Furthermore, the horse is a fine metaphor for the body, and Stephen's relationship with the horse was a good metaphor for the relationship between mind and body.

We started practising: in one fist, Steven concentrated as much tension as possible. When his fist was completely full of tension, he focused on the image of the horse in the meadow, and collected all the positive associations he had with that image in his other fist. As that image became stronger, he allowed the tension in his left fist to flow away. This is Stein's "clenched fist method" (Stein, 1963). Steven soon experienced a wonderful sense of calm. He saw beautiful colours, imagined himself brushing the horse, and his body felt truly at ease. He also felt his head clearing. Steven was open to the suggestion that if his head were to become clearer, he would have more space to absorb his lessons at school.

We practised this form of hypnosis a few times so that he would be able to do it by himself, at school and at home, without anyone noticing. That phrase "without anyone noticing" also linked up to his view of the world: he did not need to lose face, and as his therapist, I was his secret ally who helped him to develop smart strength.

Then we started to explore the possible significance of these fits in the wider perspective of his background. He talked about his family—a male stronghold, with only his mother facing her husband and three sons. His mother thought it important to do well at school. She worked with disadvantaged children and wanted to maximise Steven's chances in life. Besides, she thought the truckers' world too harsh for her son. She had seen her eldest son do well because he had been encouraged to study, so she did not feel that it was right to give in to Steven and stop pressuring him. Still, this pressure was only increasing Steven's tension. His father thought it better to let things run their course and could imagine Steven doing well as a truck driver, a world he knew very well. It became clear that the parents argued a lot about this issue, with Steven stuck in between.

Steven adored his father, and the men in the house often belittled the mother. The parental squabbles also impeded contact with school. While Steven's father wanted the school to stop putting pressure on the boy, his mother wanted him to be kept on board: "otherwise he won't get anywhere." The school, the parents and Steven became increasingly embroiled in conflict. So I checked with the school if they would be willing to cooperate in creating a career path for the transport sector, provided the parents agreed. Then I invited the parents and Steven for a discussion. It was essential to stop Steven's fits, since he would have to have been completely free of fits for some time to be allowed to work in this sector.

I talked to Steven and his parents on the subject of the "male family" and we discussed the men's tendency to dismiss the mother's views. This created space for the mother to explain her arguments. I would not let the others interrupt her. Then the father told his own story. He too hoped that Steven would get his school-leaving certificate, but he could see that pressure had an adverse effect on his son. Still, he was able to say for the first time that he admired his wife's efforts on behalf of their eldest son and was delighted with the results. This brought the two approaches closer, and Steven's mother eventually consented to her son's pursuit of a path geared towards the transport sector. The discussion also touched on Stephen's loyalty to his mother.

Then another factor emerged in the significance to be attached to the fits: although Stephen was often rude to his mother, spoke disparagingly about her and called her stupid, he felt very close to her, loved her, and attached great value to her approval. He was now able to say so openly. The tension between his father and mother, between yes and no, between his longing to work with trucks and his mother's disapproval of this choice, had blocked his future prospects. Now that his parents had created space for him, he could engage with school in the newly agreed theme-based framework or "consensual domain" (Maturana, 1988; Maturana & Varela, 1992). This domain provided space to continue therapy with Steven, developing the exercises that might help to banish the fits.

When the therapy started, Steven was having up to fifteen fits a week. Within six months, the rate had fallen to just a few each week. Steven's father told me that every time the telephone rang he was afraid of being summoned to get his son, and that every time he heard an ambulance siren, he was afraid that his son would be brought home unconscious again. I maintained frequent contact with the parents, who confirmed the steady progress and supported the chosen approach. We now agreed with the school that it was time to increase the difficulty of the material to prepare Steven better for his training in the transport sector. By then, Steven was getting the hang of releasing tension from his body by doing the exercises we had practised. He started enjoying school and getting better grades. He no longer saw school or lessons as enemies poised to deliver a knock-out blow.

He gradually managed to overcome the fits and gained a different sense of his body, more connected to the world of the horse; a horse that was powerful but looked with a friendly gaze; that was strong without needing to be aggressive. Steven himself was also now less likely to provoke aggression and was even capable of deflecting challenges he would once have settled with a fist fight. He had learned to see walking away not as a defeat but as an instance of using smart strength. He would wink and laugh when relating stories like this. The last time I heard from Stephen, it had been two years since his last attack.

### "I got off with a fright"

Tony, a man aged forty-six, was referred to the epilepsy centre after suffering epileptiform fits. Six months earlier, he had had five fits within the space of a week. Extensive hospital tests found no epileptic activity, although the fits did present as such. Each fit started with stabbing pains in his head, after which he would lose consciousness, followed by muscular spasms and much thrashing of his limbs. At the beginning he made a full recovery after each fit, but in recent months that was no longer the case. He had suffered another series of fits three months earlier, and more the previous month. The neurologist requested a consultation with a psychotherapist.

Tony and his wife sat before me. Tony complained of chronic fatigue and said that the slightest effort made him break out in a sweat all over his body: an alarming new development for a man used to regular strenuous exercise. Tony was not a man of many words, and nothing remarkable emerged from his account of his background. He and his wife seemed happy and said that they had a good family life. They had no idea where the fits could have come from: there was no indication of where they might be inscribed in his life history.

Then, right at the end of the session, Tony related almost casually that he had had an accident at work some months before. He worked in a stockroom and saw a large forklift truck heading straight for him in the narrow path between the storage racks. Realising that the driver hadn't seen him, he thought: "This is the end, I've had it". The forklift truck drove over him, and he saw his life flash by in an instant. Fortunately, the incident had ended well. A colleague had taken him to the doctor, and the examination revealed only a few bruised ribs. Tony had few emotional memories of the accident. He related: "I just went back to work. I even did some overwork that day. I got off with a fright."

I wrote the sentence down on a flip chart: "I got off with a fright." I got off, but with a fright. Tony and his wife sat there in silence and stared at this sentence on the white sheet of paper for a long time.

"You got off, but with a fright. So where is the fright now? Where has it gone?"

"Well, it's still in there," said Tony, pointing to his body.

"So what needs to happen to it?" I asked.

Tony replied: "It has to come out!!"

So right at the end of the session we had stumbled on the story underlying his fits: they had arisen from the fright that was still in Tony's body, and that needed to come out. He appeared to need some help in getting the fright to leave his body. We decided on hypnotherapy, with the following framework for therapy:

> After the accident you got off with a fright, which was a great relief. People patted you on the shoulder, spoke to you encouragingly, reassured you that you had nothing worse than a few bruised ribs. Everyone was relieved. You got off, but you got off *with* a fright, and that fright is still there; your body is weighed down with it. That's why the slightest effort exhausts you. The fear was so great that your mind wanted to forget the accident as soon as possible. The sweat that keeps breaking out may be a cold sweat, for you must have been absolutely terrified. It's possible that you briefly lost consciousness during the accident and that this repeats itself during the fits.

Tony and his wife fell silent and looked at each other. Then his wife said that they had never discussed the accident. The explanation took on a felt, physical significance. Since Tony himself had few words in which to describe his life and had no idea how to influence the fits, but was weighed down by terror within his body, it seems to me best to propose removing the terror from his body. Just as in an anaesthetic administered for an operation, a trance could be induced that would serve as an "analgesic". While he was in a trance state, the terror would be able to leave his body.

When Tony and his wife accepted this story of what had happened, the narrative circle was closed, there was a framework for therapy, and a therapeutic context had been created in which they would be working with me as the therapist alongside the neurologist.

I took plenty of time to induce a deep trance, after which I spoke the words that created a framework of hypnosis-narcosis:

> Just as an operation in a hospital can remove something from you under anaesthesia that is causing you pain and as you feel liberated when you wake after the anaesthetic wears off, hypnosis can act like a sleep in which the fright can be released from your body. When you wake up, you need not remember anything, but you will experience a sense of release.

Once a deep trance had been induced, I monitored ideomotor signals (LeCron, 1971; Edelstein, 1981; Rossi & Cheek, 1988) to check that Tony's subconscious also agreed with this story about the origin of the fits. Tony responded with affirmative signals. The context of the entire conversation naturally pointed in this direction, but to ensure perfect harmony it is important to gain the consent of the subject's subconscious to continue while he is in a trance state. I then continued:

> The fear of the accident is still in your body. The accident was so terrifying that you don't want to be reminded of it in any way at all. We're going to help your body and your unconscious to get rid of that terror. When the body is afraid, it generally trembles, and if that fear cannot escape, the body

convulses. We're going to help your body to release the fear by provoking that trembling. It can happen almost without you noticing it. Just let the body release the fright; we'll wait until it begins, and see where the trembling starts.

Tony remained still for a while and then his body started gently trembling. First his hands, then his arms and legs. After a while, his entire body was shaking violently back and forth, while at the same time Tony sat calmly observing it all: "Fancy that! Just look at all that!" With an embarrassed smile he observed his trembling body. I suggested that he take his time to allow all the terror to escape from the deepest fibres of his body, while at the same time he could calmly watch the terror leaving his body through the trembling. In other words, I appealed to his dissociative ability, asking him to remain in a deep trance, calmly seated on his chair, watching his trembling body, and on the other hand to experience the trembling as a form of release. For an escape route had been created, a vanishing point. Once the trembling had stopped, the terror would have left his body. And the fits would be a thing of the past.

It must require an immense amount of energy to keep so much terror locked inside your body. That's why you were so tired and why any kind of exertion made you break out in a sweat. You can imagine how much energy will be released now, and how much space there will be, once the terror has gone.

The trembling and shaking gradually subsided, and once it was over, Tony experienced a deep sense of calm. "A wonderful feeling," he said, smiling broadly. He still thought the trembling was an odd experience. With this feeling of tranquillity and the suggestion that the extreme sweating and fatigue could now diminish and the fits could stop, Tony returned from hypnosis.

We went through eight hypnosis sessions in total to allow his body to release the terror. A curious phenomenon of trance logic occurred at one point, when Tony was getting better, but not so fast as we had expected, and he suddenly said:

"I think that what's coming out through my hands is going back in through my legs!"

We noticed that his arms were shaking in close contact with his legs. So I suggested that he rest his arms on the arms of the chair to allow the terror to be released into the ground instead of through his legs and back into his body. Then he felt a tingling from his shoulders and down through his arms, and became intensely calm. Once we had worked twice in this way, we achieved excellent results. Tony's wife said that he was open to emotions again for the first time; that he had reacted very emotionally to the gifts he had received from his children at Christmas, and that the fatigue had gone. Soon he was enjoying ice skating. The excessive sweating and fits had completely disappeared. Over eighteen months later, he was still completely free of symptoms.

The case of Tony shows that the emphasis on language and significance in narrative psychotherapy has nothing to do with educational background or intelligence. This man lacked words to describe his life, had hitherto been content with his life, and had little else to say. In his experience, nothing in his life had influenced his fits. Yet a single sentence, spoken offhand

and almost by chance (there is a logic in chance, says Johan Cruyff) was sufficient to organise the therapy. That one sentence became an organising principle. The man and his wife together studied a key metaphor for what had taken place. In addition, the fits as a problem were externalised: it was not the *man* but the *problem* that had to be addressed.

It seems eminently plausible that the dramatic accident was the explanation for the fits. No one in their circle, even Tony and his wife, had considered what the accident might have meant, and yet he had briefly experienced the sensation that he was about to die. The experience had been stored in his consciousness in a dissociated way and could be retrieved or conjured up by random stimuli. He would then break out in a cold sweat, lose consciousness, and he appeared to physically relive the accident, as it were, outside the control of his conscious mind. The accident had inscribed itself in his body's memory, creating a kind of post-traumatic stress.

Peter Levine describes a response of this kind as a trauma reaction (Levine, 1997). It is energy that has been stored and has coagulated in the body. The fright was a movement that had been abruptly halted; unfinished, it needed to be completed. His trembling was a vehicle through which the fright tried to escape and seek resolution.

CHAPTER TEN

# Birth stories: listening to children

*"Civilisation is ensuring that everyone can be comforted at essential moments between birth and death"*

—Marc Chavannes

*Introduction*

The Story of the Weeping Camel *(with thanks to Ineke Rood)*

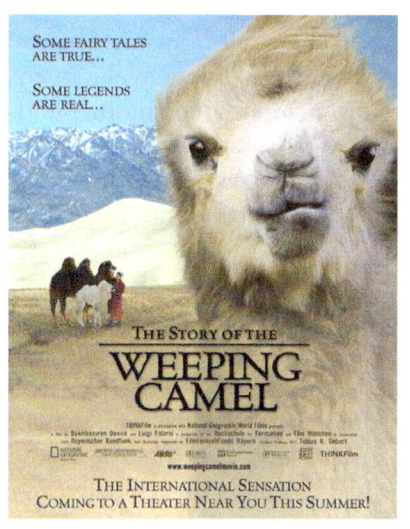

Figure 22. Film poster, *The Story of the Weeping Camel* © University of Television and Film Munich.

The film documentary *The Story of the Weeping Camel* records the use of the Mongolian hoos ritual to heal the relations between a mother camel and her newborn calf, which the mother has rejected. The film focuses on a group of nomads in Mongolia that live with sheep, goats, and a herd of sixty camels. The animals are extremely important to the community: they provide transport through the desert as well as giving wool and milk.

About a quarter of the camels are pregnant. The last camel to give birth has sought seclusion from the herd for some time now. She is emitting plaintive cries. The birth proves difficult and the nomads are obliged to assist with the delivery. After the birth, the mother rejects her newborn calf. When he is presented to her, she walks away or stamps her foot, refusing to feed him. The nomads try tying her feet together to stop her going away, but she responds with a menacing roar. When the calf then comes to feed, she produces a pitiful lament. As soon as her feet are untied again, she immediately pushes the calf away and goes off, distancing herself from the herd. The calf is bottle-fed, but after a while it refuses to feed. Alarmed, the tribesmen enlist the help of a shaman.

Rituals are performed to assuage the spirits: offerings and prayers, and solemn requests for help. However, the mother persists in rejecting the calf and in preventing him from feeding. In the end the community decides to enact a hoos ritual, and requests the help of a local musician who plays a morin khuur. The mother camel moves even further away, seeming to sense that something is about to happen. With great difficulty the nomads catch her and she resumes her pitiful lament. At this point one of the women in the tribe starts to sing, at the same time gently stroking and patting the camel. Shortly after this the musician begins to play. The ritual is extremely intense. The entire tribe attends, and the animals too listen in rapt attention.

When the singing and playing have been going on for some time, the calf is brought to its mother. By now, the calf too has become reluctant to approach. Very carefully, it is coaxed to the mother and encouraged to feed. This time the mother does not repel her calf, though she continues her plaintive cries. They are the cries of a sick camel, says the musician. As the calf feeds from its mother and the singing and music continue, it appears as if the camel is allowing the birth trauma to pass through her. Tears fall from her eyes, but she allows the calf to go on feeding. After a while the music stops and everyone waits in anxious anticipation to see what will happen. The calf continues to drink, after which mother and calf sniff each other and walk around one another, as if they have to rediscover each other. The nomads can see, and so can we, that the relationship is slowly healing. The singing, the music and the gentle touching have combined to form a healing ritual. Mother and calf now stay together, albeit tentatively at first, and it is clear that they can now bear each other's company. The calf keeps feeding from his mother, and the two actively seek out physical contact. Not long afterwards they can be left alone. The ritual has done its work.

This film shows how a "third element" can be used to heal a relationship. In this case, the third element consists of the nomad community and their animals that form a circle around the mother camel and her calf, the woman's gentle stroking, the singing and the music. At some point the musician stops playing, listens, and says that the mother camel now sounds healthy.

It was clear that the birth pains had created a breach between mother and calf, giving rise to rejection. Evidently the pain could not be healed without the intervention of a third element.

Attachment is a major research theme in psychology and psychiatry. It was Françoise Dolto who placed the young child on the agenda in France with her proposal that a child should be seen from conception as an autonomous, knowing and linguistically competent being. Even the youngest children know what is going on in their life and in their surroundings, in spite of their lack of a language in which to express it and in spite of their undeveloped cognitive faculties. If the major events they experience are not communicated to them in words, they lose their way. Premature babies who are placed in incubators experience pain, miss the physical contact with their mother, her smell and sounds. They do not understand why they are where they are. In this no man's land without significance, but with an acute awareness of pain, cold, heat, and hunger, they become confused and develop symptoms. We frequently hear about difficult births and the pain caused to mother and child, but seldom is this pain linked to the subsequent development of symptoms. In the examples discussed below, this link was made and incorporated into the therapy.

Let us briefly return to the philosophy of Deleuze and his description of the subject as a rhizome. An important part of the rhizome metaphor is the idea that the smallest real unit is the link. It is at junctions or links that singularities arise, as details, unique and remarkable moments. These nodes are immanent, always already present in the rhizome and based on relationship. They are present in the centre, in the interspace. From these nodes, more and more new lines can be drawn to the outside, creating new links. It is from the singularity that movement comes into being, the constant *becoming* and the world of possibilities. If you try to halt that movement in position, space, and time, something essential is lost, since movement takes place in the intervals between measuring points (Raessens, 2001).

The birth story in this chapter relates to a traumatic birth that disrupted the attachment relationship between mother and child. This disruption takes place within the relationship, in the intermediate space, the in-between. Even so, in psychiatry we often discuss attachment disorders as if they were a feature or attribute of a particular person, and then set out to treat the attachment disorder. But if we look at the disrupted *relationship*, focus on the *between*, our therapy will look very different.

In *The Story of the Weeping Camel*, it becomes clear that the disruption is in the relationship between camel and calf, and it is this relationship that must be treated. The traumatic birth erects an obstacle between mother and child, blocking them from accepting each other. In an interview, the documentary-maker Davaa tells the story of a zookeeper who, after watching the film, related another story, of a donkey that had gone through such a traumatic birth that she trampled her young colt to death. After this, the donkey had cried for over a year, while its cries, its language, were not understood. The documentary-maker said that the nomads, in contrast, *did* understand the camel's language, and that was why they used this ritual. They did not want to leave the camel to "weep" for years.

Birth is not only an event, but also a process of becoming. It is a constant re-enactment that reorganises itself again and again. The traumatic birth continues to form an obstacle dividing mother and child, which may indeed persist indefinitely. The child refuses to feed, does not attach to the mother, and the mother weeps. This "weeping" can lead in psychiatry to a wide range of symptoms, which may be interpreted differently from one case to the next. Where it appears relevant, I invite those concerned to consider whether the symptoms might be linked to traumatic birth processes. The third element as an event can be organised in psychotherapy by telling the birth story to the mother and child while the child sits on his or her mother's lap. This enables them to "smell" one another, ensures that they are together

Figure 23. Stefan Cools, *Untitled*.

while they concentrate on the therapist as *third* and the birth story as the *third element*. Telling this story can help to heal the relationship and while they are so close, that *between* can be transformed. The birth story, narrated by the therapist, acts as healing music, creating new possibilities and "links".

The documentary shows how new kinds of behaviour, new explorations and discoveries develop between the mother camel and her calf. The psychotherapist who looks at relationships as the third space thinks in terms of movement and process rather than fixed positions in time and space. In this way we can be inspired by Deleuze's affirmative exhortation.

The following examples reveal the connections that existed between a traumatic birth process and symptoms that soon emerged and persisted for years. A painful birth can be seen as a pain that is organised again and again. In each of the following case histories, the birth story was part of a complex case file, one that was related casually and has gone unnoticed amid the intensity of the symptoms.

### Sander and his bald patch (with thanks to Myriam Hoornick)

My supervisee, Myriam Hoornick, requested advice about a family she was counselling. When four-year-old Jonas died, Sander had just been born, and the middle boy, Bas, was two. Myriam was finding it a challenge to provide appropriate help to this mourning family. In the supervision discussion, she told me about Sander's bald patch, resulting from his constant hair-pulling. Sander was now eighteen months old. His parents could not understand his behaviour or suggest any solution. Myriam and I tried together to construct the story that the hair-pulling and the bald patch were telling, and arrived at the following interpretation.

Jonas had had a brain tumour, and chemotherapy had made him go completely bald. We posited that Sander had his own grief, and that this had not been acknowledged. His brother

Bas had actively lived through both Jonas's illness and the process of saying goodbye to him. But Sander was still very young. Could his hair-pulling and his bald patch be an act of solidarity? Perhaps he was saying to the world: "I am also grieving! I loved my brother too!"

We decided to follow this route. Myriam would hold a session with the entire family, place a lighted candle by a photograph of Jonas in the middle, and ask Sander to sit on his mother's lap. When the family gathered in this setting, Myriam told them the following story.

> I'd like to talk to you about your Jonas. I've been looking at all the photographs of him: in the bath, in Mummy and Daddy's big bed, and with Grandma and Granddad. A photo of Jonas having lots of fun making pancakes. In that photo you can also see that he is completely bald. Just as bald as this place on your head, Sander (touching it).
>
> What happened to Jonas's hair? When he was two years old Jonas became very sick. Bas was one year old, and you, Sander, were still warm and safe in your Mummy's tummy. Jonas had to go to hospital, and the doctors said that he had something bad in his head, and they had to take it out. That's called an operation. Jonas had to have an operation. Mummy and Daddy were very sad that Jonas was so ill, and perhaps they were a bit angry too. They didn't want Jonas to have to go to hospital and have an operation. Maybe it would hurt, and they didn't want that. They wanted Jonas to be a happy, healthy boy. It was a difficult time. Everyone was frightened that Jonas might not get better. You felt all that too, Sander. Even though you were safe in Mummy's tummy, you felt the talking and crying of all the people who came to visit, everyone so frightened and sad. Mummy and Daddy went to the hospital with Jonas and Bas stayed with Grandma and Granddad.
>
> Jonas had the operation, and everyone stayed close to the hospital. You all wanted to see him as much as possible. After the operation, the big thing was gone, but there were still a few sick bits left in Jonas's body. He had to stay at the hospital, and he got a bit better every day. You went to see him a lot, and there were lots of other sick children like Jonas. Finally the doctors said Jonas could come home. That was good, because it was almost time for you, Sander, to be born. You could all rest and have a nice time being together at home. Jonas still had to go back to hospital a lot, and the doctors gave him some medicine to get rid of the little sick bits that were still left in his body. It was such strong medicine that it made him very sick, and it made his hair fall out. That's why he became bald.
>
> And then you were born, Sander. Mummy was at home and Daddy was far away at the hospital with Jonas. Of course Mummy was very happy with you, Sander, and with you too, Bas. But she was also worried about Jonas, who was with Daddy. Daddy was also very happy with both of you, but also sad that he and Jonas couldn't be there with you. That was a very strange beginning of your life in this world, Sander. People around you who were happy and sad; that's very confusing.
>
> When Jonas came home you started on your life as three brothers. After a while Jonas didn't have to keep taking that medicine that made him all bald, and his hair grew back again. For a while everything seemed good and happy. You were going to go on holiday and after the holiday Jonas would be able to go to school.
>
> But then the doctors phoned and told you something really horrible. They had found out that Jonas was still very sick and that he couldn't get better. Everyone was shocked and sad and angry. It was not fair! Jonas had fought so hard for his life, and he couldn't get better. This was a terrible time for all of you. Lots of people came to help and everyone was sad.
>
> What was it like for you, Sander? You really wanted to help Jonas, but you were so small. Perhaps you were thinking: "Everyone's taking care of my brother, and I want to take care of him too. But I can't talk, I can't do anything. So I'll talk with my hair. I was so sad when I saw Jonas go all bald and I thought,

> I'd like to give him my hair." Everyone tried to take good care of you both, but perhaps people didn't realise how sad you were, because you were so small. You loved Jonas very much!
>
> So have we understood it now? Are you tearing your hair out to show how much you loved Jonas and wanted to help him, and that you wanted to give him your hair? Lovely Sander, if we've understood what you're saying, you can let your hair grow again now. You've told us all how much you loved Jonas, how much you wanted to help him, how sad you are and how you wanted to take care of him. If your hair grows back again, we'll know that we listened to your hair and understood you.

After this session, Sander's hair grew back again. He stopped pulling his hair and his bald patch disappeared.

### Nina and "the Angry"

Elisa, a woman aged thirty-five, registered for psychotherapy because she had suffered post-traumatic stress syndrome after the birth of her first child. She had no feelings for her little daughter Nina and she was locked into conflict with her. The little girl, now nearly two years old, was constantly kicking and hitting her, and had all-consuming temper tantrums. Nina also caused problems at the day care centre. She kicked and hit other children, pushed them over and sat on top of them. Her tantrums were impossible to deal with. Elisa sank into depression and her feelings were deadened. She had not been able to weep about her child's traumatic birth. It seemed likely that the little girl's symptoms were linked to that traumatic birth. Together with Elisa, I decided to tell Nina the story of her birth. Her father would also attend the session.

In preparation for this session, Elisa described the birth in a letter in which she addressed her own daughter. After a description of the gruelling initial hours of dilation in what was planned as a home delivery, Elisa wrote of the midwife's decision to move her to hospital because of an unaccountably high fever, which proved to be a Streptococcus B infection. The contractions were too weak, and many hours later concerns arose about the baby's flagging heartbeat. The tension in the room soon became unbearable, and after a long period in which Elisa kept pushing to no avail, the medics decided, without asking or even informing her, to use a vacuum pump.

> ... Suddenly the room was full of stress and things became really rough. The gynaecologist tried to pull you out, pressing her leg against the bed so that she could pull even harder. Someone else pushed down on my belly to force you out. It was really violent. I watched them pull from left to right, but nothing worked. And I hadn't had any painkillers at all! I remember Rob shouting, "Is this really necessary?!" I don't remember much apart from that. I seemed to be a distant observer, but didn't hear or feel anything. I did see you, though, when you first came out ... all floppy and purplish-grey. You weren't breathing, you had no reflexes, your mouth hung open. In my mind you were taken away from me straight away, but Rob says that you lay with me for a minute. Everyone was panicking, you were taken away and Rob went too, your Apgar score was only 3. They gave you oxygen and a heart massage and called the paediatrician. You were a real fighter! Five minutes later your Apgar score was 7 and after ten minutes it was 9. You were alive!
>
> And yet in my mind you were dead. I called Rob back to take a photo of you so that I would at least have something to remember. Ages later he came and told me that you were alive and doing well and

that you were a girl. Still, he also said you'd had too little oxygen, and they didn't know how long, so they would make a brain scan two days later to check if there was brain damage. That was another big shock and fear. Over an hour later I was allowed to see you. You drank from me for a few minutes. You looked so far away, with dark, hollow eyes. It was so short and I worried about you all night. At 4.15 I called the nurse in the incubator ward. She said you still had a fever, but were calmer. At 8.30 I saw you again for a feed and that went really well. We were separated too long, I think now, and that made the attachment more difficult.

You were in pain and moaned a lot, and kept clenching your tiny fist. Everything startled you. You were calmest lying against me, safe and sound. I felt how much you needed me and tried to do as much as possible for you. You were drinking well and soon you were allowed to stay with me.

The gynaecologist came to apologise and became emotional. I was angry. No one knew why things had gone so badly wrong. I focused on you. The scans showed no problems: no brain damage, arms bruised but nothing broken. What a relief! We could all go home!

People came to visit, and everyone was happy. But my feelings were switched off somehow. I focused on this new life with you. But I couldn't cry or laugh, and I had no energy. People said it was normal, that it would change. But it didn't, and 18 months later it got to me. I wanted to enjoy my daughter, but I was still stuck in the pain of her birth. I couldn't turn it around, and soon became irritated when you had a tantrum. Sometimes I found myself blaming you: the pregnancy was wonderful but now it was all wrong. I felt weak, exhausted, rigid.

These last few months you've become more rebellious. You don't want to get into your chair or the bath, and you've hated getting dressed ever since you were born. You've always hated having clothes pulled over your head. You kick and hit me, sometimes other people too. You sit on top of babies and are rough with other toddlers. More and more often, the word "no" sends you into a rage. You whine and claim and want to be with me all the time: sometimes you feel like a millstone.

You're super-sensitive to tension and intonation. We really want to find a way of dealing with it, so that your cheerful and engaging nature can come out more. Because you're my little girl and my princess.

We used this letter as the basis for our talk with Nina. Elisa explained to her daughter beforehand that we were going to discuss the day she was born, and asked if that was OK. Nina was cheerful when she arrived at the session, and sat on Elisa's lap, with her father next to them. I told Nina that we were going to talk about how she was born. That both she and her Mummy were still upset about it.

> 'Cos I hear that you often get really angry, Nina. I think that's because you were in a lot of pain when you were born. So was Mummy! The doctors had to work hard to help you to be born. They had to pull you hard, and it hurt Mummy so much she almost lost consciousness.

At that point, Nina started screaming, jumped off her mother's lap and said she wanted to go out of the room. She was completely out of control, in a way that often happened at home. I decided to connect her behaviour with the birth story.

So I said: "Yes, when you wanted to be born, you were stuck, you couldn't get out." Nina became even more frantic. She climbed onto her mother's lap, jumped off again, pulled her arm, wanted to go out, climbed back onto her mother's lap, stood up on her legs, looked around for her pacifier, and tried to drink from her mother's breast. Then she pushed her mother away again, got down, pulled her mother's arm, got back on her lap, lay over her legs, kicking and hitting, completely out of control.

I went on: "Yes, Nina, that's how hard you had to fight to get out! It hurt you a lot, and that makes you feel really angry. You've never understood why you were in such pain. And you hit and kick your mother as if you're angry with *her* too. Maybe you think that it was she who hurt you? Or who else can you hit when you're angry but your own dear mother, who you love?"

It took almost half an hour for Nina to calm down. Eventually she lay against her mother's breast, her pacifier in her mouth. Eyes wide open, she looked back and forth between her parents. It was if the three of them were reliving the moment of intimacy just after the birth. No, *not* reliving: experiencing for the first time. It was quiet, and there was an atmosphere of wonderful harmony. As Nina kept looking between her parents, I said: "Yes, that's your Mummy, that's your Daddy. You're a very strong girl and you had to fight hard for your life, and you did it. And Mummy had to fight hard to help you to be born and she did it too. And now you're all together. This is your Daddy and this is your Mummy, and you're safe with them."

Intensely satisfied, Nina sat on her mother's lap and sucked at her mother's breast. At the end of the session she received the tiniest Russian doll. At the beginning she had kept putting it into the larger dolls and taking it out again: in and out, in and out. Within the context of the story, it seemed that she had been acting out the unsafe attachment. Now she was happy to take the doll with her, and she gave it a place in her bedroom. The family did not talk about the session when they got home.

In the weeks and months that followed, Nina's problematic behaviour subsided. She remained quite a handful. But her tantrums were now discussed within the general theme of upbringing. She gradually stopped kicking and hitting her mother. In a few subsequent telephone calls, Elisa and I discussed Nina's progress, and we decided to ask Nina to draw "the Angry", as she called it. She made her drawing with great enthusiasm, and Elisa suggested finding a nice place in the fields outside to bury "the Angry". Together they chose a place and dug a hole, but just as they were about to put the drawing in, Nina shouted, "No, it's mine!" She decided that she wanted to keep "the Angry" with her. Back inside, they cut the drawing up and put the pieces in a pot in Nina's bedroom, where she wanted it.

This story illustrates the extent to which children take a full part in their therapy. They are autonomous and have their own input. Nina's voice said, forcefully and in complete autonomy: "That is mine! And I'm not ready to let it go yet!"

Nina's behaviour greatly improved, the disrupted attachment had been repaired, and Elisa related that they could have fun together. When Elisa became pregnant again, Nina was fully involved in the process of the pregnancy. When her sister was born, she was a loving, caring big sister. Some time later, Nina herself suggested to her mother that it was time to bury "the Angry". The single therapy session, in which the birth story was told in a safe context together with her parents, appears to have had a healing influence.

Nina's parents wrote in a letter:

> … A truly intense period, not just for Nina but also for us as her parents, has now come to an end. We admire our little girl. She's learned to control her feelings better and she has become a more stable, more cheerful child! Or as Nina herself says: "Mummy, the Angry has really gone now!"

## Demi and the ball of anger

Demi was nine years old and had severe, frequent temper tantrums, in which he became violent, hitting and kicking his mother, Yvonne. The family had gone through intensive therapy at the outpatient clinic of the paediatric psychiatric hospital. Demi had once been admitted to a unit with special learning needs and had even spent some time in a secure ward. Thus far, none of the care provided had greatly influenced the symptomatic behaviour: it had simply gone from overt to covert: Demi was now constantly kicking his mother under the table at mealtimes.

During registration at the family therapy unit, Demi's aggression was defined as the organising feature. The therapy revealed that there was tension between the parents, Yvonne and René, because Yvonne believed that there was something wrong with Demi. René saw his wife suffering physical abuse at the hands of their small son and reacted by becoming angry. Yvonne became anxious and tried to mediate. She in turn then became angry with René. The therapy in the outpatient clinic succeeded in reaching a new equilibrium of mutual support between Yvonne and René. However, Demi's behaviour scarcely changed. This indicated the existence of an independent problem. By this point, much had changed: René had become a more visible presence, standing alongside his wife. Demi's symptomatic outbursts were shorter and less violent. The interactions within the family had also improved. Yet the kicking under the table continued undiminished.

I was asked for a consultation and became a new listener to the story of and about the family. The story of Demi's birth, which had been an extremely traumatic process, attracted my attention. He had been born with severe concussion and his clenched fist against his nose had pushed it completely out of shape and to one side. Mother and child were separated immediately after the birth and both required intensive medical treatment. In the first few months of his life Demi had undergone two operations following ear infections and severe earache. Once the team had told the story of the family and the therapy up to that point, I spoke to the parents. Yvonne said that Demi had started hitting her when he was just eleven months old. "We have often talked about the birth and told other therapists about it, that we think his problems are related to the way in which he was born. But nothing has ever been done with it."

No one had ever really talked to Demi about his birth, other than in fragmentary comments and anecdotes. His temper tantrums had never been linked to his traumatic birth.

Here is a partly paraphrased rendering of the discussion we had with the parents, Yvonne (Y) and René (R). The letter J stands for my own comments. My colleagues Deet van Zaanen and Irene Bettonviel also attended this meeting.

J: There is still a big problem.
Y: Yes, there certainly is.
J: And your son Demi is eleven years old, right?
Y: He turns twelve on Tuesday.
J: But he hits out like someone of twenty-one, I understand.
R: Things are getting better; the tantrums don't last too long. They used to last for half an hour, and now I can calm him down within five minutes.
Y: But he still hits out … It can suddenly explode from one minute to the next, that aggression … a really violent aggression …

J: (*to Yvonne*) And it's mainly expressed towards you, right?
Y: Yes.
R: But recently towards me too.
Y: I notice that he now reacts to my husband more and then looks to me for support.

The team at the outpatient clinic had made a concerted effort to get Demi's father more involved in the therapy. Yvonne was now slightly less troubled by Demi's aggressive behaviour because he was now focusing more on his father. René said that he was still having trouble adapting to his new role. We noted that the fact that he now had a stronger presence as a father had calmed the situation down. (In this discussion C1 and C2 stand for Colleague 1 and Colleague 2.)

R: He hasn't got his friend any more. Now he sees that I'm his father and understands that I won't accept this behaviour any more. I also spend more time at home, you see. There was a furious storm this morning, and we got into the car and it was all over in a second. I don't understand that. It's all over in a second!
Y: And then he's cheerful again.
J: So there are two Demis?
Y: Yes, there are two …
R: (*nodding*) Yes, two!
  (*together*) A nice, calm, eleven-year-old boy …
R: When I'm alone with him, nothing ever happens.
Y: He's a really sweet boy, then, very gentle; he's really a sweet boy then …
J: (*to Yvonne*) And when you're alone with him, something happens?
Y: Not always. Sometimes everything goes well and then we have fun together and can play a game. But as soon as I put my foot down, say "Demi, you have to go to bed" or "you must get dressed" and there's some pressure of time, he can suddenly go berserk … It might be some word or some gesture that upsets him …
R: It's so strange … He comes home on time now, he stays at the table during dinner …
  (*Yvonne nods, agreeing*)
Y: (*to René*) Sometimes it's when you come into the room, he totally blows his top.
R: Yes, he totally explodes …
Y: And why?
  [Neither René nor Yvonne has any idea why their son sometimes gets so angry that he explodes with rage.]
J: Well anyway, things are getting better, and the way we're talking now, I'm sure there have been conversations like this before, and now we have to look for a new approach … and something new I heard [in the consultations beforehand] was that Demi started hitting you in the face when he was still a baby?
Y: Yes … it was before he could walk … before his first birthday … he was walking at eleven months.
J: So before he was a year old …
Y: Eleven months.

J: So let's think about that for a moment … a child of eleven months who starts hitting his mother in the face.

Y: Well, not deliberately, but grabbing hard and like, he went ballistic … I'd pick him up and he'd really go ballistic and pinch me in the face and kick and everything … He'd try and get away from me … He wouldn't let me pick him up, he really went ballistic … you could see him going completely red in the face.

C1: You've got a photo of it?

Y: Yes.

J: And I understand that he went through a lot of pain when he was little, and had operations.

Y: Yes, yes … certainly the first four years … he had about six operations.

J: And a very difficult birth, is that right?

Y: Yes, he came into the world with concussion and he was given paracetamol and that was the first day of his life … I wasn't allowed to pick him up straight away … I was allowed to feed him, but then I had to let him rest as much as possible, since he couldn't cry very well. It was always interrupted … he couldn't really cry, because it hurt too much.

J: Have you ever had a real talk about that?

Y: I've often mentioned it, that he had trouble coming into the world. But apart from that, nothing has ever been done with that, as far as I can remember.

J: So he was born with concussion … day one?

Y: Yes.

J: He got stuck in your uterus, or in the birth canal, or what happened?

Y: He was lying with his hand in his face (*Yvonne holds her fist against her nose*) and he came out like that and so he was pulled out with the forceps and … it should really have been a caesarean, but it was too late for that … so … They pulled and pushed him … so he had a really hard time coming into the world …

J: So … that must have been incredibly painful!

Y: Yes … yes …

J: For you too!

Y: Yes … for me too … I lost an awful lot of blood …

J: You must have been completely torn open, I would think, or not?

Y: Yeah, that too, right, yes …

R: But especially a baby's brains if that happens … if you've got a pointed head like that … It seems to me, if your brains are pressed together like that. … that some damage would be done …'Cos the amazing thing is, we went on a course [for parents of children with autism spectrum disorders] and all the women had had a delivery like that … all six!

Y: That's right.

R: And they all have the same kind of children …

J: … All of them similar stories …

R: And I was really struck by that … So it occurs to me, could that have caused it?

J: What do you think about the idea of putting this story at the centre of what we do here, of taking a good long look at it?

Y: Yes, I've been saying that ever since we started therapy with Demi ... I've always wondered ... is there something wrong with his brain? Isn't it possible to do a brain scan or something, or just see a neurologist ... I've often asked about that, but no one has ever taken it up.

C2: And the emotions you've gone through yourselves, your own experience ... has anything been done with that? What it meant for the two of you that your child came into the world like that?

Y: No, never.

C1
&
C2: It has often been mentioned ... a physical trauma, what might have happened ...

J: And he lay like this? (*holding my fist against my nose*)

Y: Yes, and his mouth and nose were totally pushed out of shape ... But they straightened out later.

Y: I didn't notice anything at all, at the time. At that point I was ... I didn't notice at all when he came out ... they'd drugged me up to the eyeballs ...

R: No, he didn't just flop out into the world, he didn't just come out ...

J: No, he'd already been moved, of course ...

R: And his skull was all crooked too, later ... completely flat ...

J: And his face was all pulled out of shape.

Y: Yes it was ... I've suddenly remembered ... X-rays were made of his head at the time because it was squashed out of shape; he had to wear a helmet, and the top of the skull, that's supposed to be such a nice oval shape, was all bent and his eyes were also strangely out of line. And then the man said: "Luckily his brains didn't get pressed against the skull, so he won't need an operation."

J: But mother and child were pulled apart in quite a brutal way. There was no alternative, since it was too late for a caesarean, but still ... quite brutal.

R
&
Y: (*nodding*) Yes, absolutely!

Y: And when he was two I was told to stretch his neck because it was so bent ... I was supposed to grab his head near the neck and turn his neck around, as it were. As his mother, I couldn't do it, so I left it to the physiotherapist. I also had to ... When he was lying on his back and his head had become a half moon, had grown all misshapen ... I had to do everything back to front. So instead of giving him the bottle from the right I had to do it from the left ... Everything on my left side.

C1: So all that felt unnatural to you ...

Y: It felt completely unnatural, yes ... yes.

C1: And how long did he wear that helmet?

Y: He started wearing it when he was eighteen months old and he had to wear it day in, day out.

C1: For about a year?

R  
&  
Y: (*together*) It's such a long time ago … About a year, yes.
R: He only had one helmet, didn't he?
Y: It had layers and they took off one layer at a time.
R: Oh yes, they took off one layer at a time!
J: And he's still rebellious.
Y: Yes … he's still rebellious … you can say that again …
R: [proudly] But for much shorter times … that's something we've really achieved …
J: Yes, I heard that! Now let's go back for a minute. Mother and child were pulled apart in a very brutal fashion … The child was pulled out, so hard that his entire nose and mouth were all pulled out of shape … his whole head was misshapen. So the child experienced a great deal of violence.
Y: Yes.
J: Natural violence, birth violence, but also the violence of helping hands … It was *unavoidable*.
Y: Yes, it was unavoidable.
J: It was unavoidable … But a tiny baby cannot understand … Why am I being hurt like this? But he does register the pain … Even a tiny baby knows … he has knowledge of what has happened to him … he doesn't understand, but he *knows* it happened …
Y: He knows … yes …
J: … so he wonders to himself … Why am I being hurt like this? So he's born with anger in him …
Y: He's born with anger in him … yes … I think so too.
J: … And that anger is still in him …
Y: Yes … Because that anger was … yes … Even when he was just a little a baby actually … in the first few weeks … with the maternity nurse …
J: But that anger stemmed from the concussion …
Y: Yes …
J: … His whole being was completely shaken up …
(*Silence*)
J: How terrible …!
Y: But, well, what can we do about it now?
J: That's what we're going to look at …
(*Silence*)
R: Strange … But that might explain why he always acted like that with you!
Y: Yes …
R: But *I* don't remember anything about being born … Do you actually register that, as a baby?
J: That's a different kind of memory … That's your conscious mind, which doesn't remember, but a body has a memory of its own … That's a different kind of knowledge …
R: (*nodding*) Hmm … hmm … yes.
Y: The body has its own memory?

R: The body has its own memory, I never knew that …
J: It's quite possible that he doesn't remember anything about it … But his body does.
Y: Yes, his body does remember!
J: He was born with anger without knowing where it came from. So you're most likely to express that anger to the person closest to you … From whom you were separated … and then you almost think that was the person who did it to you!
Y: Yes … That makes sense to me.
J: And that has nothing to do with you personally, but there's that pain in the relationship …
R: (*to his wife*) But I still think it's strange … He would sometimes say: "These aren't my real parents"… That's such a strange thing to say. Wherever did he get that from?
Y: Yes.
R: He said it to the doctor, and so the doctor turned to me and asked: "Is that true?"
J: Has he often said that?
Y: Yes, quite often … When he was just a few years old, he used to say: "Are you my real parents?" Yes, he got that idea into his head very early on. And so I showed him the photos … "Look … Here are the photos …" The photos of him lying on my breast … So I showed him and said: "See … that's you …" Even so, he still had that same feeling, "you're not my real parents."
C1: But that's not true, of course!
Y: No, but he certainly said it, from time to time!
J: That's something that might make you feel angry.
Y: Well, I just thought, he's doing it as a form of self-protection … you're not my real mother and so I don't have to love you …
C1: He does carry on looking [for resemblances]. At the clinic he sometimes says: "You're not my real parents … I don't look like you … Certainly not like *you* …" He didn't say that so specifically to you, René, but specifically to *you* (*looks at Yvonne*).
J: Have you ever spoken to him about this?
Y: Whenever he asked me that question, I told him: "Demi, that's not true … I certainly am your real mother …"
J: But have you ever talked to him about his birth?
Y: I have told him that he came into the world with great difficulty and that he suffered a lot of pain … And that at the beginning I was allowed to breastfeed him, but apart from that I had to leave him to rest by himself as much as possible … So I've told him all that from time to time. And … well … you don't discuss all the details of childbirth with your child …
J: Well … Day one … concussion … paracetamol … and then it went on … He also had ear surgery?
Y: Yes, just after his first birthday, he was given ear tubes, and I think it was about six months later … and he kept getting ear infections … He had so many ear infections in his first year, he had so many courses of penicillin.
R: We do realise how much pain he suffered.
Y: Yes … All those ear infections …
J: Ear infections are so painful!
Y: Yes … yes he gets them very often … that's why he had ear surgery when he was so little … he was given ear tubes … And I remember that the second time he was operated, they

also did his adenoids. More tubes … The people there said they heard him screaming in the operating theatre … And he came out screaming and covered in blood … Most children sleep for a while after the operation … But he was wide awake and screaming. So there was something there as well, I think, something not entirely …

J: We know that it had to be done, of course …
C1: But he couldn't understand that …
J: It had to be done … but it inflamed his anger …
Y: And it didn't go exactly as it should have done …
J: You'd be so furious inside you, at all those people who have hurt you so much …!
C1: I've been thinking about what you said about stretching his neck … How could anyone ask a mother to do that?
Y: Well I *didn't* do it.
C1: … On the other hand … You explained that it *had* to be done …
Y: Yes but I couldn't do it …!
J: So he lives with a ball of anger … He was born with it … And that ball of anger has just got bigger and bigger … And there are lots of people who have hurt him really badly … And very small children can't understand that …
Y: No.
J: I'm particularly sensitive to this right now, because my daughter went through surgery two days ago … She had a … She went to India and caught an infection there and it went to her back and that couldn't be anaesthetised and one doctor came, and then a second and a third … And they said: "that'll have to be cut open and we can't anaesthetise it" … And she screamed with pain … But she was able to understand that it would help her, so … And they were really kind and empathic with her … And she was incredibly relieved afterwards because the pain stopped … My daughter is nineteen, she is an adult, and she can understand … She knows "oh this is happening now, for that reason … This doctor is going to help me and right now he's my greatest enemy, but he's really my ally." But a tiny child … who hasn't yet developed the ability to think … He doesn't know … All he knows is: someone is hurting me terribly and how dare they do that? That's a ball of anger …
Y: Yes … I can imagine he has that inside him, 'cos that's what it always looks like … It can suddenly fly out in a second …
J: … and a ball of anger can be sparked … seemingly out of nowhere … and you, his mother, will be the first victim of the ball of anger, because you were the first to be torn apart …
Y: (*thoughtfully*) Yes …
J: I use strong words like that deliberately …
Y: Yes, but that's how it was.
J: And those who helped had no choice but to use violence.
Y: No choice … yes …
J: The doctor had to put the knife in my daughter and she was wailing from the pain … It made me cry too … It was terrible … But at least we knew why … But how must it have been for you? And for you, as Demi's father …? And we're talking about such a small baby …
Y: I probably had to … I've forgotten so much of the birth … I had to hear …
J: You were probably also in so much pain …

Y: I don't know … in my memory I had a very good delivery, so much for that …
J: You may have been unconscious from the pain?
Y: I don't know … I just lost part of that past … So that must have been it …
C1: Do you think that's what it was, René?
R: I remember you whacking me out of your way … I remember that … You were completely out of it, I think you were completely gone …
J: Did I hear you say *whack*?
Y: Yes … like that (*making a gesture of warding off, an "out of my way" gesture*)
R: Yes, not really whacking, but shoving, I ought to have said.
J: But that's the same principle, so your wife was also in terrible pain!
R: Yes she was … I'm sure she was.
J: And if someone comes too close at that moment, you push them away … Not because you don't want them, it's … "Get out of my way; I'm in too much pain."
R: Even though you want to help …
J: … It's an acute emergency!
R: Yes.
C2: Is this the first time that you've heard this?
Y: No … As far as I recall I just found you irritating … But I can't remember for sure.
J: You probably weren't all that gentle, since you were in terrible pain … You might have knocked him down (*laughing*).
(*Yvonne smiles, agreeing*)
R: You didn't hit me …
J: Exactly … It's not a deliberate action, hitting to express "I'm angry with you." But anyone who comes too close at that point risks getting walloped.
R: Yes.
J: Because you are in so much pain.
R: Yes, that's how she looked. I had to keep out of her way.
J: You lost part of that past … You were simply unconscious because of the pain …
Y: Yes, I didn't feel Demi come out, so I lost that too.
R: Yes, but they anaesthetised you, remember?
Y: Yes, I know I had a few injections, but I can't remember what they were for.
R: You were anaesthetised.
J: Is Demi nearby?
Y: Demi's at school.
C2: Did you want to see him?
J: I would like to talk about this with Demi. I think that if we explain it to him …
R: I can easily go and get him … I can bring him here from school … I can just go to school and fetch him.
C1: And what would you want to speak to him about, then? About this theory that we've been discussing?
J: Because he doesn't understand this himself … He doesn't know why he lives with such a ball of anger, so he thinks he's a bad child …

y: He does think he's a bad child …
j: … And his mother thinks that she's a bad mother.
y: Yes.
j: But this is a case of trauma.
r: It's just what you were saying: he feels that he's a bad child. "I want to die," he says …
y: Yes, he does shout that out.
r: Yes, when … when he was only about four or five years old … in Austria … he wanted to walk into the river …
j: He's incapable of controlling that ball of anger; it's much too big, and people think badly of him because of it, because it's not acceptable to hit your mother … It doesn't solve anything … But he's in real distress.
y: Yes … I'm never … He once stood in front of me with a knife … I've never been afraid of him … I've always felt … He comes to me to ask me something … With a message that he can't figure out himself.
c2: That's how you always interpreted it, every time?
y: … I've always felt: he won't do anything to me, this is just his own helplessness, it's an anger that is inside him … That he doesn't understand and I don't understand …
j: A ball of anger …
y: Yes …
j: … And that was already large when he was born and it grew as he grew … and that is the ball of anger of a physical trauma accompanied by the feeling of outrage: "How can anyone do this to me?" And he's incapable of controlling that ball of anger, since it's much too big and it only takes a small thing to set him off—quite suddenly—and then the anger explodes.
r: Yes, especially if you hold him tight …
j: If you hold him tight, you're repeating a trauma.

It was clear to me that there was scope to try approaching the problem from a different angle, and I told Demi's parents and supervisors that I wanted to consult Walter Oppenoorth, the "policy psychiatrist", because I thought it was important for us to speak to Demi himself. As the person with final responsibility, it was Dr Oppenoorth who had to give his consent.

We concluded the session by asking René and Yvonne to consent to involving Demi in the discussion and getting him from school. In the meantime I could talk to the "policy psychiatrist". That was important for several reasons. It clarified the hierarchical structure to the parents. I had received a request from the policy psychiatrist to explore ways of injecting fresh life into a therapeutic process that had stagnated, in the capacity of a consultant. In the session, the focus had shifted to the birth story, and if we were to talk to Demi it would stop being an exploratory investigation and be therapy, which was not the initial request to me as a consultant. It was important that I did not set off down that road without obtaining the proper consent. All the hierarchies had to be respected: the parents must give their consent for me to talk directly to their son about the theme we had broached, the school had to give the parents consent to take Demi out of school for the session, and the policy psychiatrist had to consent to me taking on the role of therapist, rather than as consultant, to see whether the therapy could be given a new lease of life in this way. The chosen procedure also safeguarded my autonomous position as consultant. I had been called in to make my own assessment and it was therefore my own professional responsibility to pursue a new avenue; after all, that was the point of enlisting a consultant's assistance.

## Reflections

It was clear that Demi had experienced immense pain. He knew what had happened to him, but only in very broad outline. The story was inscribed in his body, but had not been translated into words. Françoise Dolto says that children need to be spoken to directly, that they have a right to know all the information that relates to their existence (Dolto, 1998). It was important to devote attention to this existential, painful period of Demi's life. That had not yet been done. Might his symptoms be related to this traumatic birth? Could his habit of hitting his mother be incorporated into the story? It was clear that Demi always greatly regretted the temper tantrums directed against his mother; after each incident he sought comfort from her. Could the traumatic birth have disrupted the attachment between mother and child? This would mean that the problem was this disruption in their relationship, rather than an attachment disorder identified with Demi himself.

This interpretation gave a different significance to Demi's hitting out: it was not attached to his identity, as a bad habit that had to be unlearned. Demi saw himself as a bad person and was used to being admonished. His self-esteem and self-image were poor. He was used to being taken to task for behaviour over which he had no control.

The discussion with Demi followed later that day. Naturally enough, the boy was confused to find himself suddenly fetched from school and taken somewhere to talk about his birth. Even so, I opted to carry on the conversation that same day, since I felt that all those involved were open to a new approach.

Yvonne said: "I've always felt and always known this, and that's why I could bear it. I knew that his anger had to come out and that it was best for it to come out with me. Now I really know why." That is how strong a mother's love can be!

It was important for the parents to ask Demi's consent to discuss the birth story at this time. During this discussion, which would include Demi himself, his symptomatic behaviour—the hitting out and kicking, which without context, language or explanation and without a coherent story was leading a life of its own—would have to be addressed. It was important to talk about the exact events surrounding his birth and to acknowledge the pain that Demi had suffered. He needed to understand that the doctors had been forced to use violence to pull him out of the birth canal, to save the lives of both Demi and his mother.

It had to be explained to Demi that there was a connection between the pain inflicted on him and the impotent anger that was itself causing pain. He needed to understand how that pain had caused a ball of anger to form and grow larger and larger as he grew older. It was also important to emphasise that Demi and his mother had been separated immediately after his birth, and that each had had to bear their own pain. A child in so much pain, and without a mother to comfort him, has ample cause for rage. At the same time, he needed to understand that he evidently found it easiest to express his anger to his mother, who had always held him tight amid his pain and forgiven him when he hurt her. The aim was to help Demi to gradually dissolve his ball of anger.

J: Demi, do you know why we've taken you out of school and asked you to come here?
D: Dunno.
R: I did try to explain the whole story in the car, but …
J: Well. We've been talking to your father and mother this morning. I'd never met you. I'd never met your father or mother either. And Dr Oppenoorth asked me to talk to you to see how we could get things to go better in your family. So that's what we did this morning, Demi, and we discovered something. It was about how you were born. Because we were wondering why you get angry so often. You have all worked very hard on changing this, you and your father and your mother, but it's a bit stronger than you are, that anger. It's actually really quite huge. Well, so we asked your father and mother how you were born, and you know what we discovered?
D: No, I don't know. I was born with black hair and I was very little. And then I had concussion and I couldn't sleep and I screamed a lot. My mother told me about that.
J: But actually there's a lot more to say about that story.
D: Oh yes, and my nose and my head were all out of shape and my back and everything, and my feet were out of shape too. Did you know about that?
J: Yes, I heard about that this morning, all out of shape.
D: Yes, and it's still like that. That's why I've got those support things in my shoes, I think. At least, I used to have them, but what happened to them? (*to his mother*) Do you know? Did you throw them away?
J: (*to Yvonne and René*) And can you show me again what his little hand was like? And when he was born, with his nose and mouth all out of shape (*René and Yvonne show how baby Demi had scrunched up his fist, squashing his nose out of line*).
D: I can't help it.
J: No, you can't help it … Then it went on, because you got stuck, that little hand was stuck, and so you couldn't come out of your Mummy's tummy.
D: No! Well if I couldn't come out, what am I doing here then?
J: Well, first you were very stuck, and the doctors wanted to cut Mummy open with an operation to take you out.
D: But that hurts a lot.
J: That hurts the mother, but they give her an injection and she doesn't feel it so much. But in your case it was too late to have that operation, because you were stuck. That little fist with which you felt nice and comfy in your Mummy's tummy was all stuck and you had to come out. And you know what the doctors had to do? They had to pull you out with a special instrument.
D: Ow!
J: Yes, but if they hadn't done that, Demi, your mother might have died, you might have died. So they pulled you out. And then your Mama was completely torn open, she was in terrible pain. But you also had to be pulled through that narrow birth canal, that's what it's called, so

they had to grab your face very hard, and everything got squashed and pulled out of shape. That little baby was in terrible pain.

D: But I don't feel that pain any more.

J: No, you don't feel it any more, you don't even know about it any more. But your body knows.

D: My body doesn't know, really not!

J: And you can't remember, Demi, but that pain is still in your body. And when you feel that pain, you also feel the anger. Because you hit out a lot, and that comes from the anger. It's because there's a ball of anger inside you, which grew from the very first day of your life and got bigger and bigger every time you were hurt. That ball was already so big when you were eleven months old that when your own Mummy picked you up you hurt her face. Eleven months old!

D: But I don't remember that. And how big is that ball now? Are you going to cut open my tummy too? You're not, are you? [This idea frightened Demi and he started to cry].

Y: *(comforting him)*: No, they're not going to cut you open, Demi. We'll explain in a minute, but you're not going to have an operation.

D: No, I don't want any more, no more with that man.

J: Go and sit with your Mummy.

D: I don't have to listen if I don't want to.

The fact that Demi immediately associated the idea of pain with an operation seemed to corroborate the theory that the hospital admissions and operations had traumatised him and were still present in his body. Since he was so frightened, I identified the tears as evidence that the process had already started and the ball of anger was coming out. Demi crept away and sat crying on his mother's lap. He sought comfort and security with her and covered his face with his arms. The traumatic pain was being reactivated. Unintentionally, but this was what had happened.

Demi cried long and hard. His whole body shook, and his mother held him tight, lovingly, and comforting him. His father too was included in this circle. I chose words that connected them, referred explicitly to their relationship.

J: You all went through this together; it's something that you all share. You can now leave that period behind you and the pain can go away. The relationship between you all will be able to heal.

J: Let Demi first be sad for a while, because it seems we've already touched the pain. It's really the pain that is speaking now; the pain is actually coming out. This is the "operation" we were talking about. It's not a real operation, like in a hospital, but another kind. The pain is coming out and turning into sadness.

D: What a daft man.

J: Yes, I'm a daft man! It sounds funny doesn't it! But that little baby inside you, it understands what I'm saying. And now that anger that grew into a big ball can now grow softer and come out again. One half of you doesn't understand at all and thinks it's just crazy talk. But that little tiny baby understands, and it makes him sad. What that sadness is really saying is:

"Yes it's true, I suffered so much, I was in so much pain when I was little. That would make anyone angry and I don't know what to do about that anger, I just can't stop it. And now, sometimes if I'm held or touched, the anger can suddenly come out and then I hit my own Mummy. And I don't really want to but the anger does it, and the anger comes from that pain that I suffered. I was in so much pain, such terrible pain when I was a baby." And from now on, we're going to make that ball of anger completely soft, so that it can come out and so that you can become a normal boy who doesn't have that problem any more. You were in so much pain from the first day of your life. And when someone has been in so much pain, he can hardly help getting angry with everyone who hurts him. But a baby can't understand why a doctor might hurt you. That sometimes doctors don't even realise that a baby is in so much pain. And your body still remembers that pain. Baby Demi still remembers all that pain. It's just that the pain feels like anger now. And now we'll let it quieten down for a while.

Demi lay still in his mother's lap for a long time, with both his mother and father holding him tight, as if they could now welcome their tiny baby for the first time. In this way, the healing process of the disrupted attachment could begin. I explained to Demi that we wanted to help him get over his pain, not by operating but with words, since words can help you to get better too. Words could help to soften the anger and melt it away.

J: But to do this, you will first need to understand it … It's a painful truth that you won't want to hear. You'll cover your ears to block it out. Even so, part of you does want to know, because it's about you, and the words will help. They can help you to get better. It's time to let all that anger melt and come out, so that it stops bothering you. Then you won't have that ball of anger sitting in between you and your Mummy any more. You can just be totally a boy who loves his Mummy …

I told the parents that this was enough for the time being, that they should go home with Demi now and that they could phone Dr Oppenoorth a few days later.

I reported to Oppenoorth and we agreed that he would talk to Demi again the next day, because the experience had been so extremely distressing for him. After that, he could confirm the new framework for therapy and supervise the process as it continued.

It was a slow healing process, but over the following weeks and months, Demi improved in leaps and bounds, and at length he no longer hit his mother.

This case history illustrates Dolto's idea that if a particular existentially important period in the life of a child has not been translated into an intelligible story, symptoms arise. Dolto says that if there is a discrepancy between what the child knows and what the outside world says about it, or if a child knows something that is not spoken about in the outside world, a question mark resides in this no-man's land. Symptoms are the answer to that question mark. The small child's cognitive faculties have not yet developed enough to enable it to understand. But it knows; it has a complete knowledge of what happened, a knowledge that understands the right language. What baby of just eleven months would hurt his mother? What was the explanation?

The framework we devised set out to find an answer by providing a narrative, the story of Demi's birth. The value of the narrative lay in the client's positive response to it.

## *Comments by Walter Oppenoorth*

This intervention was quite unusual for our department. The case histories that are described by Dolto and her student Eliacheff are certainly impressive, but actually applying their theory as part of therapy is a different matter altogether!

In this case, we were dealing with a problem that appeared resistant to therapy and seemed to be pointing towards a long path of drug-based interventions that scarcely have any power to heal, a path followed with many boys who have serious aggression control problems. These drug-based interventions would need to be justified by invoking the categorical diagnostics of the DSM: PDD-NOS.

I remember the conversation I had with Demi and his mother the next day. He was just as uncommunicative as usual, and mumbled something about a "crazy man". Anxiously he asked whether he would need to have an operation. I asked what he meant and he made a gesture with his hands in front of his belly, indicating the "ball" that had been mentioned in the session the day before. I reassured him that we worked differently and repeated the story of the little baby. The story seems to have a certain logic for Demi. Still, things did not progress as clearly as suggested in Dolto's case histories. The attacks of aggression did not vanish overnight, and I recall the doubts I felt, as the family's therapist, when drawing up my report in the period following this consultation. Were we giving the parents false hope?

On the other hand, the story that had surfaced certainly provided a logical explanation, and the family members were prepared to work with the new framework as an alternative to medication. Looking back at this case with the hindsight of today's knowledge of developmental pathology based on neurobiological research, it is not surprising that Demi's affect regulation, which was so dependent on his affective relationship with his mother, had been disrupted in the first year of his life, the year that is so essential to the prefrontal circuits (Schore, 2009). The brain is malleable and can recover from injury when these circuits are stimulated at a later stage (Siegel, 2010). The many repetitions of this stimulation, in the form of loving and affect-charged interactions between Demi and his parents, as has been described so beautifully above, was necessary in order to repair this neural network. The intensive family therapy was continued for another eighteen months, and the family was delighted to see that there was a gradual improvement, in which the support provided by the new therapeutic framework was decisive. This naturally prompted us to wonder how many of the children who present with behavioural and affect regulation disorders might have suffered from some disruption in their early development.

In a follow-up session, three years later, it was clear that Demi was doing very well. He had become a "normal" boy, was doing well at school and had plenty of friends. Demi's relationship with his mother and father had been completely repaired. His mother wrote:

> Demi is fifteen years old now and he's doing really well. He's attending a regular school and he's a sweet, sociable boy. He doesn't hit me any more and he actually loves a cuddle.

Since the talk we had together, he has relived his time as a baby and a toddler again, in short bursts of time. For instance, he lay like a baby in my lap for a while, even though he's twelve years old. He was more childish, young for his age.

I read your account. It's a long story about our family. I became quite emotional, reading it again. But I'm glad it achieved such a change in our family. We're very grateful to you.

It was a long journey we had to go through, with so many care workers and different institutions, and we didn't always agree with the methods that were used. We were ignorant parents, not understanding the problem, taking the advice of the professionals. We always thought: they know what they're doing. We just rationalised our feelings away. But those feelings are so important!

We had no idea what to expect from that session with you. At the beginning we thought it was a very strange discussion. But gradually I started to understand it better and better, and I could totally see what you were getting at. My feelings said "this is it," this is what I wanted to explain to the care workers, what they needed to look at, what they had to focus on.

I hope that our story can be of some help to other families.

CHAPTER ELEVEN

# Blended families

*"The worst form of inequality is to try to make unequal things equal"*

—Aristotle

Figure 24. *Mosaic dish (detail)* by Ine van Helfteren.

## Introduction

Psychotherapists are frequently confronted with symptoms that arise within blended families. Some involve a wide range of behavioural problems in the children. Others involve depression in one of the parents following a divorce. Then there are cases involving conflict with a former partner, sometimes about the present partner. Parenting issues and access arrangements may be involved. In short, blended families are linked to a varied palette of problems in the psychotherapist's consulting room.

When two families are joined together, there is generally an assumption that the love between the new partners is strong enough to shape the new family life. In practice, however, much as the new partners may love each other, the forces at work in the histories and loyalties of all those concerned often place their relationship under intolerable strain. Amid the naivety of romantic love, the new partners frequently neglect to take the various steps that are key to establishing equilibrium in the new blended family. They may make decisions without fully appreciating the consequences for the children, without ensuring that the children can feel at home in the new constellation. Blended families need a plan, an "architecture of living". All too often no such plan exists. Rather, the new partners make great changes with optimism unclouded by reflection, in the buoyant confidence of their love. The following case histories describe situations involving major changes and decisions, with all the attendant consequences. Parents and children alike came adrift and searched for ways of living together in harmony.

### All off together to the amusement park

Thomas had two teenage children. Some time earlier he had taken up with a new girlfriend, Greta, who was also divorced and had a son, Brian, aged eight. In addition, Thomas often saw his other young son Bennie, just six years old, who had a different mother. Thomas thought it would be fun to celebrate his birthday by getting the whole gang together and taking a trip to an amusement park, to develop a sense of family and to achieve a harmonious feeling of togetherness. So off they went: Thomas with his new girlfriend and her son Brian, Thomas's two teenage children, and Bennie, the little son from a different relationship. Thomas had the best of intentions, but the trip was a disaster.

Brian felt out of place, and kept crying and clinging to his mother. Greta pressured Thomas to stay with her and Brian. Thomas felt torn, since his own children wanted him to go on the big wheel with them and Brian was too young for that. Bennie stared wide-eyed at everyone and was happy to tag along with his half-siblings. Brian kept pinching Bennie whenever Thomas and Greta were not looking. Bennie would scream and Thomas was constantly having to calm everyone down. His daughter became irritated and went off with Bennie. This made Brian cry, because he had wanted to play with Bennie. Greta became angry with Thomas because she felt he was not supporting her enough. His daughter became angry with Thomas because he was allowing himself to be manipulated by Brian, whom she considered a spoilt brat. Thomas found Brian annoying too, but did not think it was his place to rebuke the boy, and thought that Greta ought to do so. In short, what was supposed to be a fun outing became a disaster. Everyone tried to make it work, and everyone came home feeling they had come off badly.

When two families move into a house together they bring all their loyalties with them, and also the phantom presence of those who are not there in person. These loyalties keep their attention focused elsewhere, on the mother or father of their original nuclear family, on brothers and sisters who did not make the move along with them, or on previous partners who are still taking care of the children for part of the time.

*Ronald and Connie: all snug together in a new house*

Ronald and Connie decided to build a shared future and bought a new house together. Connie had two children, Sara and Tom, from her first marriage. The children's father suffered from such severe diabetes and epilepsy that he had scarcely been able to act as a father. Sara and Tom had frequently had to help their father during his seizures and were often afraid that he might die. Tom, the eldest, had therefore developed a sense of responsibility for his father and was under considerable stress. His father had since moved in with his own mother, the children's grandmother, and they often visited him there.

Connie had lived alone with her children for years. When she fell in love, the couple soon decided to form a new family together. Ronald had left his wife on amicable terms and their three children were grown up. They had never been passionate lovers, and their relationship had easily slid into friendship. Ronald decided to give his life new meaning by investing in the relationship with Connie. Still, his children and his ex-wife continued to play an important role in his life and he often visited them. This annoyed Connie, who thought that he should devote himself wholly to her and to Tom and Sara, his new family.

Tom had grown used to caring for his mother. Unwilling to make room for his mother's new boyfriend, he refused to accept Ronald's authority and turned his back to him at every opportunity. Connie was constantly trying to mediate. Both partners felt aggrieved at the other's lack of support. From Ronald's point of view, Connie was doing too little to give him a real place in the family, while Connie thought Ronald failed to appreciate how difficult the situation was for her children. Another background factor was that Connie had almost died when she was pregnant with Tom, just before his birth. This near-death experience had forged a special bond between mother and son from which Ronald was completely excluded. They all lived together, but the air was thick with tension.

The knowledge that his mother had almost died just before he was born and that his father might die at any moment from hyperglycaemia or an epileptic seizure must have weighed heavily on Tom. How happy he was that his mother had survived! Having long been "the man of the house", he resented the intruder. Besides, accepting him would feel like a betrayal of his father.

In this example, each of the partners and the son had a different set of resentments. In a sense, each was out of balance, and each found it hard to carve out the new space that was needed for a harmonious life together.

*House of two worlds*

Twelve-year-old Lawrence and his elder sister Mireille, fourteen, lived in a large new house that their father Roger had bought together with Esther, his new life partner. Esther's three children were grown up and no longer lived at home. Roger had been widowed nine years earlier and had cared for his children alone for several years, with a great deal of support from his family, his in-laws, and his deceased wife's friends. Mireille, Lawrence and Roger had picked up the thread of their lives, but the mother's death had left a gaping hole. Mireille was delighted with the advent of a new "mother" to fill this gap and accepted her enthusiastically. In contrast, Lawrence rejected the intruder and constantly said she did not belong there and ought to leave. When Lawrence was rude to her, Esther expected Roger to tell him off, but Roger found this difficult and felt torn. Mireille hoped that her father and Esther would stay together. She did her utmost to make her new "mother" feel at home, forming an alliance with her and often rebuking her father. The family became divided and the tension between Roger and Esther became unbearable.

Esther's own children were also finding it hard to accept that their mother was giving her love to a new family. Esther missed them and often succumbed to feelings of regret. She tried to see her children alone whenever possible so as to preserve her role as their mother. Her children seldom visited the new house, where they did not feel at home. Esther felt pulled in two directions, and whenever she experienced the pain of this split existence she hurled bitter accusations at Roger.

Lawrence and Esther, in particular, found their new situation extremely difficult. Lawrence not only found it hard to accept the presence of this newcomer, just a few years after his mother's death, but also, perhaps, feared that she too might "leave them". The only person on whom he felt he could depend was his father, Roger, but Roger's attention was divided between Esther, Lawrence, and Mireille. Although Lawrence was at times pleased with his new "mother", he also tested her and would not easily make room for her.

Meanwhile, Esther, who was still grieving at the lost togetherness of her own family, had great difficulty fitting into this new set-up.

In a sense, Mireille felt able to embrace her stepmother precisely because Laurence was resisting her and thus watching over the family's old constellation. The love between Roger and Esther was not in itself strong enough to withstand this complex mesh of emotions.

### Martin and Rosalie: the floor caves in

Martin lived with his new life partner Rosalie in a large house with enough space for everyone: Martin with his three children and Rosalie with her two children. But in spite of all this space, and although Rosalie did her best to cook delicious meals for the family, the house was full of tension.

Martin's ex-wife suffered from frequent psychotic episodes. At times she was unable to care for the children and roamed the village, ranting and cursing. Then there were days on which she sealed the house off to ward off some imagined menace from the outside world. The three children were ashamed of their mother, but felt the strong support of their loving father. When their mother was hospitalised, the children were frequently left alone. Martin had to provide for the family: he spent as much time as possible at home, but was powerless to prevent his children coming home to an empty house.

When Martin fell in love, he was delighted that Rosalie was willing to care for his children on a regular basis. The children were happy too, also for their father. They knew how difficult his life had been and were glad he had someone to love. Everything went well until Rosalie moved in. From then on, the children felt she was usurping their mother's place, and rows started erupting.

Then Martin sold the old house and they all moved into a new house with Rosalie, a house to which they felt unconnected. On top of that, Martin failed to acknowledge the importance to the children of their holiday home, where they had enjoyed so many good times together. At this point the children turned against Rosalie. She reacted by withdrawing and blaming Martin for the situation. Martin in turn accused his children of causing trouble. He urged them to express their gratitude to Rosalie and to apologise for their meanness to her. The children refused, leading to a rift between them and their father and to furious rows between Martin and Rosalie, who accused Martin of taking too little interest in her own children.

When a large party was organised in the holiday home, which his children saw as their own family's special place, the tension increased. Rosalie prepared the guest rooms for her own friends and asked Martin's children to sleep on mattresses in the living room. The children asked their father to stand up for them, but Martin found the tension unbearable and abandoned his own party.

## The order of love

Blended families can be regarded as complex dynamic systems. Within these systems a multiplicity of symptoms may develop, which appear in diverse guises in the consulting rooms of therapists and care workers. In many cases, the love between the new partners is not strong enough to withstand the battering that arises from clashing loyalties.

It is all too common in blended families for everyone to feel estranged or dislocated. A new equilibrium cannot be created overnight; everyone is out of balance. Cast adrift from familiar moorings, each person is trying to acquire a new sense of belonging. This quest often leads to fierce conflicts. When the new partners assume that their romantic love can withstand the tensions that will arise, they often underestimate the impact of the changes on the children, who are expected to adapt to complex new situations, including the loss of much that was familiar to them. Children are frequently expected to accept new partners while they are still grieving over their parents' separation. When behavioural problems arise there is often a failure to see these in the wider context.

Bert Hellinger refers to the "Order of Love" (Hellinger, 1989, 2005), a phrase denoting a social order that obeys certain rules. Within this order there is a hierarchy, from top to bottom, from earlier to later, and from past to present: quite simply, the first comes first. For new partners this means that the first husband or wife must be acknowledged and honoured and given a permanent place. The new partner often finds this difficult and would prefer the first partner to step aside and preferably to fade away. Great tension arises as a result. Hellinger maintains that honouring all those who belong to the system is crucial to the systemic equilibrium. When everyone's place is assured and honoured, the situation can settle into a calm state. No one must be overlooked. Those who came before have priority over those who came later. People belonging to the larger system are often excluded because it is hard to find an appropriate place for them. Here is a list of people who may be left out:

- the previous partners of one or both parents;
- children from earlier relationships, including those conceived during a marriage but with a different father, and children put up for adoption or placed in foster care;
- relatives who are never mentioned:
  - because they died young from sickness, in war, or in an accident;
  - because they committed suicide;
  - because they have been in prison;
  - because they have been given the role of scapegoat;
  - because of a protracted illness;
  - because of their sexual identity.

(see Veenbaas & Goudswaard, 2002, p. 227)

It is important that everyone has a place of their own—the appropriate chronological order. If a father leaves his family and subsequently has a child with his new wife, his first children, who have remained with their mother, have lost their place. The system is out of balance and tensions will arise if the father cannot give the children born from his earlier relationship the place they deserve.

Hellinger's ideas can help to build an "architecture of living", a plan that can help a blended family to resolve the conflicting loyalties and to arrive at a new equilibrium that does justice to all, that does not overlook or exclude anyone. The Order of Love includes children who have died in the womb or who have been unable to live because of a miscarriage or abortion. Everyone needs a place. It is important that everyone is acknowledged and honoured, the deceased and the living, those who came first and those who came later, the parents and the grandparents. It is only when those earlier members of the family system have been duly acknowledged that space can arise for a horizontal bond with a new partner.

## Architecture of living

When Ronald and Connie came to my consulting room and presented the problems described above, it was clear that a plan was needed. We had to take stock of the diverse problems and symptoms that required attention and decide on the order in which to tackle them. I started by inviting Connie and her children to the consulting room. We talked about their father, his sickness, and what it was like for Tom to be alone with his father during the latter's epileptic seizures. Then Connie spoke to both children about the illness that had almost killed her in the last months of her pregnancy with Tom. Tom had fought for his life, and mother and son had kept each other alive. This forged a very special bond between them.

We made a Russian doll arrangement to give everyone a place: a place for the children's father and their grandmother, for their mother and themselves, and for Ronald and his children.

Tom and Sara made a meticulous arrangement in which everyone's place was calculated down to the last millimetre. This introduced calm into the system. Once the arrangement was complete, Connie asked her children's permission to make a new life with Ronald. Only then was Tom able to give Ronald a place in the whole. Soon afterwards, when Ronald came home with a puppy that they could all care for together, the atmosphere was much improved. After that, Tom and Ronald developed a good relationship. They shared responsibility for the dog, and Tom asked Ronald to help him with his homework. The fact that Ronald maintained contact with his ex-wife and his children continued to generate conflict with Connie, however. In this area, we did not succeed in creating the necessary space within the therapy.

Thomas's new blended family, which had clashed at the amusement park, also came for therapy. I started by talking to Thomas and his teenage daughter, Barbara, who still found it hard to accept her parents' divorce, even though it had taken place many years earlier. She cherished her early memories of the large extended family and her parents' shared friends, a circle in which she had felt warm and safe. In consequence, she resisted it when either parent started seeing someone else. Thomas and Barbara discussed the divorce in my presence, and when Thomas broke down in tears it had the effect of calming Barbara, because she could see that her father too grieved at their loss. She then had an opportunity to talk about how the divorce had affected her. Later it became clear that her mother had not yet come to terms with the divorce and that the two of them often talked about the "good old days" together. Barbara often saw her mother in tears, and that drove her to do battle with her father, and certainly to resist any new girlfriend he might have, since the newcomer would by definition threaten the old equilibrium that she desperately wanted to preserve.

Then we set up a session with mother and daughter, since it was clear that Barbara was helping her mother to bear her sadness. We discussed how hard it was for Barbara to share this burden, and suggested that if the mother did not start living her own life, Barbara's development would be arrested. In a separate session I spoke to Thomas alone, and he was in doubt as to whether living together with his new girlfriend, Greta, as she wanted, was a good idea. Greta was very insistent and he found it hard to resist this pressure. He foresaw big problems in the upbringing of her son Brian, who claimed all his mother's attention. He was afraid that if he tried to impose his own ideas on Brian's upbringing, he and Greta would fight. Brian deeply resented the fact that his own father had not only abandoned his family but had also had two children with his new wife. He was only allowed to visit his father once a fortnight, and felt that he had lost his place. His mother was his only mainstay. He resented her forming any relationship and saw each newcomer as an intruder. His mother was tired of having to raise him alone and longed for a man's support. But when she asked Thomas to intervene and Brian ended up in tears, Greta would complain that he was too hard on the boy. This situation was of benefit to no one.

Thomas concluded that it was better to maintain separate households. He still needed to resolve certain issues with his own children and their mother, and Greta too had things that needed to be dealt with. Each of them had work to do. It was not yet possible to give everyone a place in the new family system, to create a new equilibrium.

Martin and Rosalie came to see me after the unfortunate incident at the holiday home. We decided to use the metaphor of a house to describe their family system. It was a fine old house, full of character, but badly in need of renovation. It needed more than cosmetic modifications. The foundations were not strong enough to support the upper storeys. We devised a plan, an architecture, which involved renovating these foundations. I would begin by talking to Martin and his three children to draw up their shared story together: in other words, to give the children an opportunity to speak at length with their father about their own stories.

They told him how their mother's mental illness had affected them, and the strain of being alone with her. The role of the eldest son, who found life so stressful, became clear, and his siblings thanked him for taking good care of them. Martin also thanked his eldest daughter for helping him on so many difficult occasions. The children were able to talk about the loyalty they felt to their mother and to thank Martin for having always been a mainstay in their life. They said they missed him now that he was devoting so much of his time and attention to Rosalie. They said they wanted to spend more time with him at the holiday home—just the four of them. They asked him to ask Rosalie to take a step back; that would really help to improve their relationship with their father.

The exchanges between Martin and his children were intense but they provided clarity and strengthened the "foundations". Martin's relationship with his children was repaired and consolidated, and he also felt on firmer ground in relation to Rosalie.

I saw Rosalie only once, to talk about her divorce and the place of her own children in relation to Martin.

For the "architecture of living", then, it was essential to start by reinforcing the foundations and the ground floor. If this was neglected it would be impossible to live on the first and second floors; in other words, the larger system could not achieve calm and equilibrium, a state in which everyone could settle into a comfortable place, a place that felt right.

However, Martin failed to keep his promise to visit his children (who had since moved out) more frequently. Furthermore, when he spoke to them, he often complained about Rosalie's behaviour; and yet when talking to Rosalie, he did not stand up for his children. Rosalie had asked him to remove the photographs of his children from the holiday house, and Martin had still not hung them up again as the children had requested. During the final conversation with his children in my consulting room, Martin became angry and walked out. After that, the process stagnated. His children stopped visiting him altogether, either at his house or in their holiday home. They didn't want to see Rosalie. Martin's daughter and Rosalie met once, but this meeting drove them even further apart. Then the youngest son phoned me to make an appointment. He was going to become a father, and was at a loss to decide how to communicate with his own father.

It is part of the architecture of living to thank children for their care and exertions, to extend this respect and gratitude to former husbands and wives, and to widen the boundaries to ensure that there is ample space for everyone. Determining the right order, giving everyone a place in the larger whole, is crucial. A blended family is a complex dynamic system, and as such it has to incorporate many stories. An equilibrium needs to be established amid the polyphony, the multiplicity of positions, the "multiverse" of stories and definitions of reality. Two people who want to start a new life together in such circumstances will therefore need great reserves of strength, patience and wisdom, since their new life must be built on a field that has its own pre-existing order.

*André's new family*

André, forty years old, had two children, aged seven and four. After his divorce he had lived alone for a few years and saw the children according to an agreed schedule. These access arrangements started to break down when André started seeing Margaret. Margaret was only thirty, and had had a difficult childhood. Her mother had a borderline personality and Margaret had never felt safe with her. She would always be on edge coming home from school, fearing her mother's mental state, and took care to prepare some story to keep her mother calm. Her father had a busy job, was often away on business, and left his daughter to cope with her mother. When Margaret left home and fell in love for the first time, she did not dare to tell her parents about it. She lived her private life in secrecy, in the shadows, alongside her other public life. This double life was very taxing and she was often exhausted.

Margaret blossomed when she started going out with André. This time she did dare to tell her parents, and they accepted her choice. She was happy, enjoyed their mutual love, and they had fun doing things together. She determined to be a good mother to André's children. Still, she found it more and more difficult to accept the children's behaviour. To her they seemed spoilt and rude. When she tried to correct them, it caused conflict between her and André, since the children refused to accept her authority. So she decided to distance herself when the children came to visit. She was exasperated that the children's mother kept messing about with the access and holiday arrangements, which made it difficult for her and André to make plans. The tension grew palpable. André was so eager to have a new family that he was unwilling to accept Margaret withdrawing when the children came to visit, complaining: "After all, they don't come so often!" Margaret started fantasising about having a life of her own, and considered the idea of living separately. André became afraid of losing her and tried to check up on her movements.

We discussed the enormous changes to which Margaret had adapted within a short space of time. First, there was the tension caused by telling her parents, especially her unpredictable mother, about her new lover. Then she and André had had only a brief period of time to enjoy their new love, since the children had soon become part of their life together. She was obliged to adapt and to make herself "bigger", so that she was not just André's new girlfriend but also his partner in the children's upbringing. Furthermore, she had moved in with André, and the house did not really feel like her home. She was plagued by insecurities.

In spite of their very different histories, André and Margaret assumed from the outset that their love was strong enough to guide the complex forces. We agreed that the mothering role placed too much strain on Margaret and agreed that when the children came to visit she would go and do something else. André would explain to the children that Margaret was his girlfriend and she would not take care of them when they came to visit; he would care for them himself. This gave the children a clear domain with their father that was not influenced by his new life partner. Margaret loved having time to meet up with friends or to find other forms of relaxation in these weekends, and it improved their relationship. It also enabled André to be a real father to his children and to strengthen his ties with them. The children loved having their father to themselves. The change introduced serenity into the system.

*An empty space between two worlds*

In the following example, the children were immersed in their mother's grief after their parents' divorce. They missed their father, who had formed a new family, and felt wretched in the empty space between those two worlds.

Janna was fifteen when her mother brought her to the consulting room. The GP had felt she needed support and referred her for psychotherapy. The mother, Olga, was worried that Janna spent too much time wandering about the streets by herself, fell for untrustworthy boyfriends, and sometimes suffered from depression. The girl was also doing poorly at school.

Olga and her husband Jim had separated when Janna was nine, and their two daughters, Janna and her younger sister Wilma, stayed with their mother. Once a fortnight the girls spent a weekend with their father. These visits went well until their father's new girlfriend Agnes and her son moved in with him. An antagonism developed between Olga and Agnes that soon escalated into a fierce conflict.

Then Jim and Agnes had twins. This made the situation even more complicated, since Jim had to "love all his children equally". When Janna and Wilma came to visit their father in the new situation, they had to be on their best behaviour to avoid rows. Janna felt that Agnes ignored her and that her father simply did whatever Agnes expected him to do. Janna would occasionally quarrel with Agnes, because she felt sorry for her father; she sensed his pain and saw him shaking from tension. Usually she prevented the row from getting out of hand, however, and would withdraw to another room. The situation made her unhappy and she wept ceaselessly in the consulting room as she talked about it.

> I always know how someone else is feeling straight away. At school too. I see all those insecure boys wandering about and I feel how unhappy they are. I have it with my mother and my father too. And with Agnes too. I feel how afraid she is of losing my father. I always understand what everyone is feeling. I can stand up to my mother because she stands firm and won't collapse. My father is weak and I don't dare to put any pressure on him.

Janna wept endlessly as she told me all this. She explained that she had been to a therapist before, together with her parents, but:

> They just talked about each other and got into a row right in front of me; that was no good to me at all. And there's no point in me saying all this to my father, 'cos he immediately denies it all and gets angry and starts shaking. Then I just shut up.

I decided that this meant that there was little point in inviting the girls and their parents to come for a joint session. The pain and complications surrounding the divorce were so great that it was highly probable that the battle would recommence in the consulting room. Inviting Janna together with her father Jim also seemed a bad idea, since Jim would not feel able to talk openly and would probably feel the need to protect Agnes and his love for the young twins.

It seemed best to invite Jim to come by himself, and to talk to him man to man and father to father about the different forces between which he was caught up. Discussing these forces openly in front of his daughters might feel like disloyalty to his new wife. To help Janna and Wilma it was important to guard against his losing face.

It became clear that Janna felt a great hole in her existence, a gaping hole that she filled up by focusing obsessively on clothes and make-up: her appearance. She could only see herself through the eyes of the outside world—she had almost completely become "outside world" herself. Very occasionally that sad, lonely little girl in that emptiness behind her facade came to the surface. The emptiness turned out to consist of the gap between the Janna that heard all the voices in the outside world, who felt and understood everything, and the lonely little girl who had lost her place amid the rows between her parents. Fortunately, however, she did still feel she had a place with her mother. She would sometimes lie still all evening, with her head on her mother's lap. That was a wonderful feeling for that little girl, but fifteen-year-old Janna would feel all her mother's sadness at such times, and would feel the need to stay strong afterwards.

Janna talked about the daily rows between Agnes and Jim and the tension in their house, and said how sorry she felt for her father. I told Janna that the strain was too much for her and her sister to bear. I suggested that I would invite her father to come and talk about the situation, and try to see if he could take some of the burden away from her. Janna agreed. I said that after the talk with her father I would also talk to her mother to see how we could reduce some of the pressure she felt. Then I would talk to her again, tell her what we had achieved, and we would discuss the next steps to be taken.

Janna was visibly relieved, and as the two prepared to leave, Olga remarked that Janna was intent on having plastic surgery to straighten her nose, which she felt was crooked. As Janna admitted, "It's become an obsession." I wondered if all the colliding loyalties in this complex system had somehow congealed into an obsessive preoccupation with a supposedly crooked nose.

Before I had an opportunity to invite the father to visit, he called me himself to request a consultation. When he came, he acknowledged that he and Agnes were trying to bring all the children together and to integrate them into a single harmonious family. All the children were treated equally. I remarked that it was unavoidable that "some were more equal than others." Janna and Wilma only came to visit once every two weeks, and if they received no special treatment at those times, weren't they effectively "less equal" than those who always lived with their father? And "equal in a different way" from Agnes's son, who lived with his mother but missed his own father.

Jim tried to be the same father to all the children. He agreed that this was a completely unmanaged network of clashing forces. He was very willing to work on devising a way of managing this complex field. He was shocked to discover that Janna and Wilma were worried about him, and that they continued to feel upset about the quarrelling they had seen at the weekend when they went home to their mother. What he saw as everyday squabbling made a great impression on Janna and Wilma. The other children saw the bickering as unimportant, since they knew it was temporary and the general good humour was always restored. He was shocked to hear that Janna was convinced that he was unhappy with Agnes and that she thought Agnes did not want him to show that he loved her and Wilma.

He realised that Janna and Wilma needed him to devote time and attention to them separately. It emerged from the session that he never tucked them in or sat at their bedside for a while when they went to bed. He said that Agnes never discouraged such affection but that he had tried to be consistent in treating all the children equally. "We need to orchestrate things better and I'm going to talk about how to do this when I get home."

After this, there was a session with Jim and Janna together. They made an arrangement with the Russian nesting dolls to try out ways of giving everyone the place they needed. Jim admitted to Janna that he had not managed things well and that he sometimes found it difficult to cope with all the sensibilities involved in such a large family. He said that he loved Agnes very much and that the bickering that Janna and Wilma saw was always over very quickly. He said that Agnes never tried to influence the way he behaved with them and that he was going to tackle things differently from then on.

Janna said that she loved being in the car with just her father and her sister. But as soon as they got in the door everyone wanted his attention and the intimate atmosphere they had shared with him was gone. Janna said she loved playing with the twins and never minded them being there as long as she felt that her father noticed her too—that he was pleased to see his daughters. She very much wanted to occasionally do something together with him.

Jim promised to be more sensitive and Janna felt somewhat reassured. There was a noticeable improvement over the following few weekends. Jim talked to Agnes before the girls came and spent some time alone with Janna and Wilma.

After this there was a session in the consulting room with Jim and Wilma. Wilma too made an arrangement with the Russian nesting dolls to find the right places for everyone, including herself. She felt almost invisible during the weekends with her father and did not feel that she had a clear place there. Like Janna, Wilma loved spending time with the other children, but for her the most important thing was for her father to really see her.

These were only the first few steps in the architecture: many more would follow. Jim became a more dynamic presence in his daughters' lives. But they could only achieve a real improvement if he and Olga—the girls' parents—succeeded in keeping the pain associated with their past relationship to themselves. That would not be easy to achieve.

# CHAPTER TWELVE

# Fatherly love

*"It is a wise father that knows his own child"*

—William Shakespeare, *The Merchant of Venice*, Act II, Scene II

## Introduction

In this chapter I want to use some examples from my practice to reflect on the role of fathers in the family and their relationships with their children, especially their sons. It goes without saying that the father–daughter, mother–son, and mother–daughter relationships are equally important. However, this chapter reflects specifically on the role of the father in the development of young boys in their adolescence. This chapter does not seek to make any pronouncements on alternative family structures in which children may be raised.

As psychotherapists we find ourselves confronted more and more with boys who have identity problems: boys who are doing poorly at school and playing truant, and whose lives seem to lack purpose and direction. Boys who seem unable to develop their abilities and staying power. In many of these cases the parents are separated, and the sons stay close to their mothers, growing up in a world of women—often missing their fathers. Many boys do not encounter male teachers until secondary school. Throughout primary school and after-school care they are largely raised by women. Their fathers are all too often absent, whether because of divorce or a busy job, or because they are wrestling with their own identity, and the lion's share of upbringing is left to the mothers. In all such cases, boys have to do without a male role model and without masculine strength in their lives.

While I was working on this book, I taught two seminars as further training for parental supervisors and systems therapists who worked in child psychiatry and special needs education. Hardly any men attended either of these seminars. We discussed the fact that the responsibility for taking care of families with problems frequently rests on the shoulders of women. We see a great many families with absent fathers, families with boys of all ages who pose problems of authority to their mothers. Then it is female therapists who help these mothers to try to establish their authority, and female therapists who discuss the boys' behaviour with the fathers.

Where are the male therapists who can help families, together with their female colleagues? Where are the male therapists who can urge fathers to accept their responsibility?

For years I worked together with my colleague Paulien Kuipers. It proved a valuable combination: I could conduct talks from man to man, as one father to another, while my female colleague could assist the mother. I have found it extremely helpful when both male and female language can be spoken during therapy: when men and women complement one another, respect each other, and each set an example to their children. In his book *Les pères et les mères*, the French paediatrician Aldo Naouri emphasises the key role of the father in preserving harmony in the family (Naouri, 2005). Mindful of his ideas, and of Deleuze's philosophy, I want to make a passionate plea here for fathers to be present in the lives of their sons—and also, of course, in those of their daughters.

### *The role of the father*

In the course of my work I came across a father who frequently played football with his six-year-old son. Fiercely determined to win, his son played "dirty" and did not keep to the rules. And while you might allow a very young child to win, to give him the pleasure of victory and to bolster his self-confidence, this did not apply to a boy aged six. That would not be right, said the father. The father insisted on fair play, come what may, despite his son's frequent floods of tears.

The boy would say: "Have you practised this before, Daddy?"

Father would say: "Practised? Oh yes, at least 10,000 times."

His son was very impressed, and had great respect for his father. He decided to practise more, because he wanted to be just like his father.

Minuchin's family therapy placed emphasis on the dividing lines between generations, on the domain of the parents and that of the children, and on parents collaborating as a team in their children's upbringing. He emphasised the importance of clear structure: indeed, his approach became known as structural family therapy. It developed in an age dominated by patriarchal thought. It was Minuchin's belief that the formation of a coalition across the generational boundaries led to pathology.

In practice, we see more and more fathers who want to be friends with their sons, together forming an alliance against the mother. We see fathers who refuse to take sides in conflicts between mothers and their teenage sons; fathers who undermine the authority of their son's school by standing up for him if he breaks the rules. We see fathers who are more concerned to tell tall stories about the "heroic" deeds of their own youth than to provide advice and support for the future. But a father is not his son's friend: he has a different task. As an adult and a parent, a father is responsible for providing direction and setting boundaries.

We also see many sons who stay close to their mothers if the father is absent—whatever the reason—and become "mother's little helper". This means that they stand beside their mother in a space that is far too large, a space that fills them with fear and in which they feel ill at ease. They may inflate themselves, occupying too much space and refusing to accept any authority, certainly if their own fathers no longer represent any authority. By making themselves bigger than they are, they conjure up the presence of an absent father. When the mother seeks help for her son's behavioural problems, the two will probably be seen by a female therapist. Care providers frequently omit to involve the father if he lives elsewhere following divorce or has had no contact with his son for many years. In supervision sessions I often find that there will be discussions *about* the father but not *with* him. The care providers simply overlook the importance of involving him.

The language used by care providers, with its emphasis on expressing emotions, is frequently unhelpful when dealing with teenage boys, especially if all the care providers are female. For instance, a boy is unlikely to say that he misses his father, in the presence of his mother and another woman. But the boy may experience this very silence as disloyalty to his father.

In a letter to the daily newspaper *de Volkskrant*, a secondary school teacher, Ferry Haan, wrote that he noticed again and again that the example set by a boy's father was key to his development. "Many mothers complain that they cannot 'get through' to their sons, while sons complain that their mothers' nagging drives them crazy."

*The nine-year-old knight*

Ian, aged nine, was constantly quarrelling and fighting at school. He shrugged off all attempts to correct his behaviour. After various internal discussions, a meeting was set up with the boy, his mother Anne, his teacher, the internal school supervisor, and the headmistress. All the adults present were women. In this setup, the boy was urged to try to explain his behaviour. The boy's father, Robert, had a busy job and was unable to attend. The boy withdrew into intractable silence. The adults concluded that Ian must have some psychological disorder if he could express himself so poorly and had so little insight into his behaviour. Perhaps he was autistic or suffered from attention deficit disorder.

Ian was referred to local mental health services, where he had an intake interview with a female therapist. After two sessions he was referred for diagnosis to a female colleague. The boy's refusal to say anything beyond a few essential details heightened the suspicion of autism. Arriving home after the session, Ian put on his knight's costume and rushed out to play. When the woman next door exclaimed: "Wow, you look tough!" the comment brought a wide smile to the boy's face.

The family was referred to me for therapy, and at some point Anne told the story of the knight's costume. The story made it clear that Ian yearned to be treated differently, as a "young man". Realising this, Robert promised to take a more active role in his son's life. We agreed that in future it would be Robert who would liaise with school about his son's behavioural problems. Robert also suggested that he would start putting Ian to bed himself.

Up to then, bedtime had led to recurrent scenes. Anne would put Ian to bed. Ian would refuse to let her go, and when she was finally able to tear herself away, after an hour or so, she would collapse onto the sofa in exhaustion and complain to her husband. Robert, tired after a day's work, would be immersed in his newspaper and ask to be left in peace. The exchange would escalate into a row, which could be heard upstairs. Ian would come downstairs and complain that he couldn't sleep. Robert, agitated by the row with his wife, would grab his son by the scruff of his neck, drag him upstairs and throw him onto the bed: "Right, that's enough! I don't want to hear another word from you!"

Robert would go downstairs, and the couple would maintain a frosty silence until Anne went to bed early, while Robert stayed up late, even though he had a long commute the next morning. Chronically exhausted, he used the weekend to catch up on his sleep and was unable to take his son to soccer practice.

Now that Robert was more present in Ian's life and put him to bed, the two had time to discuss the day's events, to laugh and play together. Robert set boundaries, telling Ian to go to sleep and not to come downstairs. This went well the first few evenings. Then, when Anne started to discuss Ian's emotional problems, Robert asked her to leave the matter to him. He took his son to bed, and refused to be drawn into a discussion: "We agreed that you were not going to come down any more; you're going to go sleep now." And he immediately left the room.

The atmosphere between Anne and Robert improved in leaps and bounds. Both were pleased with the way they had cooperated. But Anne did not find it easy to allow Robert to take over.

We often see cases in which the mother has completely appropriated her son. She shuts the father out, and if he is allowed to play a role, it has to be on her terms. In these situations, when the father is involved, he reacts in one of two ways: either he tries to mediate and defuse the situation, or he takes harsh action, provoking the mother to intervene to protect her son from his father. All this deflects attention from the initial theme, which is generally the boundaries to be set to the son's behaviour. When this pattern occurs, the son achieves a brief "victory" but loses his way in a space that is too large for him.

> In the film *Mon fils à moi* (Martial Fougeron, 2006), the young teenage protagonist, Julien, has been completely appropriated by his overprotective mother. The remote father ignores his son's unspoken pleas for help. The mother invades her son's life and mental space, frequently visiting his school to discuss her concerns with the teachers. Grandma, with whom Julien has a good relationship, is told not to interfere. In their efforts to avert tragedy, neither the boy's teachers nor the care services think to get the father involved.

It is hard for a father to wrest his son from the mother's arms. And it is hard for a mother to allow the father to take a more active role and to define him as "a safe pair of hands".

### Pride

While I was working on this book at my little lakeside holiday cabin, I noticed a father and his son, aged about twelve. They spent entire days fishing together. At one point I saw that they had caught a huge carp. Proudly they showed their trophy to the mother. Father and son stood shoulder to shoulder, the carp in their hands, for mother to take a picture. It was clear how proud the mother was of her husband and their son. After a few photos were taken, the man and boy carefully slid the fish back into the water and the carp swam away.

What a lovely structure, I thought. A mother who was so proud of the relationship between father and son, and a father and son who had the opportunity to show the mother the trophy arising from their shared efforts. Then I mused on where that pride "lived": was it in the landscape between the fish and the water, the son and the father, the husband and the wife?

The Australian family therapist Steve Biddulph says in an interview that boys need their mother, their father, and then a mentor, in that order. The mentor—a sports coach or music teacher, perhaps—acts as an extension to the father's safe pair of hands. A good father will support the authority of the school and that of the mentor, and support the authority of the referee rather than justifying his son's fouls.

> In an interview, the professional soccer player Willy Brokamp said that when boys are young, they should all play together. When they are older, some are selected for the team and others are excluded. Selection is necessary and is good for the boys' development. They discover the importance of technique, talent, and character. Still, all the boys carry on practising, since a team can always change: it needs reserves and substitute players. Then mothers interfere. Concerned about their sons' bruised egos, they accuse the coach of a lack of respect for daring to leave their son out of the team. Brokamp asks: Where are the fathers who set boundaries and encourage boys to practise? Fathers who can teach them to convert disappointment and frustration into energy and determination to fight back?

The Dutch historian Angela Crott wrote her PhD thesis on the image of boys in the literature of children's upbringing from 1882 to 2005 (Crott, 2011). For over a hundred years, boys were described as restless and noisy, fond of horsing about and acting tough, all such characteristics being seen as necessary steps on the way to a healthy identity. The past twenty-five years have witnessed a change in the public image of boys. With the feminisation of education, boys are increasingly likely to be labelled "aggressive" and their behaviour is often described as "deviant". Single-parent families—usually headed by a mother—are more and more common. There are fewer male teachers, who could serve as essential role models to boys. Furthermore, there is a growing emphasis on independent work at school, on self-reflection, and on the development of social and emotional skills.

Fathers remain of crucial importance to their children after a divorce. In practice, however, we often see mothers caring for their children alone. Access arrangements frequently cause conflict. But children have a fundamental right to both parents; access should not be dependent on the ex-spouse's approval. There is nothing wrong, in principle, with "Dad's world" operating according to different rules from "Mum's world". Always providing, of course, that there is no question of either neglecting or harming the child, divorced parents have the task of building up a new kind of partnership, one based on shared care, shared parenting. Even though a father may forfeit his right to care for a child, biological fatherhood cannot be cancelled out and may well continue to play a role in the child's emotional world. Some boys who grow up without a father have a difficult time. If a boy is referred to care services, it is important to get the father involved, however absent he may have been. Otherwise, the care services will take the father's place, and the boy is very likely to reject whatever help is offered.

The importance of the father's role following divorce is also clear from the findings of the PhD thesis of Esther Hakvoort, who followed a small group of blended families (Hakvoort, 2011). Children who maintained a warm relationship with their biological father did better and even built up a better relationship with their stepfather, Hakvoort concluded. The biological father was essential in helping boys to develop their social competence.

## Love and effective action

The parents of fourteen-year-old Leon were appalled when their son was arrested and revealed to be a member of a gang that conducted robberies. They had found him impossible to deal with for several years. Leon climbed out of the window and went into town at night, often missed school, drank alcohol, and smoked cannabis. The parents decided it was time to take action. When the boy was released, his father Sam picked him up and took him straight to a campsite in France, where he spent the entire summer holiday alone with his son. In this way Sam took responsibility for the boy, and by expressing love and determination he made it clear to Leo that his parents wanted him to change his life. He "detained" his son. Sam loved his son, and although Leo protested at the sudden change, a new relationship developed between them. For the first time, Sam became an active presence in his son's life, having previously entrusted the boy's upbringing largely to his wife.

## In search of fatherhood

Ralph, thirty-three years old, had recently become the father of a little girl. Seated opposite me, he said that he did not feel glad at the birth of his child.

> All my friends experience fatherhood as a divine gift. I do cuddle my little daughter, but I don't really know how to be a father. And yet I often thought I would love to have a child … How's it possible? Since my friends are so happy with their own children, I don't dare discuss my doubts with them. I'm afraid they'll think I'm a bad father.

Ralph had gone through therapy with me several years earlier; we had completed the therapy successfully eighteen months ago. Ralph had gone through a tremendous development in terms of his emotions and insight. The first time I met him, he was texting his girlfriend as he entered the consulting room because they were in the middle of a row. It turned out to be one of many rows, and for Ralph the umpteenth relationship that was dominated by rows. All this conflict weighed Ralph down.

Ralph had grown up in an atmosphere of violence. He had been teased as a small boy and was always frightened. At some point he decided this had to change. He ended up in the world of martial arts, became an extremely proficient fighter, and acquired a superbly toned body. Fighting helped him to conquer his fear. He was no longer afraid of the outside world, and if necessary he could settle rows by force. Still, his years of training also gave him the tools to defuse conflict. He built up his own business and was proud of what he had achieved. We called the therapy "mental training" that was needed to complement his physical training.

Ralph had grown up without a father. His parents separated early on, and his father took little interest in his two sons: as Ralph put it, "I had to manage by myself."

During the two years of therapy or "mental training", we had discussed his fears and anxieties and the people he had lost when he was young, one of whom had died a violent death. We talked about his concern for his mother, who suffered from depression and drank too much, in Ralph's opinion. She drank together with his brother, who had lost his way in life.

We explored the constant troubles in his relationships with girlfriends. With the support of the therapy, Ralph acquired more inner strength. He broke off his relationship and lived alone for a time. Then he met someone else, and for the first time, this relationship weathered the frequent rows and settled into more stability. He learned different responses to conflict situations, learned how to deal with his partner's verbal outbursts, and started to experience harmony in the relationship. He felt happy and was so afraid of losing this happiness that he constantly fantasised about breaking the relationship off, "because it's bound to end in failure anyway."

In spite of all this, the two succeeded in steadying and deepening this relationship. His girlfriend wanted to live with him and they discussed the idea of having a child. Ralph spoke at length about his desires and concerns. He underwent EMDR therapy to help him "get his head in the right place." At length he proposed to his girlfriend, in an extremely creative and playful way. Ralph's life was on the rails and we concluded the therapy with an air of satisfaction.

Eighteen months later, then, Ralph was back. His daughter had been born, and Ralph told me, with tears in his eyes, that he could hardly restrain himself from teasing his tiny daughter. He would occasionally pinch her, and his inclination was to leave her to cry instead of going to her. Although he did not give in to this inclination, he was very shocked at these reactions and feelings. We looked at each other intently and Ralph's tears flowed freely.

I asked Ralph: "Are you feeling the pain of what you never had? Are you experiencing a mixture of happiness with your daughter and anger at what you did without? Do you feel that she is receiving what you never had? That must be confusing."

Ralph replied: "I feel so angry at my father, who never cared about us at all. Now I don't know how to be a father and I'm mainly afraid that I'll do it wrong. I have a very good friend, Bob, who's sixty years old. When I see how he behaves with my daughter, I feel full of respect and admiration—proud of my friend! It makes me feel safer. He has five children, and when I see how much he enjoys having fun with my daughter, making contact with her, I feel more restful. It's as if he's showing me how to do it. I should have asked him to be godfather." Ralph showed me some photos of Bob holding the baby and Bob's wife smiling with pleasure. It was a touching scene.

Ralph said it was a relief to be able to speak about his doubts regarding his fatherhood and his feelings of shame at wanting to tease his little daughter. He added: "You know what it was like when I was a little boy? An uncle would come and tell me, all exciting like, that he could smoke with his eyes. Then, opening his eyes wide and fixing me with his gaze, he would push a burning cigarette into my right arm. He had such a good laugh when I jumped out of my skin … that's how things were at our place. I was used to it."

I suggested that he ask his older friend Bob and his wife to be his daughter's godparents after all. I said he should tell them his story and ask them to take him on as an "apprentice" for fatherhood. Ralph was enthusiastic about the suggestion, and was sure that Bob and his wife would be pleased too. He would have the mentor he needed and his daughter would have two more caring people in her life.

## Sons without fathers

A widow, Yolanda, with three adult children was referred for family therapy in connection with her youngest son, twenty-one years old, who could scarcely care for himself. While her daughter, aged twenty-six, was doing well in the theatre world and had a harmonious family, her two sons found life difficult. Jan-Willem, aged twenty-four, lived in what Yolanda referred to as a "mole hole"—a small dark space into which he retreated. Although he was studying for a degree, he could not graduate since he kept postponing his final exams.

Walter, aged twenty-one, also lived in a "mole hole", but a filthy one without any order or structure. As a young boy he had been a champion athlete, but after the departure of his coach, with whom he had an extremely good relationship, he had abandoned his ambitions in sport. Unable to finish school, he lived without any income, work or structure in filthy surroundings. He smoked cannabis all day and spent half the night sitting at the computer. He liked to talk about philosophy and spirituality with his mother and his siblings, but he often lost the thread of whatever topic they were discussing.

Walter came to the consulting room together with his mother and brother. He wore clean clothes and seemed to have had a shower, whereas his mother had told me he usually wore dirty clothes and went around unwashed. Yolanda told me that Walter had been living on almost nothing but pizzas for so long that his body barely functioned. If he ate a proper meal, his intestines could not digest it. In addition, he was almost always tired and lay on the sofa when he came to visit. His once muscular body was almost devoid of strength.

The father had died a few years ago, after a long and devastating illness. Walter did not realise that his father was going to die until very late, and it shocked him. He had never come to terms with his grief. Yolanda said that her husband had been a wonderful father when the children were small. He took them everywhere, spent lots of time with them, and always went to see their sports competitions. But when the children went through puberty and became rebellious, he could not deal with it. The change saddened him, and he withdrew. A few years later he fell ill and he no longer had the strength to raise his sons.

Walter told us about what he had felt when he was twelve years old, and saw his elder brother Jan-Willem battling with their father, and winning. This disturbed Walter and he distanced himself from them. Together with Jan-Willem, we all discussed what it meant if the eldest son wins a battle with his father. There are many types of "winning": physical victories, winning an argument, and winning by crossing boundaries with impunity. The boys' father, it became clear, was incapable of enforcing boundaries. Both young men said that if you win from the father you love, and with whom you have so many good memories, it stops you in your tracks. Jan-Willem said that he had come to a dead end in his life after that. Walter had withdrawn so much that he was living in complete isolation. After he witnessed the key "battle", he decided not to engage in a similar conflict himself.

Walter's development had apparently stagnated since he was twelve. After his coach had left and his father had become ill, he had lost all sense of purpose. Having become stuck at the psychological age of twelve, he could not cope with life. His life had left the main track and been shunted off into the depot. From this depot, he had not been able to find his way back to the main track.

Walter would have to be treated not as someone of twenty-one but—partly at least—as a boy of twelve, and the developmental tasks belonging to that age would require attention. We started by organising a therapeutic context.

We placed chairs around the room to visualise the different positions. If the room was seen as a tennis court without a net, the mother would be seated on the long side on the right, with an empty chair representing her late husband to her right. In the middle of the room was Jan-Willem's chair, and about a metre behind and to the side of it was Walter's chair. Jan-Willem's chair was exactly in the middle, where the net would be. He could survey the part of the court that lay before him without being able to cross the central line. Behind him, Walter watched what his elder brother was doing in his life. The mother's chair was on the other side, just past the "net". Thus Yolanda could see from the sidelines whether her sons would cross to the other side of the central "net" line.

I adopted a position on Jan-Willem's side, near the "net" line. This made it possible to visualise the family dynamics and constellation in space. Then I went and stood next to Jan-Willem and discussed with him how difficult it is to "win" from your father when you are so young—the father you love so much and with whom you once shared so much. And that father is now dead.

I said: "It seems as if your life has come to a stop and you don't know how to carry on. Is it actually OK for you to carry on with your life if you have 'won' from your father, and if your father then gets ill, and you have avoided any confrontation with him since then? Do you still dare to invest your energy in anything? Do you feel that the situation has paralysed you?"

Jan-Willem's eyes filled with tears. He said that he had not realised it before, but that this was what he had been struggling with.

Then I stood beside Walter and said how hard it had been for him to develop and to go through puberty after witnessing his father's inability to act with parental authority: "You withdrew and became totally isolated. You did not fully commit to life. Meanwhile, you noticed that your brother's life was stagnating too, that he was postponing his exams, not finishing his papers. Both your lives have faltered, and for you Yolanda, as their mother, it is too difficult to pull these adult children across the "line" into maturity."

Yolanda nodded and she too started to weep. By now, the central line we had marked out had come to symbolise the place where the sons' lives had ground to a halt.

I suggested that in staying close to their mother, the two sons were trying to take care of her, but that it was time to help them pick up the thread of their lives. I asked permission to help both young men cross the "line" where their development had stopped, and asked Yolanda if her husband would approve. She said that he would.

Both Walter and Jan-Willem felt that their existential dilemma had been well translated into the image we had created with the chairs and the uncrossable line. They both said "yes" to this visualisation of their problem. And when I asked Yolanda whether she would like her sons to start leading their own lives, she too said "yes". Indeed, she added that she wanted to start leading her own life herself.

We arrived at the following therapeutic framework: first, Jan-Willem. I agreed that he would contact his course coordinator and draw up a plan of action with her. We agreed a date on which he would inform me of the outcome.

To make a plan for Walter, we needed the help of his mother and brother. I put it to him that he could not yet cope with life: his finances were in a mess, he had no insurance, and his room was filthy. All this was perfectly understandable if we accepted that he was in a sense only twelve years old. He needed a father figure to help him get back on track, and we decided to think of a suitable foster family that could take Walter on temporarily, help him get his stalled life moving again.

After much thought it was decided to try some relatives in America: a family with a son of Walter's age, a house in which there was a lot of laughter and a love of sport. Each member of this family was very self-aware and they were devoted to the natural world and the environment. Yolanda would ask them if they were willing to take Walter into their home for a while, and after much hesitation, Walter reluctantly agreed to the plan. Still, he said he was troubled by depression and did not dare to take this step alone. We asked his sister to support him. Walter also requested antidepressants. We consulted the psychiatrist Dirk Corstens, who agreed.

Some time later, Walter was taking medication and had stopped smoking cannabis. He had spent a holiday with the American family and had functioned extremely well there. The therapy was under way.

*Giving up is not an option*

Figure 25.   Raleigh cycling team. Photo © Cor Vos.

Henry, aged thirty-one, sought therapy because of problems in his relationship with Fenna. He said that they had a good time together, but that he was insecure and needed constant affirmation. He enjoyed their intimacy and friendship and felt that they had a wonderful relationship. But Fenna found him too clinging, which was a cause of irritation. She had just graduated and found work in the city where her parents lived. So she planned to stay with her parents on weekdays, leaving Henry alone. Fenna was ambitious and excited about her future prospects; she had a bold, vigorous approach to life.

Henry admired his in-laws and felt very much at home with them, especially with his father-in-law, whom he regarded as the epitome of reliability and kindness: an energetic man who was completely devoted to his family. Henry got on well with this man, and his in-laws totally accepted him.

Fenna asked Henry to go into therapy, and Henry agreed, since he could see that otherwise their relationship had little chance of success. He would be blocking Fenna's development. He was constantly confronted with his fear of losing Fenna. This insecurity and fear paralysed him. Even so, they enjoyed their weekends together, but only at times when Fenna felt that Henry was able to cope with this change in their relationship. Things went wrong whenever he asked for affirmation or called Fenna during the week to tell her how difficult he was finding things.

Henry talked about the family in which he had grown up. He was the only son, and had a sister. Henry considered that his father always chose the path of least resistance and had not made much of his life. According to Henry, his father avoided every serious discussion and left everything to his mother. Nor did he feel his father supported him. Henry explained several times why he and Fenna were going through this process, but his father simply asked when they were going to live together again and if they had already bought a house. As a result, Henry felt that his father completely failed to understand him. We formulated the theme "masculine vigour" and the father–son relationship.

Henry said that he had often felt ashamed of his father, because of the man's limitations and his tendency always to choose the easy way. As Henry saw it, his father was never there when he needed him. He missed his maternal grandfather, who *had* supported him and set an inspiring example. He said, "Granddad always had faith in me and encouraged me to fulfil my potential. He died when I was eighteen, and since then I've had to manage by myself. I've done so, and I've achieved quite a bit. I've travelled around the world by myself, I graduated, and I've got a good job. Even so, I'm often confronted by my fears, and they are absolutely enormous."

We discussed the difficulty of surpassing your father, becoming better qualified and achieving a higher status. Many sons may find this a frightening idea. This turned out to be a theme in their wider family. Henry told the story of his cousin, who wrestled with a similar problem. This cousin was a brilliant student, and at some point he gave up his studies and ended up in a psychiatric clinic. It seemed possible that this cousin found it too difficult to compete with his father and instead left the arena by a side door: neither winning nor losing, a half-hearted solution. Another cousin, the son of a different uncle, while not ending up in a psychiatric clinic, had completely failed to fulfil his potential and was working in a job well beneath his abilities.

We defined the following context as the start of the therapy. Henry would write a letter on behalf of his grandfather. This letter would convey the message that Henry should fulfil his potential; that he should try to excel, and not resign himself to just muddling through. In addition, Henry would talk to his parents and ask their permission to pursue excellence instead of mediocrity. The idea of this conversation filled Henry with dread. He kept putting it off, and finally went to see them on the very last evening before our next session. His mother had no difficulty saying that she was proud of him and would be happy if he fulfilled his potential. But his father shuffled back and forth uncomfortably, lit a cigar and tried to change the subject. Finally, urged on by his wife, he managed to say, though with difficulty, that he would be happy to see Henry pursuing excellence and fulfilling his potential.

Then Henry told me a curious anecdote. He was a very keen racing cyclist and had just completed a ride of 150 kilometres. A sports photographer took some pictures and posted them online. Henry ordered a photo that showed him climbing the highest, steepest mountain on the ride. It was taken just as he reached the top. It was striking that the photo also showed four other cyclists who were behind Henry and who had dismounted. "Giving up is not an option," said Henry, and this appeared to be a key metaphor for his life. He never gave up, always carried on, and managed to conquer every mountain.

His father, on the other hand, did appear to be someone who had "given up" in his life. Strangely, Henry's father had also ordered the photo, but he Photoshopped it, placing his own head on his son's body, as if he had reached the top of the mountain himself. When Henry's father sent this modified photo to his son, Henry felt quite confused. However, when he arrived at his parents' house on the evening before the next session, he saw that his father had framed the original photo, thus expressing pride in his son's achievement.

We analysed the possible meaning of his father Photoshopping the picture in this way. What was he trying to convey? We concluded that his father seemed to be saying: "I wish I were like you. I wish I could do what you do. I'm someone who gave up, but you, my son, are not. I find that hard to take and it arouses contradictory feelings in me, but at the end of the day I'm proud of you and that's why I've hung the photo up. I want to give you the space you need."

We agreed that Henry would stop calling his girlfriend when he was finding life difficult. Instead, he would tell her that that he would take responsibility for this process himself, that he would conquer the difficulties that arose, and that in this way he wanted to help their relationship to flourish. We agreed that Henry would take two friends into his confidence and ask them to support him during this process. The support of friends is like that of teammates making the same journey and handing you a bidon, pushing you for a bit, or shielding you from the wind.

He could also ask Fenna's father for support, and for instance go on cycling trips with his future father-in-law, who was extremely fit for a man of sixty and could easily cycle over the top of the highest mountain. We also agreed that Henry would go his parents' house again and stand in front of the photo together with his father. He would say to his father: "Yes, Dad, I want to get the best out of myself, to get to the top of the mountain. Are you OK with that? Do you give me your blessing?"

A son needs his father's permission to become bigger than the father himself.

# *EPILOGUE*

The story of seventeen-year-old Diederik, in the case history that follows, combines a number of elements that have been discussed in the course of our expedition through narrative practice: paternal love, the vulnerable equilibrium in blended families, stagnation in development, the usefulness of nesting doll arrangements, "parts integration", and symptoms such as untold stories that have been stored in the body.

### *The boy who soiled his trousers*

Peter came to see me with his life partner Veronique and his seventeen-year-old son Diederik. Peter and Veronique had been together for eleven years, and Diederik had moved in with them twelve months earlier. Before that, he had been living in Austria with his mother, his younger brother, and his half-brother. During that time, his father had had little contact with him. During his rare visits to his father, Diederik would stay at his computer for days on end, engrossed in games. Without noticing, he would soil his trousers. He would then hide the soiled trousers, but the smell naturally led to their discovery. Diederik was called to account for his behaviour but was unable to give any explanation or to change his behaviour. Instead, he found better hiding places. Veronique had recently discovered a large number of soiled pairs of trousers in the attic. It also turned out that Diederik had done the same thing with his urine at an earlier stage, leaving pots full of urine in diverse cupboards around the house.

The boy I saw looked much younger than his age—about twelve years old, and obviously extremely uncomfortable with the situation. It was clear that Diederik was afraid of being asked about his behaviour. He expected a repeat of the talks at home, in which his only answer was to shrug his shoulders, ostensibly unconcerned, to indicate that there was nothing he could do about it. It emerged that Diederik had been exhibiting these symptoms for a very long time.

His mother had been unable to find any helpful response to her son's behaviour when he lived with her. With the passage of time, she also noticed that he was often leaving the house without washing, in clothes that were dirty and too thin for the time of year. She did not intervene, but believed that all such matters were his own responsibility. Now that Diederik was living with his father, the task of disposing of the soiled trousers fell largely to Veronique; Peter kept somewhat aloof and expected her to deal with it. Although Diederik got on well with Veronique, who was doing her best to care for him as a loving stepmother, he was evidently reluctant to accept this care from her, and she found it impossible to help him. She was at her wits' end. She continued to find soiled trousers around the house, and she quarrelled about it with Peter.

We tried to get a clear picture of Diederik's behaviour, the symptoms he was exhibiting. We started by reorganising the context by asking his father if he was willing to take over the care for his son from that point on. This care was rightly his responsibility more than Veronique's. We did suggest that Veronique could assist him and point out what Diederik needed, but she was not the boy's mother and could not play that role.

Could we place the symptomatic behaviour in a developmental context? The theme of toilet training and independently learning to defecate on the potty and then in the toilet belongs at the developmental stage of a child of two or three years of age. Could Diederik have stagnated at that phase in his development? If so, his behaviour would belong to a toddler rather than a teenager. Diederik was clearly mortified by his behaviour. His only response to the situation was to try to hide it. However, the symptomatic behaviour was beyond his control. He was afraid of the negative reactions, criticism, and punishments, and ashamed of the fact that he was constantly soiling his trousers at the age of seventeen. Diederik's father had offered to help and had applied the method of reward and punishment to help his son change his behaviour, but nothing appeared to have any effect. "It just doesn't get through to me," Diederik offered by way of explanation.

Peter added at this point that Diederik was also insensitive to heat and cold. If he was not warned, he would set off on a bitterly cold day without any winter clothes. He also lacked a sense of hunger and thirst. If he was not urged to eat, he would simply "forget," in the same way that he "forgot" to go to the toilet and "forgot" to dress warmly. It scarcely occurred to him to wash and his personal hygiene was abominable. I got the impression that Diederik had been neglected as a baby and a toddler, and that the impulses of hunger and thirst, heat and cold, and personal hygiene matters had all been stifled or extinguished.

Peter told us about the way in which Diederik had been neglected by his mother:

"If he cried, my ex-wife would not let me pick him up; in fact I was not allowed to take any part at all in the boy's upbringing. I moved out and did not see much of my children, partly because of my busy job. I was unable to play any significant role in his early childhood and now I'm trying to catch up. Still, I don't really know how to be a father to him." His eyes were brimming with tears as he said this.

A hungry child who is not fed when he cries will adjust his metabolism accordingly until he eventually loses the ability to feel hungry. A similar adaptive mechanism applies to heat and cold and to defecation. If a two-year-old child has had to walk about with soiled nappies for a long time because no one was there to take care of him, this could explain the symptomatic behaviour when the boy is older. A child who is neglected is thrown back on his own resources and is at the mercy of his own impulses. Having got stuck at this stage, seventeen-year-old Diederik had adopted the strategy of "forgetting" what had happened when things went wrong.

When this story was suggested and this significance was attached to Diederik's behaviour, Peter became extremely despondent that he had let his children down so badly. He said that the marriage had been in difficulties even before the children were born, and had gone further downhill afterwards. His wife would not allow him to pick the children up out of their cots if they cried because he smelled of cooking fat. He spent all day in his snack bar and his wife thought the smell that clung to him was bad for the children. Peter gradually withdrew from playing any parenting role. Partly because of his busy job and partly because of his marital troubles he left his wife to deal with the children. When he discovered that she had been neglecting them, he decided to bring Diederik back from Austria and to take over his care and upbringing.

Diederik made a nesting doll arrangement for the family in Austria, consisting of his mother, a younger brother, a half-brother, and his mother's life partner. Almost all the dolls were the same size. It became clear that when Diederik was with his mother he took on a mature role, taking care of his four-year-old half-brother. He said that he had sometimes been left alone for days on end and had to take care of everything himself. His other brother was either at school or upstairs at his computer.

At his mother's house, Diederik did not "forget" to go to the toilet; he did forget to eat, however, because he spent so much time by himself, and he neglected his personal hygiene. His mother either failed to notice this or paid little heed to it, seeing it as his own business. Nor did anyone else pay attention: he was left to his own devices.

When Diederik made an arrangement for the small family at his father's house, he chose a large doll for his father, an equally large one for Veronique, and a smaller one for himself as a seventeen year old. He also chose a tiny little doll to represent the boy with soiled trousers.

In line with the nesting doll arrangement depicted here, which shows the father, Peter, standing behind and to one side of seventeen-year-old Diederik, we agreed on the following therapeutic framework.

Peter and Diederik would together take care of that small boy who had fallen asleep and whose natural impulses had almost been extinguished. Together they would "awaken" that little boy. To achieve this, it was important for the almost grown-up Diederik to listen attentively to what his father said; he did now have a caring father and a caring Veronique. This meant that Diederik agreed to do as his father advised if the latter urged him to eat, drink, and take proper care of himself. Diederik would call his father and ask him for help if he soiled his trousers again. He would stop hiding the trousers. Veronique would help Peter and provide support, but father and son would take care of this task together. In this way, the normal impulses in the boy's body would be reawakened. After all, his bodily functions were perfectly healthy.

This framework gave seventeen-year-old Diederik a better understanding of his behaviour, and with his father's help he set about learning how to control it. Diederik had the appearance of a twelve year old, but by eating well and taking proper care of himself he would start to grow again. In this way the context was made therapeutic. Peter and Veronique had a clearer

Figure 26. Russian doll arrangement of Diederik.

understanding of Diederik's behaviour, and Diederik himself was now highly motivated to put an end to the soiling.

When the trio arrived for the next session, they reported, visibly elated, that the symptomatic behaviour had stopped. Nor did it resume. Still, for Diederik to kick-start his stalled development was not so easy. He still neglected to eat, wash, or put on clean clothes unless urged to do so. This seemed to be an oblique way of asking his father and Veronique to stay close to him. He had already had to do so much for himself and had spent so much time alone. This care placed heavy demands on Peter's powers of adaptation: he was unsure how best to act, but took his cue from Veronique. He had real difficulty getting used to the role of father.

Connecting the symptomatic behaviour to a developmental phase and to part of the boy's personality had the effect of removing the question of blame; the possible significance attached to the behaviour helped to defuse tension and provided clarity. The nesting doll arrangement also helped Diederik to understand his behaviour better. With this new insight, he could be encouraged to ask for his father's help. Father and son spent time together in the evenings; Peter would take Diederik to bed after they had packed the boy's school items for the next day. Together they took care of the neglected little boy. Veronique no longer had to bear such a heavy burden and was able to nurture the relationship between father and son instead of caring for Diederik. She acquired a different place in the family, one more appropriate to her position as stepmother. As this book goes to press, the three are still working hard to achieve a healthy resolution.

*CONCLUSION*

# The end of the journey: from modern to postmodern to diagonal

*"The real voyage of discovery consists not in seeking new landscapes, but in having new eyes"*

—Marcel Proust

Since this book opened by placing narrative psychotherapy in the context of postmodern thinking, it is only right that it should conclude with some reflections on the direction that Western thought might take *after* postmodernism, how this new path might help to answer some of the questions of our time, and how these answers might help to organise the practice of psychotherapy.

Given that we have described the subject as nomadic and polyphonic, and described it using the metaphor of the rhizome; given that we have characterised the subject as decentralised and multiple, with lines of flight that can start anywhere and create new connections, how should we construe the direction of the subject, the way it is ordered, its linking pattern? The world has become what the German philosopher Peter Sloterdijk calls "horizontal". He uses the term to mean—roughly speaking—an absence of transcendentalism. If the "big stories" have been deconstructed and the subject has broken away to float in a space of free thought, that subject will seek the meaning of its existence evermore urgently. Truths have become small truths. If the subject is nomadic, what is the place of the "vertical", transcendental or spiritual world? Have all stories been reduced to the same level now?

As we reach the end of our nomadic journey and the end of this book, we are back on the bench under the tree. Our thinking has been freed up, the space for assigning significance has widened—perhaps it has become *too* wide. The space that has become a fertile void has produced an adventurous journey. But is it too much? How much multivocality can we cope with?

In Jonathan Franzen's novel *Freedom*, we see a character struggling with this very question:

> He didn't know what to do, he didn't know how to live. Each new thing he encountered in life impelled him in a direction that fully convinced him of its rightness, but then the next new thing loomed up and impelled him in the opposite direction, which also felt right. There was no controlling narrative: he seemed to himself a purely reactive pinball in a game whose only object was to stay alive for staying alive's sake. … How to live? (Franzen, 2010, pp. 338–339)

Our identities have been uprooted and become fluid. Indeed, the sociologist Zygmunt Bauman tells us, we live in "fluid times" (Bauman, 2007). This fluidity makes constant adjustment unavoidable; we can scarcely settle into any specific form. Fluidity has no hierarchy, which means that we must choose, "in freedom", again and again. And what or who determines this freedom? Are we obliged to constantly seek out individual answers to each question, "doomed to freedom", to use the words of Jean-Paul Sartre?

The thrust of this book leads us to the concept of *diagonal thinking*, which links the "horizontalism" of postmodernism to the "verticalism" of the "great stories". The new journey that awaits us will be a diagonal path, which leads forwards and up. This links up with the ideas of Sloterdijk, a philosopher of our own times, and with philosophies of the art of living. Let us reflect on this concept as baggage to take along on our next journey.

In his book *Rage and Time* (Sloterdijk, 2010), Sloterdijk discusses the loss in present-day Western society of what the Greeks called *thymos*. This is a reference to the exposition of the human soul in Plato's *Phaedrus*. On the one hand is *eros*, the desire for what we lack, a desire that craves instant satisfaction, and that Sloterdijk describes as having a certain "horizontal" quality; what is desired must not cost too much effort or sacrifice. This is contrasted with thymos, a desire for justice, recognition, and respect, which can inspire inordinate effort and the ability to defer gratification. Thymos reins in the passions.

It is through thymos that the subject stands up for the *we*; for communal values and the public interest. The Greek heroes pursued thymos by authority of the gods. Sloterdijk describes this in terms of a call for a "vertical" course, forging onwards and upwards, as it were, a summons to a human being to pursue his or her mission. It is striking, adds Sloterdijk, that pride and self-fulfilment go hand in hand with receptiveness to the sacred.

In our times, thymos has been largely suppressed in favour of an eros based on desire and greed. Thymos, on the other hand, is based on pride and self-respect. Thymotic relations have to do with dedication and effort, with a concern for human dignity, with a desire for justice that goes hand in hand with assertive commitment and the adoption of a firm position. Thymos seeks recognition—inspires deeds and acts of heroism.

Thymotic force is not just a matter of restraint, persistent effort, and deferment of gratification: it also develops through reciprocity—a mental structure that makes it possible for people to cooperate. It is this that enables people to act together, confident that agreements will be kept and loyalty reciprocated. Nomadic thought fosters this reciprocity, care and responsibility, solidarity, and a sense of interdependence.

While Western thought is based on the myth of Oedipus, with its competition and power struggle—its conquest and battlefield, and endless battles with one or more losers—nomadic thought is closer to the myth of Aeneas, who carries his wounded father on his shoulders.

Rather than a battle between "us" and "them", between self and other, nomadic thought fosters a sense of connection and an interspace. Van Kilsdonk (Van den Eerenbeemt & Van Heusden, 1983) writes that our deepest psychological interpretations are based on rivalries and struggle between different ages and generations. Aeneas, on the other hand, symbolises loyalty and care, and can serve as our guide in the subconscious mind.

Bateson too says that deliberate profit-seeking actions damage the ecology and disrupt processes of equilibrium. Love and cooperation preserve equilibrium. As emerged from the discussion of Bateson's ideas about "mind", the great field of consciousness is organised hierarchically into a distinction between element and class, a distinction of meta-levels. Thus, the parent is the meta-level of the child, the teacher that of the pupil, the therapist that of the client, the supervisor that of the supervisee. The person who occupies the meta-level has the power to organise the context and can choose whether it will be a context of love and cooperation or one of power. We can elect to be guided by Aeneas instead of Oedipus, making a different choice from the old storehouse of myths.

In his more recent trilogy *Spheres* (Sloterdijk, 2011 (I), 2014 (II), 2016 (III)), Sloterdijk focuses on the question "where is the human being?" instead of "what is the human being?" He posits the notion that each person starts life "in a sphere". The first sphere is the womb, the mother–child dyad, which he describes as a place of immunity, a place that resists external influence. The sphere seeks to endure.

When this dyadic unity opens up to the outside world, development occurs through transformation: the interior world can transfer its sphere to the outside and is influenced by the outside. Development requires the presence of a third element.

In psychotherapy, this means that the interior world needs the third element in order to transform itself and to develop. The outer world enters and disrupts; the interior world must find a way of relating to the outer world, absorb it and find a new organisational form. A new phase of life, in the family or in the person's individual development, disrupts the interior world, calling for a new answer and a new adjustment. The interior world is absorbed into the outer world and becomes a new sphere. This makes growth and development possible. Stagnation shows itself in symptoms. In short, the third element is essential for growth and development, and for transformation and new stories.

In Sloterdijk's view, where people live together in solidarity, a new sphere—a new interiority—is created. He calls the sphere "the interior, disclosed, shared realm inhabited by humans" (Sloterdijk, 2011). Since *dwelling* has meant from the earliest times the forming of spheres, both large and small, people are in essence creatures who create spherical worlds and who look at horizons.

These spheres feel the outside world impinge on them; the interior space is an animated space, a space of relationships between people—an intimate space that seeks to endure unchanged and that resists external influence.

Besides the mother–child dyad, Sloterdijk also discusses the dyadic relationship between God and Adam as related in the book of Genesis. Sloterdijk refers to the dyad as the primary *dualis*—the child cannot do without the mother—by which he means that there is a duality of mind from the beginning of life. Isolated points exist only in geometry. The elementary is always a resonance of two: two poles, two elements, two individuals. The second element is therefore given from the outset. In other words, subjectivity requires "the other"; it is formed through relationship, and relationship inhabits a sphere, creates an interior space, as in a ball, from which the world can be surveyed. We search for the bell jar of significance. Its interior has a centre from which we can see the horizon. In this way, the world remains an orderly whole.

Sloterdijk describes what happens when individuals cease to relate to each other as poles in a dyadic field and enter the multipolar outside world as a drama of spherological development: "the bubble bursts" and the outer world is born. The outer world is then absorbed in this dynamic process as a third element, or a third space, and assimilated in its totality as a new "family member". Every social structure seeks its own bell jar of significance, a space in which people come together, form connections, understand one another, and develop. This space might be seen as a community that imparts meaning, a linguistic community that encases itself in a safe outer shell. So if the outer world can be absorbed, and the interior world can reorder itself through contact with the outer world, we live in a harmonious sphere.

Until the advent of the Internet, we managed to continue inhabiting those spheres. The Internet has created a virtual reality, a virtuality that can no longer be incorporated into the interior world. There is only an outside, an outside that no longer corresponds to an interior world. This is the world of *foam*, Sloterdijk's metaphor for the times in which we live. The round world, the world of the globe, has been broken open, and there is no longer a centre; the sphere has been violated. In the world of foam, it is no longer possible to draw a line to the horizon; we can no longer survey the world. Foam can accumulate and form into temporary structures. The messages are no longer transmitted from the centre but go in all directions, from one little bubble of foam to the next, just as the rhizome branches out in all directions. In the world of foam, individuals and groups are no longer capable of seeing the world as a whole. The idea of an all-encompassing world, the holistic world view, is vanishing. What this means for the individual in psychological terms is a gradual loss of the capacity, amid these foam structures, to create his or her own psychological space.

In the world of the sphere there is both horizontality and verticality. Foam, however, is exclusively horizontal and spatial, and in the world of foam, no single bubble has primacy. Groups of subjects, local communities, confront the question of how to conduct themselves in the great foam world; a question that could be seen as a challenge, prompting a world of new possibilities. Perspectives are constantly shifting and it is no longer possible to find a centre or meta-level: thinking in foam, says Sloterdijk, is navigating through unstable currents.

Where an interior world has been created and shaped, it can be taken over at any time by the outer world. This means that the interior world is nothing more than an interior of the outside world: the sphere has vanished. The world has become too big for many people, concludes Sloterdijk.

In the world of the sphere, there is an animated interior space. Within this interior space, people who live together in animated mutual relations draw a circle around themselves, a sphere that can be seen as a self-organisation. In the world of foam, this interior world is constantly being taken over and disrupted. There are no foundations any more. Sloterdijk's analysis leads him to urge certain actions: he sees the world of foam as a world of potential. In the world of foam, everyone needs to create their own complementary context. The shared living units of a more or less temporary nature live in a state of permanent hovering, in a fluid "stability". The foam bubbles float, and the world between them too is in constant flux. Everything becomes horizontal, and lightness is the raison d'être of foam. In spite of everything, Sloterdijk sees the potential here for a joyful form of knowledge, once the mourning process—mourning for the loss of the bell jar of significance and the sphere—has come to an end. And then, thought can become thinking in possibilities (Van Tuinen, 2004).

In the world of foam, subjects and groups of subjects are invited and challenged to find answers and to create their own world, their own context. Take the example of the Slow Food Movement. Carlo Petrini, one of the initiators, remarked in an interview with *de Volkskrant* (30 May 2011) that the Slow Food Movement tries to create food communities: a cluster of villages in Africa, say, or a group of fishermen, an urban farmers' market, a cooperative, or a school with its own vegetable garden. These are communities of people who treat food with care, in a sustainable and cohesive way: communities that create their own context, their own "sphere", around a particular theme. Petrini urges a return to the earth and encourages interaction between traditions and modern technologies. He gives the example of a group of people who make date jam in the deserts of Morocco and then sell it all around Europe through Facebook.

Petrini's view is that while our roots are local, our heads are in the world, and we must use technology to connect these local worlds. These connections will help to cement cohesiveness and solidarity, linking local and global concerns. In this way, lines can be drawn through the world of foam, producing a new coherence and order.

Sloterdijk sees the art of practice, in the sense of mastering a craft, as the path to this order. It is through practice that we can ascend from the horizontal world of foam to the vertical, transcendental realm. His book *You Must Change Your Life* (Sloterdijk, 2013) urges a return to the vertical. He describes the vertical tension that presses down on those who try to rise above themselves, confronting what he calls the "cultural mountain range of improbability". According to Sloterdijk, people have always cultivated the art of practice to respond to this call of the vertical, to transcend their own limitations. It is this call that inspires artists and artisans, athletes and warriors. If the world has become horizontal, open, and foam-ridden, the challenge is to create new communities—new contexts that respond to this call and will encourage the cultivation of new practices. The art of practice demands complete dedication and the learning of new skills. It will be guided by thymos rather than eros, infused with energy and fighting spirit, it will draw inspiration from mentors and will be invigorated by the continuous call to strive upwards, to reclaim the vertical.

The art of practice calls for endurance and commitment. Routines are essential. They can encapsulate knowledge, experience and skills that help us to deal with complex situations. Routines represent proficiency that has been developed through frequent repetition. They highlight experience and thus put the teacher back in the foreground. It is through teachers that an art, a craft or skill can be learned. All learning relies on practice and perseverance, on thymotic force. Eros, with its desire for instant gratification, will soon give up.

Practice does not necessarily involve spirituality. It may exist in the arts and sciences, in the world of sport—and also in psychotherapy. Each discipline develops its own verticality, which Sloterdijk calls "the practising life". However much talent one may have, acquiring skill in music—or any other discipline—calls for ten thousand hours of practice (Gladwell, 2009). Practice is not the same thing as work, since it serves a higher purpose: it responds to a transcendental call.

When Sloterdijk refers to the act of confronting the "mountain range of improbability", of doing what appears impossible, he sees it as an ethical appeal, an imperative for life. It is ascending that mountain that I will call here "diagonality"—a journey between the horizontal and the vertical.

It will be useful here to see diagonality in terms of the natural hierarchy that exists between teacher and pupil, parent and child. Spheres and contexts organise themselves into a natural hierarchy of significance. In our fluid, horizontal times, it is appropriate to highlight the role of the teacher. In the book *Wasted: Why Education isn't Educating* (Furedi, 2009), the British sociologist Frank Furedi focuses on the role of teachers, of those in possession of knowledge and experience, of those who have honed specific skills. Do they still command authority? Examining the crisis in education, Furedi sees it as symptomatic of a more fundamental problem: that of society's disinclination to value and affirm the exercise of authority by adults. He goes further and asserts that this refusal to accept authority undermines our capacity to help young people develop their potential.

Furedi says that the authority of adults is inextricably linked to the status accorded to past experience. Teachers pass on the heritage of human knowledge and culture. The devaluation of school subjects has greatly lowered the professional status of teachers. Amid confusion regarding the authority of parents and other adults, today's schools are expected to guide pupils through the socialisation process. As parental authority declines, the school and teachers—for all the decline in status—acquire a greater role in upbringing.

Furedi advocates the return of authority, but an authority that is based on a shared field of values. What he has in mind is not the patriarchy or an unquestioning acceptance of a higher authority, but the restoration of natural authority, earned through knowledge and experience, through age and seniority, through the succession of generations.

Sloterdijk describes different types of teachers, from gurus and abbots to sports coaches and music teachers, from practitioners of traditional crafts to schoolteachers. Each one guides his or her pupils to a measure of expertise, provided these pupils persevere. In the eyes of such teachers, progress is achieved through constant practice and repetition. The formation of active habits leads to better results. The pupils' own aspirations are further stimulated by the teacher's desire to spur them on to great heights. The same applies in sport, or indeed in the practice of a craft.

All learning stands or falls with practice. In the Middle Ages and Renaissance, guilds functioned as systems for the training of apprentices, who gradually mastered their craft. Sloterdijk dwells at length on the model of the guild, in which the personal and spontaneous desire of the young trainees, the urge to learn the craft, and the inspiring example of a great master, were woven with constant practice and repetition until the skills acquired had become internalised. Apprentices would spend seven years on their initiation into all the elements of their craft; not until they had completed this long training were they permitted to take the journeyman's test. Then followed a further period of training and practice, culminating in the production of a "masterpiece"—the original meaning of which was a piece demonstrating that the apprentice had mastered the necessary skills and could henceforth be considered a "master". This practice possesses a spiritual added value. There is a wonderful description of the process in Herman Hesse's novel *Narcissus and Goldmund*. At the end of his life, having led a wandering existence and studied under a succession of masters, Goldmund finally produces his "masterpiece", in the form of a sculpture of the Madonna.

Like Sloterdijk, the Israeli clinical psychologist Haim Omer seeks new inspiration for the theme of authority. His own context is the treatment of young people with behavioural and psychiatric problems whose parents have no authority over them. Such parents frequently live an isolated existence, concealing their loss of authority from the outside world out of shame. The very concealment of their problem exacerbates it. The children's symptoms reflect their lack of direction and their complete surrender to the tyranny of eros. Omer draws inspiration from Ghandi's principle of non-violent resistance (Omer, 2004, 2011), which he applies to his systemic interventions, encouraging parents to form a support community with friends, relatives, and neighbours, forming a protective circle around the child. Omer's "new authority" paradigm replaces the lost vertical authority. Rather than using coercion, parents make their presence felt and seen in their children's lives. With the community's help, they re-establish themselves as parents, reclaiming their natural seniority and authority, and developing new powers of expression and persuasion. Parents are encouraged to use thymotic forces to regain their children's respect. Such interventions exemplify the African saying "It takes a village to raise a child".

> The parents of a sixteen-year-old girl who persistently cut her arms with a razor blade were at their wits' end. They decided to go to their daughter's bedroom and to say:
> 
> "We love you and don't want our daughter to cut herself. We want to help and support you, but we will not allow you to harm yourself any longer. We are going to stay here until you give us the razor blades."
> 
> Their daughter pulled out all the stops: she swore at them, turned the TV on at full volume, retreated with her headphones on; she hurled objects around the room, some of them at her parents. The parents did not react, but continued to repeat their message: "We love you and will not allow our beloved daughter to harm herself."
> 
> The parents remained seated side by side, radiating the same unshakeable commitment. They were determined to persist until their daughter handed over the razor blades. This taxed their thymotic powers to the utmost, calling for persistence, self-sacrifice, and the suppression of emotions such as anger and fear, which might foster violence. After a standoff lasting some two hours, their daughter handed over the razor blades and the parents had won a battle, without the use of force, in which there were three winners.

I believe that this "new authority", which seeks to reinstate a form of verticality, is a way of going up the mountain. This introduces the concept of *diagonality*.

If the nomadic thought that we discussed in Chapter One has helped to liberate the subject from the verticality of the "great stories"—if the subject has become "horizontal" and the world has turned to foam—the subject faces the challenge of creating new possibilities. Perhaps these possibilities can be created by following a diagonal path up the mountain. This brings us to what is sometimes called "the art of living", an appeal to human beings to join with others in making life into a work of art.

The Dutch philosopher Joep Dohmen recalls that the Ancient Greeks saw the art of living as a quest for the good life (Dohmen, 2002). Dohmen anchors it firmly in ethics and willingness to take responsibility for one's actions. The art of living calls for the development of a personal, authentic attitude to life, one that is attuned to others. This attitude is formed by upbringing, education, and experience, and demands unremitting attention and practice—it requires a diagonal approach.

In the view of Foucault (Foucault, 1995), the art of living is a quest for the aesthetics of existence. This aesthetics of existence calls for a constant reflection on both oneself and the other, and is a pre-eminently social practice of *éducation permanente*. Here it is not eros with its hedonistic happiness that holds sway, but *eudaimonia*, the deep happiness that springs from doing what is really good for the soul. It is the happiness in which we are challenged to give of our best in everything: in our relations with those close to us and to the community, and in our work, sport, and all our other activities. Another concept that is key to the art of living is *phronesis*, meaning attention to what is appropriate right now.

In Ancient Greece, the quest for the good life involved the physical aspects of existence as well as spiritual development. The body is our primary interface with the world, our primary way of being-in-the-world (Van den Bossche, 2010). The world of sport, too—either literally or in a metaphorical sense—could be seen as a certain practice and a domain of the art of living, and here too we can ascend the mountain by the path of diagonality. Indeed, there is no alternative: we cannot ascend the mountain vertically, and yet ascend it we must. On the mountaintop awaits mastery. Each individual, each group, has a different mountain to climb.

The philosopher Marc Van den Bossche writes of sport as "an art of living" (Van den Bossche, 2010). He focuses on the physical aspects of being-in-the-world as a source of knowledge and of a measured approach. Sport, he argues, is not about winning, scores, or times, or the result. Achievements are always team efforts. Where narrative psychotherapy uses the metaphor of sport, the focus is on the therapist, the client, and the family system working together with the aim of achieving "victory"—that is, triumphing over the symptoms through dialogue and cooperation. All those concerned are united in partnership rather than being pitted against one another in conflict. This joint effort, however, is something that requires practice.

Where sport is seen as an art of living, everyone can achieve victory. The point is to get going, to start going up the mountain. To do so calls for a certain equanimity, a smile, a willingness to grapple with the struggles ahead; it calls for passion and warmth, a friendly demeanour. The point is to fight without focusing on winning, to lead a wandering existence and to fight without a predetermined goal. You might say that it is a Taoist fight, in which the journey itself is the end pursued.

Van den Bossche sees this struggle as one in which we are not trying to defeat others, but to overcome obstacles, to forge a path from one side to the other. As we move forward, we are not heading for a clearly defined destination: the triumph consists of keeping going. Nor is there an opponent: we are fighting alongside an ally.

When we speak of sport as an art of living, the focus is on the path and on relinquishing the idea of a goal. But in the actual world of sport, when the goal does matter, the point is to focus on the *process*, as the way to achieving that goal. The slogan "the end justifies the means" is therefore completely inapplicable here. The means and the end must be congruent with one another: the goal and the path to that goal must be in mutual harmony.

Take the example of Marc Lammers, who coached the Dutch national women's hockey team to a gold medal in Beijing. Lammers wrote a book on the eight-year journey that led to that title (Lammers, 2011). When his team came away from the Athens Olympic Games with a silver medal he was deeply disappointed. They had expected gold. The team had been thrilled to face Germany again in the finals, having already beaten them resoundingly in the quarter-finals. Everyone was already celebrating. In their minds, the medals had already been handed out and it was time to organise the victory party. The most important lesson that Lammers learned from this experience was that the defeat came from a failure to stay fully focused on the process. If the process was right, the result would automatically follow. Lammers regarded the silver medal as a defeat and decided to completely change his strategy. He studied a wide variety of sports, from horse riding to soccer and cycle racing. He studied training methods and technologies. He defined the situation as a crisis, but in the sense of an opportunity to change course and to think outside the box. The next stage was to develop a plan and a vision, together with the entire team. The team opted for a higher goal than winning: they decided to work together on achieving "gold!"

This decision, that enables all the members of the team to rise above themselves, becomes an organising principle. A shared goal in the distance creates a self-organisation. Each person is responsible for moving towards that goal and for calling others to account if they fail to do so. Everything along the path must be in harmony with the goal, from materials and clothing to the intensity and frequency of coaching sessions. All the values that are important to achieving this are named explicitly, creating a collective pattern of values and shared responsibility for living up to them. Lammers emphasises that you can only influence the process, not the result. The process, or plan, involves concentrating wholly on each person's strengths. This not only maximises enjoyment but it increases people's self-confidence, encouraging them to train to become better still.

It will be clear that this account can serve as a metaphor for narrative psychotherapy. In narrative psychotherapy, the focus of attention is not on a client's problems but on their capacities, and on what they would like to retain. Focusing on what you are good at increases enjoyment and confidence. It stimulates the passion to develop skills further and to persevere through hours of practice. "If it's good, make it outstanding," Lammers would say. Pay attention to whatever goes well, and do it more often, and better still. An inspired process develops when the appeal of the transcendental is linked to the person's skills and experience. If there is too little skill for the task at hand, the bar is set too high and the situation creates tension. In the opposite case, where there is no challenge, the bar is set too low and attention will wander.

We encounter a similar focus on the diagonal upward path in the philosophy of Phil Jackson, the most successful basketball coach in American history. In his book *Sacred Hoops* (Jackson & Delahanty, 2006), he argues that winning means giving up a small part of yourself to enable the team to win. Winning needs a plan, a *shared* vision. Just as Lammers knew how to draw on the qualities of one player to compensate for another player's weakness, Jackson too observes that truly great players will take responsibility for helping their teammates to improve. This collective sense of responsibility will ensure that good players become great, and that weaknesses are counteracted by strengths. That is how to build a team. Jackson refers in this context to a heightened sense of awareness and undiluted attention for the process, the here and now.

Diagonality appeals to a person's capacity for self-sacrifice—the ability to make a sacrifice to help someone else improve. In team sport, a team that focuses heavily on a single star tends to perform less well, because other players are overly dependent on that one person's achievements and see themselves as possessing less value. They become passive and may lose the power to take the initiative; they can no longer get the best out of themselves. In narrative psychotherapy, cooperation and dialogue is like forming a team to get the best out of the client. The psychotherapist joins the client's team in an effort to overcome the problem. Psychotherapy involves a great deal of practice, working together on defeating complaints and symptoms, and working on one's own shortcomings.

Van den Bossche says that sport as an art of living might be defined as a form of "physical spirituality" (2010, p. 47). Spirituality is the realm of existential questions. The art of living and spirituality are connected, since spirituality is about relationships with transcendence or higher values, whatever label one wishes to give it (De Hennezel & Leloup, 1997). The word *religion* derives from Latin *religare*, meaning "to bind". An alternative derivation, favoured by Cicero, is from *religere*, meaning "to reread". In the present context, the reference might be to rereading history or tradition, the knowledge of our ancestors, to discover deeper meanings. In this sense, rereading becomes a form of archaeological research.

In the tradition of Ancient Greece, says Leloup, spirituality meant casting off the heavier elements in the entirety of constituents that make up a human being. To be spiritual means to be one with one's breath. To be spiritual is to be in-spired, and to be inspired means to take that extra step. This brings us to the commonest meaning of spirituality: to go further, to go beyond where you are now. This is the spirituality of the pilgrim following the route to Santiago de Compostella, and hailing fellow pilgrims with the traditional greeting *ultreïa*—onward! This spirituality, which releases human beings from the heaviness of existence, is connected to the art of practice as a spontaneous, joyful practice, a practice that is desired.

## Aesthetics

Foucault suggests that the ongoing work of ethical subjectivity might consist in "making" ourselves as a work of art, and that this might be our major contemporary and aesthetic task. "From the idea that the self is not given to us, I think there is only one practical consequence: we have to create ourselves as a work of art" (see Dreyfus & Rabinow, 1982, p. 237).

If the path to the goal is in harmony with the goal itself, the whole—path and goal—possesses a certain aesthetic quality. Narrative psychotherapy seeks that harmony, that aesthetic balance, and focus on patterns, unity, bonds, organisation, and equilibrium. Narrative psychotherapy embraces the aesthetic basis of psychotherapy, and views processes of change as possessing an aesthetic dimension. It goes in search of the congruence between form and content, between process and goal, between conscious and unconscious mind, between the self and the other. It seeks connections: between the self and the body, between the self and the surroundings, and between the self and a transcendental, mystical reality.

Following Bateson, narrative psychotherapy proceeds on the basis that acting on a purely pragmatic basis disrupts the ecology, because it emphasises rational knowledge, which is only part of the totality of what we know. With this one-sided emphasis on a single part of the circuit, it seeks to maximise certain variables. Bateson maintains that our conscious knowledge can only see part of the ecology. Things of which we have more knowledge sink to deeper layers of our consciousness, areas inhabited by wisdom, art, religion, and craftsmanship. And it is in that deeper repository that dedicated practice too takes up residence. Wisdom focuses on connecting patterns, through which the organic world is organised in accordance with aesthetic principles, says Bateson. Placing too much emphasis on a single objective disrupts the process, disrupts spontaneity and enjoyment.

Narrative psychotherapy therefore looks at the relationships—the polyphony—between the voices within a single person. It focuses on relationships between life partners and those between other family members. It also focuses on the relationships between the person, the neighbourhood, work and friends; between the self and nature, and the self and the body. The world of relationships is the world of the story—a story that has a certain aesthetic organisation. The word "aesthetic" refers here to the beauty of patterns and connections—connections that reveal themselves through metaphors. Systems have aesthetic preferences embedded within their organisation, and the totality of the system is immanent in each part. Bateson believes that the connection between consciousness and aestheticism is sacred, and that this sacred connection is experienced through the body, through a significance that a person feels throughout his or her body. In this world of relationships, this multiplicity of contexts, the appropriate logic is a poetic logic that gives significance to the space in between contexts. Narrative psychotherapy tries to find the aesthetic resonance in the combined contexts.

Furthermore, narrative psychotherapy seeks to forge connections with the wider context and strives to create aesthetic solutions for pragmatic problems. Following Spencer-Brown (see Olthof & Vermetten, 1994), who says that observation begins by making distinctions, we can organise our world in countless ways, depending on the distinctions we draw. Narrative psychotherapy creates aesthetic distinctions, distinctions related to love and loyalty, connections and relationships, protection and self-sacrifice; effort and perseverance, thymotic power.

The aesthetic principle will ensure that the metaphors used will not be those of struggle and competition, but those of connection and cooperation. The focus will be on using metaphors drawn from the natural, organic world rather than the world of substance and energy. Like art, psychotherapy is concerned with the relationships between the different levels of the mental process, the relationships between conscious and unconscious, and relations with the external world. Taking the aesthetic principle of narrative psychotherapy as my point of departure, I suggest looking at narrative psychotherapy as one form of Sloterdijk's "art of practice". In this sense, narrative psychotherapists do not observe clients so much as observe what happens in the therapeutic relationship. This art of practice is the world of stories, and stories reveal how people interpret their world. Thus therapist and client can weave their stories together. Narrative psychotherapy is an exchange of stories.

In an interview in *de Volkskrant* of 6 July 2009, the Dutch composer Louis Andriessen was asked about his own favourite music, the music that moved him. Andriessen started talking about J. S. Bach, and said that he found some of Bach's arias almost unbearably beautiful. When the interviewer then asked him to define beauty, he said:

"Beauty is what we recognise but cannot analyse."
"A specific sort of emotion?" asked the interviewer.
"It seems like it," Andriessen replied. "It strikes you unexpectedly, through its combination of strangeness and familiarity. I like to use the word 'grace' in this connection. Grace means that you receive something wonderful without having to do anything for it. You know immediately when you've created something like that: that's how it has to be!"

The same feeling of emotional connection can be felt during the process of psychotherapy, when we find the right word for something; a significance that fits exactly, an aesthetic connection and a new story. It is an exciting moment when the right context has been created and the appropriate framework devised: *that's* how it should be! Then someone else comes along, with a completely different context, and the voyage of discovery begins again.

Figure 27. End of the journey.
Photo © G. L. Sijbers

# AFTERWORD

*A word from the editor and the translator*

Narrative psychotherapy is dialogical in nature, says Jan Olthof. Translation, too, is dialogical: it involves a constant dialogue not just between languages but also between cultures. Key sections of this text, which was written in Dutch, describe imaginative efforts to understand what clients *mean* when they use certain words. What does Mrs Johnson *mean* when she looks at her full wardrobe and keeps asserting sadly, "yes, but I have no clothes"? When a client's words include idiomatic expressions, conveying the spirit of these imaginative efforts in English poses difficulties that are sometimes almost insuperable. What to do with the Dutch word *afdanken*, which means "to dump" but contains the word "to thank" in it? Such echoes may be resonating in the speaker's mind. All this required a great deal of thought, and above all, discussion. So it was entirely fitting that the translation of this book became a dialogical activity between editor and translator. It was an illuminating, inspiring dialogue, and we enjoyed every minute of it.

*Gertha Sijbers and Beverley Jackson*

# REFERENCES

Aalbrecht, H. (2008). *Joost mag het weten*. Den Haag: Uitgeverij BZZTôH.
Allman, L. R. (1982a). The aesthetic preference: overcoming the pragmatic error. *Family Process, 21*: 415–428.
Allman, L. R. (1982b). The poetic mind: further thoughts on an "aesthetic preference". *Family Process, 21*: 43–57.
Andersen, T. (1987). The reflecting team. *Family Process, 26*: 415–428.
Andersen, T. (Ed.) (1991). *The Reflecting Team: Dialogues and Dialogues about Dialogues*. New York: Norton.
Anderson, H., & Goolishian, H. (1988). Human systems as linguistic systems: preliminary and evolving ideas about the implications for clinical theory. *Family Process, 27*: 371–393.
Assoun, P. L. (Ed.) (1987). *Hedendaagse Franse filosofen*. Assen: Van Gorcum.
Baartse, W. (2007). *Toeval is logisch: Johan Cruijff van A tot Z*. Den Haag: Uitgeverij BZZTôH.
Bakhtin, M. M. (1981). *The Dialogic Imagination: Four Essays*. Austin: University of Texas Press.
Bandler, R., & Grinder, J. (1976). *Patterns of the Hypnotic Techniques of Milton H. Erickson, M.D* (Volume I). Cupertino, CA: Meta Publications.
Bandler, R., & Grinder, J. (1979). *Frogs into Princes: Neurolinguistic Programming*. Moab, UT: Real People Press.
Barthes, R. (1973). *Le plaisir du texte*. Paris: Editions du Seuil.
Bateson, G. (1972). *Steps to an Ecology of Mind*. New York: Ballantine.
Bateson, G. (1979). *Mind and Nature: A Necessary Unit*. New York: Bantam.
Bateson, G., & Bateson, M. C. (1987). *Angels Fear: Towards an Epistemology of the Sacred*. New York: MacMillan.
Bateson, G. (Donaldson, R. Ed.) (1991). *A Sacred Unity: Further Steps to an Ecology of Mind*. New York: HarperCollins.
Bauman, Z. (2007). *Liquid Times: Living in an Age of Uncertainty*. Cambridge, MA: Polity Press.

Bemelmans, J. (1978). The mutual storytelling technique/De techniek van het wederzijds verhalen vertellen. *Tijdschrift voor Orthopedagogiek, 5*: 263–271.

Berg, I. K. (1994). *Family-Based Services: A Solution-Focused Approach*. New York: Norton.

Berry, W. (1977). *The Unsettling of America: Culture and Agriculture*. San Francisco: Sierra Club.

Bor, J., Kingma, J., & Petersma, E. (1995). *De verbeelding van het denken: Geillustreerde geschiedenis van de westerse en oosterse filosofie*. Amsterdam/Antwerpen: Uitgeverij Contact.

Böszörményi-Nagy, I. (1987). *Foundations of Contextual Therapy: Collected Papers of Ivan Böszörményi-Nagy, MD*. New York: Brunner/Mazel.

Böszörményi-Nagy, I., & Krasner, B. (1986). *Between Give and Take: A Clinical Guide to Contextual Therapy*. New York: Brunner/Mazel.

Braidotti, R. (1991). *Patterns of Dissonance: An Essay on Women in Contemporary French Philosophy*. Cambridge: Polity Press.

Braidotti, R. (Ed.) (1993a). *Een beeld van een vrouw: De visualisering van het vrouwelijke in een postmoderne cultuur*. Kampen: Kok Agora.

Braidotti, R. (1993b). De weg naar de nomade. Socrateslezing. Humanist.

Braidotti, R. (1994). *Nomadic Subjects: Embodiment and Sexual Difference in Contemporary Feminist Theory*. New York: Colombia University Press.

Braidotti, R. (2004). *Op doorreis: Nomadisch denken in de 21e eeuw*. Amsterdam: Uitgeverij Boom.

Braidotti, R., & Haakma, S. (Eds.) (1994). *Ik denk, dus zij is: Vrouwelijke intellectuelen in een historisch en literair perspectief*. Kampen: Kok Agora.

Brokken, J. (2006). *De wil en de weg*. Amsterdam: Uitgeverij Augustus.

Brouwers, J. (1981). *Bezonken rood*. Amsterdam: De Arbeiderspers.

Bruner, J. (1999). *Acts of Meaning*. Cambridge, MA: Harvard University Press.

Bruner, J. S. (1986). *Actual Minds, Possible Worlds*. Cambridge, MA: Harvard University Press.

Campert, R. (2000). *Kus zoekt mond*. Amsterdam: Rainbow Pockets.

Carroll, L. (1992). *Alice in Wonderland and Through the Looking Glass*. New York: Alfred A. Knopf.

Cauffman, L. (2010). *Simpel: Oplossingsgerichte positieve psychologie in actie*. Den Haag: Boom/Lemma.

Cavafy, C. P. (1992). *Collected Poems* (Trans. E. Keeley, & P. Sherrard; Ed. G. Savidis, revised edn). New Jersey: Princeton University Press.

Charlton, N. G. (2008). *Understanding Gregory Bateson: Mind, Beauty, and the Sacred Earth*. Albany: The State University of New York Press.

Chopra, D. (1989). *Quantum Healing: Exploring the Frontiers of Mind/Body Medicine*. New York: Bantam.

Chopra, D. (1993). *Ageless Body, Timeless Mind: A Practical Alternative to Growing Old*. London: Rider/Ebury Press. London.

Crott, A. (2011). Van hoop des vaderlands naar ADHD-er: Het beeld van jongens in opvoedingsliteratuur (1882–2005) (Thesis). Nijmegen: Radboud Universiteit.

De Coninck, H. (2011). *Geef me nu eindelijk wat ik altijd al had: De mooiste gedichten*. Amsterdam: Arbeiderspers.

De Hennezel, M., & Leloup, J. (1997). *L'Art de Mourir: Traditions Religieuses et Spiritualité Humaniste Face à la Mort Aujourd'hui*. Paris: Robert Laffont.

Deleuze, G. (1993). *The Fold: Leibniz and the Baroque*. London: The Athlone Press.

Deleuze, G., & Guattari, F. (1976). *Rhizome: Introduction*. Paris: Éditions Minuit.

Dell, P. (1985). Understanding Bateson and Maturana; towards a biological foundation for the social sciences. *Journal of Marital and Family Therapy II 1*: 1–20.

Derrida, J. (1978). *Writing and Difference*. London: Routledge.

Derrida, J. (1982). *Margins of Philosophy*. Chicago: University of Chicago Press.

De Shazer, S. (1982). *Patterns of Brief Family Therapy: An Ecosystemic Approach*. New York: Guilford.
De Shazer, S. (1985). *Keys to Solution in Brief Therapy*. New York: Norton.
De Shazer, S. (1988). *Clues: Investigating Solutions in Brief Therapy*. New York: Norton.
De Shazer, S. (1994). *Words Were Originally Magic*. New York: Norton.
Dohmen, J. (2002). *Over levenskunst: de grote filosofen over het goede leven*. Amsterdam: Ambon.
Dolto, F. (1998). *Kinderen aan het woord*. Nijmegen: Uitgeverij SUN.
Dormaar, M. (1989). February man revisited. In: M. Dormaar, *Consensus in Psychotherapy*. Maastricht: Proefschrift Rijksuniversiteit Limburg.
Drees, A. (1984). Personal communication.
Drees, A. (1991). *Der "Potentielle Raum" in klinischer Psychiatrie: Unveröffentliches Manuscript*. Duisburg: Bertha Krankenhaus.
Drees, A. (1995). *Freie Phantasien in der Psychotherapie und in Balintgruppen*. Göttingen-Zürich: Vandenhoeck & Ruprecht.
Dreyfus, H. L., & Rabinow, P. (1982). *Michel Foucault: Beyond Structuralism and Hermeneutics*. Chicago: University of Chicago Press.
Eco, U. (1990). *The Limits of Interpretation*. Bloomington: Indiana University Press.
Edelstein, M. G. (1981). *Trauma, Trance and Transformation: A Clinical Guide to Hypnotherapy*. New York: Brunner/Mazel.
Efran, J., & Lukens, R. J. (1985). The world according to Humberto Maturana. *The Family Therapy Networker, 9(3)*: 22–29.
Eliacheff, C. (1993). *À corps et a cris: Être psychoanalyste avec les tout-petits*. Paris: Éditions Odile Jacob.
Elkaim, M. (1997). *If You Love Me, Don't Love Me: Undoing Reciprocal Double Binds and Other Methods of Change in Couple and Family Therapy*. New York: Jason Aronson.
Epston, D. (1994). Extending the conversations. *The Family Therapy Networker 18(6)*: 31–37, 62–63.
Erickson, M. H. (1967). Pediatric hypnotherapy. In: J. Haley (Ed.), *Advanced Techniques of Hypnosis and Therapy*. New York: Grune & Stratton.
Erickson, M. H. (2006). *An American Healer* (Ed. B. H. Erickson, & B. Keeney). Sedola: Rolling Rocks Press.
Erickson, M. H., & Rossi, E. L. (1979). *Hypnotherapy: An Exploratory Casebook*. New York: Irvington.
Erickson, M. H., & Rossi, E. L. (1980). *The Collected Papers of M.H. Erickson on Hypnosis, Following I-IV*. New York: Irvington.
Flemons, D. (1991). *Completing Distinctions: Interweaving the Ideas of Gregory Bateson and Taoism into a Unique Approach to Therapy*. Boston: Shambala.
Foucault, M. (1971). *L'ordre du Discours*. Paris: Gallimard.
Foucault, M. (1995). *Breekbare vrijheid: de politieke ethiek van de zorg voor zichzelf*. Amsterdam: Boom.
Foucault, M., & Deleuze, G. (1981). *Nietzsche als genealoog en als nomade*. Nijmegen: Sun.
Franzen, J. (2010). *Freedom*. Toronto: HarperCollins.
Furedi, F. (2009). *Wasted: Why Education isn't Educating*. London: Bloomsbury.
Gardner, R. (1971). *Therapeutic Communication with Children: The Mutual Storytelling Technique*. New York: Jason Aronson.
Gladwell, M. (2009). *Outliers: The Story of Success*. New York: Little, Brown.
Goffman, E. (1961). *Asylums: Essays on the Social Situation of Mental Patients and Other Inmates*. New York: Anchor.
Goffman, E. (1963). *Stigma: Notes on the Management of Spoiled Identity*. New York: Simon and Schuster.
Hakvoort, E. (2011). Parenting and child adjustment after divorce (Thesis). Amsterdam: University of Amsterdam.

Haley, J. (1973). *Uncommon Therapy: The Psychiatric Techniques of Milton Erickson, MD*. New York: Norton.
Haley, J. (1981). *Reflections of Therapy and Other Essays*. Washington: Family Therapy Institute.
Halsema, A. (1998). *Dialectiek van de seksuele differentie: De filosofie van Luce Irigaray*. Amsterdam: Beau.
Hammarskjöld, D. (1957). A room of quiet. www.aquaac.org/un/medroom.html [last accessed 26.10.2016].
Hammarskjöld, D. (1964). *Markings*. London: Faber and Faber.
Hartland, J. (1971). Further observations on the use of the "ego-strengthening" techniques. *American Journal of Clinical Hypnosis*, 14: 1–8.
Hellinger, B. (with G. Weber, & H. Beaumont). (1989). *Love's Hidden Symmetry: What Makes Love Work in Relationships*. Phoenix, AZ: Zeig, Tucker.
Hellinger, B. (2005). *Der große Konflikt: Die Antwort*. München: Goldmann Verlag.
Hemmerechts, K. (1998). *Taal zonder mij*. Amsterdam: Atlas.
Hermans, H. J. M. (Ed.) (1995). *De echo van het ego: Over het meerstemmige zelf*. Baarn: Ambo.
Hermans, H. J. M., & Hermans-Jansen, E. (1995). *Self-Narratives: The Construction of Meaning in Psychotherapy*. New York: The Guilford Press.
Hermans, H. J. M., & Kempen, H. J. G. (1993). *The Dialogical Self: Meaning as Movement*. San Diego: Academic Press.
Hermsen, J. (2009). *Stil de tijd: Pleidooi voor een langzame toekomst*. Amsterdam: Arbeiderspers.
Hoffman, L. (1981). *Foundations of Family Therapy: A Conceptual Framework for Systems Change*. New York: Basic.
Hoffman, L. (2002). *Family Therapy: An Intimate History*. New York: Norton.
IJsseling, S. (1990). *Mimesis: over schijn en zijn*. Baarn: Ambo.
Irigaray, L. (1985). *This Sex Which is Not One*. New York: Cornell University Press.
Irigaray, L. (1993). *Je, Tu, Nous: Towards a Culture of Difference*. New York: Routledge.
Irigaray, L. (1996). *I Love to You*. New York: Routledge.
Irigaray, L. (2002). *Between East and West: From Singularity to Community*. New York: Columbia University Press.
Irigaray, L., & Burke, C. (1980). When our lips speak together. *Signs*, 6(1): 69–79.
Jackson, P., & Delahanty, H. (1995). *Sacred Hoops: Spiritual Lessons of a Hardwood Warrior*. New York: Hyperion [reprinted 2006].
Keeney, B. (1983). *Aesthetics of Change*. New York: The Guilford Press.
Keeney, B., & Ross, J. M. (1992). *Mind in Therapy: Constructing Systemic Family Therapies*. Pretoria: University of South Africa.
Kenny, V. (1988). Steering or drifting? The organisation of psychotherapeutic conversations. In: E. Rosseel, F. Heylighen, F. de Meyer (Eds.), *Self-steering and Cognition in Complex Systems*. New York: Gordon and Breach.
Klukhuhn, A. (1995). Het einde van de vooruitgang. *De Volkskrant*, 23 December.
Klukhuhn, A. (2003). *De geschiedenis van het denken: Filosofie, wetenschap, kunst en cultuur van de Oudheid tot nu*. Amsterdam: Bert Bakker.
Koolhaas, A. (1986). *Vanwege een tere huid*. Amsterdam: G. A. van Oorschot.
Kristeva, J. (1987). *In the Beginning Was Love: Psychoanalysis and Faith*. New York: Columbia University Press.
Kuipers, P., & Olthof, J. (2005). Het landschap van de klacht. In: E. Reimers, L. Cottyn, & M. Faes, *Spelen met werkelijkheden*. Houten: Bohn Stafleu Van Loghum.
Kundera, M. (1991). *Immortality*. New York: Harper Perennial.

Kundera, M. (1996). *Slowness*. London: Faber and Faber.
Kundera, M. (2002). *The Art of the Novel*. London: Faber and Faber.
Kunneman, H. (2009). *Voorbij het dikke-ik: Bouwstenen voor een kritisch humanisme*. Amsterdam: Uitgeverij SWP.
Lakoff, G. (2004). *Don't Think of an Elephant: Know Your Values and Frame the Debate*. Vermont: Chelsea Green.
Lakoff, G., & Johnson, M. (1980). *Metaphors We Live By*. Chicago: University of Chicago Press.
Lammers, M. (2011). *Winners Have a Plan: Losers Have an Excuse*. Utrecht: Tirion Sport.
LeCron, L. (1971). *The Complete Guide to Hypnosis*. New York: Barnes & Noble.
Lenaerts, P. (2009). Het derde element: over het gebruik van poëzie in de appreciërende en samenwerkende systeempsychotherapie. *Systeemtheoretisch Bulletin XXVII:3*: 273–294.
Levine, P. (1997). *Waking the Tiger: Healing Trauma*. Berkeley, CA: North Atlantic.
Lyotard, J-F. (1984). *The Postmodern Condition: A Report on Knowledge* (Trans. G. Bennington, & B. Massumi). Minneapolis: University of Minnesota Press.
MacDonald, A., & Fox-Davies, S. (1993). *Little Beaver and the Echo*. London: Walker Books.
Maturana, H. R. (1988). Reality: the search for objectivity or the quest for a compelling argument. *The Irish Journal of Psychology, 9*: 22–83.
Maturana, H. R., & Varela, F. (1992). *The Tree of Knowledge: The Biological Roots of Human Understanding*. Boston: Shambhala.
Meijer, M. (1996). *In tekst gevat: Inleiding tot een kritiek van representatie*. Amsterdam: Amsterdam University Press.
Minuchin, S., & Fishmann, H. (1981). *Family Therapy Techniques*. Cambridge/Massachusetts: Cambridge University Press.
Myss, C. (1997). *Anatomy of the Spirit: The Seven Stages of Power and Healing*. London: Bantam.
Nachmanovitch, S. (1982). Gregory Bateson: old men ought to be explorers. *CoEvolution Quarterly* (Fall): 34–44.
Naouri, A. (2005). *Fathers and Mothers*. London: Free Association.
Nieuwenhuis, J. (2004). *Johannes de Ziener*. Kampen: Uitgeverij Kok.
Oaklander, V. (1978). *Windows to our Children: A Gestalt Therapy Approach to Children and Adolescents*. Gouldsboro, ME: Real People Press.
O'Hanlon, B., & Wilk, J. (1987). *Shifting Contexts: The Generation of Effective Psychotherapy*. New York: The Guilford Press.
O'Hanlon, W. H. (1994). The third wave. *The Family Therapy Networker, 18*: 19–29.
O'Hanlon, W. H., & Weiner-Davis, M. (1989). *In Search of Solutions: A New Direction in Psychotherapy*. New York/London: Norton.
Okri, B. (1997). *Tussen de stille stenen*. Amsterdam: De Volkskrant.
Olthof, J., & Rober, P. (2001). Het nomadisch team: op zoek naar een vruchtbaar therapeutisch narratief. *Systeemtherapie, 13*: 156–167.
Olthof, J., & Vermetten, E. (1994). *De mens als verhaal: Narratieve strategieën in psychotherapie voor kinderen en volwassenen*. Utrecht: De Tijdstroom.
Omer, H. (2004). *Non-Violent Resistance: A New Approach to Violent and Self-Destructive Children*. New York: Cambridge University Press.
Omer, H. (2011). *The New Authority: Family, School, and Community*. New York: Cambridge University Press.
Oppenoorth, W. (1990). Twee vormen van disfunctioneel ouderschap: Een intergenerationele ontleding. *Tijdschrift voor Systeemtherapie II 1*: 27–34.

Oppenoorth, W. (1992). Intergenerationele erkenning als behandeling voor parentificatie. Rotterdam: Internal note Rotterdam's Medical Pedagogic Institute, dept. Internal Family Treatment.

Oudshoorn, D. N. (1979). De verhalentechniek van Richard Gardner toegepast bij een jongen met een lichte hersendysfunctie. *Tijdschrift voor Psychotherapie 5*: 285–294.

Oudshoorn, D. N. (1980). Het gebruik van verhalen als vorm van kinderpsychotherapie. In: A. Cools & D. van Herwaarden (Eds.), *Kinder- en jeugdpsychotherapie*. Deventer: Van Lochum Slaterus.

Pakman, M. (2004). On imagination: reconciling knowledge and life, or what does "Gregory Bateson" stand for? *Family Process, 43*: 413–423.

Paz, O. (1974). *Children of the Mire: Modern Poetry from Romanticism to the Avant-Garde*. Cambridge: Harvard University Press.

Peirce, C. S. (1960). *Collected Papers of Charles Sanders Peirce* (Volumes V and VI). Cambridge: Harvard University Press.

Pirandello, L. (1992). *One, No One, and One Hundred Thousand*. New York: Marsilio.

Raessens, J. (2001). *Filosofie en Film: Vivre la Différence: Deleuze en de Cinematografische Realiteit*. Budel: Uitgeverij Damon.

Rhode-Dachser, Ch. (1982). *Expedition in den Dunklen Continent: Weiblichkeit im Diskurs der Psychoanalyse*. Heidelberg/New York: Springer Verlag.

Rich, A. (1986). *Of Woman Born: Motherhood as Experience and Institution*. New York: Norton.

Ricoeur, P. (1969). *The Symbolism of Evil* (Trans. E. Buchanan). Boston: Beacon Press.

Rober, P. (2005). Family therapy as a dialogue of living persons: A perspective inspired by Bakhtin, Voloshinov, and Shotter. *Journal of Marital and Family Therapy 31*: 385–97.

Romein, E., Schuilenberg, M., & Van Tuinen, S. (2009). *Deleuze Compendium*. Amsterdam: Uitgeverij Boom.

Rosen, S. (1982). *My Voice Will Go with You: The Teaching Tales of Milton H. Erickson*. New York: Norton.

Rosenblum, B., & Kuttner, F. (2006). *Quantum Enigma—Physics Encounters Consciousness*. Oxford: Oxford University Press.

Rosenhan, D. L. (1973). On being sane in insane places. *Science, 179*: 250–258.

Rossi, E., & Cheek, D. (1988). *Mind-Body Therapy: Methods of Ideodynamic Healing in Hypnosis*. New York: Norton.

Saeys, A. (2004). Het psychologisch discours in dialogisch perspectief: Mikhail Bakhtins taalfilosofie en de psychoanalyse van de schizofrene psychose (Thesis). Leuven: Katholieke Universiteit Leuven.

Scheepers, M. (1987). Gilles Deleuze. In: P. L. Assoun (Ed.), *Hedendaagse Franse Filosofen*. Assen: Van Gorcum.

Scheff, T. (1975). *Labelling Madness*. Englewood Cliffs, NJ: Prentice Hall.

Schierbeek, B. (1965). *Een broek voor een octopus*. Amsterdam: De Bezige Bij.

Schore, A. N. (2009). Right brain affect regulation: an essential mechanism of development, trauma, dissociation, and psychotherapy. In: D. Fosha, D. Siegel, & M. Solomon (Eds.), *The Healing Power of Emotion: Affective Neuroscience, Development & Clinical Practice* (pp. 112–144). New York: Norton.

Seikkula, J., & Amkil, T. E. (2006). *Dialogical Meetings in Social Networks* (Systemic Thinking and Practice Series). London: Karnac.

Sermijn, J. (2008). *Ik in veelvoud: Een zoektocht naar de relatie tussen mens en psychiatrische diagnose*. Leuven: Acco.

Shotter, J. (2010). *Social Construction on the Edge: 'With'-ness-Thinking and Embodiment*. Ohio: Taos Institute.

Siegel, D. J. (2010). *The Mindful Therapist: A Clinician's Guide to Mindsight and Neural Integration*. New York: Norton.

Sloterdijk, P. (2010). *Rage and Time: A Psychopolitical Investigation*. New York: Columbia University Press.
Sloterdijk, P. (2011). *Bubbles: Spheres Volume I: Microspherology*. Los Angeles: Semiotext(e).
Sloterdijk, P. (2013). *You Must Change Your Life: On Anthropotechnics*. Cambridge: Polity Press.
Sloterdijk, P. (2014). *Globes: Spheres Volume II: Macrospherology*. Los Angeles: Semiotext(e).
Sloterdijk, P. (2016). *Foams: Spheres Volume III: Plural Spherology*. Los Angeles: Semiotext(e).
Spencer-Brown, G. (1969). *Laws of Form*. London: Allen & Unwin.
Stein, C. (1963). The clenched fist technique as a hypnotic procedure in clinical psychotherapy. *American Journal of Clinical Hypnoses, 6*: 113–119.
Tamaro, S. (1995). *Follow Your Heart*. London: Secker & Warburg.
Tellegen, T. (1990). *Langzaam, zo snel als ze konden*. Amsterdam: Querido.
Tellegen, T. (2000). *Gedichten 1977–1999*. Amsterdam: Querido.
Tellegen, T. (2003). *Wie A zegt*. Amsterdam: Querido.
Tellegen, T. (2005). *Daar zijn woorden voor*. Amsterdam: Rainbow Pockets.
Tellegen, T. (2010). *Het vertrek van de mier*. Amsterdam: Querido.
Tranströmer, T. (2011). *Memories Look at Me: A Memoir* (Trans. R. Fulton). New York: New Directions.
Van de Ven, P. (1975). *Vriend als vijand: Naar een paradoksale terapie*. Bloemendaal: H. Nelissen.
Van de Ven, P. (1982). *Ludagogie: Spelen met kans*. Bloemendaal: H. Nelissen.
Van den Bossche, M. (2010). *Sport als levenskunst*. Rotterdam: Lemniscaat.
Van den Eerenbeemt, E. M. (2009). *Door het oog van de familie: Liefde, leed en loyaliteit*. Amsterdam: Bert Bakker.
Van den Eerenbeemt, E. M., & Van Heusden, A. (1983). *Balans in beweging: Ivan Boszormenyi-Nagy en zijn visie op individuele en gezinstherapie*. Haarlem: De Toorts.
Van der Hart, O., & Schurink, G. (1987). *Strategieën in hypnotherapie*. Deventer: Van Lochum Slaterus.
Van Lommel, P. (2010). *Consciousness Beyond Life: The Science of the Near-Death Experience*. New York: HarperOne.
Van Tuinen, S. (2004). *Sloterdijk: Binnenstebuiten denken*. Kampen: Klement.
Van Wolde, E. (1991). *Meneer en mevrouw Job*. Baarn: Ten Have.
Veenbaas, W. (1994). *Op verhaal komen*. Utrecht: Scheffers.
Veenbaas, W., & Goudswaard, J. (2002). *Vonken van verlangen: Systemisch werken: perspectief en praktijk*. Utrecht: Phoenix Opleidingen.
Veronesi, S. (2011). *Quiet Chaos*. New York: Ecco.
Vincenot, A. (1990). *Renaissance: Drie teksten van Irigaray: Vertaald en becommentarieerd*. Amsterdam: Perdu.
Watzlawick, P., Beavin, J. H., & Jackson, D. D. (1976). *Pragmatics of Human Communication: A Study of Interactional Patterns, Pathologies, and Paradoxes*. New York: Norton.
Watzlawick, P., Weakland, J. H., & Fisch, R. (1974). *Change: Principles of Problem Formation and Problem Resolution*. New York: Norton.
Weick, K. (1995). *Sense Making in Organisations*. London: Sage Publishers.
White, M. (2007). *Maps of Narrative Practice*. New York: Norton.
White, M., & Epston, D. (1990). *Narrative Means to Therapeutic Ends*. New York: Norton.
Winsemius, P. (2004). *Je gaat het pas zien als je het doorhebt: Over Cruijff en leiderschap*. Amsterdam: Balans.
Zeig, J. (1980). *A Teaching Seminar with Milton H. Erickson*. New York: Brunner/Mazel.

# *INDEX*

Aalbrecht, H., 195
abduction
    logic of, 111–123, 129–131 *see also:* Bateson, G.;
        metaphor: logic of
active(ly) not-knowing, xxvi–xxvii, xxx, 37, 41
*Alice in Wonderland*, 55, 64
*Alles ist der Patient*, 25–26 *see also:* Drees, A.
Allman, L. R., 98
    aesthetic preference, 98
    cited works, 98
Amkil, T. E., 35, 63
Andersen, T., 6, 39
    cited works, 6
    reflecting team, 6
Anderson, H., 6 *see also:* problem-determined
        system
*annähern*, 165, 167
architecture of living, xxxii, 274, 278, 280
*arriver entre*, 8 *see also:* Deleuze, G.
art of living, 302, 307–308, 310 *see also:* Foucault, M.
art of practice, 164, 310–311
"as if", 9, 124, 222–223
    world of, 15, 21, 95, 112, 118
assemblage, 121, 192–193
    infra-, 201

inter-, 201 *see also* line(s) of flight
intra-, 201
Assoun, P. L., 7
attractor, 72–73, 133, 137, 191, 223
Auerswald, D., 4–5
autopoietic system, 6

Baartse, W., 61, 164
babushka dolls, 17 *see also:* matryoshka dolls;
        nesting dolls
Bakhtin, M. M., xviii, 35–40, 42, 63, 70
    cited work, 35, 63
    dialogical self, 35, 38
Bandler, R., 12
Barthes, R., 29, 37
    cited work, 29
Bateson, G., xviii, xxxi, 4–5, 13–15, 111–115,
        117–118, 122–123, 133, 207, 303, 311
    cited works, 14–15, 70, 83, 111–115
    dialogical encounter, xxxi
    difference which makes a difference, 118
    ecology of ideas, 113–115
    interface, 13–15
    logic of abduction, 111–123
    mind, 112–113, 115, 117, 303

research group, 4–5
syllogism in grass, 114
Bateson, M. C., 15, 83, 111
Baudrillard, J., 28
Bauman, Z., 302
Beavin, J., 5
Bemelmans, J., 99
Berg, I. K., 6
Berger, J., 67
Bergson, H., 60–61, 70
Berry, W., 233
blended families, xxxii, 272, 274, 277–280, 290, 297
Bor, J., 30
Böszörményi-Nagy, I., 5, 92
Braidotti, R., 7–8, 11, 16, 18, 29–31
    cited works, 7–8, 11, 16, 29–30, 66
Brokken, J., 44
Brouwers, J., 13
Bruner, J., xix, 6
Burke, C., 18, 127

Campert, R., 107
Carroll, L., 55, 64
    Cauffman, L., 92
Cavafy, C. P., viii
Charlton, N. G., 13, 114–115
Chavannes, M., 249
Cheek, D., 246
Chopra, D., 58, 68–69, 71, 76
Chronos, 61, 180
clenched fist method, 242
consensual domain, 31, 55, 243
context marker, 117–118
Cools, S., 252
Crott, A., 289
Cruyff, J., xviii, 61, 82, 162–165, 247

De Coninck, H., xviii, 44–45, 173
De Hennezel, M., 310
De Saussure, F., 58
De Shazer, S., xviii, 6, 39, 58, 92
deduction, 113
Delahanty, H., 309
Deleuze, G., xviii, 4, 7–10, 16, 18, 22–23, 31, 44, 64, 66, 82, 107, 121, 174, 192, 201, 251–252, 286 *see also:* nomadic thought; rhizome

*arriver entre*, 8
assemblage, 121, 192, 201
cited works, 7–8, 10, 15
deterritorialisation, 8, 201
*entre-temps*, 23
line(s) of flight, 9, 44, 82, 174, 201
ritournelle, 201
territory, 201–202
Dell, P., 6
Demnig, G., 96
Derrida, J., 4, 37, 58, 112
deterritorialisation, 8, 201 *see also:* Deleuze, G.
developmental psychology, 196–197
diagonal thinking, 302
diagonality, 306–308, 310
dialogical
    encounter, xxxi, 22
    interaction(s), 35–37
    relationship, xxx, 11–12, 35, 38
    self, 35, 38 *see also:* Bakhtin, M.
*différance*, xxx, 3–4, 7, 9, 67, 91
discourse, 18–19, 37, 151, 169
    classical logical, 113, 118, 121, 129–130
    dominant, 6–8, 16, 58, 82, 91, 202
    language of, 15
    male, 7, 16
    order of, 29, 55 *see also:* Foucault, M.
    paternalistic, 95
    patriarchal, 18
distinction, 113, 121–122
    draw(ing) a, 13, 112, 121, 311 *see also:* Spencer-Brown, G.
Dohmen, J., 308
Dolto, F., xxvi–xxvii, xxxii, 14, 151, 169, 250, 266, 269–270
dominant problem story, 90, 121, 165, 182
Dormaar, M., 175–176
Drees, A., 19–21
    cited works, 20, 25–26
Dreyfus, H. L., 310
*durée*, 60, 70–71
dyadic relationship, 107, 303

Eames, C., 111
Eco, U., 28–29

ecology of ideas, 113–115, 119 *see also* Bateson, G.; mind
Edelstein, M. G., 101, 245
Efran, J., 6
*élan vital*, 61
Eliacheff, C., 13–14, 270
Elkaim, M., 25
EMDR (eye movement desensitisation and reprocessing), 75, 191, 291
enactment, xxxi, 213–215, 219, 222–223, 225, 227
    *see also:* Minuchin, S.
*entre-temps*, 23 *see also:* Deleuze, G.
Epston, D., 6
Erickson, B. A., 119
Erickson, M. H., xxvii, 4, 10, 119–200, 210, 214, 236, 241
    cited works, 10, 210, 236, 241
    "my friend John" strategy, 236
    utilisation approach, 210–211, 241
externalisation, 6, 223
externalising the problem, 90–91

family therapy *see also:* Hoffman, L., Minuchin, S., development of, 4–6
firstness, 59, 107
Fisch, R., 4–5
Fishmann, H., 213
Flemons, D., 81, 122
Foucault, M., 4, 6–7, 10, 12, 29, 55, 84, 91, 308, 310
    *see also:* parrhesia
    cited works, 7, 10, 29, 308
    order of discourse, 29
Fox-Davies, S., 160
Franzen, J., 302
free space, 7, 18–19, 21, 27–28, 70, 84, 101 *see also:* transitional space
    subject–object–, 12, 26–27, 60, 71, 181
"friend as foe" strategy, 237
Furedi, F., 306

Gardner, R., 99
Gielliet, O., v, 33
Gladwell, M., 164, 305
Goffman, E., 138
Goolishian, H., 6, 91 *see also:* problem-determined system

Goudswaard, J., 278
Grinder, J., 12
Guattari, F., 201

Hakvoort, E., 290
Haley, J., 4–5, 200
Halsema, A., 17
Hammarskjöld, D., 18, 98
Hartland, J., 101
Hellinger, B., 277–278
Hemmerechts, K., 45
Hermans, H. J. M., 35, 38, 43
Hermans-Jansen, E., 43
Hermsen, J., 60
heteroglossia, 35, 42
Hoffman, L., xxvii, 5–6, 39, 91
horizontalism, 302
Hutschemakers, J., 128–129
hypnotherapy, xxvii, 210 *see also:* Erickson, M. H.

identified patient, 162, 164–166
IJsseling, S., 26
induction, 113
interface, 13–14
interpretation
    process of, 51
    world of, 56–57, 62
interspace, the, 11–15 *see also: entre-temps*
intertextuality, 8, 36, 40
Irigaray, L., 4, 7, 11–12, 17–18, 67, 127

Jackson, D., 4–5
Jackson, P., 309–310
Johnson, M., 95

Keeney, B., 81, 124, 212
Kempen, H., 35
Kenny, V., 91
Kingma, J., 30
Klukhuhn, A., 30
knowledge, 23
    archaeology of, 66
    body as a source of, 10–11, 29
    conscious, 311
    contextual, xxxii, 3
    embodied, 38, 43

local, 8, 15, 29
narrative, xix, 179
nomadic, 79
Koolhaas, A., 49
Kristeva, J., 11, 36, 67
intertextuality, 36
Kuipers, P., 23, 119–120, 191, 213, 286
Kundera, M., xxx, 178
Kunneman, H., 73
Kuttner, F., 69

Lacan, J., 40, 44, 58
Lakoff, G., 95
Lammers, M., 309
landscape of the body, xxvii, 66, 68, 73
LeCron, L., 245
Leloup, J., 310
Lenaerts, P., 94
Levinas, E., 30
Levine, P., 247
line(s) of flight, 9, 44, 82, 121, 174, 191, 201–202, 301 *see also:* Deleuze, G.
linguistic domain, 35, 40, 44, 82, 95–96, 182, 202
logical types, 111–113
hierarchy of, 117
Logos, 7–8, 16–17
Lukens, R. J., 6
Lyotard, J.-F., 4, 7

MacDonald, A., 160
master signifier, 37, 39, 42, 58, 95, 99, 107
matryoshka dolls, 197 *see also:* babushka dolls; nesting dolls
Maturana, H. R., 5–6, 243
meaningful Rorschach, 124, 212
Meijer, M., 28, 35–36
metaphor
description of, 43–44
key, 47, 69–70, 76, 94–95, 182, 238
logic of, xxvi, 15, 81–82, 111–116, 118, 122, 131
power of, 95
metaphorical
(core) expression(s), 43–45
(core) statement, 116
midfield play, 95, 162–164, 182–183, 219 *see also:* soccer metaphor

mimesis
strategy for change, 16, 18
mind *see also* Bateson, G.
conscious, 223, 234, 247, 310
subconscious, 303
unconscious, 213, 310
Minuchin, S., xxxi, 4–5, 213–214, 286
cited work, 213
idea of enactment, xxxi, 213–215, 219 *see also:* enactment
Montalvo, B., 5
multiple self, 39, 197
"my friend John" strategy, 236 *see also:* Erickson, M. H.
Myss, C., 125

Nachmanovitch, S., xiii
naïveté,
first, 219
second, 23, 219
wisdom of, 219
Naouri, A., 286
narrated facts, 182–183, 186, 188, 190
narrated reality, xxx, 57, 174, 179
narrative
circle, 99
cycle, 28, 177
element(s), 95–96, 98
knowledge, xix, 179
language, 15, 92
lines, 174, 192
paradigm, 3
perspective, xxii, 3
phase, 27, 30
self, 38
spot, 75
subject(s), 89
text, 52
thought, xxix, xxxii, 4, 182, 201 *see also:* nomadic thought
narrative, a
definition, xxix–xxx
developing, 154
narrative psychotherapy
philosophical background, 6
practice of, 22–23, 81

narrative space, 82, 84, 88 *see also:* third element; third space
narrativity
    definition, xxix
    in action, 29, 214, 219, 223, 226, 229
    of the body, 68, 125, 196
    nesting dolls, 17, 94, 107, 187–188, 197–198, 200, 227–229 *see also:* babushka dolls; matryoshka dolls
    Russian, xxxii, 107, 197, 227–228, 284
new authority, 307
Nietzsche, F., 4, 10, 67
    "Three Metamorphoses", 23
    will to truth, 7
Nieuwenhuis, J., 34
nomadic
    becoming, 8, 66
    knowledge, 79
    phase, 25, 27, 30
    processing of material, 182
    team, 24–30, 81, 159
    use of language, 81
nomadic therapeutic team, 24
nomadic thinking, xxx, 66, 81, 130
nomadic thought, xxx, xxxii, 4, 24, 182, 201, 302–303, 307 *see also:* Deleuze, G.; narrative: thought
    development of ideas, 4, 6–11, 19–22

Oaklander, V., 99
off-screen, 192
O'Hanlon, W. H., 91–92, 117
Okri, B., 56
Olthof, J. B. G., 2, 15, 23, 25, 35, 75, 99, 311
Olthof, J. B. M., 206, 123
Omer, H., 307
Oppenoorth, W., 137, 145, 265, 267, 269–270
Order of Love, 277–278
organising space, 214, 219, 227
Oudshoorn, D. N., 99

pacing, 12
Pakman, M., 111, 113
parentified position, 137, 195
parrhesia, 12, 27, 84 *see also:* Foucault, M.
passive parentification, 140

Paz, O., 122
Peirce, C. S., 59, 107, 113
Petersma, E., 30
Pirandello, L., xviii, 30, 39
Plato, 30, 66, 302
polyphonic self, 38 *see also:* narrative: self
polyphony, 8, 280, 311
    horizontal and vertical, 63–64
postmodernism, 4, 6, 301–302
present absence, 123–124, 127, 220, 230
primary process(es), 26–27, 114–115
principle of slowness, 178
problem-determined system, 6 *see also:* Goolishian, H.
problem identity, 6, 91, 93

Rabinow, P., 310
Raessens, J., 192, 251
Raveel, R., 127–128, 174
reader-focused reading, 39
real, lived time, 60–61
reasoning
    abductive, 113–114
    deductive, 113
    inductive, 113
reflecting team, 6
refrain, 201–203 *see also: ritournelle*
resonance, 25–27, 124
    aesthetic, 311
rhizome
    metaphor of, 8–9, 31, 251, 301, 304 *see also:* Deleuze, G.
Rhode-Dachser, Ch., 7
Rich, A., 10–11
Ricoeur, P., 23, 219
*ritournelle*, 201 *see also:* refrain
Rober, P., 25, 35, 37
Romein, E., 22, 193
    cited works, 22–23, 64, 66, 121, 193, 201
Rosen, S., 200
Rosenblum, B., 69
Rosenhan, D. L., 138
Ross, J. M., 212
Rossi, E. L., 10, 210, 236, 241, 245
Russell, B., 111

sacred space, 83
Saeys, A., 35
Satir, V., 5
Scheepers, M., 7
Scheff, T., 138
Schierbeek, B., 59
Schore, A. N., 270
Schuilenberg, M., 22–23, 64, 66, 121, 193, 201
Schurink, G., 43
Seikkula, J., 35, 63–64
semantic space, 37, 47, 57, 59–60
sensemaking, 214, 219, 226
serendipity
    aesthetics of, 56, 179
    logic of, 120
Sermijn, J., 197
Shotter, J., 64
Siegel, D. J., 72
silent space, 70–72, 76–77
Sloterdijk, P., xviii, xxxii, 108, 164, 301–307, 311
    cited works, 108, 115, 164, 302–303, 305
slowness
    principle of, 178
    wisdom of, 178
soccer metaphor, 82, 137, 162–163, 219 *see also:* midfield play
Spencer-Brown, G., 311 *see also:* distinction: draw(ing) a
Stein, C., 242 *see also:* clenched fist method
Stolperstein, 96
*Story of the Weeping Camel, The*, 249–251
syllogism in grass, 114 *see also:* Bateson, G.
systems thinking, 4–5

Tamaro, S., 179
team as therapeutic medium, xxv, 15, 19, 21, 24–26, 60–61, 159, 176–179, 182 *see also:* nomadic therapeutic team
Tellegen, T., 52, 55, 65, 89, 113, 115, 124, 178
    cited work, 51–52, 65, 89–90, 113, 124, 126, 178
text-focused reading, 39–40, 60
textual analysis, 3, 35, 39–40, 43, 45, 47, 79, 95, 162
therapeutic context, 163, 175–176, 182, 188
    creating a (new), 137, 164
    structuring (of) a, 133, 150

therapeutic framework, 28, 137, 163–164
    principles of a, 174, 177–181
    process of developing a, 162, 175–177, 182
    structure of a, 183, 188, 191
therapeutic medium, 25–26, 60–61
therapeutic space, entering, 162, 168
therapeutic system, xxviii, 151, 175
third element, 81–82, 94, 99, 107, 250–252, 303–304 *see also:* narrative space; third space
third space, 81–84, 89, 164 *see also:* narrative space; third element
    landscape of, 106
    orientation towards, 94
    story as a, 99
    story tracks as a, 96
    symptom as a, 162
thirdness, 107
thymotic
    force, 302, 305, 307
    power, 307, 311
    relations, 302
transitional space, 26
Tranströmer, T., 13, 114

utilisation approach, 210–211, 241 *see also:* Erickson, M. H.

Van de Ven, P., 237
Van den Bossche, M., 308, 310
Van den Eerenbeemt, E. M., 92, 303
Van der Hart, O., 43
Van Duin, A., xviii, 118
Van Heusden, A., 92, 303
Van Kilsdonk, J., 303
Van Lommel, P., 69
Van Tuinen, S., 22–23, 64, 66, 121, 193, 201, 305
Van Wolde, E., 77–78
vanishing point, 174, 182–183, 186, 188, 191–192
Varela, F., 5–6, 243
Veenbaas, W., xxix, 278
Vermetten, E., xxv, 3, 15, 25, 35, 75, 99, 311
Veronesi, S., 124, 126
verticalism, 302
Vincenot, A., 16

Von Foerster, H., 6
Von Glasersfeld, E., 6

Watzlawick, P., 5,
Weakland, J., 4–5
Weick, K., 214
Weiner-Davis, M., 92
White, M., xix, 6, 90, 93 *see also:* externalising the problem
    cited works, 6, 90, 92–93
Whitehead, A., 111
Wilk, J., 117

Winderman, L., 91
Winnicott, D. W., 26 *see also:* transitional space
Winsemius, P., 61, 162–163
wisdom
    earthly, 3, 11, 15
    embodied, affective, 3, 11
    of the naïveté, 219
Wolters, J., 44

Zeig, J., 241